# Gentleman Jack and Rough Rufus

–

## The Rise of Black American Wrestling

# Gentleman Jack and Rough Rufus

-

## The Rise of Black American Wrestling

By

Ian Douglass

Edited by Oliver Lee Bateman

Copyright Ian Douglass 2025. All Rights Reserved.

Published by:
Darkstream Press

www.darkstreampress.com

All rights reserved. This book may not be reproduced in whole or in part in any form without written permission from the author.

This book is set in Garamond.

10 9 8 7 6 5 4 3 2 1

ISBN 979-8-218-61562-8

This book is dedicated to the memory of

# Jamie Melissa Hemmings AKA "Jem"

June 13, 1981 — February 10, 2025

You once wrote that one of my books was "like an all-inclusive reading vacation."

The joy of your friendship made everyone feel like they were on a wonderful vacation.

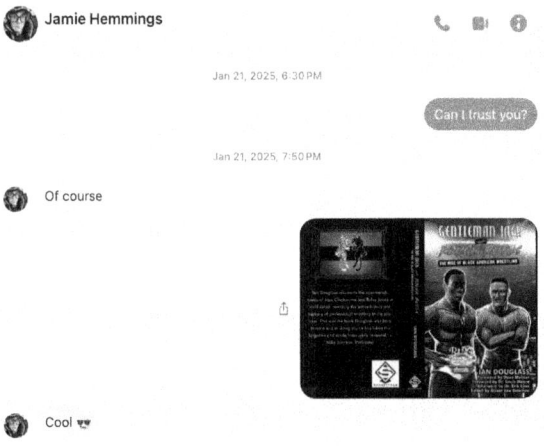

# Table of Contents

| | |
|---|---|
| Foreword | 2 |
| One | 9 |
| Two | 33 |
| Three | 55 |
| Four | 80 |
| Five | 104 |
| Six | 128 |
| Seven | 150 |
| Eight | 171 |
| Nine | 195 |
| Ten | 213 |
| Eleven | 236 |
| Twelve | 258 |
| Thirteen | 282 |
| Fourteen | 305 |
| Fifteen | 328 |
| Sixteen | 355 |
| Seventeen | 379 |
| Eighteen | 404 |
| Nineteen | 428 |
| Twenty | 449 |
| Epilogue | 471 |
| Afterword | 475 |
| Editor's Note | 478 |
| Author's Acknowledgements | 481 |
| Credits | 482 |
| About the Author | 483 |

# FOREWORD

I've read a number of Ian Douglass' books on pro wrestling, and the key component is that they are filled with great stories, sometimes funny, often perceptive, and always well researched. This current book intertwines the history of Black pro wrestlers, along with important culture references during the time period with the lives of two key players: Joe Godfrey, better known as the original Rufus Jones, who wrestled around North America from 1937 to 1951, and Elmer Claybourne, who wrestled as Jack Claybourne, who worked all over the world, and was often billed as the "Negro world champion." But it also looks at the plight of Joe Louis, one of the biggest sports stars of his generation, who, after his boxing days were over and the IRS came calling, went into pro wrestling.

The two were the predecessors of far bigger stars like Bobo Brazil, Bearcat Wright, Sweet Daddy Siki, Sailor Art Thomas, and Dory Dixon, who were all major stars and drawing cards in championship challenges against their era's world champion "Nature Boy" Buddy Rogers.

Unfortunately, covering the plight of these athletes, subject to stereotypes and discrimination, is a lot less fun than the books Douglass has written with Mike "Buggsy McGraw" Davis, Brian Blair, and Steve Keirn, or on the wild history of pro wrestling in the Bahamas.

The one thing with pro wrestling is that the so-called color barrier that existed in the major pro sports in the early part of the 20th century didn't exist in the same way, but racism toward those stars and stereotypes associated with them proliferated far longer than it should have.

Blacks weren't the only stereotyped athletes in the early days of pro wrestling, which was built around ethnic stars in many parts of the country. Like with boxing, appealing to the ethnic fans of a market was considered a key. Unlike in team sports, boxing had the ability to control outcomes through matchmaking to a degree. But with pro wrestling, it was inherent. The promoters picked the winners and losers. They decided who would be the stars, and if you could sell tickets, you could have a long career. With pro wrestling, there was one rule above all others: If people will pay to see you perform in main events, you will get work as a main-eventer.

Some of the promoters in the early days may have been racist, while others may not have been. But whether they were or weren't, they all prayed to the God of the dollar bill. A promoter could very well have been racist or prejudiced against all sorts of minorities, but the rule of thumb was that if they could make money, that would override everything. But the issue was also whether or not the promoters *believed* Black wrestlers could draw money, and were even willing to make an attempt to attract fans with Black wrestlers.

Few today have even heard of the Rufus Jones chronicled in the book. Historians and long-time fans would certainly remember his namesake, Carey Lloyd, who was known as Rufus R. Jones, The Freight Train. He took on the Rufus R. Jones name in 1969 and was very quickly a major star until a combination of age and the dying of the territories ended his career in 1989. He was popular across all fans, regardless of race, but like so many stars of that era, he was also perpetuating in-ring stereotypes that dated back generations to his namesake.

Doing that enabled him to be a main-event player almost everywhere he went for the next decade.

Sam Muchnick had perhaps the best reputation nationally as a wrestling promoter, and St. Louis as a wrestling city was considered the epitome of class pro wrestling. I certainly never heard anyone say that Muchnick was racist. Yet in the rich history of that city, no Black wrestler ever main evented at Kiel Auditorium until Sweet Daddy Siki in 1966.

At the same time, Muchnick would tell his bookers to always protect the top Black talent he brought in — whether it was Jones, Bobo Brazil or Rocky Johnson — from clean losses as much as possible. And still, in the history of Muchnick's Missouri State title as well as the NWA world heavyweight title — the former which he controlled and the latter in which he was among the key people in the decision-making process for determining its holders — you see no Black wrestlers in either title lineage until Muchnick's retirement as a promoter in 1982.

The original Rufus was the prototype of the role that virtually every Black star well into the '80s played, built around the idea that they all had hard heads, and that their head-butts would be popular and devastating finishers. The other common trait, not in everyone, but in *many*, was the idea, reinforced from boxing, of boxing movements and backgrounds, high flying dropkicks and muscular physiques. Claybourne, a contemporary of Jones, exemplified these traits until the huge Brazil took his mantle as pro wrestling's leading Black superstar in the '50s, '60s and '70s.

While wrestling was open to anyone who could draw long before baseball, the national pastime, that didn't mean the talent wasn't subject to the horrors of the worst part of our culture.

To understand not just pro wrestling, but the culture, it's imperative that the lessons of what these men went through and the truth of what it was like didn't die with them.

To me, Douglass' book is important reading both for wrestling fans and those interested in Black culture through the lens of pro wrestling, an American entertainment genre. The book looks at cultural changes during the lives of these men, from segregation, racist taunts, and being told that they were "too Black" to be the highest-paid stars in the game. This culture in wrestling survived until recent years, when Michael Hayes, a WWE executive and match producer, told Mark Henry — one of the strongest men in the world and someone who achieved world championship status in 2011 while also at times being called "Sexual Chocolate" and "The Silverback" and "The King of the Jungle" — that Hayes was "more of a n----r than [Henry] was" before headbutting him. This incident happened as late as this century.

The book recaps Jones' and Claybourne's lives, travels, heartache, and heartbreak in a world that gives them work, but at the same time was not ready to allow them to be stars. You can chalk up the promoters as the bad guys. Some of them surely were. But it was the culture at the time and the belief of those promoters that the audiences would only accept them in a certain role, which seldom allowed them to be the lead star of a territory.

My generation grew up with stories about slavery and racism. Yet, in just a few years, we watched as Muhammad Ali went from being the most hated athlete in American culture to perhaps its most beloved. Every baseball fan of that era was taught about Jackie Robinson and how important he was to baseball and all that he had to overcome. We also learned about the legends of Josh Gibson and Satchel Paige, who were two of the greatest of all-time in that sport, but who were not allowed in the major leagues in their heyday due to their skin color. But for whatever reason, stories that I read about when it came to baseball and football players in the South well into the '60s were more vivid when described to me first hand.

Arthur Thomas ("Sailor" Art Thomas) was by legend, one of the top bodybuilders in the country in the '50s, but won no major national competitions. As the story goes, judges would place him highly in contests that he should have won handily, but would not give first places to Black bodybuilders. Thomas was in his mid-30s when he broke into pro wrestling. Aside from perhaps Earl Maynard, a former Mr. Universe, who made his bodybuilding name in England where such racism in that genre wasn't as rampant, was lauded as having the best physique in the business.

Keep in mind, the wrestling business had many former bodybuilding contest winners. Yet, none of them in the pre-steroid era looked as impressive physically as Sailor Art, even well into his 40s. In that era, before steroids changed the very nature of bodybuilding, it was not uncommon for bodybuilders to move into pro wrestling. When your job is to attract fans and your work attire are brief trunks, a good physique was always a valuable calling card.

Bruno Sammartino was arguably the biggest pro wrestling star of his era. He started as an ethnic hero to Italians as he migrated from that country when he was young, to Pittsburgh, where he lived the rest of his life.

Sammartino didn't know English and was picked on for being different. He discovered weights, and became one of the strongest men in the world. He was recruited into pro wrestling where he first became an ethnic hero before later becoming something of a cultural icon in the Northeast. He remains one of the biggest drawing cards and most legendary figures in pro wrestling history.

It's hardly a surprise that Thomas and Sammartino would become friends, since getting to the gym was important to both of them even with the brutal travel schedule of wrestlers in the early 60s. Plus, Sammartino grew up a fan of bodybuilding and competed in it himself. He knew of Thomas, who was 11 years older than he was, from that world. He knew of him being screwed in that world due to his skin color before Thomas became a pro wrestling star.

Sammartino would tell me this story with such passion, like your favorite uncle talking about his life experiences and pain he went through.

He and Thomas were traveling together through New Jersey, and Sammartino had a favorite Italian restaurant, not just in the area, but it was his favorite restaurant in the Northeast and would go there whenever he was in the area.

Sammartino by this point was WWWF champion, the predecessor of today's WWE. He was a celebrity of pretty significant proportions and was among the highest paid athletes in the country since his income was based on a percentage of the gate and he headlined and drew well in the biggest arenas in the Northeast. The owners of the place of course loved him and treated him like royalty. The patrons in those days were both friendly and in awe of him.

Sammartino enterd the restaurant with Thomas, and this was in the 1960s in New Jersey, not in the South where stories like this were more common. He said the owners greeted him like they always did, and remarked how it was so great to see him again. But then they told him that they couldn't serve his friend.

Sammartino at first thought they were busting his balls, like it was a practical joke, although he told me he didn't find it funny. But not for a second did he believe they were serious. Even if people were racist, as many were, he felt by the way he was treated and his standing in Italian culture, that his friend and guest would be welcome.

Then Bruno realized they were serious. His heart sank, and he would talk about that painful experience four and five decades later, and how humiliated he felt because as much as they hurt him, he just couldn't imagine how his friend must have felt.

Sammartino told me that he never went back to that restaurant.

When Ian first told me about his book, I immediately thought of this story because it wasn't one I read in a cold history book, but one I was told by someone with the passion and pain in his voice about something that happened in the Northeast during my lifetime.

It's important this part of our history isn't forgotten.

Dave Meltzer
*The Wrestling Observer*

# 1 – A Panther Problem

Beginning in November 1983 and extending into April 1984, "The Soul Patrol" — a tag team consisting of Rocky Johnson and Tony Atlas — made World Wrestling Federation history by forming the first Black tandem to successfully capture a tag team championship of any kind in the powerful wrestling promotion that had dominated the Northeastern United States for several decades.

Depending on personal preference, it would be perfectly reasonable to categorize this tag team championship reign, which preceded the first reign of Hulk Hogan as WWF World Heavyweight Champion, as the inaugural tag team reign of the WWF's push toward recognition as a truly national wrestling promotion.

Following the arrival of Hogan to the WWF in January 1984, the company's meteoric rise would eventually culminate in record-breaking revenues, the mainstreaming of pro wrestling, the formation of a publicly traded company known as World Wrestling Entertainment, and worldwide recognition as the leading brand in sports entertainment.

Given the fraught history of Black performers in professional wrestling, and the frequent reluctance to bestow championship reigns upon all but a select few Black wrestlers, the title reign of Johnson and Atlas on such a popular platform certainly could have been interpreted as a changing of the tides.

Few would have suspected that the opposite would have been true; following The Soul Patrol's breakup in April 1984, it would be another nearly 10 years before the next Black tag team — Men on a Mission — would break through to become the next Black wrestlers of any kind to hold sanctioned WWF championship gold.

The decade-long title drought of Black wrestlers in the world's premier wrestling organization notwithstanding, there are other features of The Soul Patrol's formation that are worth interrogating, beginning with the performance styles of the two men comprising the team.

Rocky Johnson was an Afro-Canadian who made his wrestling debut in Canada during the mid-1960s before venturing out to Western Canada, the Pacific Northwest, Detroit, New York, and eventually California, where he became a massive star.

Virginia native Tony Atlas, who was 10 years Johnson's junior, began his career in the Mid-Atlantic region of the United States in the mid-1970s, and developed the rudiments of his wrestling routine while seldom venturing outside of that region.

Prior to the official formation of their tag team in the fall of 1983, Atlas and Johnson spent very little time together in the same territories, and only shared the ring with one another on a handful of confirmed occasions. Yet, for some bizarre reason, their wrestling styles appeared to be nearly identical long before they ever united in a professional capacity.

Certainly there are subtleties and nuances to their performances that vary, but the similarities in mannerisms and move selections — including dropkicks, flying takedowns, boxer shuffles, and an array of headbutts delivered from postures ranging from standing to leaping — were far too similar to have been coincidental.

Moreover, a broadening of the analytical lens finds that a great many of the Black babyface — or "good guy" — wrestlers of the era, regardless of their height, weight, or point of origin, display a strong penchant for boxing mannerisms, dropkicks and headbutts, with the latter usually backed by some underlying pseudoscientific belief in the natural thickness of Black skulls.

How was it that Black wrestlers whose careers and trajectories had very little overlap still managed to develop performance styles that were nearly identical to one another's? The quest to find the answers to those questions forces us to travel back to a point in time that precedes the Soul Patrol's formation by five decades, and to immerse ourselves within the peculiar set of circumstances under which the first significant, recognizable wave of Black Americans began to engage with the performance art known as professional wrestling.

It is quite challenging to properly contextualize the emergence of Blacks within the ranks of professional wrestling without first understanding the atmosphere within which they made their debuts, and the circumstances that contributed to that environment.

As professional wrestling evolved from a form of legitimate catch-as-catch-can combat to a brand of predetermined entertainment, there were several Black wrestlers who emerged on local and regional levels to capture the interest of local fans, with a few occasionally breaking through to grasp semi-mainstream attention.

The first of the men to truly do this was "The Black Panther" Illa Vincent, who rose to prominence in Europe under the name "Illa Kuba," and who first set foot in the United States preparing to grapple in 1911. Standing 6'0" and weighing over 200 lean, muscular pounds, Vincent cut a striking figure, and was both taller and larger than nearly all wrestlers of the era, not to mention considerably darker.

A fluent German speaker who was often denigrated as a "smoked German," Vincent took up residence in Chicago where his presence piqued the media's interest. He was also quickly reclassified as a Cuban national, and had to contend with mocking barbs from sportswriters who couldn't believe a Cuban could be so dark, and were apparently blissfully ignorant of Cuba's 12 percent Black population level in the 1910s.

While no other Black wrestlers of the era achieved the original Black Panther's level of regional or national recognition — like Harry "Tarzan" Wilson, Arthur Gates, and Lee Umbles — these men all proved to be adept enough at wrestling to attract some level of public interest, and were typically awarded victories over opponents of other races and nationalities with some consistency.

Even though some of the aforementioned wrestlers rarely won conclusively due to the widespread use of the best-of-three-falls system, whereby a wrestler needed to win two out of three falls in order to claim a match outright, capturing a single fall in a losing effort was usually regarded as a partial or symbolic victory for all of these combatants. Still, none of them ever came particularly close to being able to call himself the true champion of a prominent region or wrestling territory.

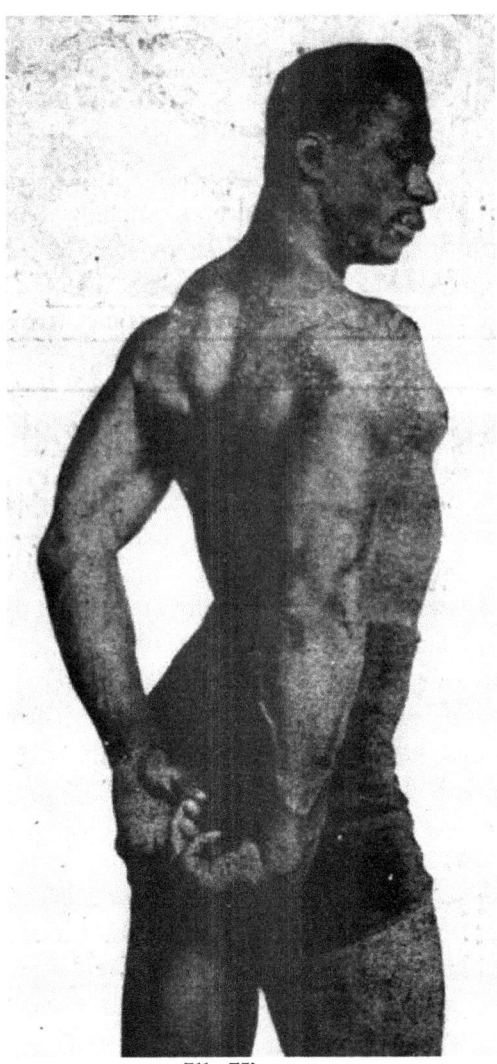

**Illa Vincent**

Historically, this perception is often changed with the emergence of Reginald Berry, who wrestled most frequently under the stage name of Reginald Siki. The "Siki" was borrowed from Senegalese fighter Louis Mbarrick Fall, who fought in Europe under the name "Battling Siki," just as many of the names and tropes utilized by early Black wrestlers in particular were baldly lifted directly from their boxing precedents and gently altered into a wrestling context.

In the case of Louis Fall, he had come by his popularity through a shocking knockout of popular French boxer Georges Carpentier in 1922, which earned him the world light heavyweight championship. His career and social life both imploded in the aftermath of that victory, but by then Fall had moved to the United States and become a media sensation.

While Battling Siki's escapades on the streets of New York were being eagerly lapped up by the American press, Reginald Berry adopted the Siki name and captured headlines while touring with the wrestling organization spearheaded by the famous Zbyszko brothers, Stanislaus and Wladek.

Over the course of his appearances on behalf of the Zbyszkos, Siki created quite a stir. He had a tall, lean, chiseled physique reminiscent of Illa Vincent's that was similarly atypical for the era, and which set him apart from the noticeably smaller Black American wrestlers that preceded him.

Moreover, Siki's association with the premier traveling wrestling troupe of the day resulted in his name being disseminated on an international basis, and the travels of the group provided Siki with the opportunity to appear in major cities primarily across North America, Europe, and a few other select locations around the world.

The trailblazing activities of Siki are often remembered fondly considering his emergence as the first Black professional wrestler to both achieve and sustain true intercontinental notoriety, but a deeper analysis of his match results reveals a somewhat less rosy picture.

Specifically, for all of the unmistakable success and fame Siki enjoyed as a standard bearer for Black wrestlers, he ultimately lost almost every high-profile match he engaged in on North American soil during the first decade of his wrestling career, generally from 1922 straight through his mid-1930s departure from the United States.

In sum, while Siki was essentially the Black representative for what was presented as a traveling brigade of all-star wrestlers — each of whom was touted as the champion of his respective nation or race — Siki was never portrayed as a palpable threat to the dominant wrestlers within that assemblage.

Siki's lack of major North American victories notwithstanding, another issue emerged in the aftermath of his success. The fake Senegalese wrestler had proven to be such a reliable attractor of Black wrestling fans in several of the cities where he appeared that wrestling promoters decried the paucity of Black wrestlers who could be promoted to attract Black wrestling fans in Siki's absence.

Southern California wrestling promoter Lou Daro spoke with *The California Eagle* in 1928 about how anxious he was to have Siki back because of how strong of a draw he was in the Los Angeles area, and how he "deplores the fact that there are so few Negro wrestlers."

Daro also reached out to the Associated Negro Press to say that he "failed to see any logical reason why colored athletes do not seem to take to wrestling," and enlisted the news service to spread the word that he would provide "plenty of good matches" to any qualified Black wrestler who could be found.

While Reginald Siki is credited with being the first Black wrestler to achieve true multiregional stardom within the United States, his presence alone was not sufficient to prompt a noticeable uptick in the number of Black wrestlers receiving prominent placement on wrestling cards. If a stable generation of young, Black performers was going to enter the professional wrestling business, a separate catalyst would be required.

That catalyst would come from a source that was in one respect highly predictable, yet still wholly improbable.

While Reginald Berry had already drawn inspiration from the popular boxer Battling Siki when creating his Reginald Siki persona, the most direct push toward an increased presence of Black wrestlers is attributable to the events that drew one of the most dominant and popular Black heavyweight fighters of the era into the wrestling world.

If it seems plagiaristic for so many names and ideas from Black boxers to be reused by Black wrestlers, one of the reasons for this may be the high rate of name theft that occurred within the boxing world itself. One of the most obvious examples of this occurred when Feab Smith Williams took inspiration from mid-19th-century Black Canadian fighter George "Old Chocolate" Godfrey and appropriated the name George Godfrey for himself for the duration of his own professional boxing career.

Even as he rapidly piled up victories throughout the 1920s, Godfrey was dogged by accusations that he accepted bribes to extend the lengths of his fights, or that he would throw blatant low blows in order to get himself intentionally disqualified from fights that he had been winning.

Such was the case when Godfrey fought top contender Primo Carnera, and Godfrey threw a left hook to the groin of the future world heavyweight champion in the fifth round after Godfrey had undeniably dominated the early action of the fight.

An independent review of the event concluded that the fight had been fixed, and ruled Godfrey's low blow had indeed been intentional. As a result, Godfrey was suspended from boxing in the majority of the major states where fights were held.

In the aftermath of his suspension, Godfrey was forced to fight outside of the lucrative fighting states of New York, New Jersey, Pennsylvania, Massachusetts, and Illinois. It was at this stage that Godfrey was presented with another option for making money inside of the squared circle.

According to Jim Rooney of *The Springfield Union* who interviewed Godfrey, the fighter was "hanging around a gymnasium one day, doing nothing as there was nothing to do," when a wrestling promoter approached Godfrey and asked him if he had ever wrestled before. Godfrey replied that he had wrestled while serving in the Navy, presuming that traditional folkstyle grappling was the sort of wrestling the promoter had been talking about.

The announcement of Godrey's wrestling debut was made on January 16th, 1931 from Mexico City. He was said to be competing the very next night against American wrestler Jack Russell.

"I'm through with boxing," Godfrey was quoted as saying by the United Press. "The best white fighters in the United States absolutely refuse to meet me, and I'm fed up on just shadow boxing."

Godfrey was not actually through with boxing by any means. Two weeks earlier, he had knocked out Salvatore Ruggirello just over two minutes into round one of their 10-round fight, and he already had a fight booked in February for the vacant Mexican heavyweight boxing championship. Still, the idea that the highest ranked Black heavyweight fighter in the world would completely forsake boxing for professional wrestling certainly added weight to the announcement.

Godfrey won his debut wrestling match, and the word of his pro wrestling debut was carried all across North America. In response, promoter Carlos Henriquez immediately announced his plans to bring Godfrey to the United States because his drawing power would be best utilized there. As this was happening, the joint boxing-wrestling commissions of several states made de facto anti-Godfrey rulings, preemptively banning mixed Black-White wrestling matches simply to prevent Godfrey from sidestepping his boxing suspension.

By the time Godfrey finally made his American wrestling debut, other wrestling promoters from around the country had already taken steps to capitalize on the buzz that the fighter had generated. As one example of this, just 10 days after "The Black Panther of Leiperville" announced his intention to wrestle and subsequently made his in-ring debut in

Mexico, a very different Black Panther — who also just so happened to be a Black American — was suspiciously rushed to the ring in Centralia, Washington to compete against Mervin Barackman.

This Black Panther of Washington was joining another Black wrestler known as the Black Panther — Jim Mitchell of Louisville — who first began wrestling sporadically in 1929, but whose activities also experienced a notable uptick in frequency after the insertion of Godfrey into the wrestling ranks in 1931.

It's important to make a note about the significance of the Black Panther title when applied to Black American fighters, irrespective of Illa Vincent's first use of the title in a wrestling capacity.

In August 1927, a major Associated Press editorial from Bill Ritt appeared in newspapers all across the United States to explain in detail how in every decade of the early 20th century a "Black Panther" had emerged to stalk and hunt the reigning White world heavyweight champions. Jack Johnson had carried the title unofficially, Harry Wills had formally carried the title, and George Godfrey had now positioned himself as being worthy of the name.

"George Godfrey is the new Black Panther's name," wrote Ritt. "George is a great hulking chocolate-hued boy who hails from Leiperville, Pa., a 224-pound fighting man with maybe not so much science, but possessing great punching power and the build to take it. Though he's new to the top of the business, Godfrey is a veteran of many years of fighting."

Two months after this editorial ran, aside from the massive increase of local Black boxers adopting the name of Black Panther, wrestling promoters also began referring to Reginald Siki as "The Black Panther of Wrestling" for a three month stretch in Massachusetts, demonstrating how quickly a concept that had been inspired in one corner of the boxing world could become ubiquitous in that space before spreading into wrestling circles.

When Godfrey finally arrived in New Jersey, he brought with him a freshly won championship belt that signified his Mexican heavyweight boxing championship victory — the product of a 53-second knockout of Ricardo Rosel.

"The Philadelphia negro scored fourteen victories in a Mexican wrestling tour and hopes to win a place among the performers in one of the eastern mat trusts," reported *The Atlanta Journal*.

Once the opponent for Godfrey's U.S. debut in Newark, New Jersey was declared to be John Grandovich, "the heavyweight champion of Yugoslavia," Dixon Stewart of United Press wrote a syndicated piece that received wide-scale circulation. In the editorial, Stewart once again referred to Godfrey by his feline nickname, and also unwittingly made a prophetic statement about how Godfrey and future Black wrestlers were likely to be presented as they pressed forward into wrestling ventures.

"Promoters are undecided as to Godfrey's billing, but the unwritten rules of wrestling require that all performers be titleholders, and the 'Black Panther' probably will become Negro heavyweight champion," prophesized Stewart.

This sentence from Stewart would be remarkably prescient with respect to the representations of Black wrestlers for the three decades that followed. In the meantime, as Godfrey was getting down to the serious business of preparing for his American wrestling debut, a fresh crop of Black wrestling talent was preparing to make its mark on the Great Depression era.

It was into this environment that Siki and Godfrey both had a hand in seeing that a core group of Black wrestlers who became regular attractions for the better part of the next 20 years fully emerged.

The greater professional wrestling scene first became aware of the existence of Elmer Claybourne of Mexico, Missouri in January 1932, when the Great Depression was in full swing, and one out of every four American workers was unemployed.

As hard as living conditions were for most Americans, it can be of further use to reflect on the fact that the career of the future "Gentleman Jack" began in the same year as the commencement of the infamous Tuskegee Experiment, in which hundreds of Black American men were enrolled in a government study believing they were going to receive treatment for the debilitating condition that afflicted them, only to be denied both a proper diagnosis of their illness and the means of treating it so that their deterioration and eventual deaths could be studied.

When Claybourne made his wrestling debut as a nearly 22-year-old Black man, he had grown up under the oppressive Jim Crow laws of Missouri — implemented in the decades following the Civil War, beginning in the 1870s — and within a federal system that officially viewed his life as less valuable than that of White citizens. As a consequence, he was acutely aware of the steep uphill climb he faced both in his profession and in his daily life.

*The Minneapolis Tribune* and *The Minneapolis Journal* described how local middleweight wrestler Harry Kamatchus of Mankato — billed as the world champion of the 156-pound weight division — had defeated the "Kansas City Negro" Jack Claybourne in consecutive falls to conclude an exhausting match. The first fall went over 37 minutes, and the second fall lasted an additional 42 minutes.

The name Jack was actually a true nickname, as Claybourne had no middle name. He may have had this legally amended sometime after 1941, since he is alluded to in government documents as "Jack E. Claybourne" or "Elmer Jack Claybourne" in his later years.

That same month, Claybourne began wrestling in a few locations inside of his home state of Missouri, within a reasonable drive of his hometown of Mexico. In the town of Moberly, he debuted under his actual name of Elmer Claybourne, and *The Monitor-Index and Democrat* of Moberly proclaimed Claybourne to be "best of his race at the mat game in this section of the middle west."

Competing against Billy Wolfe, Claybourne lost a multi-fall match that lasted well over an hour, dropping the first fall in 29 minutes and the second in 39 minutes. *The Monitor-Index and Democrat* observed that the 21 year-old Claybourne "possesses great strength, but lacked the skill and knowledge of the grappling game to successfully combat the punishing holds that Wolfe continuously fashioned on him."

Claybourne also wrestled that month at the City Hall of Chillicothe, and after he "vanquished Charles Knoche with a toe hold," Claybourne was described by *The Chillicothe Constitution-Tribune* to have "evinced more speed than local fans have seen in some time and proved himself a favorite with the crowd."

Such was the case during a bout emanating from Council Bluffs, Iowa, in late March 1932. Pulling curtain-raising duties, Claybourne impressed the audience of 2,000 fans while sparring with Curley Smith, and *The Council Bluffs Nonpareil* cited Claybourne's performance as a highlight of the show.

"A crackerjack opening bout between Curley Smith and Jack Claybourrne, Kansas City Negro, went to a draw and drew a big hand from the crowd," reported *The Nonpareil*. "The colored boy was the favorite and kept Smith well in hand by tossing him from the ring occasionally. According to Promoter Grace, the Negro will be seen again in the local ring."

However, wrestling wasn't the only ring-based endeavor that Claybourne was involved in at the time. In a pattern that would play out repeatedly during the early years of his career, Claybourne would find himself donning the leather gloves and participating in boxing matches that were often inserted into wrestling cards and participated in by combatants who were ostensibly competent at both disciplines.

While the authenticity of any boxing match included on a professional wrestling card should automatically be called into question — and especially when one or more of the fighters involved is known to be a professional wrestler — at least the earliest recorded boxing match of Claybourne's career appears to have been legitimate based on its description. Unfortunately for Claybourne, it also suggests that he wasn't a particularly gifted boxer.

At the Athletic Hall in Moberly, Claybourne boxed under his real name of Elmer Claybourne, and lost decisively to Cyclone Williams in their 10-round match. The writer for *The Monitor-Index and Democrat* made it clear that Elmer "could not trade punches successfully" and that Williams "was taking it easy" throughout the contest.

"Williams proved a remarkably clever boxer, with a lot of power to his punches," added the fight report. "He jolted Claybourne severely in the third round, putting him down and all but knocking him out. Claybourne rallied some in the latter rounds, but Williams was master of the situation at all times."

Back in Wells, Minnesota in April, and competing against Harry Kamatchus yet again, Claybourne was yet again defeated in straight falls even after putting forth a valiant effort and displaying a commendable level of conditioning.

"Harry Kamatchas, called the 'Greek Demon,' defeated 'Happy' Jack Claybourne in straight falls, the first fall taking 24 minutes and the second coming after 32 minutes of the fastest wrestling ever seen in Wells," stated *The Wells Mirror*. "Kamatchas, the champion, was, as usual, the master of the situation most of the time, but Claybourne displayed some wonderful showmanship as well as some fast, clean wrestling."

As Claybourne became a regular participant in shows at the Memorial Building in Kansas City, the promoters followed what was a common practice of billing Claybourne from one of the areas in which he had most recently wrestled. This is why throughout his first year of wrestling regularly in Kansas City, the Missouri native was introduced as being a resident of Minneapolis, Minnesota, a Northern city with a Black population of less than one percent in 1930.

Even though he won 50 percent of his matches at best in 1932, Claybourne still emerged as a situational world champion by the end of the year. Labeled as the "colored world's champ" from Montgomery, Alabama, Claybourne staged a match in the first week of 1933 in the entirely White town of Marysville, Kansas against "Marysville's wrestling mechanic" Charles Deabenderfer.

Inexplicably, the event was advertised as a title defense by Claybourne despite the fact that Deabenderfer was White and would not have been eligible to win a wrestling title reserved for Black athletes. *The Marshall County News* cast Deabenderfer as the clear underdog against Claybourne, who the fans were told had "recently been in 40 matches in which he had never lost a match."

Given the obvious priority of showcasing Deabenderfer's abilities in front of his hometown fans, the local grappler unsurprisingly defeated Claybourne in front of nearly one-third of the town's population of 4,000 residents. *The Advocate-Democrat* described the bout as taking place under "catch-as-catch-can *Police Gazette* rules," which Claybourne later professed to be unfamiliar with, and added that he would like to have a rematch "under Texas rules."

Based on *The Advocate-Democrat*'s description of the action, the "*Police Gazette* rules" of the bout required that the referee only be present to adjudicate the submission victories. During the third fall of the match, Deabenderfer dropped Claybourne off of the ring ropes "with such force that he bounced back to the mat in a helpless mass," and Claybourne eagerly acknowledged his defeat when Deabenderfer "piled on top of him" afterwards.

Claybourne had lost, but *The Marshall County News* claimed that the wrestler "pleased the crowd with his shifty feet and good sportsmanship, and he was granted a second opportunity to claim victory in front of a Marysville audience when he wrestled Herbert "Young Gotch" Hartley.

Seizing his opportunity, the fleet-footed Claybourne put together a performance that dazzled the audience with his technical wrestling prowess and strength, blended with his speed, and an impressive amount of showmanship for such an inexperienced grappler.

According to the account provided by *The Marshall County News* of Marysville, Kansas, "Happy Jack" dropped the first fall to Gotch via toehold, and then beat his adversary from pillar to post throughout the final two falls without the broad grin ever departing from his countenance.

"Wading into the second engagement with as much pep as he started the fray, Jack slapped, mauled and threw Gotch around in a fashion that should be considered naughty in the book of etiquette," joked *The News*. "He so completely outfigured and outmaneuvered the pale face that Gotch gave up in three minutes and seven seconds."

Once he had used his superior grappling technique to submit Gotch with an alligator stretch to conclude the second fall, Claybourne bullied his adversary through the use of brute force in a style that caused *The News* to report that nothing as spectacular as that third fall had been seen at the Marshall City Auditorium during that entire wrestling season.

"After 'Happy' had mauled the toe specialist about the mat as he pleased, he finally grasped him by the arms and legs," continued *The News*. "Then, lifting the white boy high above his head, Jack swung him in a dizzy circle, first to the right, then to the left, and threw him to the floor. Jack jumped on Gotch, and the match was over insofar as decisions are concerned."

In another bout that took place in Marysville shortly thereafter, *The County News* reported that Claybourne defeated "Flying" Parson Aldner, winning his two falls with an alligator stretch and a body smother, with the second fall occurring after Aldner got into an altercation with the referee.

Claybourne also appeared regularly in Moberly, Missouri, a short 40-mile drive from his home. *The Monitor-Index and Democrat* said of Claybourne that "no faster man has ever performed in the local ring than Happy Jack." This description was provided in conjunction with Claybourne's victory over fellow Black wrestler Dan Watts of Sedalia, which was acquired by way of a body slam in the first fall and a double arm lock in the second fall.

One consistent observation about Claybourne during the earliest stages of his career was his unmatched speed and how well it translated to the appreciation with which fans received his matches, even among audiences that were entirely White in their racial makeup.

In Emporia, *The Daily Gazette* described how "the speedy colored boy from Chicago" outmaneuvered Harry Olson to win the second and third fall of their bout — with a double hammerlock and a body slam — and how their bout was "well-received by a big crowd."

Only a few months into his first year as a grappler, Claybourne was already being credited with innovation. In describing what Claybourne offered to wrestling fans of Kirksville, Missouri, an early May edition of *The Daily Express & News* said that Claybourne "has a famous hold in which he uses his legs while flying at his man, and in a manner not done by anyone else."

Claybourne was quite dark when placed along the spectrum of Black American skin shades, and his skin color was undoubtedly used as a selling point for his appearances. As *The Daily Gazette* casually observed in its "Localettes" section,

"Happy Jack Claybourne, who claims the Negro wrestling championship, is the darkest light heavyweight ever seen in an Emporia ring."

In the all-White town of Council Grove, Kansas, the sighting of a wrestler bearing Claybourne's complexion was apparently worthy of front-page news. *The Council Grove Republican* introduced "Happy" Jack Claybourne, stating that the "184 pounds of ebony muscle" had earned his nickname through his "habit of dealing with rough stuff with a broad smile."

"He is also a boxer with a long string of knockouts to his credit," added *The Republican*. "Numerous opponents who have met him under Texas rules have declared that the lack of gloves was the only thing that kept the wrestling bout from being called a boxing match."

Claybourne made good on his debut as "the first colored wrestler ever to appear in Emporia" by defeating J.E. Ethridge with an alligator clutch and an airplane spin. For his next bout in the city, Claybourne would be competing against the man who was presumably the *second* Black wrestler to appear in Emporia when he met "the Black Panther of Ft. Worth" in the main event of the evening.

This Black Panther was *not* from Fort Worth by any means, but was actually the Black Panther who had debuted in Washington after the announced wrestling debut of boxer George Godfrey. It was "The Black Panther" Alex Kaffner, who would eventually become one of the longest-tenured performers in Wisconsin's history, and would later have his name permanently set as "The Black Panther of Wisconsin."

During the Roaring '20s, the absence of any noteworthy Black wrestlers aside from Reginald Siki became a source of frustration for promoters, with their numbers being so few that it essentially rendered the concept of race-exclusive Negro championships as ridiculous.

Back in 1923 when Siki's career was first gaining traction, columnist John J. Peri of *The Stockton Daily Evening Record* quipped that colored wrestlers were the scarcest things in the world, "next to hen's teeth and left-handed third basemen." The fact that two young, competent Black wrestlers were squaring off with one another in the heart of the country was a testament to the fact that a new era had dawned.

During his time sharing cards with Claybourne in the Midwest, Kaffner vacillated in his use of various iterations of both his first and last names. Just prior to his relocation to the Midwest, Kaffner had used the name Alexis Kaffir while being depicted as either an Egyptian or a Senegalese grappler in the Rocky Mountain region. Depending on the venue, the city, or the promoter he was working for in the areas around Missouri, Kansas and Nebraska, Kaffner may have been referred to as Alex, Alexis, Lex, or Ellis, appended with the surname Kaffner, Keffner, Heffner, Kaef, or Kaffir.

Few descriptions of the encounters between the young Black grapplers successfully made it into print, but the surviving accounts suggest that the bouts were stellar. During a main-event affair between the two at the Royal Theater in Emporia, *The Daily Gazette* described how Alex and Jack traded the first two falls with separate alligator clutches before Claybourne closed the show with a back-body slam.

A very colorful description of a different bout between the two was printed in *The Council Grove Republican* in the aftermath of one of their matches in Council Grove, Kansas, albeit one punctuated by analogies of the era that leaned heavily into the use of racial imagery.

"Customers at the wrestling matches last evening came to the conclusion that Happy Jack Claybourne and the 'Black Panther' (Alex Kaef), the two colored headliners, were raised on the milk of rubber trees on the dark continent. It was a logical conclusion," began the report from *The Republican*.

The article proceeded to describe a multi-fall contest in which the two Black combatants bounced each other off of the mat with little regard for one another's personal safety. After Claybourne secured the first fall with a "double Japanese toehold," Kaffner rallied to win the second fall with an airplane spin. That's when the action truly became frenetic.

"In their try for the deciding fall, the colored wrestlers literally wrestled all over the armory," continued *The Republican*. "Spectators, with aid of (referee) 'Tiny' Elza, heaved the pair back in the ring without bothering to untangle them. After Claybourne had dented the platform several times with the Panther's head, the latter's shoulders stayed on the mat for the official count of three."

**Alex Kaffner**

Chaos seemed to be the norm whenever Claybourne and Kaffner squared off. Kaffner struck fast during their April rematch and took the first fall with a Boston crab, which required Claybourne to score a pinfall to even the tally. With the score tied, the action predictably spilled outside of the ring once again.

"The two wrestlers and the referee, Les Holzapfel, were staging a track meet around the ring with Holzapfel in the lead," reported *The Republican*. "The latter took a corner too fast, skidded and went down. Alex stumbled over him and fell flat on the mat. Taking advantage of his opportunity, Happy did a dive onto the Panther, knocked out his wind, and pinned him for the required count of three."

In addition to being a speedster, Claybourne also demonstrated the ability to entertain a crowd through humor. During a bout against Svend Petersen in Council Bluffs, Iowa, *The Nonpareil* described how Claybourne "danced around the ring, kicking his feet high in the air, and laughing uproariously when Petersen tickled him in the ribs."

In this same Iowa venue, Claybourne was forced to rely on his gymnastic abilities to lure White fans into his corner after the audience became miffed by the non-appearance of advertised headliner Roughhouse Nelson for a bout with Frenchy LaRue.

*The Nonpareil* illustrated how after Claybourne seasoned the main event with "a clever little tumbling routine to vary the monotony," the audience "soon forgot its apathy to the Negro, and before the match was over, was booing LaRue vociferously."

Throughout this period, Claybourne continued to dabble in boxing — especially when he made appearances in Iowa. Yet again, competing under his real first name of Elmer Claybourne, he was stopped in the second round of a fight scheduled for 10 rounds in Mason City, Iowa in April 1933.

Even as 1934 rolled around, Claybourne was still being advertised more as a converted boxer than as a mat aerialist. Still appearing in Council Bluffs, Claybourne was advertised in *The Nonpareil* with "nimble footwork and fast punching hands" being his primary assets during wrestling matches as he continued to box at the Acacia Garden.

This led to a period in which Claybourne was advertised as "rassler and boxer" in Iowa's newspapers, stemming from the continued mixing of predetermined wrestling and legitimate boxing matches within the same Midwestern shows, and interspersed within the same rings.

Among the difficulties this causes is in determining how many of the boxing matches the wrestlers participated in, if *any*, were authentic. For instance, when Jack Claybourne was credited with knocking out Don Baer in the sixth round of their boxing match in Shenandoah, Iowa in April 1934, it's difficult to know if Claybourne should have been congratulated for knocking out his opponent, or if both men should have been applauded for the quality of their acting.

After spending the first half of 1934 functioning as something of a hybrid fighter, Claybourne made a geographic move that probably stretched the outer boundaries of his personal comfort zone when he started appearing regularly in Montana.

Wrestling against "The Black Panther" Alex Kaffner had helped Claybourne to bolster his reputation as one of the best active Black wrestlers in the business, at least within the confines of the Midwest. Ironically, it would be in Montana that Claybourne would help himself to Kaffner's nickname and start being referred to regularly as the Black Panther himself, first appearing in Big Sky Country as "The Black Panther" Jack Smith.

For several valid reasons, many professional wrestling historians strongly associate "The Black Panther of Louisville" Jim Mitchell with the Black Panther name. Mitchell is credited with using the Black Panther name as early as 1929, at least one-and-a-half years before any of his wrestling peers, although certainly not before Illa Vincent, Reginald Siki, or the first use of the name by boxer-turned-wrestler George Godfrey. However, Mitchell's use of the name was certainly the most consistent.

With that being said, it is rare to find a major Black pro wrestler who competed for more than two years between 1931 and 1950 who was not promoted under the name of the Black Panther at least once. The members of this Black Panther fraternity include Reginald Siki, Jim Mitchell, Jack Claybourne, Alex Kaffner, Tiger Flowers, Tiger Jack Nelson, Seelie Samara, King Kong Clayton, Gorilla Parker, and Don Blackman *at a minimum*.

A July edition of *The Harlem News* of Harlem, Montana described Jack "The Black Panther" Smith as "a powerful negro wrestler with ears like toadstools on a stump." Despite sharing its name with Harlem, New York — a Manhattan neighborhood populated by more than 300,000 residents in the 1930s, 70 percent of whom were Black — Harlem, Montana was occupied by scarcely more than 700 residents during that same decade, all of whom were either White or American Indian.

The name Jack Smith disappeared right before pro wrestling's newest Black Panther appeared in the much larger city of Great Falls, with its population of 29,000 — several hundred of whom were Black. Promoter Bill Root said that he scouted "the shiny colored wrestler from St. Joseph, Mo." over the course of "his travels during the summer," and rated him as a first-rate showman.

Wrestling in Montana exposed Claybourne to environmental hazards that he would have been unlikely to experience when traversing shorter distances between Midwestern states. In September, Jack was one of three wrestlers booked by Root who was unable to attend a show they were scheduled for, although each wrestler presented a different reason for not being able to participate.

"Mickey McGuire got lost on a hunting trip in Oregon, the Black Panther got mired in a snowstorm enroute from Kansas, and Mack Beckley is in the hospital," explained *The Great Falls Daily Leader*.

When Jack finally arrived in Great Falls, and his bout with "Totem Pole" Anderson was rescheduled, he pulled out a victory in a city that applied the same round-based system utilized in boxing to its wrestling matches. This methodology inserted multiple opportunities for wrestlers to be saved by the bell into the performance, heightening the drama whenever it appeared a grappler was on the verge of being pinned, or more frequently when they were locked in holds they couldn't escape from, and were hoping the round would expire before their pain tolerance did.

Claybourne and Anderson had exchanged falls through submission holds in the early rounds, with the Panther taking the first fall with a surfboard hold, and Anderson forcing Jack to yield to a short-arm scissors. Then Anderson resorted to dirty tactics and started choking the Panther in the ropes with "a noose hold."

"When the referee objected, Anderson concentrated on him. The result was that [referee] Higgins, a heavyweight mat man in his own right, took a couple of swats at Anderson and sent him spinning," stated *The Great Falls Tribune*. "The black boy took advantage of Anderson's momentary dizziness and put on a Boston crab and rolled the Totem over for the finish."

In his very next outing in Great Falls, the Panther continued along his winning trajectory by taking two falls from Lou Kotonen with a bodyslam and a toehold. Then the action shifted to Montana's capital city of Helena in October, where *The Daily Independent* described Claybourne's feet as being "longer than a mule's ears," while also clearly identifying "the 168 pounds of brawn and ivory" as the babyface in his bout with Totem Pole Anderson. *The Independent* insisted "there will be plenty out there hoping the colored boy smears Totem all over the Arctic Circle."

By all accounts, Jack's actions that evening in Helena satisfied the bloodlust of the audience. After losing the first fall to Anderson with a "rolling keylock," the Panther "used a flying Dutchman and a body press" to even the fight. Then, in the fifth round of the battle, the Panther hoisted Anderson onto his shoulders, spun him around with an airplane spin, and turned him over to "send Anderson crashing to the canvas on the back of his neck, knocking him out."

Back in Great Falls, Claybourne was given the appearance of being the most dominant wrestler in Montana during that tour when he won a six-man "wrestle royal" to begin the evening, and then destroyed Tiger Backley during their bout later in the night. *The Tribune* described the Panther as spinning Backley around in the airplane spin "in the most approved roller skating fashion," after which, "Backley went down hard and failed to come out for the start of the next round."

Once the Panther had concluded this herculean effort in front of a Great Falls audience, a follow-up edition of *The Daily Leader* described him as "apparently invincible."

Hyperbole aside, history would eventually show that Claybourne was far from physically invincible. What's more, he would soon be required to show that he possessed the internal resilience to endure the racist assumptions of writers, publicists and promoters as he completed his first visit to America's West Coast.

## 2 - Tiger Style

While Jack Claybourne was completing the initial steps of a wrestling career that would make him the quintessence of what a heroic Black wrestler should be, the development of his villainous equivalent would take a far more circuitous path.

The fact that Joseph Alvin Godfrey of Malden, Massachusetts played the roles of both Tiger Flowers and Rufus Jones is a reality that escaped the attention of wrestling historians for nine decades, yet the clues required to make those connections were always present.

The known handwriting samples of Godfrey and Flowers were evaluated by a forensic specialist in Charlotte, North Carolina, who concluded that there were not enough samples available to make an official confirmation in accordance with the standards of the profession, but the writing style was so similar that the shared identity theory couldn't be ruled out.

Then again, the handwriting analysis was only conducted in the interest of being extremely thorough. More telling is the straightforward fact that Rufus Jones and Tiger Flowers used the exact same promotional photos — with matching left ears that were deformed by cauliflowering to a grotesque degree — while at least one newspaper directly outed Rufus Jones for appearing in other territories as Tiger Flowers.

All the same, a misunderstanding of the cultural significance of the name Tiger Flowers, coupled with the way it was later used by other Black performers, was apparently sufficient to throw many sleuths off of the most obvious suspect, who hid for years in plain sight.

The source of the name Tiger Flowers is no secret, as it was first used by the famous Black fighter Theodore "Tiger" Flowers. Hailing from Camilla, Georgia and making his pro debut in 1918, Flowers experienced a meteoric rise in popularity and captured the world middleweight boxing championship by dethroning Harry Greb in Madison Square Garden in 1926.

This achievement — accomplished in Flowers' 130th fight in eight years of ring activity — made him the first Black American to win the world middleweight boxing championship. It also marked the first time a boxer from the state of Georgia had captured a world boxing championship, at least according to the recollections of the sportswriters of the day.

Just one year later, Flowers would die of complications from retinal surgery, removing him from boxing while he was in his competitive prime, as he went to his grave with a record of 15-0-2 over the course of his previous 17 fights.

The Georgia native — who was referred to as "The Deacon" due to devoutly religious displays that were observable during his pre-fight routines — was one of the most prominent names in boxing circles, and an instant legend in the households of Black Americans who followed professional boxing.

In an era when Blacks were prohibited from competing in the top divisions of all major professional sports, boxing was the sole source of athletic escape in many Black households, and the one outlet through which Blacks could be seen to get the best of Whites through displays that were both violent, and justified by the rules of the game.

Consequently, several young Black fighters assumed versions of the name Tiger Flowers themselves, and attempted to ascend the boxing ranks. Variations of the name, like "Young Tiger Flowers" and "Baby Tiger Flowers," sprouted up across the boxing world. This is aside from those young fighters who blatantly took the full name Tiger Flowers for themselves without any modifications, not unlike the many Black boxers and professional wrestlers who performed under some version of the Black Panther title.

While such a practice may seem particularly untoward, especially when it comes to lifting a portion of someone's real name, it was arguably less flagrant than when Feab Smith Williams adopted the entire name of George Godfrey as a tribute to Black Canadian fighter George "Old Chocolate" Godfrey and helped the name to reach greater heights of prominence.

**Young Joe Godfrey as Tiger Flowers**

Just as Reginald Berry had adopted the name Siki to make a connection with fallen boxing legend Battling Siki and apply it to his identity as a professional wrestler, so too did Joe Godfrey adopt various versions of the name Tiger Flowers for use in a wrestling capacity.

In order to fully understand statements made by Joseph Alvin Godfrey later in his career, it's critical to understand that the first time he made clear use of the name Tiger Flowers was not the first time he capitalized upon the famous fighter's recognizable surname. February 1933 marked the debut of Flowers as "a dusky middleweight from Cuba" in New England.

Known varyingly as Ed Flowers and Nick Flowers, and often with "The Black Panther" added to his name, Flowers was thrust straight into the mix with Ted Germaine, Joe Costello, and the rest of the top wrestlers in the region.

Details from Flowers' matches throughout the spring and early summer months are difficult to come by, but a report from *The Boston Globe* in early May indicates that he had "stripped Al Vantres of his middleweight crown" during a match in Fall River.

Since the middleweight championship of the region that was offered by promoter Charley Gordon was listed as a world championship, Flowers became perhaps the first openly Black wrestler of his generation to be granted a run as an advertised world champion.

Flowers' first reign as a world champion appeared as if it would not last more than two weeks; Vantres defeated Flowers in Boston's Mechanic's Building in early May to reclaim the championship. Apparently, promoter Gordon changed his mind, and informed *The Boston Globe* days later that Vantres was "over the middleweight limit" at the time of the match, and that Flowers was still the world titleholder.

In these early stages of his career, Flowers was touted as a masterful wrestler. *The Greenfield Daily Recorder-Gazette* described his opponent Marshall Muse as being of no match for "the Cuban from Salem," as Flowers dismissed his challenge in straight falls with an armlock-bodyslam and a "back fall."

After two months of dueling with Ted Germaine, the top star in the region regained the world middleweight championship from Flowers on July 7th in Salem by winning the first and third falls.

Flowers continued to war with Germaine — a notoriously rough wrestler — and the rest of the grapplers on Charley Gordon's roster as they engaged in a promotional war with the roster of competing promoter Paul Bowser.

One of the best displays of Flowers' early competency as a wrestler was on display at the very end of November. That's when Flowers wrestled Paul Adams for one hour and nine minutes in Greenfield's Washington Hall before emerging victorious.

"Wrist locks, double arm holds, spread eagles and numerous other holds never seen here before were applied," reported *The Recorder-Gazette*. "Flowers finally won the bout after Adams had tried a couple of holds that Flowers broke out of. As quick as a flash, Flowers applied a reverse arm hold on Adams, the South Hadley mat artist tried to break away, but instead Flowers brought his arms between his legs and like a shot of lightning flopped Adams over backwards and landed on him for the fall, the time being 69 minutes."

Right in the middle of Flowers' rookie year in New England, a Black wrestler by the name of Joe "Chocolate" Gans was briefly introduced as the light-heavyweight colored champion. It was a seemingly superfluous title considering that Flowers had already held the top race-neutral championship of the region without any qualifications based on skin color.

Early in 1934, Ed Flowers was phased out of action in New England, as was his name. Surprisingly, Flowers then wrestled at least twice under his real name of Joe Godfrey, in what appear to be events promoted outside of the Charley Gordon banner.

It's possible that Godfrey wanted to avoid any unnecessary feather-ruffling by wrestling under his established name in opposition to the promoter who helped him gain traction in the industry.

The two matches were held in Saugus, Massachusetts at the Cliftondale Community House, very close to Godfrey's hometown of Malden. One of the bouts concluded in a brawl with Bill Anderson that needed to be broken up by representatives from the Saugus Police Department.

These two appearances by Godfrey under his real name were interspersed between the initial matches wrestled by Godfrey under the name Tiger Flowers in New York.

In February 1934, Tiger Flowers recorded a victory over Otto Van Burg at the Jamaica Arena in the borough of Queens in New York City. This initial reference to Flowers the wrestler only referred to his stated nationality of Cuban rather than his race. Almost immediately, Flowers had his status nominally upgraded to that of the Cuban light heavyweight champion in keeping with the international all-star nature of pro wrestling from that era.

When Flowers defeated Phil Koesch that same month at the Convention Hall of Camden, New Jersey, Flowers acquired the victory with a double-bar lock, suggesting that he possessed some level of mastery in the technical aspects of wrestling.

Perhaps out of the necessity of distancing the pro wrestler Tiger Flowers from the countless boxers making use of the same name, the first addition was made to Godfrey's pseudonym prior to a New York bout in March, with the addendum of "Johnstone" tacked onto the end. This would only be the first of several concurrent names employed by the same wrestler in different locations around various East Coast locales.

Flowers then wrestled to a draw with a grappler that he would have several encounters with, Maurice LaChapelle. Although he was often stated to have been of French extraction, LaChapelle was actually Zoltán Kájel of Hungary. This is representative of the fact that the application to false national origins within the wrestling world was broad, and applicable to wrestlers of any race.

During a follow-up appearance by Flowers in Camden, *The Courier-Post* made it clear to readers that the "clever colored foe" of Johnny "Popeye" Carlin was also Black in addition to being of faux Cuban extraction.

"In jousting with Flowers, Carlin is facing another worthy rival," glowed *The Courier-Post*. "The colored youngster is one of the cleverest light heavies ever to appear in this city, having won his first bout and drawing in his second with Maurice LaChappelle of France last Monday night. The latter bout was a whirlwind match from start to finish, and the draw decision met with popular approval."

The article went on to explain that it should be no surprise to fans if Flowers won his bout with Carlin, given that he was "built like a young Hercules" and "displayed great ability as an orthodox wrestler." A later *Courier-Post* piece would refer to him as "a perfect specimen of humanity" due to his chiseled physique.

Aside from displaying tremendous technical prowess and a powerful figure, another trait Flowers soon presented to the fans was his remarkable toughness. In a 30-minute Convention Hall draw with Pat Faletti, he made his ownership of that attribute crystal clear by exchanging stiff shots with Faletti in front of 3,500 fans, leaving both men the worse for wear.

"It was a fast, rough match, and Faletti finished with a deep gash over his left eye, while Flowers was bleeding from the mouth," described *The Courier-Post*. "Faletti, who was making his debut, started slugging early in the bout, and dropped the colored youngster on numerous occasions with terrific rights to the head and body. Flowers finally met the Italian at his own game and gave him as good as he received."

Later, *The Courier-Post* would say that Faletti was so aggressive during the show-stealing bout that "Flowers finally reached the stage where he either had to punch back or be knocked out, with the result that the bout became a brawl."

A Camden Convention Hall loss by Flowers to Harry "Speedy" Schaffer in late March revealed a few other characteristics of the young Black wrestler. Tom Ryan of *The Courier-Post* emphasized Flowers' insistence on maintaining a squeaky clean wrestling style no matter how dirty his opponents' tactics became.

Ryan wrote that "2,800 fans witnessed Schaffer subject the clean-cut colored youngster to a savage, off-color beating before winning each fall," noting how Shaffer "could have been disqualified at least 50 times for biting, punching, kneeing, and using strangle holds."

It was a reluctance to engage that was often displayed by Black wrestlers in that era. Perhaps fearing swift, physical reprisal from White fans against Black wrestlers who were seen as overly aggressive, wrestling promoters were frightfully reluctant to permit Black grapplers to tread too far into villainous territory. Instead, they were required to display implausible levels of restraint despite enduring degrees of cheating that would push ordinary athletes past the breaking point.

For example, the Black Panther Jim Mitchell retaliated to dirty tactics from a different Speedy — "Speedy O'Neal" — during a match in Kokomo, Indiana in 1932. Early in the bout, O'Neal used a series of headbutts to discombobulate and then defeat the Panther for a fall, with the headbutt being construed as a dirty move. At the conclusion of a bout in which Mitchell had "stayed with his fast, scientific grappling," the Panther responded to O'Neal's earlier series of headbutts with two of his own, and then pinned O'Neal to raucous cheers.

These uses of borderline tactics were rare, and Mitchell can only be found resorting to the use of headbutts early in his career when retaliating against an exceedingly dirty opponent, and even then, only on the rarest of occasions. In 1934 in Battle Creek, his use of the move against Red Sims surprised sportswriter G.B. Dolliver Jr., who called it "a new trick of Jimmy's, which we'll call a head-bump for lack of anything better." In general, match descriptions show that Mitchell received far more headbutts than he administered during the early stages of his career.

Aside from this, Mitchell was developed and promoted in a fashion that fit the mold established by Reginald Siki. A description of Mitchell by *The Kokomo Tribune* of Indiana from 1932 described him as a scientific wrestler who had trained in Europe, and who "knows enough of a dozen different languages to at least order ham and eggs." Simply swapping the name of Jim Mitchell with that of Reginald Siki would have rendered this endorsement identical to those written of Siki a decade earlier.

While Flowers had showcased his great reluctance to get down and dirty with his opponent during that match in South Jersey, he also displayed a physical trait that caught Tom Ryan's attention when the writer noticed what the specific target of many of Schaffer's illegal punches had been.

"A punch early in the match opened Flowers' left ear, which is one of the finest 'cauliflowers' in the mat industry, yet, despite the painful injury, the colored youth stuck to his guns and went down fighting gamely each time he was pinned," noted Ryan.

On top of his musculature, the strikingly cauliflowered left ear of the original Tiger Flowers would become one of the principal means of identifying him. For what it's worth, the legitimate fear held by wrestling promoters that the heelish actions of a wrestler might spark real conflict with the audience is justified by the outcome of this very bout.

*Philadelphia Inquirer* reporter Ronald Friedenberg observed that a "burly fellow" who "was particularly abusive" challenged Schaffer to a fight after the wrestler had finished abusing Flowers. This led to Schaffer stripping off one of his two pairs of tights and inviting the fan to fight him in the ring. Fortunately, the fan declined the invitation.

In April, Flowers began wrestling in New York with greater regularity, and extended his appearances to different venues around the city. This included what would retroactively be an ironic ending to a match that took place inside of a small venue in Manhattan.

"A head-on collision between Tiger Flowers Johnstone and Herman Donchin resulted in both of them being counted out and a draw being rendered at the St. Nicholas Arena last night after 28 minutes 20 seconds," reported *The Brooklyn Daily Eagle*.

As a new Black entrant to the entertainment scene of New York City, Flowers was simply keeping pace with the zeitgeist of the city. Just one month before Flowers made his debut, the 125th Street Apollo Theater reopened as a performance venue catering to Black audiences with Black entertainers and an all-Black staff. It would soon become a cherished symbol of Black art, entertainment and culture.

May would be the month that the first in a slew of fake baptismal names would be bestowed upon Flowers, with one New York promoter labeling him Charley "Tiger Flowers" Johnstone. While this was the most common spelling of Flowers' surname, Johnston and Johnson also became common alternatives. For example, the Johnston spelling was used when describing Flowers' act of brutalizing Axel Madsen after the latter had bridged his way out of half a dozen pinning attempts.

"Shortly after the 25-minute mark had been reached, Madsen scored with flying mares," observed *The Brooklyn Time Union*. "However, Johnston whipped back from a mare to score with a flying tackle, and that was the beginning of the end. Battered by tackles, Madsen fell easy prey for the series of slams which followed, and was easily pinned by the body slam."

Changes to the names that bookended Tiger Flowers weren't the only alterations that were made to the wrestler's title. Also in May, Flowers was squarely inducted into the pantheon of Black wrestlers who would be forced to wear the name of "Black Panther" when *The Bergen Evening Record* described him as "Tiger Flowers Johnstone, The Black Panther," making Flowers a bearer of the name in two states.

It was an inherently awkward use of the name that simultaneously ascribed two very different breeds of the Panthera genus to the same person, and was far from the only time that the labels would be paired so clumsily. On more than one occasion, Black wrestling star Tiger Jack Nelson would have his name appended with "The Black Panther" in advertisements for his matches in California.

Flowers would also be lumped into the company of the other Black stars of his era in another way. In the promotion for a Hasbrouck Heights show in New Jersey, in which half the wrestlers on the roster were touted as the representative champions of their respective nations, Flowers at least temporarily shed his false Cuban identity and was advertised as the "colored champion."

Of course, there were inevitably descriptions of Flowers that combined all of those identities, like when *The Bergen Evening Record* labeled Flowers as a grappler "who lays claim to the light heavyweight championship of Cuba and Harlem, is one of the most subtle, scientific grapplers of the present age. He is as spry as a panther and just as foxy. Moreover, he's a great showman, and that is a great addition to a grappler."

Regardless of how he was advertised prior to the opening bell, Flowers developed a favorable reputation for being one of the standout wrestlers on the card once his matches were underway. Reporting favorably about Flowers' match with LaChappelle in Teterboro, *The Bergen Evening Record* noted that "the bout lacked the tragedy, clowning, burping, and grunting associated with the other bouts, but was waged scientifically. There wasn't a rough moment in it, but the masters put on an excellent show that was called a draw. Both were given a wild ovation."

So noticeable was Flowers' reliance on his technical wrestling prowess at this early juncture that promotion for him began to lean all the more heavily into spotlighting those abilities. *The Evening Record* anointed him as "an expert wrestler with all the science and ring lore of a Londos or a Lewis — and just as tough when opponents try to spread him."

It was quite premature to compare Flowers to full-fledged legends like "The Golden Greek" Jim Londos or Ed "Strangler" Lewis, both of whom were beloved White champions whose names were recognized across the continent and around the world. Moreover, making such comparisons carried other potential risks, like offending White wrestling fans who wouldn't take kindly to having a Black wrestler compared so favorably with their heroes.

Given the palpability of the underlying racial tension that lingered in many of the urban metropolises of the United States in the 1930s, it was seemingly inevitable that someone would make an overt threat to the proprietors of any form of combat theater in which a Black wrestler was even occasionally seen to be getting the better of his White opponents.

In June, prominent wrestling promoter Jack Pfefer of Teterboro submitted one of those threats for public consumption through *The Bergen Evening Record*.

"Guess you haven't been reading the Bergen County newspapers lately, else we don't think you would have the nerve to bring Tiger Flowers Johnstone over to wrestle at Teterboro Saturday night," began the letter. "We still have a few more crosses to burn and we never run out of matches. This is just a friendly tip so take it while the taking is good and call the match off. (Signed) K.K.K."

The letter was published by *The Bergen Evening Record* along with the response from Jack Pfefer, who declared that he would not be intimidated by "night prowlers" with "pillow cases and bed sheets over their heads," and that Flowers would indeed be appearing as advertised.

In addition to addressing the threat made by presumed members of the Ku Klux Klan, the article by *The Evening Record* also delved into the fact that Flowers had been picking up "a lot of easy money posing for some of the most noted sculptors in the country."

As tempting as it might be to attribute bravery to both Pfefer and Flowers for insisting that the show must go on beneath a cloud of intimidation, the aforementioned threat must be taken with a huge grain of salt considering its alleged target.

Over the course of the next decade, Jack Pfefer would gain a reputation for being something of a swindler and charlatan in promotional circles. While credited as one of wrestling's original innovators with respect to the use of pageantry to attract fans, Pfefer would likewise be cast as someone who would stoop to any level to garner attention for his wrestling product.

Therefore, the legitimacy of any such threats being directed at Pfefer must also be questioned, especially when *he* was the person alerting the media to the existence of the threats, and responding with such bluster.

When Flowers appeared in the Pennsauken Township Arena and wrestled under the auspices of promoter Charley Grip, he would have his name modified again. This time, the surname of Johnstone was dropped altogether, and he was provided the first name of Ted — a common abbreviation for Theodore — to make him a closer match to the original Theodore "Tiger" Flowers, the boxer who inspired his name.

Flowers usually appeared to hold his own during the introductory matches that exposed him to fresh audiences at new venues, but he quickly fell into the pattern of losing the overwhelming majority of his bouts. When he did win, it was often under disputed circumstances that made it clear that he was the inferior wrestler. Such was the case when he wrestled Max Martin of Ohio at the Jamaica Arena.

"The Ohioan had Johnstone beaten to a frazzle," wrote J.J. McAlester of *The Brooklyn Times Union*. "A series of flying tackles had left the Cuban lying half way out of the ring, stunned and ready for the cleaners."

The referee administered the 10-count to Flowers as he rested on the floor beside the ring, and as the count reached nine, Martin turned away and began to celebrate. Just as the referee uttered the word "Ten," Flowers burst beneath the ropes, applied a flying body scissors to the surprised Martin, and won the match with a pin.

"The fans who jammed the house to the guards, despite the heat, were of the opinion that Johnstone had been counted out and hooted the verdict," added McAlester. "Martin, in the dressing room, stated that he turned away from Johnstone only when he thought the referee had finished counting. The clamor raised by the fans should earn the genial brother of Sergt. Bob Martin another crack at his fluky competitor."

Another reason for Flowers requiring some name modifications was made evident by some of the other flawed comparisons that were used to explain the level of skill that Flowers brought to the wrestling ring.

In one of his articles, Stan Baumgartner of *The Philadelphia Inquirer* referred to him as "Tiger Flowers, the Kid Chocolate of the mat," which seems like a harmless hodgepodge of names at first glance. In actuality, it was a perplexing pairing of names that was designed to attract the attention of boxing fans.

In effect, Baumgartner was using the name of a deceased world champion fighter and pairing it with the name of arguably the most dominant super featherweight boxer active in the world at the time — Eligio "Kid Chocolate" Montalvo of Cuba. Theoretically, Baumgartner justified this naming practice on the basis that Tiger Flowers the wrestler was supposedly an Afro-Cuban like Montalvo.

It was at this point when the name confusion surrounding Tiger Flowers the wrestler truly escalated, as he returned to using the name Ed prior to a bout with LaChappelle at Pennsauken arena. If the same wrestling fan tracked every performance by Flowers across four different locations over the course of the same week, they would find the wrestler introduced as Tiger Flowers, Ed "Tiger" Flowers, Ted "Tiger" Flowers, and Charley "Tiger Flowers" Johnstone, depending on the venue they were seated in.

## Gentleman Jack and Rough Rufus

Jack Claybourne began 1935 in a very different part of the country from Flowers, as he continued to tour Montana as the Black Panther, and was undoubtedly the first Black wrestler to appear in many of the cities and towns around Big Sky Country. Cases in which the news publications imposed racist language upon his bouts were infrequent, but they undoubtedly occurred.

In Belgrade, the writer of *The Belgrade Journal* described Claybourne as a "big Buck Negro." He then attributed the quote to Claybourne's opponent, Montana middleweight champion Eddie Meyers, that Meyers would "make this black cotton-picker wish that he had never seen Montana," later adding that he would "tie up the black boy and send him home to his mammy in St. Joe."

Even in cases where there was no way to pass the racist quotes onto a wrestler, the writer for *The Belgrade Journal* still employed language intended to force readers to draw prejudicial inferences. For example, when Claybourne prepared to wrestle against Oklahoman Bill Cazzell, the writer included the statement that "fans expect to see the Oklahoma white boy throw the cotton picker plenty hard."

Ironically, "white boy" Bill Cazzell would routinely wrestle as an American Indian in other parts of the country, and would coincidentally appear as a masked wrestler known as the Black Panther in a few of the Southern states.

Predictably, the use of plainly racist language would be something that Claybourne would have to get used to when wrestling in states with only a scant few Black inhabitants. Jack soon began splitting his time between Oregon and Montana before transitioning over to Oregon on a relatively full-time basis.

In some cities in Oregon — including Salem — Claybourne originally wrestled as Jack "Snowball" Clayton, while still being simultaneously labeled as the Black Panther. Fortunately, the use of this objectionable nickname only persisted for a short time, as "snowball" was a derogatory term for American Blacks that extended back to the 18th century.

Sadly, the ethnic slurs didn't end there. In Salem, Claybourne was stamped as "Mose" by *The Oregon Statesman*. One of the sources for the term "Mose" came through the comic strip "Musical Mose," which was written and illustrated by mixed-race Louisiana Creole cartoonist George Herriman — a man for whom questions of racial identity always occupied a prominent place in his work.

In the syndicated strip, the Black American protagonist Mose was a musician who repeatedly attempted to impersonate other ethnicities — usually Whites — only to suffer regular, harsh beatings as a consequence of having his Black identity found out.

Fortunately for Claybourne, his wrestling talent appears to have been respected from the moment he arrived, and he swiftly piled up victories. In Corvallis, the "jet-black colored chap who is built like an Olympic athlete" was immediately given a win over a former football player from Oregon State University.

"[Claybourne] met Bill Kenna, former State College football guard, but the ex-collegian was no match for the smooth working Claybourne, and after dropping the first fall, the colored grappler returned to the ring to annex the next two falls and the match," recorded *The Daily-Gazette Times*.

As Claybourne was booked for return engagements in Corvallis, *The Gazette Times* was tasked with offering readers a deeper dive into Jack's backstory, and also the appearance of "the dynamiting negro middleweight."

"Claybourne is around the six foot mark and weighs a little over 170 pounds," described *The Gazette Times*. "He is the blackest, liveliest negro grappler that has ever shown his wares in Corvallis, said local promoters here today. Everywhere Claybourne has wrestled, the fans have packed the arenas upon the occasion of his return engagements. He resorts to a very clean type of wrestling, breaking cleanly and conducting a tough but clean campaign throughout his entire match."

Sadly, the promoters in Corvallis also attempted to use the same article to apply the nickname "Midnight" to

Claybourne because of the dark shade of his skin. In an Oregon city with exceedingly few Black residents in the 1930s, apparently the presence of a dark-skinned Black man in Corvallis was an attraction in its own right.

**Jack Claybourne's "Fevven Sakes" promotional photo**

In April 1935, a large photo of Claybourne was included in *The Sunday Oregonian* of Portland, with his eyes directed at something off to the reader's left, and his palms pressed together in front of his body at chest level. The caption-writer for *The Sunday Oregonian* saw fit to interpret this as a prayerful posture, and captioned the photo "Fevven Sakes, Lawd, Help Me."

The clear intent was to suggest that Claybourne was offering up to God "a fervent plea for divine protection" from the other participants in the battle royal he was set to engage in at Portland's Labor Temple.

However, by rendering the sentence "For heaven sakes, Lord, help me" as "Fevven sakes," the caption writer was imposing the catchphrase of Mushmouth — a character from the *Moon Mullins* comic strip — onto Claybourne. In the comic strip, Mushmouth is the morbidly obese, lazy, oafish, Black sidekick of the White titular character.

Along with the radio sitcom *Amos 'n' Andy*, in which White voice actors Freeman Gosden and Charles Correll offered up their best minstrel show exaggerations of Black speech patterns, comic strips were often the sole sources of exposure that many Whites living in isolated regions of the United States and Canada had to representations of Black people.

Because of this, harmful stereotypes of Blacks established during the era could reach households that actual Black people would never have been invited into, resulting in wrestlers like Claybourne being forced to contend with these prejudices — and often to cater to them — in the hopes of ingratiating themselves with paying audiences composed exclusively of White wrestling fans.

This is a facet of the U.S. entertainment landscape that wouldn't really begin to get rectified until the Negro Actors Guild of America — founded the following year in New York City — would begin to acquire influence, generating more opportunities for Black performers and improving their representations in theater, film, and radio.

As for the article itself, it can be extrapolated from the writing that promoter Herb Owen was using the late addition of the man who was now occasionally being called "the Black Panther from Michigan" into the battle royal to test the waters of including a Black wrestler in the main events held in

Oregon's largest city. In the process, he explained away the absence of Claybourne from prior main events as being the byproduct of racist attitudes harbored by some of the wrestlers on his roster.

"Bulldog Jackson, Rod Fenton and other 'meanies' wanted nothing to do with the Michigan blackbird, giving the color line as a flimsy excuse," stated *The Sunday Oregonian*. "But Promoter Owen outsmarted the dodgers by signing them for the free-for-all and then unexpectedly substituting Claybourne when it was too late for the 'villains' to back out."

Claybourne gave a decent showing in that April battle royal, outlasting four other men and making it to the final pairing before he was pinned by Del Kunkel after "a series of body slams and piledriver holds."

If Claybourne's inclusion in the main event was viewed as justice being served, then it was an extension of events that were transpiring within the U.S. justice system. That same month, the Supreme Court rendered its unanimous decision on the *Norris v. Alabama* case in which nine Black teens were falsely accused or raping two White women, and the local jury selection process had ensured an all-White jury for their trial.

This Supreme Court decision established racial diversity as an expectation during jury trials, primarily to prevent all-White juries from imposing judgements on Black defendants solely on the basis of their prejudicial attitudes toward them.

Citing Claybourne's bravery as justification for including him in more main events in Portland, Owen immediately thrust Claybourne into a main-event bout with villainous Rod Fenton, "holder of the mythical meanie championship."

"The Black Panther showed in the battle royal that he fears no one," said *The Sunday Oregonian*. "He slugged toe-to-toe with the villains and dealt out more punishment than he received. This factor makes the 'experts' give him an even chance to topple the detested Fenton."

Claybourne had already acquired the habit that would also see him often referred to as "Jumping Jack," as he would finish off his adversaries with either one dropkick, or an extended sequence of dropkicks depending on the tone and progression of the match.

If an opponent was still relatively fresh, a first dropkick might drop the surprised adversary to the ground, a second dropkick would cause the opponent to recover more slowly, and then Claybourne would quickly land a final dropkick to the chin of his stunned, staggering, or kneeling opponent to bring the fall to an end.

It didn't take long for Claybourne's dangerous feet to come into play during his bout with Fenton. *The Oregonian* stated that Claybourne "had the crowd with him from the start," and "battered Fenton to the floor in 7 minutes 12 seconds, using dropkicks to flatten his opponent."

The same match showcased how Claybourne's dropkicks could also lead to his undoing. In the second fall, Claybourne began his series of dropkicks when Fenton "caught his ankles and turned him over for a Boston crab hold." With Claybourne now slowed and weakened, Fenton landed several punches to Claybourne's chin during the third fall and then pinned him for the victory.

There were other negative consequences to Claybourne's succession of deadly, yet theatrical kicks. One day later, Claybourne and the dropkick barrage he unleashed upon Fenton were cited as evidence for how fake the modern wrestling of the mid 1930s had become in an editorial by George Putnam in *The Capital Journal* of Salem, Oregon.

"The negro battered the white to the floor in 7 minutes and 12 seconds using 'flying drop kicks' to flatten his opponent," wrote Putnam. "He tried dropkicks again but was 'outsmarted.' When the negro leaped feet first at him, the white caught his ankles and turned him over for a 'Boston crab hold.'"

Putnam observed that the affair contained "little wrestling in it," and that wrestlers of the era were actually "actors staging a rehearsed show" for "the entertainment of morons." In this way, Putnam argued that the modern performers were distinct from the wrestlers of 20 years prior, the majority of whom participated in matches with outcomes that were equally as predetermined, but with cooperation that was less detectable to the uninitiated.

If nothing else, this anecdote serves to reinforce the notion that there has almost always been tension between the wrestling purists of each era who concluded that their preferred style of wrestling was the best, and regarded changes as unwelcome. As time progressed, they sought to discredit any stylistic changes that caused observers to further doubt the authenticity of the in-ring combat.

Back in Corvallis, promotional efforts centered around providing onlookers with opportunities to gaze upon Claybourne's darkness, as *The Daily Gazette Times* ensured fans that their "demand for color" would be satisfied by Claybourne's presence in the ring when he faced Dorry Dutton.

"There is listed tonight Jack Claybourne, the blackest black one will ever see, and probably one of the best athletes," promised the article. "Claybourne is a big fellow, fast and quite efficient in the ring. He does not try much of the dirty type of wrestling, being content to let the regular run of the events take care of themselves."

Claybourne won the bout with Dutton, and continued to give a good accounting of himself throughout the summer months. Midway through August, Claybourne experienced the crowning achievement of his stay in Oregon when he won a six-man battle royal at the Multnomah Civic Stadium, an outdoor athletic field.

The final three competitors in the ring were Claybourne, Danny McShain, and Bulldog Jackson. The latter two grapplers had seemingly reached an agreement to eliminate Claybourne together "until McShain decided to get rid of Jackson in a sudden about-face maneuver."

"About the only satisfaction Jackson got from the melee was knocking McShain slightly groggy in an unscheduled scuffle outside of the ring after his elimination," continued *The*

*Oregonian.* "It was enough to give Claybourne a decided advantage and the winning fall in four minutes more with a dropkick and body press."

Claybourne was proving that he could weather the storm with respect to how a Black American could handle himself in environments that were at least somewhat racially insensitive, if not outright hostile. Within mere months, he would be tasked with portraying two distinct ethnicities in areas where his presence was not only unwanted, but was technically unlawful.

## 3 - La Pantera Negra

The Black Panther of Michigan may have developed into an occasional title for Claybourne while he was in Oregon, but Tiger Flowers *actually* ventured into Michigan early in 1935 and extended the range of his travels. It was here that he would drop the 'T' and 'E' from his surname and simplify his ring name to Tiger Flowers Johnson. He would also seemingly dabble in some new wrestling tactics, as he "butted his way to victory" over Fred Kimble during his debut at the Arena Gardens roller rink on Detroit's Woodward Avenue.

When Flowers moved on to the Western Michigan, he would follow in the tradition of the Black wrestlers who had preceded him in those rings, like "The Black Panther of Tennessee" Jack Nelson, Gorilla Parker, and "The Black Panther of Louisville" Jim Mitchell, by also assuming the title of colored heavyweight champion.

Additionally, Flowers would also benefit from the common promotional tactic of being favorably compared to his Black peers in a way that ran the risk of simultaneously diminishing them in the eyes of the same fans. To accomplish this, *The Herald Press* of St. Joseph informed fans that Flowers had defeated both the Black Panther and Gorilla Parker prior to his arrival, when there is no evidence Flowers had even been within shouting distance of either man.

To be clear, it was a widespread practice for wrestling promoters to refer to all of their new arrivals as being the latest and greatest grapplers to ever appear in the area. The way the practice differed in the specific case of Black wrestlers is that they were exclusively compared to other Black wrestlers in the overwhelming majority of cases. The practice of degrading an entire class of wrestlers with each successive appearance by a new Black wrestler ran the risk of invalidating the credentials of the wrestlers of similar hues that preceded them.

During the same tour, multiple Western Michigan news publications like *The Battle Creek Enquirer* and *The Herald-Press* called out the overuse of the Tiger Flowers name in combat sports, and referred to the wrestler Flowers as "another of the scores of professional athletes named Tiger Flowers," and clarifying that this Flowers, like the others, had "copied his name after the brilliant Negro boxer, now dead."

**Tiger Flowers flexes for the camera**

Within the St. Joseph Armory, Flowers would experiment with another method of concluding matches. After surrendering the first fall of the bout to Ralph Garibaldi, Flowers worked his way through a sequence for achieving both victory and defeat that would soon become a regular routine in Jack Claybourne's playbook.

"The Italian won the first fall in 16 minutes with his old Indian death lock; Flowers evened matters five minutes later, flooring Garibaldi with a series of three drop kicks," illustrated *The Herald Press*. "Garibaldi won the deciding fall in a rather freakish manner, flopping Flowers with a leg pull after the Negro had attempted another series of drop kicks."

Wrestling in Oakland County just north of Detroit, Flowers would be involved in an incident that the Associated Press would carry to several states. Throughout his match with Frank Malciewicz, the clean-cut Flowers endured repeated fouls, with the Pontiac crowd growing increasingly more infuriated by Malciewicz's cheating. When referee Charles Southerland finally threw the match out and awarded the decision to Flowers after one final foul, the crowd decided to exact revenge on Flowers' behalf.

"The fans, irked by the methods Malciewicz used against his opponent, Tiger Flowers Johnson of Cuba, charged the ring," reported the AP. "Malciewicz was badly bruised before police could quell the rioting patrons."

Back in Detroit, Flowers would finally interact with one of the other Black stars of his generation when he shared the card with Gorilla Parker. It's quite possible that Parker — who frequently went by William "Gorilla" Parker, adopted the Gorilla nickname as a nod to the famous Black boxer William "Gorilla" Jones of Memphis, Tennessee.

Like the real Tiger Flowers, Gorilla Jones held the world middleweight boxing championship, defeating Oddone Piazza for the honors in January 1932. Even before capturing the world middleweight championship, Jones had amassed a remarkable string of victories and was already regarded as one of the best fighters of the world.

It is presumably due to the success of Gorilla Jones that Henry Daniels of Frederick, Oklahoma first took the name William "Gorilla" Parker and began his run through the Midwest, starting in Detroit.

A short wrestler who was generously listed at 5'6", Parker was one of the most well-muscled wrestlers of the era, and was often likened to a billiard ball that caromed around the ring, albeit as a figurative ball of muscle.

This initial campaign by Parker included several matches with "The Black Panther of Tennessee" Tiger Jack

Nelson, culminating in the closest thing to a legitimate match for an unofficial colored world light heavyweight wrestling championship in existence at the time, which Parker won.

**Gorilla Parker**

Despite the conspicuous presence of two competent Black wrestling stars on the match cards, Flowers and Parker were kept separate from one another even as the tour dipped into Ohio, before the pair ultimately wound up back together in New York, New Jersey, and Pennsylvania. It was also here that Parker would revert to using his East Coast name of Zimba Parker.

Flowers' venture away from New York City was fortunate inasmuch as it kept him far away from the city during the infamous Harlem riot of 1935, which was considered by many historians to be one of the first modern race riots of the 20th century.

The Great Migration — a decades-long event encapsulating the movement of Southern Blacks to primarily urban centers in the Northern states — resulted in massive demographic shifts in the neighborhoods of several major cities. In the Harlem neighborhood of Upper Manhattan, the population shifted from 33 percent Black in 1920 to more than 70 percent Black by 1930.

On March 19th, 1935, the detention of a Black Puerto Rican teen who was shoplifting in the White-owned Kress Five and Ten store across the street from the Apollo Theater resulted in threats of physical harm being made to the teen by the manager of the store. Even after the teen was released, rumors that the teen had been beaten and potentially killed by the store's employees spread, resulting in the offending store being looted, along with several other White-owned businesses in Harlem.

The riot was brought under control before the day ended, with three deaths, 100 injuries, and 125 arrests. The Harlem riot was noteworthy for the focus on damage to property as opposed to the intentional infliction of physical harm, coupled with the primary clash taking place between low-income Black citizens and the police force sent to restrain them.

Regardless, when New York's most popular Black wrestler returned to the city, it was in the aftermath of the event that was said to have killed the hope and optimism of the Harlem Renaissance.

That lack of hope and optimism was seemingly reflected in Flowers' win-loss record. His second East Coast swing was certainly less successful than his first, as he routinely dropped matches to his White opponents. In fact, the primary beneficiary from the presence of multiple respected Black light heavyweights being active in the Northeast region appears to have been Maurice LaChappelle.

*The Courier-Post* of Camden called attention to the fact that LaChappelle had knocked off one Black wrestler after another to cement his status as the top light heavyweight in the region, with Flowers and Parker serving as his vanquished adversaries.

In many ways, the most significant and enduring event that would occur for Tiger Flowers in 1935 would be in September, with the reveal of an artistic production that would add credence to the claim made during the previous year that Flowers' modeling services were in high demand.

At the 27th annual Stockbridge Art Exhibition, one of the "notable pieces" reported on by *The Berkshire Eagle* of Pittsfield, Massachusetts was a bust of the head of "Tiger Flowers Johnstone, a colored wrestler" by Emily Winthrop Miles. The bust of Flowers would include a peculiar feature that would truly distinguish it from similar busts — the severely cauliflowered left ear of Joseph Godfrey, which would be one of his signature traits throughout his career.

The works of Miles would go on to be displayed in several art museums across the Northeastern U.S., including the head of Flowers, which would eventually find a home in the Fogg Museum of Harvard University.

The reveal of the bust of Flowers' head would rekindle the flattering discussions of his features, with *The Herald-News* of Passaic stating that "[Flowers'] physical makeup is one that would create envy, so much so in fact that recently he was voted the most perfectly developed athlete his weight in

America at a meeting of sculptors for whom the 'Tiger' has been a model for some years."

Miles also completed drawings of both Tiger Flowers and his young wife, but the drawings were incorrectly identified as the boxer Theodore "Tiger" Flowers and his wife Willie Mae. Since Joseph Godfrey was serving as the model for the bust and drawing under the name Tiger Flowers, the model identified as the wife of Tiger Flowers is very likely to have been Godfrey's wife Ursaline.

The very same month that the bust of Tiger Flowers was unveiled to art aficionados, *The Moncton Daily Times* informed its readers that one of their local favorites, Vic Butland, had become a huge hit in Montreal, and that he was set to wrestle against Tiger Flowers, revealing that Flowers had also taken his act to Canada.

Advertisement for a Tiger Flowers appearance in Ottawa

Few match results are available from Flowers' tour of Quebec, but one crucial description of one of his matches survived. An October edition of *The Montreal Gazette* reported how Tiger Flowers had been disqualified from his bout against Fred Slavik at the Mount Royal Arena. In an outcome that strongly foreshadowed events that were to come, Flowers was disqualified "for butting the referee with his head."

While Flowers' wrestling career had seemingly involved a detour into modeling, Jack Claybourne's career direction during the remainder of 1935 had taken multiple turns. *The Oregon Daily Journal* had very abruptly begun to describe the dark-skinned Claybourne as being "very Ethiopian-like in color," and when he soon departed from Oregon and traveled to the Texas-Mexico border, that was a facet of his characterization that survived the journey.

Not only was Claybourne said to appear Ethiopian once he arrived in Texas, but he was declared to have been an Ethiopian straight from the Horn of Africa. It was a national designation that was very much a product of the political climate of the 1920s and 1930s. It had also had an influence on the presentation of Black wrestlers during the previous generation.

When Ras Tafari Makonnen first rose to prominence in Ethiopia in the 1920s, Reginald Siki's country of origin was retroactively changed from Senegal to Ethiopia in order to keep pace with current events. When Makonnen subsequently emerged as the Emperor of Ethiopia in 1930 and changed his name and title to Hailie Selassie, he attracted even more attention from the global media.

At the commencement of the second Italo-Ethiopian War, which was instigated by the fascist Italian government of dictator Benito Mussolini, seemingly every active Black wrestler from North America — including Alex Kaffner, Tiger Jack Nelson, Gorilla Parker and Jack Claybourne — was granted some sort of connection to Ethiopia for the sake of modernizing their characters to keep pace with the news cycle.

In the case of "The Black Demon" George Hoddison, the Massachusetts-based grappler would make the change a permanent feature of his presentation when he began appearing under the Ethiopian-inspired names of Seelie Samara — or Zelis Amhara in Quebec — Ras Samara, and Hailie Samara.

In Juarez, Mexico, in October 1935, the ersatz Ethiopian Claybourne was enthusiastically embraced by the Mexican fans when he made his debut there.

"Juarez wrestling fans shouted 'Viva Ethiopia' and lifted 'The Black Panther,' Negro wrestler, to their shoulders last night at the Pan American Stadium when he won a match from a wrestler billed as Renato Garibaldi, Italian," reported *The El Paso Herald-Post*. "'Down with Mussolini' shouted the fans, when the Negro pinned his opponent's shoulders to the mat."

The punchline to the article arrived in its closing sentence, when it was revealed that the "so-called Italian wrestler" was "Jack Purdin, blond American."

In stark contrast to the way he was received in Juarez, Claybourne was outright banned from appearing on the other side of the Rio Grande in El Paso, Texas. Even though Claybourne had been previously advertised to appear, promoter Jack McIntosh pulled Claybourne from a late-October show once he discovered that the wrestler was Black.

In his vain attempt to reacquire his position on the card, Claybourne reportedly made a statement to *The El Paso Times* that he "isn't a negro" in the classic sense of the term because he was of "Cuban lineage." Apparently this was born out of the belief that culture trumped skin color with respect to racial designations, and possibly because Afro-Cuban fighters like "Kid Chocolate" Montalvo had been observed to achieve greater public acceptance than Black American fighters.

This was further discussed in the November 8th edition of *The Times*. Promoter McIntosh expressed his own confusion over the situation — likely for show — stating that he hired the Panther thinking that he was bringing in a Cuban, only to discover once Claybourne reached Texas that "he was as black as the traditional ace of spades, and had all of the earmarks of an American negro, barred from wrestling and boxing rings in Texas."

The far more likely scenario is that it was McIntosh himself who attempted to pass Claybourne off as a foreign wrestler in order to sidestep the ban on the U.S. side of the river, and was unsuccessful in his attempt. McIntosh was probably quite familiar with the fact that the population of Cuba was approximately 10 percent Black in the mid-1930s, and therefore knew that a Cuban with a dark complexion was nothing out of the ordinary, least of all in Cuba.

There were other events brewing on the opposite side of the Atlantic Ocean in 1935 that compromised the career of a Black wrestler, and would eventually have a hand in the way Black American wrestlers were booked.

Jim Wango, a Black wrestler who was often labeled as a citizen of France, took part in a wrestling tour of Europe that brought him to parts of Switzerland and Germany, and resulted in him moving from total obscurity to becoming a major political talking point in the United States.

After Wango had either won or drawn in all of his tournament matches held in Nuremberg, Germany, he was prevented by German police from continuing to wrestle in Nazi Germany on the grounds that his appearance caused "public unrest."

"This occurred after Julius Streicher, the anti-Semitic propagandist, had visited the hall and delivered a speech to which he declared that it was only 'an advertising stunt,' and 'an appeal to the inferior when a nigger was allowed to compete with whites,'" reported *The Newcastle Evening Chronicle*. "Respect was due to every race, said Streicher, but it would have been better if the negro had been left at home."

Greater elaboration of Streicher's statement was provided when the full report from Nazi newspaper *The Fränkische Tageszeitung* was made available to the Associated Negro Press.

"Those who organize wrestling matches between Negroes and white men are damaging the white race," insisted Streicher. "It is contrary to the spirit of Nuremberg to see white men defeated in wrestling by black men. People who applaud when a black man has floored a man of our race are not of Nuremberg. Moreover, a woman who applauds no longer can have anything to do with Nuremberg."

The Nazi publication added that the key factor contributing to Wango's in-ring success had been the unfair advantage conferred by Wango's epidermis. *The Fränkische Tageszeitung* quite literally stated that Wango's skin "being oily and smooth, permitted him to slip literally from the clutches of his adversaries."

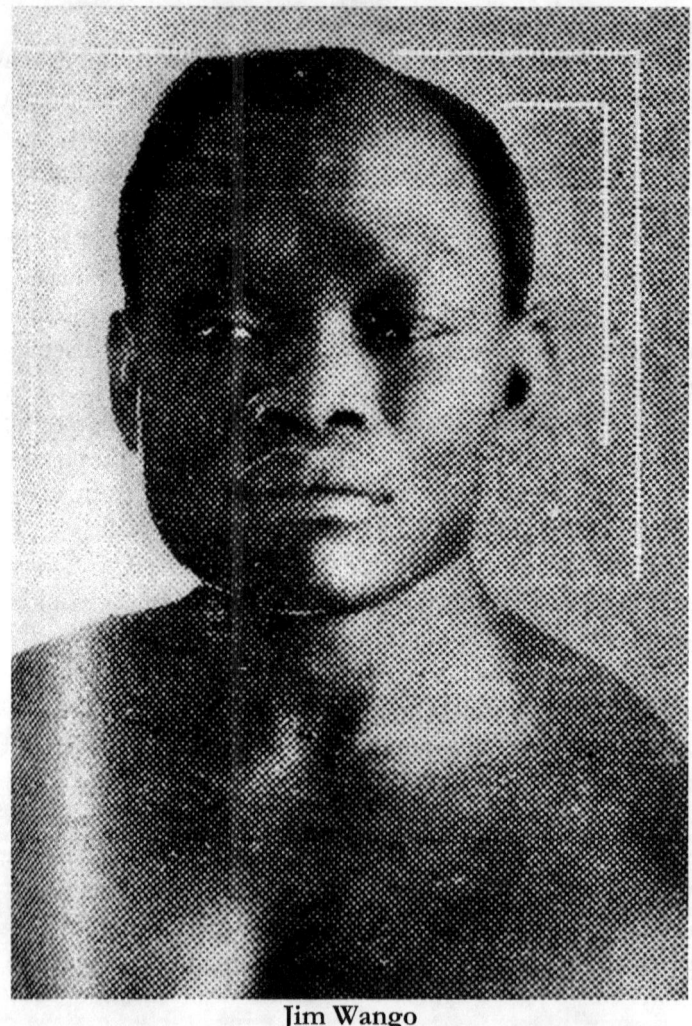

**Jim Wango**

Overseas anecdotes like this would eventually result in scenarios where Black wrestlers would be forced to uphold the honor of their race by competing against "Nazis" like "Young Hitler," as LeRoy "King Kong" Clayton would be called upon to do during his lengthy tours of Montana.

Around the same time as his appearances in Texas, Claybourne wrestled in New Mexico for promoter Johnny Flaska as "the Black Panther of Portland," or "La Pantera Negra" in Spanish. *The Albuquerque Tribune* introduced him as "the Joe Louis of the wrestling world," who was seeking an opportunity to capture the light heavyweight championship.

"Flaska said Sunday the Panther has challenged such men as Hugh Nichols and Leroy McGuirk," added *The Albuquerque Journal*. "He has been a terror on the Pacific Coast. He specializes in the drop kick and shoulder buck. He is a black Adonis."

Comparisons to Joseph Louis Barrow — shortened to Joe Louis for simplicity's sake — were beginning to become commonplace for Black wrestlers who had previously been compared to George Godfrey and Harry Wills. With the rapid rise of Louis into the mainstream of heavyweight boxing, almost every Black wrestler would find himself advertised as the "Brown Bomber" or "Dark Angel" of wrestling in order to capitalize on a flattering comparison with the world's most famous Black athlete and borrow his nicknames.

In his New Mexico debut at St. Mike's Gym, La Pantera Negra defeated Ibeen Seleem in "a fast rough battle," capturing two falls out of three in just over 45 minutes. A few days later, promoter Flaska was said by *The Tribune* to have realized that he had access to "the best wrestling showman" seen in New Mexico "in many a day" in the person of La Pantera Negra, and would now set out to find adversaries worthy of him.

Vic Weber of New York was soon deemed to be an opponent who presented a challenge worthy of the Panther, and through the first fall of his match with the Panther in Santa

Fe, Weber gave every indication that he was up to the challenge.

*The Santa Fe New Mexican* detailed how Weber took the first fall from Claybourne with a series of "wrist whiplocks," and was well on his way to winning the second fall when the Panther outmaneuvered him and won the match.

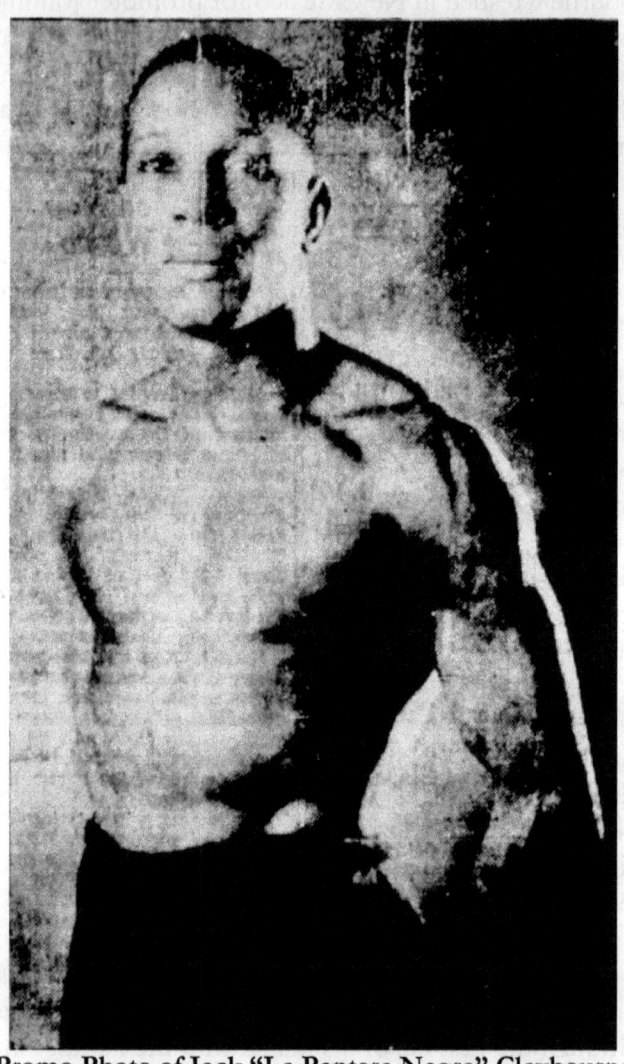

Promo Photo of Jack "La Pantera Negra" Claybourne

"At the close of the second round, Weber picked up the Panther and tossed him out of the ring, but the colored grappler hung on and jerked him over the ropes also," elaborated *The New Mexican*. "As Weber tumbled out, he hit the edge of the ring platform with the small of his back, which kayoed him and disabled him for the rest of the evening."

Writing about the Panther in late October, a sports columnist operating under the pseudonym Mahatma Gandhi dedicated his column to recent events in local wrestling, and referred to Claybourne's iteration of the Black Panther as "The Black Panther, colored boy, from points in Ole Kaintuck."

Whether Gandhi was encouraged to list the state of Kentucky as Claybourne's origin by someone else, or he was completely making it up, it is a classic example of the sort of red herring that has caused tremendous confusion amongst wrestling historians hoping to keep the activities of the different Black Panthers neatly arranged.

With Jack Claybourne, Alex Kaffner, Jack Nelson, and Jim Mitchell — who was *actually* from Louisville, Kentucky — all making the rounds, it can be quite easy to mistakenly credit certain Black Panthers with matches that took place several time zones away from where they were actually active.

When he actually offered accounts of Claybourne's matches in Carlsbad, Gandhi also leaned heavily into racial imagery. When Claybourne would defeat a White opponent, Gandhi would issue a remark like "a black panther had a nice white meat supper last night."

Gandhi also doubled down on the classification of the Black Panther as an "Ethiopian warrior," and even referred to a show-opening battle royal consisting exclusively of untrained Black "wrestlers" as "proteges of the Black Panther."

It was a common practice in some areas — and *especially* in Southern states — to open wrestling shows with untrained Black kids seeking a cash prize, and resorting to fisticuffs to violently batter one another until only one remained standing.

The advertisement for this particular show referred to this collection of Black young men in far less flattering terms than Gandhi initially selected, and instead identified them as "five burly black boys banging away."

In a later promotional piece, Gandhi mockingly referred to his favorite fighter amongst the five Black young men featured in the forthcoming battle royal by the name "Dempsey Tunney Firpo Louis" — a mishmash of the names of four famous fighters. To be clear, he never actually identified which of the fighters he believed would win, but in the aftermath of the show, Gandhi simply wrote, "My boy won the battle royal."

Soon after this show, Claybourne dramatically displayed the downside to wrestling as an aerialist, when he crashed and burned outside the ring during his match with the rugged Mike London, resulting in his first loss in a Santa Fe ring.

"The Black Panther held his own through the first round to win in 19:30 with a jackknife bend," reported *The New Mexican*. "He started a series of flying tackles in the second, which apparently had London groggy. The bewhiskered roughster ducked the last tackle, and as the Panther sailed over his head, he bobbed up like a jack-in-the-box. The thrust, plus the negro's momentum, carried the Panther clear over the topmost strand into the laps of the ringside spectators. In landing, his neck struck the top of a chair, knocking him out."

The ending to this bout may have been used to cover for some other malady that befell Claybourne. He remained inactive for much of November, and a scheduled return at the end of the month fell through due to what *The Journal* reported to be "an infected arm."

As Claybourne prepared to make his return from injury in December, he allegedly issued a lengthy statement to *The Daily Current-Angus*, which was included in the column of Mahatma Gandhi:

"I appreciate that the white wrestling fans of Carlsbad have been favorable to me; I realize that it is hard for a colored athlete to get equal treatment from the fans, and because the fans of Carlsbad did give me a fair break in their treatment in my other starts there I feel like I want to really do my best when I show there again. I am happy to come back to Carlsbad Tuesday night to wrestle the white star, Frank Wolff, and while I have a lot of respect for Wolff's ability on the mat, I hope and think I am a shade better, and that I can eliminate him as a threat to the title held by Mr. Leroy McGuirk when I meet him on Tuesday night.

"I really have hopes that in spite of my color, I can show enough stuff to beat both the Wolff and Francisco Aguayo, outstanding challengers for Mr. McGuirk's title, and if I can beat both of them, I think I can force McGuirk to give me a match and a chance at the title. I am very sorry about my last start there having been stopped on account of my bad arm, and I feel like I was doing the best I could under the circumstances, but of course the athletic commission knew better and all I want is another chance to show the fans of Carlsbad, of all races, that I can really take it and dish it out. I will be there, making every minute interesting for the white mat star, and I will appreciate it if the fans will just continue to be fair and impartial. I am not afraid of what the Wolff will do to me; I can take good care of myself on the mat, and I will be in there trying to make up for the disappointing showing I made in my last appearance in Carlsbad."

The odds that Claybourne actually issued this statement are microscopically small, as are the odds that he uttered the supposed follow-up message that was written in an overtly stereotypical and buffoonish style that contrasted sharply with that of the initial statement:

"Ah really intends to beat Mr. Wolff dis evenin' when we meets at de armory, and I would appreciate it, Mr. Gandhi, if you would tell de folks here in Carlsbad dat I certainly does appreciate dere kindness and fairness. I'll give dem a show tonight lak dey ain't never seen here before."

Against Wolff — a former world junior heavyweight champion — Claybourne offered his best effort and came up just short, losing in three falls to one of the foremost wrestling stars operating in New Mexico. Things got off to a rough start for the Panther, as he fell behind quickly, losing the first fall to Wolff with a combination "hammer and face lock."

"The Panther sprang from his corner at the starter's bell after the five-minute rest period, and in ten seconds butted the Wolff around the ring four times and fell on him for the second fall, a sensational fall, and one of the shortest ever staged in the local arena," continued *The Current-Angus*. "Wolff came out fast in the third fall, and for several minutes both men were very busy breaking and applying holds. The negro fell victim a second time to the combination arm and face hold, and was forced to concede the fall after less than twenty minutes for the third stanza. In defeat, the negro showed a great deal of speed and class, and will yet have to be reckoned with by the champion of the world, Leroy McGuirk, as will his victor of last night."

On his way out of New Mexico, Claybourne lost two additional matches in memorable fashion, the first of which came at the hands of Francisco Aguayo even though the Panther won the second fall of the bout in 20 seconds by connecting with "seven flying tackles in a row."

"The Panther struck his head on a two-by-four as he was thrown from the ring, and was knocked out, but he gamely returned to the ring twice more to take all Aguayo could give before losing the fall," reported *The Journal*.

From a stylistic standpoint, Claybourne's wrestling methodology as an Ethiopian-Cuban appeared to have been much the same as it had been when he wrestled as a Black American. The most descriptive bout he participated in during his controversial tour of the southern border was his swansong against "Murderous" Mike London at the Pan American Stadium, in a match that nearly devolved into a riot.

"London took the first fall in 7 minutes 30 seconds with his usual run of eye gouges, punches, and other mauling tactics," reported *The El Paso Time*s. "The Panther, coming out for the second, caught Mike unawares and downed him in less than a minute with three dropkicks and four flying tackles."

That's when a tumultuous third fall began. Both men threw each other out of the ring a handful of times, and then London retrieved a handful of gravel from the floor of the venue and rubbed it in Claybourne's face. The referee took exception to this action by London, and when he expressed his displeasure to London, the wrestler responded with shocking violence.

"When Referee Tip Tipton interfered, Mike grabbed a beer bottle from a ringsider and smacked Tipton with it," continued the article. "The bearded slugger kicked a woman ringsider in the face, threw the Cuban out of the ring a couple more times, and won the fall in 6:15."

After a brief foray that brought him deeper into Mexico, Claybourne returned to Oregon late in 1935, and "barely arrived at the arena" in time for his match due to a "long bus ride." *The Oregonian* reported that Claybourne dropped a quick match to Clayton Fisher in nine minutes, and then claimed his back had been wrenched so badly that he was unable to return for the second fall.

Quickly regaining his footing in the Pacific Northwest, Claybourne upended the 6'4" Totem Pole Williams in consecutive falls during Portland's Christmas show, taking the first fall with an airplane spin and the second with a series of shoulder tackles. He also defeated Thor Jensen on the Christmas Day event in Eugene.

As 1936 opened, Claybourne was placed in a bizarre position of representing "the Ethiopian side of a mat battle" against Italian wrestler Ernie Piluso, in a match that Herb Owen claimed to have arranged "as the result of many requests" from fans. In a very clumsy bit of ad hoc politicizing, Owen rushed the pair together to play out the ongoing military hostilities between Ethiopia and Italy inside of a wrestling ring.

"Claybourne and Piluso stick to science unless they are forced to open up in self-defense, but their struggle will be anything but a pink tea party," insisted *The Sunday Oregonian*.

"They are primed to extend themselves to the utmost to bring victory to their respective nationalities."

At least Piluso was of Italian descent, even though he was born in Portland and was not an Italian national. As for Claybourne's proposed connection to Ethiopia, there is no evidence that a single American slave of African descent had a direct ancestral line that originated in Ethiopia prior to enslavement. This fact alone makes the implication that Claybourne's actions would be fueled by some wellspring of Ethiopian patriotism wholly preposterous.

Regardless, when Piluso won the match due to some clever maneuvering that landed him on top of Claybourne as the latter was applying a full-nelson, *The Oregonian* stated that Piluso had "won a major battle for his countrymen in the Italo-Ethiopian controversy," and without any of the "atrocities of war" being evident in the wrestling match.

Apparently seething due to the outcome of the bout with Piluso — presumably because he was mortified at the thought of having let down his adopted countrymen — Claybourne demolished Al Aho in only 32 seconds during his next appearance in Portland. The Panther tapped into his background as a boxer and flattened Aho with a series of uppercuts, recording "one of the shortest falls on record at the Labor Temple" in the process.

Back on the East Coast, Tiger Flowers' 1936 began with a homecoming. In February, Flowers finally made it back to Massachusetts under his famous stage name in a performance capacity several months after the bust of his head had preceded him. He wrestled and won on the undercard of a show at Mechanic's Hall in Boston that presumably marked the first hometown appearance by Flowers since his name change from Joe Godfrey, as he was wrestling less than 30 minutes from the house he grew up in.

It was during this tour of Massachusetts that Flowers would get his another sniff at a universally recognized championship, wrestling U.S. champion Paul Adams in the Mechanic's Building on April 21st. Flowers was competitive enough to take the second fall of the bout with a flying beal and a body press before finally being defeated.

Returning to his familiar East Coast haunts later in the year, Flowers resumed his practice of losing the overwhelming majority of his matches. Ironically, even in the midst of his extended losing streak, he drew the same repeated comparisons to Joe Louis as his more outwardly successful Black contemporaries.

The irony of the situation stems from the fact that Louis had lost only one of his first 27 fights up until that point, whereas Flowers only occasionally emerged from his bouts victoriously. Despite the clear disparity in the success rates of the two competitors, Flowers was quoted in *The Lancaster New Era* suggesting that comparisons to the most highly ranked Black heavyweight fighter since Jack Johnson were beneath him.

"They tell me that I'm following in the footsteps of Joe Louis, but I'm a few steps ahead of Joe," Flowers allegedly remarked. "It will be perhaps a year or so before Louis ever gets a crack at the [Max] Schmeling-[Jim] Braddock winner, but I plan to win the heavyweight title within the next six months or whenever the promoters can get [Dave] Levin to meet me."

Considering the fact that Flowers had never wrestled in the heavyweight division before, let alone strung together many victories as a light heavyweight, the notion that he would suddenly move up a weight division *and* win that weight division's world championship — all within six months — probably sounded preposterous to any fans who followed his career closely.

Flowers then returned to Canada in the summer of 1936. This time, he came in billed as the "Southern states champion," and was brought in alongside alleged Ethiopian Zelis Amhara, which was a name that the "Black Demon" George Hoddison was trying on for the first time.

Amhara's actual identity was George Hardison, who was from Greenfield, Massachusetts by way of Fort Myers Georgia. Hardison would soon bring that name back to the

United States with him, and in 1937 he modified the name when he made the jump from the smaller markets of Massachusetts to Boston. From then on, he wrestled as Seelie Samara, or some close approximation of that name.

Meanwhile, Claybourne's summer began with a departure from Oregon and a return to New Mexico, where he restored his identity as the Cuban Black Panther. With Claybourne resuming his work for promoter Johnny Flaska, *The Albuquerque Journal* left a clever hint as to this particular Black Panther's true identity in advance of his bout with Matsura Matsuda, saying that "the Panther is of the Jumping Jack type."

The bout with Matsuda ended in what was quickly becoming a standard finish for Claybourne. *The Albuquerque Tribune* reported that the Panther connected with several dropkicks, then attempted to dive onto Matsuda. The Japanese grappler dodged the aerial maneuver, and the Panther flew into the ringside aisle, and needed to be carried bodily back to the locker room.

Once summer arrived, Claybourne resumed his work in Oregon, and *The Oregonian* welcomed him back "after almost a year's absence from the Northwest" that had actually only been four months long. Making his return to Eugene, Claybourne "turned loose the full fury of his dropkicks on Red Fenton," beating Fenton so soundly in the first fall that the grappler refused to return for the second round.

*The Daily Gazette-Times* greeted Claybourne with several analogies related to his color, saying that the "coal-black negro grappler" offered "plenty of speed, ability and showmanship" that all combined to "add plenty to the color the grappler already contains."

In a follow-up piece, the same writer seemed hell bent on branding Claybourne with the label of "Black Jack," and refined his earlier statement by adding that Claybourne was "black as the ace of spades, but full of plenty of color as far as wrestling ability goes."

In the midst of an ongoing feud between Claybourne and Danny McShain, during which Claybourne made increased use of acrobatic "tumbleweed tactics" like rolling around on the ground and popping to his feet, *The Eugene Guard* got in on the act of attributing uncomfortable quotes to Claybourne that echoed the popular stereotypes of the era.

"I'se willin' to meet any of the boys undah theah own rules," Claybourne allegedly stated. "Ah don' claim to be the world's greatest rasslah, but Ah ain't afeard and Ah'll try!"

The match following this was a no-referee bout that McShain had supposedly requested, but Claybourne won it regardless. *The Guard* stated that the Black Panther looked "better than ever before" as the match unfolded, and that he recovered from "a series of terrible head-first slams over the rope" to ultimately "blast the Scot into quivering submission."

"The negro won the first tumble in 17 minutes with a series of dropkicks after chasing McShain about the outside of the ropes," *The Guard* continued. "The Scot evened it 13 minutes later with a deadly barrage of fists, a series of whip slams, and a piledriver. The last fall took seven minutes, and it saw the Panther recover from a head-first smash into the radio table to mow down McShain with three terrific sonnenbergs (flying shoulder tackles). Referee Walt Achiu, who remained outside the ropes except when necessary to break one of the four forbidden holds, didn't interfere with the villain any more than necessary, and McShain had no one but himself to blame for the loss."

Claybourne also turned the tables on Mike London relative to the way the pair were booked in New Mexico, where London always defeated him. Instead, Jack regularly bested London, and after one such victory in Eugene in which Claybourne again flashed his boxing mastery, *The Guard* printed that "the blazing star of Africa, once removed, still hangs in the Oregon wrestling sky."

"Claybourne opened the hostilities in the main event with a new hold — for him — a headlock reminiscent of the deadly Jack Hagen crusher," added *The Guard*. "After 15 minutes of tense mat work, he wore the Crybaby to semi-consciousness, and London gave up. The Lodi, Cal. villain evened it 5 minutes later when he clamped on a Boston crab, but Claybourne took the decider in 7 with a right to the back of the neck followed by a press, and assisted in part by the referee, Walt Achiu, who got tired of taking London's rough stuff."

    In an August bout against Pascual Castillo, Claybourne treated fans to what had seemingly become his favorite method for losing a match when he introduced Oregonians to the crash-and-burn stunt that he had utilized so effectively in the Southwest to get himself counted out of the ring, and then to explain his multi-week absence from action.

    "With 17 minutes gone, Claybourne missed a mighty sonnenberg, and wafted headlong into the radio announcer's table, landing lightly, like an elevator falling," reported *The Register Guard*. "The Panther struck squarely on his head, bounced to the floor, and lay there as cold as last week's papers. Referee Achiu counted him out, and then attempted to revive him. Claybourne came to by degrees, and at one stage of his return to consciousness labored under the delusion that he was wrestling every occupant of the press row."

    While Claybourne's style was widely regarded as being amongst the cleanest among wrestlers — which was probably out of necessity due to the lingering fear of the sort of reaction that an overly aggressive Black heel might elicit from an all-White audience — he also displayed the ability to mix things up and exchange punches with his villainous adversaries when the need arose. When Panther Claybourne faced George Bennett in Corvallis, Claybourne's path to victory required him to outpunch his opponent in a slugfest.

    It all began when Bennett "bit a hunk out of the black panther's leg," resulting in Claybourne becoming incensed and tossing Bennett all over the ring, all over the ringside seating area, and then tossing him back into the ring for a body slam and a pin.

"A series of low punches left Claybourne groggy at the beginning of the middle fall, which Bennett took in three minutes with a Boston crab," continued *The Daily Gazette-Times*. "The final fall was as rough as the first and second, but Claybourne at last punched his opponent to the floor and won the fight to the intense satisfaction of the crowd."

In a similarly physical matchup with a surprising conclusion, Claybourne defeated "The Chicago Gangster" Al Williams in a rare best-three-out-of-five-falls match, and was credited by *The Register-Guard* with "eliminating the blonde villain as a title contender."

Williams opened the mat with "rough stuff," earning the first fall in just four minutes after repeatedly throwing Claybourne over the top rope and out to the floor. The Panther came back and evened the scoring with "a bow-and-arrow through the ropes."

"The third one also went to the Panther, this time in six with a series of dropkicks," continued the report. "Williams outfoxed the black-skinned matman for the fourth and evening fall, rising from a fusillade of rights and lefts to nail a deadly Boston crab. Both grapplers and Referee Elliott mixed in a free for all following the back and forth tumble. Claybourne ended the bout five minutes later when he took advantage of a smashing right hand, delivered to Williams by Elliott. The Gangster had insisted on pushing the referee, and Elliott promptly felled him. Claybourne sailed across the ring and pinned Navy Al before he had a chance to regain his feet."

In Portland, *The Morning Oregonian* announced that a rematch between Mike London and Jack Claybourne had been spiced-up by a statement provided by London, that he had "never been defeated by a colored boy," and had "no intention of starting now."

Certainly the two had wrestled before, with Claybourne winning their most recent meeting, but no encounters between the two men had ever occurred in Portland. Regardless, the timing of the verbal jab by London was a clear allusion to a boxing match held less than a week prior between former world heavyweight boxing champion Jack Sharkey and Joe Louis, and *The Morning Oregonian* said as much. Louis dominated Sharkey during that fight, flooring him four times, and knocking him out in the third round.

With that sort of an introduction, it was practically implied that Claybourne would win the match. Instead, London won the final fall of the bout when he "tossed dusky Jack Claybourne on his ear outside the ring to take the third and deciding fall of the main event." Afterwards, a fan attempted to land a punch to London's face, and police quickly intervened "and kept it from turning into a riot."

Both Claybourne and Flowers had already made distinct impressions on the wrestling profession, but there was much more to come. Each man was on the precipice of making a geographic move that would significantly shape their individual careers and styles. The end result would be the immortalization of both men as the archetypes of heroism and villainy within the Black pro wrestling subgenre.

## 4 - The Big Midwestern Move

In New York, Tiger Flowers was spending his autumn engaged in an indirect form of campaigning for the 1936 U.S. presidential race. This was revealed when syndicated columnist Westbrook Pegler reported on what he perceived to be the absurdity of the marriage of former world-champion-boxer-turned-wrestling-promoter Jack Dempsey's tour to the reelection campaign of President Franklin Roosevelt, who was campaigning for his second term in office.

When the tour reached Schenectady, New York, Flowers was identified as one of the six wrestlers performing at the event, and Pegler sarcastically joked how Dempsey "referees the contests, kisses the babies, delivers orations on red-blooded Americanism, and autographs old envelopes in complete vindication of Mr. Roosevelt's policies." Pegler was seemingly aghast at the effectiveness of celebrity appearances and live entertainment with respect to helping to accumulate votes that should have been won through intellectual appeals.

Over the course of the fall and stretching into the winter, Flowers' losses continued to mount. While still eager to associate Flowers with Joe Louis for promotional purposes, the wrestling promoters of York, Pennsylvania could not justify the comparison on the basis of their shared success rates, and opted to approach the comparison from a different angle.

"Flowers is called the 'Brown Bomber' of wrestling, not because he uses fisticuffs for victory, but rather the cool, systematic methods he employs in battle," printed *The York Dispatch*.

Appearances of Flowers in New York became far more sparse in the beginning of 1937. He wrestled in a few matches in March during the spring before disappearing altogether after April. It would be a few years before the real Tiger Flowers would return to the region under that familiar name. During the intervening period, he would learn to wrestle under an entirely new persona, using a wholly different style that had likely been inspired by Ted Germaine, who would eventually be publicly credited with teaching Joe Godfrey the art of wrestling.

On the other side of the country, Jack Claybourne was spending his fall in a setting totally different from that of Flowers, making his first appearances in Northern California as "the Black Panther of Alabama," with *The Morning Union* of Grass Valley acknowledging him as "one of the first Negro wrestlers to appear in the local ring," as well as describing him as a wrestler with "a national reputation for cunning and viciousness."

In his first match in California, Claybourne wrestled Abdel Khan to a standstill, and for the entirety of his time wrestling in Marysville, he was known as "Jack Clarborn." He then won the first bout of his California swing in Modesto when his opponent Klem Kusek replicated Claybourne's stunt of taking an errant headfirst dive into press row, and achieved a more convincing win over Kusek a few nights later with a first-fall dropkick, and then a series of "football charges" in the second fall.

Within the space of just a few short weeks, Claybourne's successes in the region had *The Appeal-Democrat* labeling him as "the king-pin of local matmen." Yet, while Claybourne's success was consistent across the nearby venues within Northern California, his stated point of origin was not. Depending on which of the two Northern California towns he was booked in — Chico or Marysville — Jack was Clarborne or Claybourne from either Alabama or Portland, even though Chico and Marysville were separated by only 50 miles.

During this period, Claybourne established himself as a grappler capable of "bringing with him the fast fight for which negroes are reputed," and he also successfully communicated his other attributes, as both a performer and a gentleman.

Claybourne's match with Jack Dunlop in the Grass Valley Memorial Building was reported by *The Morning Union* to be "a match of pure comedy," in which Claybourne "could have thrown his opponent any time and only fooled with him long enough to give the crowd a good laugh."

On a different night, *The Enterprise* reported that Claybourne defeated John Nemanic, who was said to have been returning to wrestling after recovering from a serious knee injury. After being announced as the winner, Jack hastily rushed over to congratulate Nemanic on his return, taking care to remark to the fans at ringside, "He is a good little man."

At the same time, at least one sportswriter took issue with Claybourne's nickname. The writer for *The Appeal-Democrat* said of Claybourne that there was "nothing panther-like about him," and noted that while he was "fairly fast moving," he was not ferocious, but was instead a "gentleman with considerable knowledge of the wrestling lore."

It was possibly the same writer who remarked that "there just wasn't any color" displayed during Claybourne's victory over Gust Johnson in Marysville, although he seemed to have difficulty deciding if it was a good thing that that two wrestlers "didn't chase each other out of the ropes," "didn't make faces at the customers," and also "did not pull all sorts of monkey tricks to stir the fans' blood pressure."

This local dominance by Claybourne was cited as the reason why promoter Cal Herman remarked that he needed to persuade some wrestlers from nearby San Francisco to visit the area in order to present the Black Panther with a suitable challenge. This eventually brought a masked wrestler known as the Black Secret to the region.

*The Appeal-Democrat* noted that the two "blacks" were "the two ranking wrestlers" of the local area, and also represented the best performers to appear there in recent weeks. Fans were also informed that the Secret would have been required to remove the mask from his head the instant he lost a match, as was the local custom.

"Mr. Secret is not black, however, as he advertises," continued the article. "He is a gentleman who prefers to hide his face with a mask while he wrestles. No one knows why he has this mental quirk because most fans would not remember the mug even if they did see it. He will have a tough opponent in the Panther, who is one of the few Negroes in the professional wrestling business. Jack Clarborn is the Panther's name, and he hails from down 'Bama and Missysip way. He is a tall, well-built lad; fast for his size."

*The Searchlight* of Redding offered an article focusing on the stylistic differences between the two "black" wrestlers.

"The Panther, champion of the colored light heavyweights, has never been seen to perform foul work in the ring here, while the Secret has done little else," the article noted. "The colored boy, however, can absorb a heap of punishment and can dish out more than the ordinary opponent can stand."

The Secret was successful in knocking Claybourne from his local perch prior to the Panther's return to Oregon, and when he returned to the Beaver State in December, Jack was greeted by the drastically different style with which certain areas of the state treated race. In Salem, the writing team of *The Oregon Statesman* greeted Claybourne by reinstating its use of a racial slur to describe him, calling him as "the grinning snowball from Missouri."

In December, wrestling fans of Eugene were presented with the most direct display of presumably staged prejudice yet, when middleweight champion Jack Lipscomb "attempted to draw the color line" so that he wouldn't be forced to defend his championship against Claybourne.

According to *The Register-Guard*, Lipscomb said his intent was "making the wrestling business safe for the white race," and that it was an injustice that a champion "should be forced into a match with a contender of another race." The article concluded that Claybourne would enter the affair with a seven-pound weight advantage and "plenty of righteous wrath on his side."

Once again, with the stage perfectly set for the attainment of a symbolic accomplishment achieved through a Black wrestler's conquest, the booker went in the opposite direction. Even though Claybourne drew even with Lipscomb in the second fall of the match with "a blasting series of dropkicks," Lipscomb caught the Panther by the legs in midair when he attempted the same sequence of maneuvers in the third fall, and forced him to submit to a Boston crab."

Claybourne recovered from the disappointment the following week in Salem by outlasting five other men to win a battle royal that marked the conclusion of his major engagements in 1936. Then, as 1937 opened, Claybourne spent the month of January helping to strengthen the positions of wrestlers like Jack Lipscomb and Ben Sherman in the eyes of fans by losing matches to them as he made his way out of the Pacific Northwest.

After concluding his business in Oregon, Claybourne traveled south to California yet again, where he was advertised as "The Black Panther of Portland," and was accidently described as a masked wrestler by *The Chico Enterprise.*

Fortunately, an edition of *The Enterprise* released shortly thereafter identified the inbound wrestler as "The Black Panther, alias Jack Claybourne, negro grappler," or there might have been some confusion as to his true identity. With more than one Black Panther stalking the various wrestling territories, it can be quite challenging to keep their identities straight.

The earliest attention garnered by Claybourne during his visit to California involved a risky crash landing he took during a match with Larry Tillman at Marysville's E Street Arena. Claybourne dove at Tillman through the ropes, as had become his custom, and when Tillman slid out of the way, Claybourne landed "in the splintered wreckage of three orchestra seats."

According to *The Appeal Democrat,* a groggy Claybourne collected himself and returned to the ring where he was easy pickings for Tillman, and had to be carted back to the dressing room after the pinfall was recorded against him.

After crashing and burning in Northern California, Claybourne once again returned to New Mexico, while also adding Arizona to the list of states he is confirmed to have wrestled in. In Santa Fe, he reintroduced the local wrestling fans to his fast and athletic grappling style while defeating Tuffy McMullen.

"Despite McMullen's attempted rough stuff, the negro grappler was easily the better man," said *The Santa Fe New Mexican*. "He won both falls by wafting through the air with the greatest of ease and planting his No. 14 shoes in McMullen's face with irresistible force, a tactic known technically as a dropkick. The Panther kicked and McMullen dropped both times, the first in 13:45, and the second in 5:55."

Over the short span of time Claybourne spent reconnecting with audiences in the region, *The Albuquerque Journal* said that Claybourne "thrilled the cash customers with flying dropkicks and other aerial fireworks" as he ascended to the number-two ranking amongst light heavyweights in the area.

Claybourne returned to the Midwest for the first time in several years during the summer of 1937, still going by the name of the Black Panther, and sowing greater confusion as to which Panther was which. In Illinois, Claybourne wrestled as the Black Panther in a state where Illa Vincent had popularized the name in a wrestling context way back in 1911.

In Wisconsin, Claybourne was referred to as the Black Panther in a state where Alex Kaffner had consistently gone by the name "The Black Panther of Milwaukee" for four straight years, and was continuing to wrestle under that name in cities like Milwaukee and Racine. While most of those cities referred to Claybourne as a product of Portland, Oregon, he was known as "the Australian Black Panther" in Green Bay.

Meanwhile, when "Black Panther" Jim Mitchell entered Oregon in 1937 in the aftermath of Claybourne's tenure there, local promoters had to go out of their way to assure fans that Mitchell was "the original" and "the real McCoy," not to mention a superior Panther to Claybourne. For full context, this attempt at clarifying that Mitchell was the truest of the Black Panthers was taking place just a few hours south of

Washington, where Alex Kaffner debuted under the Black Panther name in 1931.

In August 1937, *The Kenosha Evening News* repeated the claim that Claybourne, "sometimes called the Black Panther of the Northwest," is destined to go as far in wrestling as Joe Louis has in boxing.

By this point in 1937, Joe Louis had knocked out "Cinderella Man" James Braddock to win the world heavyweight boxing championship. This feat made Louis the first Black fighter to earn this elite distinction since Jack Johnson lost the title in April 1915. This achievement by Louis also caused a doubling down on promotional efforts to creatively tie Claybourne and his Black wrestling contemporaries to Louis.

The comparisons to Louis went well beyond the mere juxtaposition of achievements. During this era, any Black wrestler — regardless of the actual shade of their skin — might have been stated to resemble Louis by promoters eager to somehow capitalize on Louis' rapid rise in popularity. The fictitious connections to Louis ranged from personal friend to sparring partner, and the relatively light-skinned King Kong Clayton — who actually had a background as a certified fighter of considerable skill — was even stated to have been the Brown Bomber's first cousin.

Wrestling in a region extending from Wisconsin to Ohio, with Milwaukee, Chicago and Cleveland representing the largest cities he appeared in, Claybourne was fitted with the tag of "world championship contender" by multiple newspapers. These same papers also inextricably linked a colorful new set of nicknames to Claybourne, like "Jumping Jack" and "The Black Kangaroo Man."

This stretch of activity through the Rust Belt states saw Claybourne introduce a new set of Midwestern fans to his high-risk, high-reward style. In most instances, he would dropkick his way to victory. On other occasions, his high-wire act would prove to be the key to his own undoing.

Facing Jim McMillen in Milwaukee, Claybourne seemingly added a fresh twist to his practice of losing in as spectacular a fashion as he could. The United Press recounted how Claybourne missed one of his dropkicks so badly that he flew out of the ring and into the stands, resulting in two spectators he struck in the front row becoming slightly injured.

Similarly, in McHenry, Illinois, *The McHenry Plaindealer* described Claybourne's bout with Mike London as "the most spectacular contest of the year" primarily due to the fact that Claybourne closed the show when he "missed a tackle and landed in the third row ringside."

When Claybourne and Kaffner reconnected for a bout in Gary, Indiana in December 1937, they were initially banned from sharing the ring with one another. According to reporting from the Associated Negro Press, Indiana state athletic commissioner Sam Wurbarger prohibited the match from taking place.

"It is the policy of the state athletic commission to refuse permission to colored athletes to wrestle in the state of Indiana in mixed matches," cited Wurbarger.

Apparently, Wurbarger could not fathom that the two headliners of the charity affair were *both* Black, and that no mixed-race matches in violation of Indiana law were being staged. The enforcement of a restraining order was necessary for the bout to continue as planned.

Although absurd, this was hardly an isolated incident in Indiana. Despite a burgeoning Black population in industrial cities like Gary, the Hoosier State in the 1920s and 1930s was a hotbed of systemic racism, where the influence of extremist groups seeped into every facet of public life. In one outrageous episode from the era, the Ku Klux Klan nearly maneuvered to purchase nearby Valparaiso University — a move that illustrates the Klan's ambition to impose its America First ideology on respected institutions of higher learning.

In other Midwestern markets, Claybourne's method of dropkicking, which would usually see him throw both feet forward and land flat on his back rather than rotating in mid-leap and landing on his stomach, would motivate some promoters to bill him as an Australian who patterned his kicking style after the method employed by kangaroos.

Along the way, more and more media outlets picked up on the habit of referring to "The Kangaroo Man" Jack Claybourne as Australian. With few Americans ever having visited Australia or seen photos of the aboriginal Australians during that era, they were reliant upon newspaper descriptions of Australia's residents to provide them with the details.

At the time, it was understood by some that there was very little physical difference between Sub-Saharan African populations and Australian natives, and most news reports treated the titles of African and Australian as representing a distinction without a difference.

"The aborigines have bushy, black hair, dark skin and eyes, and the thick noses and lips of the negroid races, peculiarities that are common to most of the natives of New Zealand, and of all the South Sea Islands as well," declared an 1893 article printed in *The Inter-Ocean* of Chicago.

The same article presented as factual the notion that the average Australian native had been an average of six-and-a-half feet tall, with heights of eight feet being relatively common among them. An actual scientific study on the heights of Aboriginal Australians conducted in the 1920s recorded an average height for the men of 1,668 millimeters, or approximately 5'5" at the time, but this was yet another instance of facts not being allowed to interfere with an entertaining and effective story.

Regardless as to the reality of the situation or the accuracy of the depiction, Claybourne would ultimately spend a significant portion of his career cast in the role of an Australian native in markets looking to further glamorize his ethnic background.

While Claybourne's athletic style was taking portions of the Midwest by storm, it is difficult to compare the importance of what he or any other wrestler did that year with the career reimagining that Joe Godfrey underwent in Michigan under the name Rufus Jones.

Although there was an influential theologian named Rufus Jones whose lifetime and career overlapped with Godfrey's, as well as the creation of the identity of Rufus Jones the wrestler, the inspiration for that particular stage name is certainly the 21-minute film *Rufus Jones for President*, which starred Ethel Waters and marked the debut of entertainment icon Sammy Davis Jr.

Released in 1933, the film's plot involves a young Black boy named Rufus Jones who falls asleep in his mother's arms and dreams that he is elected president of the United States. In spite of the excellent singing by Waters and two spectacular tap dancing routines from the seven-year-old Davis, the film is replete with Black American stereotypes involving gambling and the overconsumption of watermelon.

For what it's worth, *Rufus Jones for President* was filmed in Brooklyn, New York, which allows for the possibility that Godfrey may have been an extra in the film, as he would later claim to have received on-screen roles in Hollywood movies. However, this is pure conjecture, and the first recorded matches of both Joe Godfrey and Tiger Flowers took place in New England and overlap with the release of the film.

Late in the summer of 1937, Godfrey re-debuted in Michigan as "Rough" Rufus Jones of New York City. However, his characterization as Detroit's newest Negro star from the Northeast didn't last long. Within weeks, Jones was being billed as "an unethical wrestler" from "Red Run, Georgia."

While Red Run was a fictitious place, it's possible that its name was selected for the reason that a "red run" in mountain sports implies that difficult skiing — or in this case, tough sledding — awaits those who dare to tangle with the terrain. The leading theories for the selection of Georgia as the location for Red Run are the fact that Godfrey's mother Lillian was herself a Georgia native, as reported by the family's 1920

U.S. Census entry, and also that Georgia was the birthplace of Tiger Flowers the boxer.

**Rufus Jones still sporting his uniquely cauliflowered left ear**

Jones made quite an impression during his first month in Michigan with his far dirtier grappling style. Within two weeks, *The Detroit Free Press* was already reporting that Jones had fouled young Babe Kasaboski so much during their match at Detroit's Arena Gardens that the venue's fans got fed up and stormed the ring to intervene.

Throughout the summer and fall, Metro Detroit newspapers fleshed out the fictional backstory of the 23-year-old Jones. He was an ex-minister-turned-wrestler who hailed "from the cotton fields of Georgia." He had been wrestling on the carnival circuit since the tender age of eight, and had engaged in more than 1,000 matches by the time he'd reached Detroit. His repertoire consisted almost exclusively of roughhousing tactics, and he had a special weapon at his disposal — a "flying headbutt maneuver."

In the early going, Jones even wrestled against familiar opponents, like the Mid-West Wrestling Association's world light heavyweight champion Maurice LaChappelle. The only difference this time was that Jones was no longer wrestling as a technical babyface, and had instead established himself as "a first class villain" in the words of *The Saginaw News*.

Interestingly enough, the battle between the two familiar adversaries was not billed as a title bout on the basis of the fact that LaChappelle and Jones were respectively billed as the "White world's light heavyweight champ" and the "Black world's light heavyweight champ." While suggesting that no unification between two race-based championships was even possible, the outcome of the bout could still indicate that the champion of one race was superior to the other.

LaChappelle emerged victorious from the bout, with *The Saginaw News* even going so far as to say the quiet part out loud, boasting that LaChappelle "upheld the white man's prestige, with the aid of the referee, by taking a decision over Rufus Jones, colored heavyweight 'champion' Monday night at the auditorium."

While the report from *The News* went so far as to add the mocking quotation marks around the word "champion" when alluding to the claim that Jones was a champion of sorts, it at least acknowledged that LaChappelle's victory was the result of a disqualification rather than a conclusive win by pinfall or submission.

In late October, Jones received a massive endorsement from a key figure within the Black community of Detroit when Harold "Poppa Dee" Johnson was introduced as his manager. Johnson was well known in Detroit's boxing circles as a manager to Black fighters, while also serving as a ring announcer for many local fights. Being linked to Poppa Dee had the net effect of causing Jones to be embraced as the unofficial in-ring representative of Detroit's Black inhabitants.

From a character perspective, the loveable Poppa Dee was there to curb Jones' tendency to turn every contest into an unstructured free-for-all, which would play out in front of local audiences in an intentionally comedic fashion.

On the night the announcement was made, Dee arrived at the Garden Arena accompanied by Roscoe Toles, a local heavyweight boxer who had amassed a stellar record since being taken in by Dee. Once he arrived, Dee spoke to Jones within earshot of the media, and explained how he could be of assistance to him.

"You can give those wrestling fans plenty of action without making yourself out [to be] such a mean devil," the avuncular Dee explained to Rufus in front of reporters from *The Detroit Free Press*. "What you need is a manager like Poppa Dee."

Prior to Jones' bout that night with the Great Mephisto, Dee reportedly climbed into the ring and explained to referee Philbin that his new protege was going to become "Gentleman Jones," and would conduct himself in a manner befitting that new title.

"A moment later, the match was on, and Rufus Jones forgot every instruction that Poppa Dee had whispered," continued *The Free Press*. "Roscoe Toles at the ringside shook his head in chagrin as Rufe violated every known rule of wrestling. He had the crowd jammed against the ring shouting curses and threats. Nobody was in his seat after the match was underway for 10 minutes. Mr. Jones didn't have a friend in the house except Roscoe, Poppy, and a twelve-year-old sister, Henrietta Jones."

A more in-depth explanation of the relationship was offered by the city's Black newspaper, *The Detroit Tribune*. It was through that publication that Metro Detroit's Black fans were informed that Jones had "left the old plow 'a-tumbling down in de fiel'" in pursuit of the riches that were presumably earned by those who participated in wrestling contests in the big cities.

Poppa Dee told *The Tribune* that Jones had heard the tale of Illa Vincent, "the only colored wrestler who ever attained national honors among the heavies," and that Rufus was attempting to emulate Vincent's mat exploits.

In order for this story to be true, Jones would have needed to make the acquaintance of someone with an exceptional memory. As headline-grabbing as Vincent's wrestling activities in the United States were, the entirety of his Stateside career was confined to a two-year period that concluded two months before the now 25-year-old Jones was even born.

In addition, both Reginald Siki and George Godfrey — to the extent that the latter could be classified as a wrestler — were certainly more recent and prominent examples of Black wrestling heavyweights who had attracted mainstream attention, and at levels that superseded those of Vincent.

Continuing, *The Tribune* elaborated as to how the fact that Jones was now a main-eventer in the area's wrestling rings was "testimony of his ability to grapple with the best in the country," while citing how "the large throngs which pack out the Arena to pray for his defeat" only translate into greater popularity for Jones.

"In the rasslin' game, the more unpopular the rassler is with the fans, the larger the crowds will be when he grunts and groans," insisted *The Tribune*.

In the meantime, Jones was allegedly training in seclusion alongside Dee, who was teaching him to master a hold called "The Lemon Squeezer," which Dee had supposedly taught to Vincent years earlier.

If there was any presumed link between "The Lemon Squeezer" and any tactics that Jones would soon add to his repertoire and unleash upon his opponents, it apparently came in the form of a specific type of headbutt. This move, which would eventually become commonplace, was not yet widely practiced as an intentional offensive maneuver, and certainly not in abundance during matches.

While the headbutt had been introduced as a part of the offense of Michigan native Gus Sonnenberg — former world champion, college and pro football star, and a wrestling legend who was exceedingly popular in the Boston area where Jones grew up — headbutting as a routine combat method was all but unheard of in most corners of the wrestling world.

In fact, many of the sportswriters who covered wrestling had not yet agreed upon its orthography, or even its terminology, resulting in many different terms being used to describe the maneuver.

It's essential to note that there had been another frequent user of the headbutt in the Boston region aside from Sonnenberg — a Black wrestler whose development had occurred parallel to that of Tiger Flowers — and who perhaps not so coincidentally used the surname of "Jones."

Buck Jones began wrestling in New England in December 1934 as "a colored giant gent," and he soon developed a style as a serious Black ruffian while Flowers was busy wrestling in New York.

During early bouts with Bull Curry over Boston's badman title, Buck Jones displayed an outsized fondness for headbutts, which was apparently motivated by the naturally greater thickness of Buck's head in comparison to Curry's — at least according to the narrative being delivered by *The Evening Express* of Portland.

"Jones came back from his pasting with renewed vigor for the second fall, and decided to war on Curry with head butts," added the article. "As Mr. Curry's pate being considerably softer than the Negro's, it was very good judgement on Jones' part, and at every chance he banged his bean against Curry's, much to the gentleman's disgust."

Buck Jones and the future Rufus Jones wrestled against one another several times during Flowers' return to Boston early in 1936, so there was certainly enough interaction between the two that they may have influenced one another.

Then again, Flowers' first recorded instance of intentionally headbutting a referee in Montreal is recorded just prior to the revelation that Buck Jones had become the headbutting king of Boston. It may simply be that Charley Gordon and Ted Germaine liked their heels to be adept with the use of their heads in the area that made headbutting famous.

Back in Michigan, by mid-November, *The Lansing State Journal* had also made note of the fact that Rufus Jones had mastered a "flying head-butt," during which he left his feet to gain momentum before bringing his own skull crashing down atop his opponent's scalp.

Jones' creative use of the headbutt was noteworthy, but it was not yet a maneuver that defined him. As he blazed a trail of carnage through the state of Michigan, Rufus would still conclude most of his matches with accepted wrestling techniques, like when he downed Mike London in December, planting him in the center of Lansing's Prudden Auditorium with an airplane spin followed by a body slam.

It was in late December 1937 that Jones' name first began to receive mentions in relation to the one race-neutral championship in Michigan that he was apparently qualified to compete for — the unofficial "Bad Man Title" bestowed upon the most successful rulebreaker in the state.

At the time, the holder of this "championship" was "Wild" Bull Curry — real name Fred Koury — a Connecticut-born wrestler of Lebanese descent who was a well-established ruffian. Curry's distinctive look was capped off by the bushiest set of eyebrows in all of wrestling.

Just two months older than Jones, Curry had a four-year head start on Jones in Michigan, and had been in the running for the title of the area's top heel for the majority of that time.

"The Red Run negro thinks Curry is just a false alarm when it comes to real downright roughing and intends to prove his contention tonight," remarked *The Lansing State Journal*. "Fans who have watched Jones in action believe the Hartford grappler is due for the surprise of his life. Rufus is not only a good wrestler, but speedy as well, and the 'Wild Bull' may not find his two-fisted attack as effective against the negro as it has been against other opponents."

The earliest bouts between Jones and Curry in Lansing in early 1938 ended in disqualification wins for Curry, followed by supposed post-match brawls in the showers. However, that was just a prelude to the drama and the exaggeration that would ensue when the two began headlining against one another in Detroit.

On the eve of the pair's late February contest at the Arena Gardens, *The Free Press* printed a dubious set of career records for each of the villainous wrestlers, and some of the claims made in the report are downright ludicrous.

"In seven years of wrestling, Bull Curry has engaged in some 700 wrestling matches," estimated *The Free Press*. "He has won 300 of them. The other 400 he was winning when a referee stepped in to award the victory to his opponent, first disqualifying Bull for rough and illegal tactics."

"In 18 years of wrestling, Jones has engaged in more than 1,000 matches," continued *The Free Press*. "He has won a majority of them, but the matches he lost usually were bouts in which he was disqualified. Jones has been grappling professionally since he was 8 years old. He traveled with a carnival and a circus from the time he was born through his fourteenth birthday."

In the meantime, Poppa Dee's role as Jones' official cornerman came to an end, as he was said to have been banned from participating in any further wrestling events by boxing commissioner Frank MacDonnell.

"Poppa Dee, you are to remain away from the ringside," MacDonnell ruled, as reported by *The Free Press*. "You'll get yourself killed trying to help those wrestlers. You are too old to get yourself mixed up in any of those ringside brawls. You let Rough Rufus handle his own affairs."

*The Free Press* then offered a description of how matches unfolded while Rufus was under the tutelage of Dee, summarizing the humor of their two-man routine, which featured repeated attempts by Jones to undermine the instructions of his mentor.

"Rufus, at odd times, has tried to reform," added *The Free Press*. "He stopped biting referees as his first concession to Papa Dee's ideas. Then he promised not to hit wrestlers in the clinches. Later, however, when Papa Dee wasn't looking, Rough Rufus returned to his old tactics, and today he remains as one of matchmaker Eddie Lewis' prize devils of the mat."

Detailed descriptions of that bout between Jones and Curry are elusive. However, the following edition of *The Saginaw News* referred to Rufus as "champion Bad Man of Detroit's Arena Gardens," while adding that Jones had defeated Curry in Detroit. At the conclusion of that bout, Curry had chased Papa Dee away from ringside, resulting in a countout victory for Jones.

For subsequent bouts, Dee's ringside ban would be in place, with *The Free Press* suggesting that Dee's activity in and around a wrestling ring was unbecoming of someone who was supposed to be acting in a serious role as a manager of legitimate fighters.

"I learned enough about color with those rasslers to go back to boxing just for the laughs I'll get out of it," Dee told *The Free Press*.

Venturing outside of Detroit, Saginaw, and Lansing, Jones also made his way to new venues in Southwest Michigan, appearing in Battle Creek, the home of the famous cereal-makers at the Kellogg Company.

In the aftermath of Jones' bout with English wrestler Walter Percy, *The Battle Creek Enquirer* remarked that Jones "as expected did just about everything except wrestle" during a match in which Jones captured the only fall with a body slam. Still, *The Enquirer* caught on to the fact that in-ring acumen was only one aspect of the value Jones brought to his performances.

"Percy landed several drop-kicks, but most of the entertainment was furnished by Jones' grimaces in feigned anguish when in one of Percy's figure four scissors or crotch holds," noted *The Enquirer*.

Future reports of Jones' activity would lend credence to the idea that he was gradually grasping the concepts that would make him one of wrestling's premier showmen. In the meantime, C. Lavern Robbins of *The Battle Creek Moon-Journal* would focus on the post-match antics of Jones, who he said "lived up to his advance publicity of being a mean mat villain."

"As the bell sounded the end of the time limit, Percy cracked Jones with a left uppercut," recounted Robbins. "Jones tried to hit back, and then Percy knocked Referee Vern Clark of Detroit down for trying to interfere. Jones and Percy squared off again, and then Jones knocked Clark down."

Seeing his referee being pinballed around the ring by the two wrestlers, promoter Farmer Nick entered the ring only to be knocked down by Percy, and then inspector Earl Brutche entered the ring, grabbed Jones, and with the help of Nick, pulled him out of the ring.

"The affair ended without any injuries, but the fans had entertainment galore for a few seconds," concluded Robbins.

When the wrestling season opened across the Ambassador Bridge in Windsor, Ontario, Canada in February 1938, Jones took part in a remarkable main-event bout against the Great Balbo to kick things off. When Balbo captured the initial fall with flying tackles, Jones "heaved a chair at him to show he didn't like being pinned," in the words of *The Windsor Star*.

Falling behind on the fall tally, Jones soon evened the bout with punches, kicks, and flying tackles, while growing increasingly dirtier with his choice of tactics as the match progressed. As was his custom, he turned every object at his disposal to his advantage.

"Jones had come out for the bout with his right wrist taped, but apparently he wore the tape as a weapon rather than for protection of any injury or sore," continued *The Star*. "He rubbed it across Balbo's eyes at every opportunity, till finally, in the third set-to, Balbo grabbed his arm and yanked the tape off."

With the tape now in his hands, Balbo retaliated against Jones with tactics identical to those that had first been employed against him. Unfortunately for Balbo, he was not as gifted at shielding his illicit activities from the view of referee Johnny Banks, who disqualified him and awarded the final decision to Jones.

"Balbo 'burned up' over the decision and was loath to let up in his wicked offensive," continued *The Star*. "He kept after Jones for several minutes after the bout ended, despite attempts by Referee Banks and a ringsider to calm him down. When last seen, Jones was in full flight headed to the dressing room, with Balbo tearing after him and a highly excited crowd of fans licking their chops after the somewhat bloodthirsty finish."

The following month, Jones and Balbo had a rematch in Windsor, and were tasked with presenting an exciting main event to the Windsor Chryslers — champions of the Michigan-Ontario Hockey League — as well as the players' wives and girlfriends. To accomplish their appointed task, the two wrestled for a full 90 minutes without either man scoring a fall.

According to *The Star*, the pair "stuck to orthodox wrestling" for the first 60 minutes before the contest devolved into something more closely resembling a typical Rufus Jones match. The dramatic change in the tone of the bout occurred when Balbo grabbed Jones, hurled him out of the ring, and followed him out to the Windsor Arena floor with his fists flying. From there, both wrestlers cheated with impunity, and took turns declining offers from referee Ted Greise to disqualify their opponent for the use of exceedingly rough tactics.

**Rough Rufus**

"Jones had Balbo almost out on his feet in the last minute or so by butting Balbo's head with his forehead, and Greise wouldn't go for that, stepping in to rescue the Italian," continued *The Star*. "Since this rescue act was perhaps instrumental in saving Balbo from defeat, Jones was quite angry, and showed it. The outcome was that for a few minutes after the final gong, both Balbo and Greise belabored the Negro, Greise even going so far as to take off his shirt."

On his very next trip to Saginaw, Jones was described as "the black villain" by *The Saginaw News*, in comparison to Patrick Finnegan, who was characterized as "lily-white," and "heroic." Jones lived up to his villainous billing during the bout, losing the final fall through a disqualification ruling handed down by referee McGregor. That's when the real action started.

"Rough Rufus objected so strongly that he felled the referee with a lusty jab, and the fiasco was on" described *The News*. "During the melee, Jones tore a leg from McGregor's pants and used it to wrap around his adversary's head in a well-acted attempt to throttle him. If McGregor's efforts lacked the sincerity and showmanship of the finished mat artists in his match with Rufus, he nevertheless provided a packed audience with a novel ending to an otherwise mediocre card."

After heading back to Battle Creek and engaging in another knock-down, drag-out brawl with Frankie Hart that required the intervention of ring officials and police officers to quell a potential riot, Jones had his actions called into question by someone identified only as "Woman Sports Fan" who attended Jones' matches and evidently thought his violent antics were real. Apparently, she also felt that such unruly displays had no place in polite society.

"If Rufus Jones won the fall, he did so by hair-pulling, biting, eye-gouging, kicking and knee prodding," began the complainant. "If it is legal to throw a man by the hair or the head, gouge his eyes and brutally throw him to the mat, then according to [referee] Ted Greis, Jones won the fall."

The writer of the letter then noted that there were reports of unoccupied seats at the arena, expressed the opinion that the downturn in attendance was linked to barbarity such as that wrought by Jones, and recalled instances when five different wrestlers needed to be carried back to the dressing room from the ring due to concussions and other assorted injuries suffered during bouts.

"We have had some clean and handsome wrestlers this season, but only to be pitted against murderous opponents," the letter-to-the-editor continued. "It is a disgrace to our community and to the auditorium where such events are staged. Bull fights are banned, but the misery of the bulls is soon alleviated by slaughter. If there are any ordinances or legal rules in wrestling, why not have them enforced?"

Almost as if he was attempting to deliberately stoke the ire of this disgruntled fan or any others that objected to his provocative, rule-bending style, Jones' next bout in Battle Creek with Frankie Hart was punctuated by actions that were equally as inflammatory.

"Jones held the advantage in the second fall and had Hart pinned in a successful hold until he started fouling his opponent," reported *The Enquirer*. "That started a free-for-all between the grapplers in much the same manner as last week's ended, and (referee) Frakes found it impossible to keep the two men separated after awarding the fall to Hart on a foul."

Jones lingered in the ring after the bout in protest and assailed inspector Earl Brutsche with "profane language" until Brutsche withdrew a blackjack from his belt and held it threateningly. At this point, Jones immediately withdrew from the ring and returned to the dressing room.

It was then that Rufus Jones ran headlong into Jack Claybourne in Michigan, and with so few Black wrestlers in the business at all, let alone two of such skill who presented as polar opposites, the luxury of simultaneously having two different Black wrestlers of such disparate temperaments was immediately a popular topic in the press.

While Jones had failed Papa Dee's test to be reformed into "Gentleman Jones," he would now face a clean-cut prospect who was already everything Dee had hoped he would eventually become in the form of the newly titled "Gentleman Jack."

"The newcomer, unlike Rough Rufus, is of the hero type," declared *The Detroit News*. "His greatest pride is a medal from Sydney, Australia, A.A. He was named the outstanding sportsman who appeared at the club in 1937. Gentleman Jack will make his Detroit debut against Tony Martini."

With two Black wrestlers of the caliber attained by Claybourne and Jones coming into their own at the same time, and now performing in a wrestling hotbed in and around a major American city, the stage was finally set for a series of matches that would reshape expectations for the sort of match two Black wrestlers could be entrusted deliver when given the opportunity to work together.

## ♪ - The Natural Rivalry

The title of "Gentleman Jack" that now decorated advertisements for Claybourne's matches had become synonymous with him in February 1938, just prior to his bout with supposed former UCLA football player Alonzo Wood.

"One of the cleanest wrestlers in the business, Claybourne has been called the finest piece of mat machinery the colored race has ever produced," glowed *The News Journal* of Mansfield, Ohio. "'Gentleman Jack' is a spiffy dresser, colorful both in and out of the ring, and wears a perpetual smile as big as his face."

The newly minted "Gentleman Jack" would have little trouble with his opponent Wood, as *The Journal* would report that Claybourne moved around the ring "with the speed and grace of a lightweight," and that Wood "ran directly into the feet" of Claybourne in the final stages of both of the evening's falls, becoming yet another victim of Claybourne's dropkick barrage.

This period of activity in the Midwest saw Claybourne listed as weighing anywhere from 175 pounds to 195 pounds. Capitalizing on these phoney and drastic weight fluctuations, Jack might wrestle as a heavyweight in Illinois one night, and then compete as a light heavyweight in Ohio the next. *The Dayton Daily News* actually went to the trouble of pointing this out.

"Claybourne... has been appearing mostly against heavyweight opponents," observed the publication. "Bordering on the heavy and light heavyweight line, he can swing into either division with ease and without sacrificing any change in wrestling technique."

This valuable ability to convincingly straddle two weight divisions was owed to the fact that Claybourne's brand of acrobatics was atypical even amongst wrestlers far lighter and shorter than he was, as the majority of wrestlers conformed to a straightforward grappling style. At the same time, Claybourne's 6'1" frame placed him within the 95th percentile of the tallest wrestlers of his generation, regardless of race.

**Gentleman Jack**

As Claybourne continued to be known as an Australian who bounced around like a kangaroo, the name given to his dropkick was further cemented as a "kangaroo kick." It was referred to as such when he competed against Sterling Davis in Mansfield, Ohio.

"They grappled for 13 minutes before Claybourne let loose with a series of 'kangaroo kicks,' and completed the fall with a 'jack knife,'" reported *The Mansfield News-Journal*. "The second fall, which also went to Claybourne, was a repetition of the first, and required 9 minutes."

Often being positioned as a respectable threat to titlists in most jurisdictions, Claybourne still had a clear line of distinction drawn between himself and the wrestlers that had been anointed as superstars. This was made crystal clear when Lou Thesz — appearing under the name "Don Louis Thesz" — squared off with Jack just one month later. Already a former world heavyweight champion at only 22 years of age, Thesz had no difficulty with the light-heavyweight Claybourne, disposing of him with "a grand slam" in just 5:10.

Brushing aside this setback, Columbus-based wrestler and former state light-heavyweight titlist Cleat Kauffman declared to the local press that Claybourne would soon be wearing the light heavyweight crown, and that he was going to be retiring from active wrestling in order to dedicate himself to helping Claybourne reach his full potential. However, before that could happen, Jack would depart for Michigan to engage in a series of bouts that defined him both as a wrestler and as a gentleman.

Before a clash between the two Black wrestlers viewed as natural adversaries could materialize, both would have other business to attend to. In the early stages of the summer, Rufus Jones returned to Port Huron, Michigan, where *The Herald Palladium* reminded local wrestling fans of exactly what had transpired that had caused Rufus to be absent from their local rings for an extended period of time.

"Jones is the grappler who gained headlines all over the country six months ago when he introduced a new dodge in the wrestling art," said *The Herald Palladium*. "The colored man pulled a police nightstick from his trunks and tapped an opponent upon the head during the heat of the match. Rough Rufus was set down by the state boxing commission for three months for the little trick, and was threatened with a life ban if he ever tried it again."

Of all of the dirty tricks Jones liked to employ in the ring, one of his favorites at this juncture of his career involved rubbing the tape from his wrists across the eyes of his opponents. He would usually work the crowd into a froth using other illegal tactics before finally brandishing his tape as a weapon, causing the audience to bubble over with rage.

Such was the case when Jones wrestled Toshito Matsura of Japan in Battle Creek, resulting in a situation where the fans "took over the show," according to *The Battle Creek Enquirer*. Jones had gouged Matsura's eyes, pulled his nose, and then rubbed his taped right wrist across Matsura's face until the crowd couldn't bear to watch another moment of the injustice.

"About 20 of them climbed through the ropes, and then it was that Mr. Jones put on a great show of fear, his eyes rolling apprehensively as the indignant fans sought to get their hands on him," illustrated *The Enquirer*. "(Farmer) Nick and his attendants finally quieted them, cleared the ring at last, and Mr. Matsura seized the cue to belabor his foe and therefore took the tying fall with a body press."

Implicit in the description of this match is that Jones and Matsura — even after their match had been interrupted by the intrusion of no fewer than 20 fans into the ring — still had the wherewithal to compose themselves and conclude the second fall with a satisfactory finish. What's more, they *still* returned to the ring after the riot was suppressed to wrestle in the third and final fall.

"Apparently unmindful of the fans' threats, Mr. Jones started right in where he left off when they came back, and after a few moments of slugging Mr. Matsura all about the ring, the referee yanked the Jap's right arm aloft, gave him the fall and match, and ordered Mr. Jones back to Georgia," concluded *The Enquirer*.

When Jones traveled east and made his first visit of the year to Kitchener, Ontario, his appearance exposed the lack of creativity promoters exhibited with respect to identifying Black combat athletes, or at least when it came to making rational comparisons between them. *The Kitchener Daily Record* referred to Jones — one of the most despicable heels in all of professional wrestling — as "the Brown Bomber of professional wrestling."

It was a straightforward allusion to the now 35-1 heavyweight champion of the boxing world, "The Brown Bomber" Joe Louis, whose reputation had always been that of a clean fighter. The seeming requirement that Black athletes could only be compared with others of the same racial classification resulted in the most villainous Black wrestler on the planet being unironically compared with a paragon of good sportsmanship like Louis.

Sadly, the overwhelming popularity of Louis was overshadowing what was potentially a far more remarkable achievement in the fighting world. In 1938, Henry "Homicide Hank" Armstrong completed the remarkable feat of winning the lightweight championship of the world while simultaneously holding the featherweight and welterweight championships.

In other words, in the era when boxing only had eight weight divisions, Armstrong won the championship at 126 pounds, jumped 20 pounds to capture the world title in the 147 pound welterweight division, and then cut weight to win the 135-pound championship of the lightweight division. It was a truly astonishing feat, and one that went largely unappreciated in light of Louis' success as a heavyweight.

No matter who he was being compared or contrasted with, Rufus was undoubtedly a showman who could tap into a bottomless bag of tricks to get a reaction from an audience. As his seasonal return to Kitchener indicated, Jones could draw the sought-after responses from the mouths of audience members even if he was fishing for laughter rather than a string of obscenities.

"The fans at last night's show got a chuckle out of the proceedings just prior to the final bout," reported *The Daily Record*. "Rufus Jones showed up with a couple of sets of long fingernails. He does enough damage with the short ones, so Promoter George Hill decided to do some 'pairing.' He borrowed a knife from (chairman of the local physical education committee) Mel Swartz, and promptly proceeded to trim the protesting Jones' fingernails."

In June, Jones shared a card with Claybourne while challenging world light heavyweight champion Bill Weidner in a title match. At the baseball park in Hamilton, Ontario, Jones submitted the first fall away to a Weidner toe hold, and then turned in a signature performance when action resumed in the second fall.

"After the rest period Jones went after the champion in rough fashion, but Weidner put on the barrel hold and gave the challenger many an anxious moment before he succeeded in breaking it," reported *The Hamilton Spectator*. "Jones then went to work in goat fashion and butted the champ around the ring, finally scoring the second fall of the bout in seven minutes."

After Jones' violent cranial usage evened the fall count, the challenger continued the use of his aggressive tactics, and "roughed it up with every person in the ring — Referee Sinclair included — and was not subdued until the champion applied his famous leglock."

Following his loss to Weidner in a match for an official championship, Jones would have to satisfy himself by defending his distinction as the top Bad Man in the region against his erstwhile nemesis Bull Curry. After Rufus took the first fall "by choking, kicking, and almost everything forbidden by the rules," Curry evened the bout with a bulldogging headlock. Then the two men began taking turns hurling one another out of the ring.

"[Curry] jumped out, put a headlock on Rufus, dragged him between the ringside seats, and ran him head first into boards that serve as the dasher when the Arena is fitted for hockey," elucidated *The Windsor Star*. "Referee [Joseph] Lauzon tried to stop him, so Bull rammed Joseph's head into the boards, too. Matchmaker Bill Thornton got the same treatment when he also essayed a peacemaker role. Then Curry turned to Jones again and jumped on him as he lay on the floor among the ringside seats."

Both men beat the referee's count back into the ring, but with Rufus looking "like easy prey," Lauzon decided to disqualify Curry for his actions on the outside of the ring and awarded the bout to Jones. As Curry tore the shirt from Lauzon's torso in protest of the decision, Jones turned and bolted back to the dressing room, with Curry following hot on his heels once he realized his foe had retreated.

During July, Jones also snuck back into Montreal during his Canadian travels and temporarily reclaimed his Tiger Flowers name during a 25-minute loss to Farmer Mack.

At this point the feud between Jones and Claybourne kicked into high gear. The claim that the two were natural adversaries was buttressed by the insistence that there was an authentic colored world light heavyweight championship that both wrestlers were attempting to acquire.

In the absence of such a title, it would be presupposed that Black wrestlers could not coexist with one another without at least satisfying their curiosity as to who among them was the best combatant of that shade. It was a competitive feature that was racially distinct within wrestling circles; White wrestlers never seemed to openly express the desire to see who among them was the best wrestler of a paler hue.

There are few examples, if any, of a White wrestler being assigned the title of German champion and then defending that mythical championship against another wrestler of German ancestry inside of a North American ring. Only amongst Black American wrestlers was it deemed a necessity that they should face off to establish supremacy.

While Black wrestling titles were seldom created with any continuity or represented by physical belts or trophies, their situational existence ensured that Black wrestlers would always be pitted against one another for the sake of novelty. As such, it also created scenarios where the relationships between Black wrestlers were often seen to be naturally contentious in ways that other intraracial relationships were not.

Yet, the racial stratification of the time had also normalized the isolation of Black athletes within their own sports leagues, and also into separate brackets for boxing competitions. As such, a backdrop was established permitting Black wrestlers to participate in an unofficial Blacks-only league within a league that other wrestlers weren't privy to.

The underlying empirical differences between the authentic Black sub-leagues of other pro sports and the mythical Black sub-league of professional wrestling was the parity in other sports between the very best White and Black athletes. Negro League baseball teams more than held their own when matched against all-White Major League teams.

Similarly, evidence had been clear for decades that the best Black fighters and holders of the world's colored boxing championships were frequently equivalent or superior boxers to their White counterparts, with fighters like Joe Gans and Jack Johnson achieving colored world champion status before finally being granted opportunities to win the mainstream titles, and subsequently dominating their respective weight classes.

Conversely, Black world titleholders in the artificial world of pro wrestling frequently lost to their White competitors, reinforcing the notion that a Black wrestler who was of a championship caliber in comparison to peers of his own race was at best only slightly above average when contrasted with the full range of non-Black wrestlers.

In fact, the few exceptions involving race-neutral black titleholders that exist prior to this point still somehow manage to prove the rule. First among these exceptions is Viro Small, whose victories in collar-and-elbow wrestling contests during the 1880s — at such a time when he was referred to as "the collar-and-elbow champion of Vermont — were presumably real and not predetermined by third-party scriptings.

By December 1937, only a few race-neutral North American championships had been briefly held by Black wrestlers, and they are easy to split hairs over as to how historically significant they should be regarded.

Wrestling pioneer Clarence Bouldin — who no less of an authority than the legendary heavyweight champion Frank Gotch once praised as the best pound-for-pound wrestler in the world — held multi-year claims to the titles of world middleweight champion and world light heavyweight champion between 1905 and 1908.

The problem with viewing Bouldin's title reign in the same light as Black title reigns that would come later is the fact that he was born to a White father and Black mother, and masked his Black identity beneath his stage name of "The Cuban Wonder." At the time of his death in 1967 at the age of 94, Bouldin was believed to have been White, and declared himself to have been White on all legal documents after 1900.

With respect to the first reigns with top championships that were held by Black wrestlers whose heritage was publicly acknowledged, Ed Flowers' two-month reign with the world middleweight championship of New England in 1933 is on the list, as is the one-month reign as light heavyweight champion of Montana by boxer-turned-wrestler LeRoy "King Kong" Clayton.

It was a title reign that overlapped with Clayton's frequent dabblings as a boxer in the same region, as Clayton was probably the Black pro wrestler whose boxing pedigree was the purest, and he was something of a two-sport star, participating in real boxing matches in both Montana and Alberta during his pro wrestling career.

The remaining two reigns were world title reigns of Seelie Samara, including his dubious heavyweight title reign in Boston, which is one of the most generous applications of the term "world heavyweight champion" ever committed to record even in professional wrestling circles.

Wrestling for what was by that point the organization that was the clear loser of the interpromotional wrestling war with Paul Bowser in Boston, Samara was appointed to the position of world champion of the United States Wrestling

Association — a name that the Massachusetts Wrestling Association and its promoter Charley Gordon used very briefly — upon his arrival rather than winning the title in the ring. He was not required to visibly defeat a White wrestler to gain the championship.

A few months later, when a merger between the competing organizations took place, Samara's title reign was completely forgotten and never referenced again, and he was soundly bested in straight falls by Bowser's appointed champion, Steve "Crusher" Casey.

When weighed against the criteria generally applied to determine the credibility of any wrestling title — let alone a supposed world championship — Samara's election to the status of a world titleholder based on his brief possession of an insignificant championship that was quickly discarded does not hold up as the groundbreaking feat it may first appear to be.

Far more credible were Samara's eventual world title reigns in Montreal during 1939, when he held the foremost world junior heavyweight title recognized in Quebec over the course of two reigns lasting just under three months.

By this point, Jack Claybourne had now been well established in the area as a representative of South Africa rather than Australia, and had also educated the fans to the danger posed by his "African twin-boot hold" from the moment he first used it to subdue Tuffy Cleet in front of 3,000 fans at the Detroit Arena Gardens in May. Even at that early juncture, *The Free Press* had outright stated that Claybourne had earned a match with "his Negro rival, Rough Rufus Jones."

*The Hamilton Spectator* declared "Jones was looked upon as a speedster, but when Claybourne appeared on the scene, he began to steal Jones' thunder." To those who perceived this statement to be true, Claybourne usurped an even larger share of that thunder when he forced Jones to submit to a Boston crab to win the semi–official colored title.

Before the pair clashed just across the Detroit River in Windsor, Ontario, *The Windsor Star* elaborated on the heated rivalry that had been brewing between the two, beginning its article by opining that "rivalry between colored athletes often reaches an amazingly high point." *The Star* also added that it was "very seldom that colored men meet in wrestling or boxing," with the point regarding boxing being demonstrably false.

"Claybourne, from South Africa, is an amiable, easy-going grappler not easily angered; Jones, from Georgia, is an excitable and troublesome rascal," added *The Star*. "Claybourne is proud of his position in the mat world; Jones is envious of it. Claybourne is a hero, whereas Jones is a villain. Where Jack gets cheers, Rufus gets jeers — and criticism in physical forms less pleasant."

The two fittingly dueled to a draw during their first meeting in Detroit, with the match ending on a "head on collision" between the two that resulted in a double knockout. Regardless of the official result, all of the talk after the match was about the sensational "hurdle hold" employed by Gentleman Jack to nearly score a fall against Rough Rufus just prior to the bout's conclusion.

"Rough Rufus was hiding behind the six-foot-two frame of Referee Verne Clark. Time and again, Gentleman Jack tried to circle Referee Clark, but try as Mr. Clark would, he could not get out of the way. Rough Rufus dodged with Clark," described *The Free Press*. "Disgusted, Gentleman Jack, unable to get around Clark, suddenly gave a leap, vaulted nimbly over the referee's head, and came down with a body scissors on the surprised Rufus. Jones eventually broke it, and a moment later the collision occurred."

Claybourne won the Detroit rematch between the two Black grapplers, along with their first bout in Canada. Their next bout, hosted by the Hamilton Sporting Club, was billed as a multi-fall match for the colored light heavyweight title, and Claybourne landed the only fall in what was called a fight that was "so intense that neither grappler paid the slightest attention to the final bell and had to be pried apart when the limit was up."

Jack defeated Rufus by taking him down with a series of flying headlocks and then locking him in a crab hold. Seemingly infuriated by losing a fall to the Gentleman, Rufus escalated the violence of the match to suit his style.

"On his return to the ring, Rufus continued his rough tactics, using eye gouges and rabbit punches on the South African, and resorted to the ropes frequently," stated *The Spectator*. "Jones applied a punishing self strangle, but Claybourne returned the favour with a series of elbow smashes. Running the ropes, Jones jumped out of the ring followed by Claybourne, continuing the bout for an interval on the ground. On their return to the ring, neither man was able to secure the advantage, and Claybourne was banging Jones' head against the posts at the gong. The bell had no effect as they continued to trade elbow smashes a short time after the gong."

Jack had temporarily emerged as the victor, but the momentum would swing when the scene shifted to Kentucky. When Jones arrived in Louisville intent on battling Claybourne, *The Courier-Journal* lauded his "unblemished record" of "300 victories in four years of competition." His phony undefeated streak was kept intact when he bested Claybourne, whom *The Courier-Journal* described as "the fastest thing since Jesse Owens kept the crowd in an uproar, with his rubber-legged antics and kangaroo kicks."

Jones smashed Claybourne to the canvas to take the first fall, and Claybourne retaliated with his dropkicks to take the second. In the third, Claybourne missed a dropkick and landed on his head, allowing Jones to retain the Negro heavyweight championship that he had allegedly arrived with.

This sequence of interactions during the summer of 1938 between Rufus and Jack marked the first series of exchanges between two of the four core members of the Murderers' Row of professional wrestling. In a North American sports context, the name "Murderers' Row" is almost universally applied to the infamous batting lineup of the 1927 New York Yankees, and particularly the first six hitters:

Earl Combs, Mark Koenig, Babe Ruth, Lou Gehrig, Bob Meusel, and Tony Lazzeri.

Only in the sport of boxing did Murderers' Row denote a different collection of elite athletic talent, and even then, only the most learned boxing fanatics are aware of the group's existence. In boxing circles, Murderers' Row — often modified to *Black* Murderers' Row — refers to a set of phenomenal fighters spearheaded by Charley Burley, Eddie Booker and Lloyd Marshall.

All were Black fighters who were considered among the best of their era, yet these feared fighters were never given opportunities to compete for the sanctioned world titles, and instead were relegated to continually fighting one another for what amounted to the championship of their personal peer group.

In professional wrestling, a variation of this theme with an adjusted understanding of its meaning is neatly applicable to the grouping of Jack Claybourne, Rufus Jones, Jim Mitchell, and Seelie Samara, with Jack Nelson, King Kong Clayton, Gorilla Parker, Alex Kaffner, and Don Blackman potentially serving as affiliate members.

The core four members of this group would spend the better part of their careers engaging with one another — as both allies and adversaries — and trading mythical championships that were spontaneously created for them. Each was a Black wrestler who was generally excluded from winning championships for the bulk of their careers, which was owed to reluctance on the part of promoters and bookers to crown Black grapplers as the supreme stars of their territories.

In all fairness, the reluctance to crown them may have been influenced by a legitimate fear of losing money due to the presumed hesitance of White wrestling fans to support Black dominance with their hard-earned dollars. Evidently, this was also one of the fears that made fight promoters fearful of the idea of putting the top White fighters in the ring with the best Black fighters, for fear that the outcome of a fight that could not be controlled might result in title reigns that paying fans would not be willing to support with their attendance and financial resources.

Back in Michigan and Ontario, the audiences had now developed an appreciation for the full range of Rufus Jones' talents, and the descriptions of his routine provided by the local newspapers began to reflect the medley of different approaches he could take as a match unfolded.

"The Georgia Negro, whose given name is generally prefixed by the word 'Rough,' well merits the tag, for his style certainly bears a resemblance to drawing-room manners," opined *The Star*. "On the other hand though, Rufus is a humorist, and one of the very few men in the game who possesses the odd knack of being able to anger and amuse a crowd in turn during a single evening."

In concluding the advertisement for Jones' bout with the Great Balbo, *The Star* further remarked that Jones "once shocked a local turnout by a like display of mat etiquette and proved the he really had a considerable store of real wrestling ability," underscoring how Jones could deliver whatever meal the audience had a taste for on any given evening.

Then in November, Jones lost a main-event, best-of-three-falls match in Battle Creek to Abe Greenberg, which would rank as just one of many main-event bouts by Jones in the state of Michigan if not for the description of the bout's second fall. Down one fall to zero, Jones used his head in an unorthodox fashion to even the score.

"Jones won the second fall in five minutes with a body slam and press after butting Greenberg in the head several times," recorded *The Battle Creek Moon-Journal*.

It's true that Jones had drawn attention to the leaping delivery of his headbutts before, but this report from *The Moon-Journal* describes one of the first instances of Jones stringing together several headbutts in succession to overwhelm his adversaries.

In Port Huron, Jones once again waged in a battle that was said to be for the Bad Man championship. This time, his opponent was Abe Greenberg. *The Port Huron Times Herald* stated that the Thanksgiving contest would pit Greenberg, "the ace rough and tumble Jew," against Rufus Jones, "a Negro pretender to the throne."

Before the bout, *The Times Herald* attributed the statement to Jones that he would emerge from the bout with Greenberg as the "king of villains," and that's precisely what he did. After Greenberg took the first fall with kicks to the ribs and other rough tactics, Jones retaliated in falls two and three "with the same kind of attack" to emerge victorious and retain his unofficial championship as Michigan's premier mat evildoer.

In the fall of 1938, the New England area was graced by the presence of Tiger Flowers, or at least someone wrestling under the name Tiger Flowers. This version of Flowers appeared at the show of Sam Price at the Boston Arena on Wednesday, October 19th, and remained in the region until winter ended in early 1939.

While this makes it impossible that this iteration of Tiger Flowers was Joseph Godfrey, who was highly active in his Rufus Jones persona in the Midwestern states, there are plenty of reasons to think that the Tiger Flowers who appeared in New England during this time was not the original version.

When this Flowers appeared on a Chick Hayes card in Portland, Maine, it was stated that his recent appearance in Boston had been his debut in that city. In fact, the original Tiger Flowers had debuted in Boston six years earlier.

By the time January rolled around and the new Tiger Flowers got around to wrestling Curly Donchin, it was advertised that the two had never wrestled one another before despite the original Tiger Flowers having squared off with Donchin several times in every year from 1934 to 1936.

Finally, unlike previous versions of Tiger Flowers who was at least competitive in his losses, this iteration of Tiger Flowers was not. In his lone feature performance during this run, against the aforementioned Donchin, he was dismissed fairly easily in straight falls.

Again, it's worth noting the prevalence of the names "Black Panther" and "Tiger Flowers" amongst boxers of all skill levels. As the Black Panther title had essentially entered into the realm of public domain use in both ring-based sports, there's no reason to believe that the same wouldn't be true of the name Tiger Flowers.

On top of that, there is at least one other clear example of a wrestling promoter attempting to substitute one Black wrestler for another under the same name and hoping that no one would notice.

Early in 1937, LeRoy "King Kong" Clayton was first introduced to Montana's wrestling fans as Tiger Jack Nelson, as if he was identical to the Black wrestler from Los Angeles who had toured the Mountain West region just a few years prior.

Not only was Clayton about a decade younger than Nelson, but he was also at least five inches shorter with a far thicker frame. Frankly, the only thing the two wrestlers shared was a similar complexion; there was *no* confusing the two for anyone who had ever seen both in person.

*The Helena Daily Independent* was forced to walk back its identification of King Kong Clayton as Tiger Jack Nelson in a very awkward and ham-handed statement.

"It is well known that the colored man wrestles under two names," argued *The Daily Independent*. "Some promoters bill him as Tiger Jack Nelson while others prefer the more spectacular name of King Kong Clayton, a moniker dubbed onto him during the heyday of the King Kong movies. Regardless of what name he wrestles under, Tiger Jack is a wrestler of the first division and many of the boys have found out to their sorrow that he beats them either at straight wrestling or in the more spectacular antics of the matmen."

The fact is that every appearance by Joe Godfrey as Tiger Flowers had been for Charley Gordon or an affiliated promoter; the fact that Sam Price was actively competing against both Gordon and Paul Bowser for wrestling supremacy in Boston makes it all the more likely that he was using a fake Flowers.

Down in Ohio, Claybourne would undergo a rather bizarre name change that was as radical as the difference between Tiger Flower and Rufus Jones. As opposed to making appearances in Cincinnati under his real name — which he had steadily worked under for six years — Claybourne would wrestle under the alias of "Pablo Hernandez," and would be presented as a Black grappler from Cuba.

The Cuban wrestling style of Hernandez was seemingly identical to the American style of Claybourne, as the reports from *The Cincinnati Enquirer* depict Hernandez as dispatching his opponents with "a series of flying tackles."

Claybourne would appear in Cincinnati in his Cuban guise in parts of 1938 and 1939, ostensibly appearing as a Black Cuban alternative to Jim Mitchell, who frequently appeared in Cincinnati, and even teamed with Claybourne while he wrestled under the Hernandez name.

In January 1939, Jones and Claybourne both appeared in Chicago and emerged victorious in their respective bouts. For the first time, Jones was referred to as a product of Boston, which is a rather reasonable stretch given the short driving distance between Boston and Malden, Jones' actual hometown.

With contests for the colored championship being far more sporadic given the paucity of participants in what could only generously be referred to as a colored wrestling division, the "Bad Boy title," which *The Times Herald* referred to as a "synthetic" championship, was treated with far more seriousness. Furthermore, the acknowledgement of the honorary title's existence provided ample justification for promoters to pair villainous, roughhousing wrestlers together without any further justification than their desire for heel supremacy.

All the same, the imaginary nature of the championship meant it would often go months without being discussed, let alone defended. Local promoters would also seemingly assign it to any heel wrestler at their own discretion, and transfer it at their leisure, without any in-ring activities being required to make the transition happen.

In a bout on the last day of February, Jones took full advantage of both the environmental hazards and those that were introduced by the participating audience during a show held at the Municipal Swimming Pool in Hamilton, Ontario.

Battling through his semifinal bout with Hamilton resident Jimmy "Red" Simms, which *The Hamilton Spectator* praised as "the outstanding bout on the card," Jones took the first fall easily, and then he and Simms "battled in and out of the ring until they both went tumbling into the pool."

"The dive apparently cooled both off and refreshed them, and Simms went to work with body slams and haymakers to even the scrap up in six minutes," continued *The Spectator*. "An excited spectator tossed an overshoe into the ring in the third round, and Jones used that to attack both Simms and the referee. Simms, however, grabbed the Georgia man and held on until the time limit."

In March, Jones' fellow Black Bostonian and Murderers' Row associate Seelie Samara arrived in Detroit, providing a fresh opponent for Jones to face in colored championship matches.

Advertised as being quite literally as "the strongest Negro in the world," Samara was possibly the first full-fledged Black wrestling star since Siki to be consistently labeled as a heavyweight. He was billed as a powerful, musclebound wrestler first and foremost, and received more descriptions touting his size than any of the other Black wrestlers in his peer group.

Samara's style was also consistent with that of other powerhouse wrestlers of the era, yet he often displayed his technical prowess, frequently relying on leglocks to earn his victories.

Jones and Samara made their first contact as opponents during tag team matches in Detroit. When Jones teamed with the Cardiff Giant and Samara paired with Leo Wallick, the quartet participated in what was said to be the first mixed-race tag team match in the history of Detroit, where both teams consisted of White and Black members.

Soon, Jones ventured southward and into Ohio, where he had his first interaction with "The Black Panther" Jim Mitchell, marking the beginning of a pairing that would last many years and take on several different forms.

The two prepared to face one another in Dayton in what was advertised as "marking the first time two colored wrestlers have been brought together into the same ring locally" by *The Dayton Daily News*. Meanwhile, *The Dayton Daily Herald* upgraded the significance of the bout by declaring it to be a contest with the colored light heavyweight championship on the line.

Curiously, which of the two men was supposed to have been the reigning titleholder on the evening of the bout was never mentioned, but by the end of the night it didn't matter. *The Herald* reported that the "extremely cagey Negro" known as the Black Panther had taken Rufus to task with "a series of rope flips" to win their bout in 13-and-a-half minutes.

Jack Claybourne would have his first engagements with Jim Mitchell during this time, but he arrived at the Black Panther's doorstep by walking a somewhat different path.

As 1939 opened, descriptions of Claybourne's matches reveal a grappler who had truly become a master of his craft. *The Times Herald* of Port Huron, Michigan described Jack as a wrestler who was "noted for his speed and sensational attack," who also "knows all the razzle dazzle holds." Of Claybourne's holds that the publication could name, they listed the flying tackle, the drop kick, the backbreaker, and the "airplane scissors," before adding that Claybourne knew at least a dozen other holds that they couldn't name.

Those same descriptions also reveal a wrestler who continued to have no problems hurling himself through the air and risking life and limb. During a January bout in Davenport, Iowa, *The Davenport Democrat and Leader* described how

Claybourne forfeited a title bout against Ray Clements when he crash landed after a missed flying tackle and injured himself.

By the same token, Claybourne's body was punished even when he absorbed landings that would have been categorized as "safe." The wrestling rings of the era were almost always boxing rings with gently padded surfaces and almost no give to them. Yet, Claybourne's selection of a specialty move had him willfully careening through the air and crashing onto his back, sometimes more than a dozen times in a single match.

*The Green Bay Press-Gazette* described a Claybourne match against Lou Mueller from February 1939 in which Claybourne landed 10 dropkicks on Mueller during the first fall alone. After dropping the second fall to Mueller, Claybourne then won the third fall and the match "on another series of drop kicks in 7 minutes 30 seconds."

In April, Claybourne returned to Louisville to battle Jim Mitchell on the latter's home turf. The match would be something of a homecoming for Louisville's Black Panther as well, as *The Courier-Journal* reflected fondly on the earliest in-ring days of "the licorice-colored lad," along with the fact that he was known locally as "The Black and White" without a formal ring name due to his tendency to wear white wrestling tights that contrasted starkly with is dark skin.

Mitchell was now defending his version of the world Negro light heavyweight championship. In light of this, it was undeniable what the outcome of their bouts would be; the only uncertainty would be how competitive Claybourne was allowed to make them.

*The Courier-Journal* reported that Claybourne was generously permitted to take the first fall from Mitchell with an airplane spin before dropping the final two falls and ultimately losing the match. The pair then wrestled several additional times in Northern Ohio, with seemingly all of them concluding in 30-minute draws without a clear victor.

Claybourne dutifully lost to the hometown hero yet again, just as he had over the previous summer, surrendering two straight falls to Mitchell after concluding the first fall of the match with an airplane spin. The two would reconnect in Akron during the month of June, wrestling to a 30-minute draw in a setting with considerably less fanfare attached to their meeting.

Well before that rematch would occur, Claybourne would conduct an interesting round of business with wrestler Turp Grimes. Originally, advertised as tag team partners, the two would have a public falling out in Dayton when they lost to the team of Whitey Walberg and Olaf Olsen, and Grimes blamed Claybourne for their shared loss. Claybourne accused Grimes of failing to work as a responsible teammate, and challenged him to a tag team match where each man would choose a new partner.

This strategy backfired on Claybourne, as he and his partner Cleat Kauffman fell in defeat to the new team of Grimes and Walter Achiu. Believing that he would fare better against Grimes in a one-on-one scenario, Claybourne challenged Grimes to a singles match only to be turned back again, and in an outrageous example of an official's indifference to rule breaking.

"Turp used a golf ball in beating Claybourne down in the final fall of the match, but the damage was slight and Referee Howard Wagner let the misdemeanor slide," reported *The Dayton Herald*. "A body slam a few seconds later gave Turp the winning fall."

Subsequent matches would give fans the impression that Claybourne simply wasn't built for team competition. This became evident when Jack teamed with his former adversary Mitchell to oppose Stacey Hall and the Great Mephisto.

"The Negro team was moving along on even terms when a misguided punch started the fireworks and set the stage for its defeat," declared *The Dayton Daily News*. "Claybourne drew a bead on Hall's jaw and let fly, but the blow went awry, landing instead on the Panther, who figured the wallop intentional and a double-cross. It was an easy matter then for Hall and Mephisto to nail the disorganized pair."

Up in Brantford, Ontario, Rufus Jones was receiving rave reviews for his main-event matchup with Cowboy Hughes, which had the fans on their feet throughout the bout and concluded with a draw.

"Jones wrestled clean for about ten minutes, then went haywire using the tape on his wrist to blind his opponent, and then eye-gouging," wrote *The Expositor*. "Jones won the first fall in 24 minutes with a self-strangle. Hughes won the second fall in 13 minutes using a self-strangle and a body stretch. After the gong rang to end the bout, both of these boys put on a private show of their own, which pleased the fans."

If the crowd-pleasing nature of Jones' performances wasn't made plainly evident through the reports that were written about him in the Canadian press, there were times when the Canadian sportswriters printed clear words to that effect. In one particular April edition of *The Windsor Star*, the writer openly contemplated the comedic potential of an upcoming tag team bout involving Cowboy Hughes, Prince Ilaki, Leo Wallick and Alex Kasaboski, and said that he hoped they would be as fun as the foursome of Hughes, Ilaki, Jones and Samara.

"Words fail one in attempting to describe the action provided by that first quartet to put on such a bout in Canada," added *The Star*. "Just picture a ring embracing a Wallace Beery, a Bill Robinson, a Joe E. Brown, and a couple of Marx Brothers, with a pair of pseudo-serious Joe Penners trying to patch things up between them, multiply by two, and you have a fair idea of what took place. Dippy? Yeah. But what fun!"

Having just compared the wrestlers to an all-star slate of comedic actors of the era, the writer turned his attention to Jones, saying that his absence from the proceedings would be the most glaring, "for Rufus is almost in a class by himself when it comes to a combination of villain and comedian."

During a bout in Brantford, Ontario in May, Jones displayed his versatility by delivering his best impression of Jack Claybourne at the conclusion of a bout with the Mighty Maniaci. After the Italian evened the fall count at one apiece with a flying tackle and a cradle hold, *The Expositor* described how Jones "floored the Mighty Italian with drop kicks, a dangerous practice, but effective in the art of opponent elimination."

Back in Michigan, it was finally Jones' turn to have his fists retroactively receive a respectful education when it was announced by *The Ironwood Daily Globe* that he had "started his career as a boxer, but took to wrestling after watching the matmen work out a few times."

The fact that boxing was the only major sport in which Black athletes were regularly allowed to showcase their abilities against all comers while getting paid to do so also made boxing the only believable connection a wrestling promoter could make between a Black wrestler and a relatable athletic skill outside of the wrestling ring. Attempting to fake a connection between a Black wrestler and a professional sport other than boxing would have been instantly dismissed as fraudulent.

As a result of this, nearly every Black wrestler of the era was at some point stated to have been a convert from the sweet science of boxing over to wrestling, and in several cases it was actually true. However, even with Jones being advertised as a skilled pugilist, it did nothing to dissuade fans from attempting to take their own shots at him.

In an event in Sault Sainte Marie, Michigan that was said to have nearly ended in a riot until police intervened, Jones was on the ropes — both literally and figuratively — in his bout with world light heavyweight champion Leo Wallick. The titlist had already defeated Jones in the first fall with his "sledgehammer hold," and had caused Jones to retreat into the ropes to avoid a pounding during the second fall.

"[Jones'] two feet were on the middle rope when Wallick lunged at him feet first to knock him out of the ring," recounted *The Evening News* of Sault Sainte Marie. "Jones was unable to return and was counted out by Referee Vern Clark of Detroit."

It was that very moment when a pair of spectators chose to take a shot at Jones, with police having to break up the melee and restore order so that Rufus could return to the locker room safely.

The Murderers' Row of professional wrestling was now fully engaged and interactive, and as the United States inched toward a second world war, they would continue to raise the bar for Black wrestlers while also having their careers heavily defined by their dealings with each other. Eventually, one of them would amplify a single element of his act to become even more of a must-see attraction, while also bringing a longstanding anti-Black stereotype to the forefront.

## 6 – Knothead

Rufus Jones had already developed a reputation as a dirty wrestler, but he was about to take that description and have it reimagined in a truly literal way. In June 1939, Rufus competed against Al Krusher in the first mud wrestling match ever held in the Detroit Arena Gardens, and persisted in maintaining the action even as the level of danger present in the bout was unexpectedly increased by an unanticipated equipment malfunction.

In coloring the scene for readers, the writer from *The Detroit Free Press* leaned very heavily into skin-color comparisons to get their point across as to how the color of the mud blotted out the natural coloring of the White wrestler and referee involved in the match.

"Two minutes after the mud bout started, you couldn't tell Mr. Krusher from Rough Rufus, while Referee Vern Clark, attired in bathing trunks for this educational affair, managed to keep his manly chest white," reported *The Free Press*. "As the mud splattered, it was easy to understand why the Hindus who began mud wrestling more than 3,000 years ago seldom wore many clothes. To make the mud match more entertaining, an overhead light bulb exploded into the ring. That didn't deter the wrestlers. They went right ahead, mud, glass and all. Krusher won when Jones, who was about to throw the Londoner, slipped."

The write-up from United Press International also used the bout as an opportunity to engage in some racial humor. In the aftermath of Krusher's victory, the UPI described how referee Clark first raised the arm of the victor, and then scraped the mud from his face to identify precisely who had won the bout.

"It was Al Krusher, who had been white when the fight started, but after the first two minutes you couldn't tell Krusher or Clark from Jones, a Negro," concluded the UPI.

It would be June when Rufus Jones and Seelie Samara would finally compete for the mythical colored light heavyweight championship in Battle Creek. The two had engaged in a series of matches across Canada, usually ending in draws after each man had taken a fall.

Funnily enough, in the midst of their activity in Canada, Jones and Samara were both advertised to wrestle on the same Montreal card under their original Canadian stage names of Tiger Flowers and Zelis Amhara at the Saint-Jacques Market Hall.

Amhara had been competing weekly in Montreal in addition to appearing in the other locations in Michigan and Ontario, and seemingly invited Jones to appear with him under the Tiger Flowers name he had previously used in Montreal between 1935 and 1938.

As advertised, Amhara faced Harry Madison, and Flowers was scheduled to face Charley Layden, but *Le Devoir* reported that Flowers could not make it to the event due to an illness in his family, and Turk Lammy was required to substitute for him. Anyone lacking the knowledge that Jones and Flowers were the same person would simply have thought Flowers was emerging from hibernation to make a rare appearance.

The most intriguing thing about the bouts between Jones and Samara was some of the language used to sell their matches to the public. In pre-1940s Canada where the total Black population of the entire nation sat at just over 20,000 residents within a populace of 11.5 million — less than two-tenths of one percent — it was apparently still possible to stoke the fans' interest in a match based on the depth of the Blackness of the participants.

Prior to an early June bout at the a baseball stadium in Hamilton, Ontario, *The Hamilton Spectator* described the medium brown Jones as "darker than a night at the dungeon" despite his skin shade falling very close to the middle range of skin shades amongst North American Blacks.

The description of the match in Hamilton between the two Black wrestling stars accentuates the stylistic differences between the two. Samara opened the match by brutalizing Jones with clubbing rights and several body slams, only for Jones to up the ante with rule-bending tactics.

"The second stanza saw Rufus run amok by punishing Seelie with a series of hard rights to the chin, along with body slams to take the round in five minutes," stated *The Hamilton Spectator*.

When the two appeared together on the same card in Kitchener, *The Kitchener Daily Record* referred to Samara and Jones collectively as "representatives of the Southern race," reflecting not only the perception of otherness that certain areas of Canada still harbored for Blacks at the time, but also the lingering belief that Blacks were categorically still tied to a Southern slave origin.

This sort of blanket identification failed to take into account the diversity in experiences and points of origin of Blacks in general. These broad generalizations neglected to account for the fact that the overwhelming majority of the Blacks living in the areas of the United States adjacent to Canada had been free since 1860 at the latest. What's more, if Samara had truly been of Ethiopian extraction as stated, a North American slave origin would not have applied to him in the slightest.

Just as Jones' bout with Jim Mitchell in Ohio had been a title bout with neither man entering the contest advertised as a champion, neither Jones nor Samara was said to be in possession of the title heading into the match.

Perhaps sensing the lack of legitimacy of the supposed title and the informal way in which the bout was declared to have been a title contest, or maybe because it was rightly questioned how a bout between two wrestlers who lost so frequently could have been for a respectable title, the writer for *The Enquirer and Evening News* of Battle Creek derisively stated that the match was "for the Negro championship of something or other."

## Gentleman Jack and Rough Rufus

In the main event of the first wrestling show held at the outdoor arena at the corner of South Division and South Avenue Street in Battle Creek, Jones defeated Samara for the mythical colored light heavyweight title, albeit the result of an unsatisfying disqualification ending in the third fall.

Samara captured the first fall with a headlock, while Jones countered in the second fall with what *The Battle Creek Moon Journal* referred to as a series of "monkey shakes." Finally, Samara was disqualified for choking Rufus and repeatedly slamming his head into the ring posts.

"Fans booed the decision since Rough Rufus had manhandled Samara quite a bit earlier in the fight, and if anyone was to be disqualified, numerous ringsiders thought it should be Mr. Jones," added *The Enquirer*.

Samara managed to win the Battle Creek rematch between the two, but his victory wasn't any more convincing than Jones' victory over him had been. *The Enquirer* reported that Jones had essentially defeated himself by locking Samara in a reverse body hold while inadvertently rolling backwards with Samara on top of him so that the referee could count the pinfall.

After having his falling out with Mitchell, Jack Claybourne would also find himself engaged in combat with Samara, except that these matches would take place in Louisville, and the first in-ring meeting between Samara and Claybourne in August 1939 ended in a Claybourne victory. *The Courier-Journal* illustrated how Jack rebounded from surrendering the first fall to Samara by capturing the two successive falls with a "kangaroo kick" and his own version of a "monkey shake" respectively.

Claybourne would then have another match at the Allen Athletic Club of Louisville against Mitchell, with advertisements stating that both men were hoping to win the bout and move on to "a return engagement with the recognized world's Negro heavyweight champion, Rufus Jones."

The multi-fall bout would be contested with a 55-minute time limit in place, and the lone fall registered would be awarded to Mitchell shortly after the 40-minute mark, as he caught Claybourne with a flying mare for the pin.

In the meantime, Jones spent August displaying his resourcefulness, and showcased as much in a match against Eddie Virag when he tactfully implemented a counter to the hold that Virag used to defeat him in the opening stanza.

"Eddie Virag scored the first fall on Rufus Jones with a full-nelson, but lost the second when the same hold backfired," stated *The Kitchener Daily Record*. "The Southern boy tried his gouging tactics later in the bout and had Virag partly blinded. However, the bronzed Hungarian managed to get the full-nelson on Rufus again, but in some manner the chocolate-colored boy pulled him to a corner, threw his feet against the post, shot Virag backward, and the latter fell hitting his head hard on the canvas. The fall won by Jones required but two minutes."

In October, Michigan welcomed another young Black wrestler who is rarely connected with the core group of Black talent that started wrestling in the early 1930s, Don Blackman, who was wrestling as "Dynamite" Blackman. The feature article on Blackman that appeared in *The Michigan Chronicle* referred to Blackman as a five-year mat veteran who was 26 years old.

In actuality, this would have been a far more accurate description of Jones, who was actually 26 years old with just over five years of ring experience at the time the article was written. Meanwhile, Blackman was actually 27 years old, and without any evidence that he had wrestled anywhere prior to his appearance in Detroit in the fall of 1939, at least not under any variation of his real name.

At the same time, Blackman's general size and appearance, coupled with his origin on the East Coast of the United States, makes him an excellent candidate to have been the wrestler who appeared briefly as Tiger Flowers in the

Northeast during that latter part of 1938 and very early in 1939.

In an interview years later, Blackman would claim to have caught the bus from his hometown of Birmingham, Alabama to New York City when he was only 17 years old, at which point he began training to be a professional wrestler "just to get in shape." If true, this means that Blackman would have been a fully trained wrestler by 1930, and physically capable of performing in the role.

Over the course of his feature article from *The Chronicle*, Blackman made a few statements that would support this theory, citing New York, New England and Cuba as three locations that were critical to his development, with New York being the most frequent wrestling area of the original Tiger Flowers, New England being the region in which the Tiger Flowers who emerged in 1938 and 1939 engaged in all of his matches, and Cuba being the original nation offered as a birthplace for the Tiger Flowers character.

The same article saw Blackman denouncing Rufus Jones as "one of the dirtiest wrestlers he has ever seen," after Blackman had concluded a public training session at the YMCA of Saginaw.

Despite what seemed like an aggressive callout of Jones, Blackman didn't last in Michigan for more than a week before heading out to the West Coast to wrestle under the name of "The Dark Angel" — another one of Joe Louis' recurring nicknames.

Instead of quarreling with Blackman, Jones would instead continue to compete primarily against his Black contemporaries, especially in Canada. There was an odd October night in Waterloo in which Rufus pulled double-duty, working as an official before entering the ring to wrestle Jack Claybourne.

The substitution of Rufus as the replacement referee for the bout between Buzz Jones and Mighty Meniaci was deemed necessary when the real referee failed to arrive at the arena on time due to the dense fog that was reported in the area. *The Kitchener Daily Record* actually conceded that Rufus "didn't do a bad job of refereeing the opening bout," suggesting that one of wrestling's most vile villains actually called the bout squarely down the middle.

From there, Jones returned to form during his battle with Gentleman Jack. *The Daily Record* described it as "the wildest show of the night, with Gentleman Jack leading Jones on a merry parade." With Claybourne leading the bout one fall to zero, Rufus grabbed Jack by the hair and tossed him out to the arena floor. When the incensed Claybourne climbed back into the ring and returned the favor to Rufus, fill-in referee Meniaci disqualified him and awarded the fall to Jones.

"Claybourne was furious," added *The Daily Record*. "He sent Jones reeling with a hard smash and then turned on the referee. Jones recovered and gained his feet only to go smashing back to the mat with Meniaci following suit. Finally, Jones made a dash for the dressing room and Jack followed, jumping over the ropes. At this point the brawl was halted by police officers who separated the two."

In October, Jack and Rufus were also on opposing sides of an elimination tag team match in Windsor, with the writer of the promotional piece for *The Windsor Star* having the wherewithal to recognize that ethnic differences applied to Blacks just as plainly as they did to other groups.

"[The match] pits two Negro-White teams against each other, and to add to its colorful qualities, it brings into contention four different nationalities," the article explained. "Hart is a Hollander, Kasaboski is a Polish-Canadian, Jones is an American Negro, and Claybourne an African Negro. With all those spices, it should prove a tempting dish before the expiration of the hour time limit that has been allowed for its consumption."

The bout itself was a further display of Jones' versatility as an entertainer. Early in the match, Jones was playing the role of the cowardly instigator, urging his partner Kasaboski to attack Claybourne while Rufus kept a safe distance. On two of those occasions, Jones actually shoved his partner forward, and both times Kasaboski's chin was met by the raised feet of Gentleman Jack. Kasaboski understandably grew weary of this tactical approach.

"If words couldn't convince Rufus that Kasaboski didn't like the Jones strategy, action could. He turned on his partner in crime, gave him a mighty elbow sock, and crashed him to the mat," illustrated *The Star*. "It was Claybourne's big chance. He took it. He piled on top of both his opponents, and before they knew it Jones had been pinned."

Claybourne was ultimately awarded the victory when Kasaboski got fed up, attacked the referee, and drew the disqualification.

Jones may have suffered the loss, but *The Star* would credit him with being "unquestionably the most entertaining team wrestler yet to be seen in these parts — and there have been more than a few of them."

For his troubles, Claybourne was rewarded with a title bout at the Kitchener Auditorium against the Great Mephisto, but the champion was a no-show, resulting in Jack competing against Frankie Talaber in a non-title affair.

"It took the dusky Claybourne only 16:29 minutes to dispose of his opponent from Chicago," reported *The Kitchener Daily Record*. "The big South African broke arm holds repeatedly by swinging one foot over his opponent's head and stepping into the clear. A reverse body drop gave Claybourne the first fall, and he won the second after only 5:38 minutes with a rolling hold."

In Hamilton, Claybourne faced an opponent who could match his speed when he met Jimmy "Red" Sims at the Municipal Pool. The bout featured "well-known holds as arm stretches, arm scissors, rolling cartwheels and leg and toe holds," before Claybourne "with amazing speed, put on a thunderbolt hold to make Jimmy say quits in 23 minutes." Up one fall to none, Jack then rode out the remaining time to earn the victory.

November saw Claybourne adding yet another maneuver to his regular arsenal — a rolling knee bar submission hold. In Battle Creek, Michigan, he used it to very effectively neutralize Frankie Hart, capturing two straight falls with the hold.

"Claybourne clamped on a punishing leg stretch against Hart in the first fall and finally forced the Dutchman to yield after 20 minutes of fighting," wrote *The Battle Creek Moon-Journal*. "The second fall was a repetition of the first, with Hart yielding to save himself punishment on the leg."

The end of 1939 also treated fans to a sight so rare that it had never been seen before, and would never see again, when Jack Claybourne, Rufus Jones, Jim Mitchell and Seelie Samara all competed against one another at the Detroit Arena Gardens in a blindfold battle royal.

While it may have been intended as a callback to the racist practice of having a group of unskilled Black combatants brutalize one another at the outset of a pro wrestling event, this moment in 1939 is best viewed through the lens of progress. After all, a considerable amount of change had to occur within the wrestling industry in order for four full-fledged Black wrestling stars to simultaneously compete within the same wrestling ring. Just one decade earlier, promoters had considered it a luxury to find even one.

Departing from the Midwest, Claybourne both concluded 1939 and began 1940 wrestling in New England, and in his Lynn, Massachusetts debut, he concluded his match using what was for him an atypical hold that relied on brute strength, forcing Joe Campbell to submit to a full-nelson after applying it for a full three minutes. After submitting to Jack and losing the opening fall, Campbell "was so badly used up that he was unable to continue and conceded the match."

"Claybourne, a dusky gladiator, is a classy performer and is bound to make trouble for the junior heavyweights as long as he remains in this neck of the woods," predicted *The Daily Evening Item*. "He knows the sport thoroughly, is fast as lightning, and a standout defensively. Campbell was outclassed, and the victor made a hit with the slim crowd."

## Gentleman Jack and Rough Rufus

In New England, the essence of Claybourne's status as a Black wrestler was far different than it had been in the other territories he had frequented. Even from the time of his earliest bouts in the Midwest, there had usually been another Black wrestler for him to share the ring with on occasion, and he was usually making appearances in states with Black populations of a respectable size, even if their numbers weren't reflected amongst the paying patrons.

**Close-up photo of Jack Claybourne**

## Gentleman Jack and Rough Rufus

In both the Pacific Northwest and Southwest, Claybourne was always the sole Black wrestler on the cards, and often appeared in states with Black population levels that were so low that they bordered on non-existent. In several of the communities he visited, it's possible that Claybourne's face had been the first visage sporting that dark of a hue that many of the locals had ever seen firsthand.

New England was different. The region had seen its share of Black wrestlers, and had served as the debut region to two of the most famous in Rufus Jones and Seelie Samara. Boston had also developed a sizable number of Black residents, and the percentage of the city composed of Blacks was rapidly swelling to 10 percent, meaning that there was no particular novelty to the mere sight of a Black man in much of New England. Claybourne would be wrestling without the luxury of having any other Black wrestlers on the cards with him.

Claybourne certainly enjoyed Boston well enough; he acquired a residence at 750 Shawmut Avenue in the Roxbury neighborhood of Boston, and established it as his permanent residence for close to a decade.

After working his way through multiple rounds of the region's light heavyweight tournament that he had supposedly joined in progress, Claybourne eliminated himself from the finals of the competition in his customarily dramatic fashion while wrestling against Winn Robbins. With the loss, Claybourne vaulted Robbins into a match with champion Salvatore Balbo.

"Claybourne missed a flying shoulder tackle, striking his head and shoulders on the apron and falling to the maple floor," reported *The Daily Evening Item*. "He was carried to the dressing room quarters and revived. The accident occurred after the warriors had gripped for seven minutes in the rubber fall of the windup match, and Robbins was declared the winner of the elimination tourney."

Claybourne piled up additional nicknames like "Dark Victory" and "The South African Show Stealer" during the early stages of his time in the Northeast. He also tacked on a growing number of losses in high-profile matches, and when he finally received the opportunity to capture one of the world championships defended in the Northeast, his bout ended in a fashion that was becoming painfully predictable.

In Portland, Maine, Claybourne was facing the world junior heavyweight champion of the area, Johnny Iovanna. Jack had Johnny reeling from several dropkicks when he attempted a flying shoulder tackle and found himself sailing out to the arena floor. Claybourne was unable to recover before being counted out of the ring, enabling Iovanna "to continue to call himself the world's junior heavyweight wrestling champion," in the words of the Associated Press.

Things turned around in mid-February when Claybourne succeeded in winning an elimination tournament in Holyoke to earn a shot at the light heavyweight championship of Salvatore Balbo. This time, Claybourne would show that he was every bit as capable a wrestler as Balbo, wrestling him to a 90-minute draw that showcased Claybourne's skill while still permitting Balbo to escape with the championship belt.

Making his debut in Biddeford, Maine for promoter Gerard Campobasso, Claybourne was named as "the most colorful junior heavyweight wrestler in the world," and "the holder of the junior heavyweight title." However, this was apparently a reference to the fake European championship Jack was advertised with upon entering the territory rather than any of the sanctioned light heavyweight or junior heavyweight titles being regularly defended throughout the region.

Along with referencing the backstory that Claybourne was of South African descent, and was educated at Oxford, the story supplied in *The Biddeford Daily Journal* furthered Claybourne's backstory for the fans, including how the wrestler had allegedly taken up the sport while attending Oxford, and had then won several tournaments, culminating in his acquisition of the European junior heavyweight championship.

"War conditions drove Jack to this country, and he tells of a funny incident, while coming to our shores three months ago," added the article. "It seems the Danish ship he came over on was stopped by a German sub a day out from the port. The sub commander with several sailors came aboard to look the contents of the ship over, and to see if they were carrying any contraband of war. The German commander spied Claybourne, and with outstretched hands greeted him and recalled when they had wrestled as opponents in an amateur tournament staged in Berlin. Though Claybourne is a British subject, the German officer wished him luck and Godspeed, and stated he hoped they would meet when this war is ended."

It's unlikely that many wrestlers, including Claybourne, had the time to keep up with the stories that were being submitted about them through wrestling promoters operating in different cities, and were caught completely off guard when asked about the details of their lives by fans on the streets.

Evidently, when Harvey Southward of *The Daily Evening Item* attempted to confirm some of the details of Claybourne's origin in the jungles of South Africa, Southward reported, "Jack Claybourne, the grappler, claims he never was in the African jungle, and that furthermore even though he was a wrestler, he never ate a man, or even had what is known as missionary soup."

Over in Ontario the word circulating throughout the province at the beginning of 1940 was that Rufus Jones had decided to reform and compete as a clean wrestler, which *The Windsor Star* agreed to be "a good idea, because Jones is one of the nastier fellows when in the mood."

The idea of a reformed Rufus carried over into Brantford, which printed the probably unintentionally true statement that "Jones used to be a clean, right-living kind of tussler, but later went haywire and was termed a 'bad man.'" Since Joseph Godfrey had wrestled exclusively as a heel since the time of his name change to Rufus Jones, the writer of the piece was either mistaken, embellishing for sake of effect, or harkening back to earlier Canadian appearances by Tiger Flowers.

Sadly, the writer from *The Brantford Expositor* once again displayed a level of insensitivity with respect to racial and ethnic identity that was typical of the era during the reveal that Jones would be competing against East Indian wrestler Nanjo Singh.

"The latter is colored, and of course Nanjo has a deep tan, too, so the boys and girls hope the trunks are different hues in order to note what is going on," said the article, as if there would be no other physical differences that the fans could use to differentiate between the grapplers.

One of the physical cues that fans might have picked up on to tell Jones apart from his opponent might have been his increasing size. *The Expositor* noted in a subsequent report that Rufus had "always been a pretty sort of fellow" when he used to appear in Brantford, but had grown "quite chubby" with the passage of time.

In March, Jack Claybourne continued his quest for a championship when he faced Jackie Nichols of Maine, the local hero who had won the world junior heavyweight championship from Iovanna just one week prior. The title match in Portland had just passed the one-hour mark when Claybourne attempted one of his favorite moves: A surprising leap-frog over the back of the referee to plant a dropkick into the face of an unsuspecting opponent.

"Using Dolan for a prop, [Claybourne] vaulted over the surprised referee, intending to upset Nichols with his move, but the latter, aware of the stratagem, moved in close to Dolan, and like the man on the flying trapeze, only the trapeze wasn't there, Claybourne went sailing over both to land hard, and to find Nichols sitting on him for the spill," illustrated *The Portland Evening Express*.

The next month in Portland, Claybourne had a violent departure from his gentlemanly tendencies after being dropped on his head three times during a bout with Paddy Mack. The match kicked off a violent feud with Claybourne responding to what he interpreted as a deliberate and gratuitous attempt to injure him.

"This, no doubt, did Claybourne no end of harm, for after being thrice deposited, he went into a roaring tantrum," described *The Portland Press Herald*. "He walloped Mack twice as a starter, and then he turned on rotund Bill Dolan and set that worthy down in a hurry. By this time, it was plain to see that Claybourne was not himself, so a couple of matmen climbed in to try to quiet him. But Claybourne was seeing red, white, and blue by this time, and he pounced on both, they being Jim Cortland and Paul O'Shea. While on the canvas, O'Shea grabbed the burly Negro, Cortland piled on, and Claybourne was subdued. While the matmen held grimly on, a physician examined Claybourne, brought him out of his 'spell,' and he was carried downstairs still writhing and quivering from all the bumping and battling."

*The Evening Express* followed up on the incident, stating that Claybourne had "required a medical diagnosis after his head had been banged up and down on the ring floor by Mack, who was practicing a new and vicious method of subduing his opponents."

*The Press Herald* teased the rematch to fans by building its promotional campaign around Claybourne's revenge-seeking efforts, suggesting that "a mild mannered and sweet dispositioned young colored 'gemman'" like Claybourne would willfully settle into the role of "badman" on this occasion in order to give Paddy Mack his comeuppance.

According to *The Press Herald*'s match report, Claybourne began his quest for justice by attempting to box Mack, who was not at all interested in throwing hands with the enraged Gentleman. Then, when referee William Malone stepped outside of the ring to confront a fan who had called him a "coward," Claybourne and Mack both attempted illegal tactics in the referee's absence, with Mack getting the better of the situation. A neck twist and knee strikes stopped Claybourne for the first fall.

"In the second fall, Jack started in again by trying to box Paddy, and his cocked right had the Irishman scared, and finally downed him for a moment," continued the article. "Jack promptly floored him again with a drop kick, and the bewildered Philadelphian sought the safety of the aisle. But

Jack came right out after him, and finally caught him, chased him into the ring, and stopped him in 5 minutes and 8 seconds with a full nelson."

At this very moment, the bout was interrupted by "an unruly customer" who had to be helped to the door by the application of a police officer's hammerlock hold. Following the interruption, Claybourne absorbed some additional rough treatment from Mack before ultimately scoring the victory.

"At the start of the third fall, it looked as if the Irishman would win, for he was using a hard hammerlock on Jack, and had him in the aisle several times," added *The Press Herald*. "But Jack used his head as a battering ram, and recovered quickly from being tossed through the ropes to come back with a flying butt, which he followed with a body press to win the bout in 8 ½ minutes."

Once he left New England, Claybourne spent the bulk of his traceable time during the remainder of 1940 in the Canadian province of Quebec, where he once again impressed fans with his sharp wrestling ability and high-flying athleticism. By this point, Seelie Samara had already twice won and lost the world junior heavyweight championship defended in Montreal. Interestingly, Samara's title success caused Claybourne to be viewed as an emergent threat in the area, and one of the reasons for this was seemingly because of his race.

"Claybourne is an ace, one of the most spectacular wrestlers to ever come to Montreal," stated *Le Devoir* of Montreal. "He is a man of color, an athlete of the breed of men who inflicted the most scathing failures on [Harry] Madison. We only have to remember the terrible fights fought here by the wrestlers Tiger Flowers and Zelis Amhara. Claybourne is undoubtedly as good as them, and probably surpasses them in classic wrestling science. But Madison is still considered by many experts to be the best 200-pound wrestler in the world. He is the one who currently holds the title, and if there is a black man who has any chance of taking it from him currently it is probably Jack Claybourne."

Unfortunately for Claybourne, he would not be as fortunate in world junior heavyweight title matches contested in Montreal as Samara had been. While the bout played out in a fashion that swayed every onlooker to the point of view that Claybourne deserved to be the world champion, the end result still left Claybourne leaving the Marche Saint-Jacques Gymnasium as the defeated challenger.

"After the two men had fought with equal chances, having each taken a fall, the referee [Saxon] received an accidental blow from Claybourne, and the official was momentarily placed out of action," reported *Le Devoir*. "While Saxon was regaining his senses, Claybourne had pinned Madison's shoulders to the mat, but without the knowledge of the referee. While the Irishman was holding the Negro to the mat, Saxon was able to realize what was happening, and he awarded victory to the champion."

The year 1940 would also bring fewer confrontations between Claybourne and his Black wrestling peers, but would sow more confusion about his true heritage. This was sparked by the overreach in attempting to exoticize a Black man from Central Missouri into something more appealing to predominantly White audiences on America's East Coast.

A potential reason for this may have been that wrestling promoters who had previously labeled Claybourne as a South African realized that the segregationist laws of pre-Apartheid South Africa would not have permitted someone of Claybourne's skin shade to represent the dominion as an approved ambassador of the people. As a result, he was recast as a Zulu tribesman, representing the largest Black ethnic group of South Africa as opposed to appearing as an agent of the minority White leadership.

Of course, Claybourne couldn't have been just any Zulu. *The Springfield Union* described him as "a Zulu warrior, educated in England, and holder of the European junior heavyweight crown," in June 1940. The coverage from *The Springfield Daily News* went one step further, making Claybourne "a graduate of Oxford University and son of a Zulu chief."

This addition of a spurious continental championship that was never defended in the ring may have been intended to grant Claybourne a level of worldliness on par with Reginald Siki, who legitimately spoke several European languages, who had acquired a championship in a European ring on at least one occasion, and who had gone silent after World War II had broken out in Europe.

It would eventually be revealed that Siki had been forced to endure constant harassment at the hands of the Nazis after the war had broken out, and things would eventually get much worse. It would later be disclosed that Siki was detained in a Nazi prison camp in Tittmoning, Ober-Bayern, Germany in 1942, and he would thankfully be freed as the result of a prisoner exchange in the spring of 1944.

As unfortunate as Siki's predicament had been, there were worse fates that could have befallen him. The true original Black Panther of wrestling, Illa Vincent, was reported to have taken a traveling troupe of women wrestlers into Russia and made quite a bit of money from the endeavor, only for the western world to completely lose track of him after the Bolshevik Revolution.

Given what is now known about what happened to people of great wealth who happened to inhabit Russia during that time period, there is a strong possibility that Vincent failed to escape Russia with his life. This persists despite the rumor that he was later spotted teaching wrestling classes in Egypt.

With respect to the faux European championship of Claybourne, all it truly accomplished was to position Jack as a ready-made challenger for the world light heavyweight and junior heavyweight championships defended in New England. In reality, the phony title was completely bereft of value; Gentleman Jack spent 1940 losing to every single holder of the respected championships, including Johnny Iovanna, Jackie Nichols, and Salvatore Balbo.

Further west, Rufus Jones was being exoticized in a different way, as he was inexplicably identified as "the Ethiopian" prior to a bout with Leon St. Pierre, just like so many of his Black grappling peers had been. That would be among the kindest terms used to describe Jones, as he would have to endure some unkind names and labels, several of which made no sense whatsoever.

In September, the promotional article from *The Hamilton Spectator* went out of its way to suggest that the medium-brown Jones was among the darkest colored people on the planet, referring to him as a man "on whom charcoal makes a white mark." Two days later, the same paper attached a new color-based nickname to him when they dubbed him "the black terror."

Unfortunately, the names kept getting worse. Ahead of a bout against Hamiltonian Johnny Silvy that Jones evened with a series of dropkicks and a reverse headlock, *The Spectator* gifted Jones the new semi-permanent nickname of "the Georgia Gorilla."

An air of unpredictability continued to permeate Jones' matches, and it became evident that absolutely anything could and did occur in them. In an early October match in Hamilton, Rufus was disqualified for whacking his opponent Walter Roxey over the head with a parasol that had been lobbed into the ring by a woman seated in the front row.

In October, Jones finally made his first appearance in Wisconsin, where *The Journal Times* of Racine introduced him to mat fans as "a good-sized lad" who "knows the ins and outs of the wrestling game to a T."

Rufus lost his very first match in Wisconsin, dropping falls to John Swenski by disqualification and countout, with *The Journal Times* remarking that he wrestled "in a maniacal way." During his following outing against Tony Bernardi, Rufus won both falls. The first came by way of a leg lock, and the second occurred when Jones capitalized on an errant leap from Bernardi and pinned him before he could recover from his crash landing.

Jones' next outing in Racine once again showcased his unique brand of humor when he let the praise from the crowd sway him into wrestling in a squeaky clean fashion.

"Jones and Haddock had been signed as two rough boys who were going to beat the tar out of each other," explained *The Journal Times*. "Jones, however, decided he liked the applause of the crowd when he accidentally broke clean during the early part of the match. From then on, the usual slugging, kicking and eye-gouging was discarded by the colored boy, and he left the ring as a hero for the first time this season."

**Rufus Jones kisses a rabbit's foot for good luck**

In a follow-up report, *The Journal Times* lamented the babyface behavior by Jones, saying that he "turned goody goody boy," and that it "wasn't as good a show that way" even though he was able to prove to fans that he could wrestle competently when required to do so.

The kind behavior from Jones simply proved to be the calm before the storm. In his next outing, Rufus unleashed an onslaught on his opponent in a heretofore unforeseen fashion. It was a style that would eventually come to define him, and *The Journal Times* noted that his style had "no buts about it, but plenty of butts."

"Dizzy had been up to his usual tactics of hair pulling and use of the ropes, and it finally got on the wrong side of the dusky lad's skin," the paper explained. "At the first opportunity, Jones grabbed Davis by the ears and soundly rapped him on the head, using his own noggin as a battering ram. Davis took about five good solid knocks like that and then went down on his knees. He got up once more, and again Jones battered him down by socking his head against Davis'. This time, Dizzy stayed down for the count."

Davis mounted a comeback in the second fall, choking Jones, and inspiring *The Journal Times* to employ the racialized humor of likening the image of Jones' tongue sticking out of his Black visage as being as conspicuous as "the white spot on the eight ball." Once he managed to free himself from Davis' grip, Jones returned to his headbutting attack.

"Again and again, he pounded his solid head like a sledgehammer against Dizzy's head, battering him to the floor," the article continued. "Then he picked him up and pounded some more, until the referee raised the colored boy's hand in victory."

This bout introduced a standard Jones trope, involving a marked overreliance on headbutts to pummel opponents into submission, along with a method of winning matches dishonorably, by forcing a referee's stoppage due to either concussion concerns, or blood loss.

Following that sudden outpouring of headbutts, *The Journal Times* took to referring to Jones as "Knothead," suggesting that the wrestler's butting explosion would become an ordinary occurrence.

"Rufus, whose name might be spelled 'rough house,' uses his head when he wrestles, but not in the manner others do," stated the article. "Rufus uses his head as a battering ram to beat his opponent to the floor by bumping his head."

Jones and Claybourne were both now masters of their wrestling craft who were beginning to innovate to tremendous effect, and attract paying customers to watch them perform. Regrettably, it would become crystal clear that there were some trappings of wrestling success that would continue to evade them no matter how much money they steered into the pockets of wrestling promoters.

## 7 – The Untitled

After setting audiences ablaze through the gratuitous and creative use of his head, Rufus Jones soon began wrestling in other areas of Wisconsin, including Sheboygan, where his hometown was announced as Lynn, Massachusetts. The city of fewer than 100,000 residents was a rather obscure reference, and there would have been no reason to apply it to Jones if it hadn't been the site of his first few matches that made it into the newspapers, when he wrestled under his real name of Joe Godfrey. It also happened to be a short 20-minute drive from Godfrey's true hometown of Malden.

Meanwhile, Jack Claybourne had returned to his home in Roxbury that was itself within a short drive of Godfrey's hometown of Malden. At the tail end of 1940 and heading into 1941, columnist Austin Goodwin of *The Portland Evening Express* remarked of Claybourne, who was returning to New England "after an absence of six months," that he had "surprised the fans with his improvement and finesse in the gentle art of catch-as-catch-can."

It may have been that Claybourne had improved as a wrestler, but it is also possible that Claybourne was in the midst of recovering from one of the serious injuries that plagued him during his career. More than a decade later, during a candid interview with *The Afro American*, Claybourne would profess to have broken "both my legs, my right arm, and several fingers during my career," as a consequence of insisting upon practicing a high-risk wrestling style.

Injury or no injury, the description of his January bout with Navy champion Pat Beel — a 90-minute draw — included no details of high-flying daredevil antics, and consisted only of straight wrestling. The lone fall Claybourne recorded was once again achieved by way of full-nelson hold as opposed to the classic standbys that necessitated him leaving his feet.

Along these lines, the promotional pieces written in advance of Claybourne's appearances during this time suggest that he may have slowed things down out of necessity. Rather than emphasizing speed and athleticism, *The Portland Press Herald* focused on Claybourne's strength, calling him "the boy with the powerful arms," who had a "beautifully built body, plumb chock full of muscle," and who used all of that strength in service of his "unbreakable full-nelson."

Whether the change in Claybourne's approach was dictated by the promoters in Maine, or whether it was out of necessity due to an injury, it was soon over. At the tail end of January, *The Fitchburg Sentinel* revealed that Claybourne had returned to "his well-known trick of jumping over the referee in order to get to his opponent" when he battled Charley Strack, and added that Jack "bounced around the ring like a jack rabbit" to the delight of the fans when he tangled with Marvin Westerberg.

Making his New Jersey debut in February 1941, Claybourne was presented as the "African Streamline" — a comparison to a sleek modern railway train — and was described as "one of the most sensational wrestlers in the country" within the sports section of *The Bayonne Times*. Then the publication went further than any other in providing New Jersey's latest Black wrestling star with an elaborate and ludicrous backstory.

"[Claybourne] has the tread of a man accustomed to the jungle, which is natural enough as he spent his early years in the Tanganyika country, a paradise of big game as he acted as a spotter for hunters," began *The Times*, as its writer relocated Claybourne's point of origin more than 2,000 miles from South Africa and into modern Tanzania. "Dangerous work for a lad, but it developed his body, made him quick to react to imminent danger, and in every way prepared him for the mat game, which at the time was far from his mind."

*The Times* pressed on, describing how Claybourne "the lion boy" was wrestling in bouts in Tanganyika, and became such a legend amongst the locals that he was plucked out of the region and ferried off to the United States to compete in U.S. rings.

As nonsensical as their story sounds, it was far from the most absurd origin story applied to a wrestler of Black American descent for the sake of coloring their backstory. In 1937, the newspapers in Helena, Montana circulated the tale that King Kong Clayton — an exceptional boxer born in Cincinnati, Ohio — wrestled under the hypnotic control of a Haitian voodoo princess, and drank a concoction of her creation before each of his matches.

The stories got even wilder when Claybourne visited New York, and in February, Buster Miller of *The New York Age* savagely mocked Claybourne's proposed backstory while divulging how promoter Jack Pfefer was taking credit for the discovery of Claybourne.

"In accents strongly reminiscent of fried chicken and cornbread country, Jack (Claybourne, not Pfefer) curls your hair with tales of how he used to hunt lions with his father in the old country," explained Miller. "He is a bit hazy on how he learned to grapple, preferring to ascribe his success to lessons received at the hands of an anonymous sailor. Jack avers that his favorite 'holt' is an 'African bear hug,' whatever that may be. At any rate, this will be surprising news to zoologists who have searched Africa in vain for signs of a bear. And won't they be startled to find out that Jack's 'lions' are called 'possums' in their native habitat."

Fables about an African origin aside, Claybourne's tactics impressed everyone who watched him perform. *The Bayonne Times* added that Jack had "tricks of his own on the mat which are unique," and was "remarkably elusive," which served as a fine complement to his unmatched speed.

Out in Wisconsin, Rufus Jones was still tinkering with his wrestling style, and despite the instant uproar caused by Jones' sudden outburst of headbutts, such displays had not yet become commonplace in his act. Instead, Jones temporarily adopted a neckbreaker as his match-ending maneuver of choice. He used the hold to effectively neutralize Al Williams in Sheboygan's Eagle Auditorium on January 1, 1941, after Williams had spent the early part of the fray turning Jones' habitual eye-gouging tactics against him.

"Jones stood for that kind of fighting just so long, and then tore into Williams and mussed him up easily, finishing the battle with his celebrated neckbreaker hold," reported *The Sheboygan Press*. "This hold, when applied, usually means the end of the match, and that was the case yesterday. Williams was through for good when he was on the receiving end of the neckbreaker, and Jones had donned his robe and left the ring long before Williams could get up off the canvas and make his way to the corner."

This isn't to suggest that Jones had even temporarily stopped resorting to the use of headbutts. During a bout with Dizzy Davis in Sheboygan, Jones fell back on the violent use of his head after securing the first fall with the neckbreaker, repeatedly headbutting Davis to no avail, and eventually succumbing to his adversary's backbreaker. Fortunately for Jones, he was saved by referee Farmer Mack during the third and deciding fall.

"Davis was roughing up Jones quite a bit when he was warned to fight clean by the referee," the report continued. "Davis hauled off and socked Referee Mack and then went to work on Jones again. Mack got up off the canvas and landed a haymaker to Davis' jaw, knocking him to the floor, and Jones pinned him for the count to win the match."

In February, Jones and Claybourne both found themselves on the same card in New Jersey, with Claybourne being labeled "The African Thunderfoot." Not to be outdone, Jones was supplied with a Caribbean origin when he was temporarily dubbed "The Jamaican Tiger." The two then met up in Bristol, Pennsylvania for a match that *The Bristol Courier* advertised as "the first time that a pair of colored grapplers have faced each other on the local canvas."

Jones returned to his familiar haunt of Windsor in the spring, where *The Windsor Star* picked up on the new tool in Jones' arsenal that he introduced against Walter Miller during the opening fall and continued to utilize throughout the match..

"In the opening set-to, Rufus had profited at times by an unorthodox but neat trick that consisted of him bumping his ebony noggin on his foe's more brittle brow," noted *The Star*. "He'd used it again in the mid-session. In the final canto, he really brought it into play."

The only catch was that Rufus *also* dispensed an alarming number of headbutts upon the forehead of referee Joe Lauzon, usually after trapping Miller's neck in the ropes, and then assaulting Lauzon whenever he tried to prevent Miller from being strangled.

"Two or three setbacks like this and Joseph decided enough was enough," continued *The Star*. "He awarded the fall, and bout, to Miller. Rufus, of course, didn't like that. He slugged the chunky arbiter a couple of times. Joe, a bit of a flier-off-the-handle himself, chased Rufe to the corner. Here, a fan butted in and hit Rufus in the face. At that, Rufe wanted to take on the fan, but abandoned the idea when several other fans ran up to the ring to the support of their fellow."

Jones soon returned to the wrestling rings of Ohio to duel with Jim Mitchell, except this time Jones was fully immersed in his routine as wrestling's most prolific headbutter. *The Marion Star* promoted the pair as arch enemies, seemingly based solely on the fact that the "sepia-hued matmen" shared the same racial designation.

"Until Jones stepped onto the local stage, the Panther had the field all to himself, being the only colored warrior to get more than passing attention," insisted *The Star*. "Jones' arrival, although no words have passed between the pair, creates a situation which had the Panther ready to jealously defend his prestige. He might well feel, who is this upstart, this usurper, who has come to invade his domain? And he'll be out for a clean-cut victory over Jones."

Heaven forbid that two Black wrestlers attempted to coexist in the same wrestling industry at the same time, let alone in the same state. However, before concluding the feature article, *The Star* elaborated on the stylistic differences between Rough Rufus and the Black Panther.

"Jones is a ruffian of the first water; his favorite 'nut cracker' is a tactic that could have been developed only by a tough ringster," the article continued. "It consists of cracking his foes' craniums with his own tough knob, something none have been able to take and survive. If the duel were to be confined to scientific grappling, the Panther would hold a long edge. Jones hasn't shown any inclination to put up that kind of a battle in any of his appearances, but prefers to resort to those attacks, which despite being illegal, result in victory more often than not."

Even more bizarre than the repeated references to Black wrestlers being Ethiopian around this time was the allusion to Mitchell — a Kentuckian with a long track record of wrestling in the Midwest — as Algerian.

Located in the Maghreb region of North Africa, Algeria was populated almost exclusively by Arabs and Berbers with skin shades distinctly lighter than those of most Subsaharan Africans. The turmoil in Algeria caused by the defeat of France by Nazi Germany quickly vaulted Algeria — which had been regarded as an extension of France of a higher status than other French colonial possessions — into the media spotlight.

Likely lacking an understanding of Algerians' physical characteristics, at least a handful of wrestling promoters were all too comfortable equating Algerians with their darker-skinned neighbors to the south, supposing that people looked roughly identical in all regions of Africa. Likewise, Seelie Samara also found himself wearing the Algerian label during long stretches of his career.

Absurd origins notwithstanding, Mitchell was the winner of the bout with Jones at the Marion Armory, befuddling his opponent with an assortment of holds and then forcing him to submit to a headlock. From there, Jones upped the ante with aggressive tactics, and rained a barrage of blows down upon Mitchell. Just as Mitchell began to fight back, the sea of fans that had been churning in the ringside area began to bubble over, requiring the intervention of the police to calm the waters.

"They crowded to ringside, and no less than three clambered through the strands to see justice done," reported *The Star*. "None of them got mixed up in the melee, however, to the credit of Patrolman Smith. He unceremoniously conducted Jones on a one-way tour to his dressing room, bringing the mixup to a close. Jones left nothing undone to earn the disqualification, but hollered long and loud that he had been robbed by the decision."

Technically, if the match had been real, Rufus would have had a point. The referee threw the match out only after ringside fans had inserted themselves into the fray to interfere by attacking Jones on Mitchell's behalf.

Jones regained his momentum later in April by making efficient use of his head in a bout against Gil Lacrosse. On multiple occasions, Jones found himself in hot water, and each time, he relied on his head to provide a path of escape.

"Jones tied the Bostonian in a hammerlock at the start of the duel, but Gil escaped and retaliated with a leg grip that looked like a winner," reported *The Star*. "The dusky warrior choked his way to freedom and then proceeded to wind things up at the 15-minute mark by bringing his 'cranium cracker' into play."

Lacrosse evened the match almost immediately by catching Rufus when he charged in to start the second fall and covered him, and then he continued to press the advantage by pummeling Jones outside of the ring. Just as it looked like Jones was on the ropes, he surprised Lacrosse with a second "cranium cracker," which sent his opponent down for the three count.

Jones' next match would be a tag team contest that placed him on a team with Bob Castle against two Southern opponents, Tex Riley and Billy Rayburn. *The Star* played up the angle that Riley and Rayburn ostensibly hailed from areas of the United States where Jim Crow racism was the law of the land, and stated that Jones' foes were "naturally allergic to his kind."

Incredibly, despite being hindered by an "allergy" steeped in racism felt toward their Black opponent, Riley and Rayburn were not automatically cast as heels even though their anti-Black racism was implied. Instead, the pair was positioned as the sympathetic babyfaces of the match who would have to avoid the "knob bumpers" and "skull-busters" of Jones if they wished to emerge victorious against the man who would have enjoyed fewer rights under the laws of their respective home states.

Jones and Castle lost the bout, and it was reported that Jones laid the blame for their loss at the hands of "the gentlemen from the South" squarely at the feet of Castle. Cast as a whiner and complainer, it was said by *The Star* that Jones "squawked" until he was allowed to select Mike Kilonis as a replacement partner for a rematch. Jones was once again turned back, even after selecting a new teammate.

For some reason, Jones wasn't permitted to team with the partner he collaborated with frequently in Canada — or even the partner he used in other cities in Ohio — who happened to be none other than "The Black Panther" Jim Mitchell.

In a display of booking that would come to typify the unique partnership arrangements adopted by pre-1960s Black wrestlers as they toured select regions of North America, Jones and Mitchell would be cast as the best of friends in Windsor, only to spontaneously develop a deep hatred for one another the instant they traveled back across the Ambassador Bridge and drove to the central part of Ohio.

While the mid-May match between Jones and the Panther in Lima was advertised as "the first time two colored grapplers have appeared against each other on the Lima mat," the two were regularly teaming up to dominate their opponents in Northern Ohio, with *The Sandusky-Register-Star-News* suggesting that the presence of Mitchell as a partner "discouraged rough tactics" on the part of Jones.

According to the report from *The Register-Star-News*, Jones secured two pinfall wins for his team by using the cleanest tactics he had employed in a long time, relying on armlocks to score two eliminations, while Mitchell contributed a backbreaker and a bodybreaker to contribute his share to the winning effort.

During this same period of time, Claybourne had traveled back to Louisville, Kentucky for a proper feud with Seelie Samara over the Negro world heavyweight wrestling championship, which Claybourne was said to be bringing with him.

Now nearly a decade into his wrestling career, Claybourne was being described as a 228-pound heavyweight, and while weights in wrestling are listed at whatever figures the promoters desired to announce to the fans, photographs of Claybourne from the era do suggest that he was considerably heavier in 1941 than when he debuted as a 170-pound light heavyweight.

Jack's opponent Seelie Samara was now going by "Haile Samara" to strengthen his claim to Ethiopian status. *The Courier-Journal* went so far as to say that even though Claybourne "whipped Joe Louis" in an unsanctioned boxing match, he had never beaten Samara due to the Ethiopian giant's "unorthodox style," and positioned Gentleman Jack as an underdog against his opponent "who can't read or write, or speak more than a few words of English."

It's possible that everything about this sentence was a lie, as Claybourne had certainly never outboxed Joe Louis, George "Seelie Samara" Hardison could presumably read and write perfectly well, and Claybourne had not only defeated Samara before, but had done so in that same city just one year prior.

This encounter between the two would yield an identical result, as Claybourne would win their best-of-three-falls contest. In the rematch, Samara would even their summer series and relieve Claybourne of what was arguably the most credible Negro world's heavyweight title defended anywhere on the continent at the time, fictional or otherwise.

"The 'champion' took the first fall in 24:28 with a flying body pin, then Samara retaliated to take the second in 12:10 with a whip hold, and made short work of the third, which he took in 4:56 with a reverse body pin," recorded *The Courier Journal*.

**Seelie Samara**

Samara's time as Negro world champion in that setting was short-lived, as Claybourne regained the title at the Allen Sports Arena in the early days of September. *The Courier-Journal* suggested that Samara had been riding high after the British had successfully booted Benito Mussolini's Italian forces from Ethiopia, liberating his homeland, and that the Negro championship had briefly made him the champion of a free land before Claybourne had left him feeling crestfallen.

"Samara used a flying tackle and a body pin to score in 15:21, but the 'Gentleman' rallied to win the second with a rolling headlock in 12:08, and then secured the deciding fall with a body kick and slam in 22:32," explained *The Courier-Journal*.

Many miles removed from Louisville, Claybourne engaged in a "duel of dropkicks" against Lee "The Butcher" Henning that once again gave Claybourne an opportunity to display his toughness after the action spilled outside of the ring.

"[Claybourne] picked himself out of the press row, and climbed back to the ring apron to headlock Henning over the ropes," described *The Buffalo Evening News*. "As the Butcher tried to climb back, a dropkick toppled him to the floor for keeps."

Heading back to the Midwest, Claybourne was scheduled to rekindle his feud from eight years earlier with Alex Kaffner at the Hammond Civic Center in Hammond, Indiana, only for *The Times* to announce that Kaffner had injured his foot in Omaha, and would be replaced by Seelie Samara.

Once again going by the Black Panther, Claybourne repeated his victory over Samara by bodyslamming him in 20 minutes to settle the feud for the time being.

Somehow, in the midst of this Midwestern tour by Claybourne, wrestling promoter Larry Gall snuck a story into *The Sheboygan Press* that Claybourne was a "former Olympic sprint champion *and* intercollegiate wrestling champ."

In the grand scheme of things, this pair of stated accomplishments may have been more ludicrous than the proffered tale that Jack was a native South African lion spotter. By 1941, the list of Black American Olympic sprint champions was very short, and it consisted of Eddie Tolan and Jesse Owens, with Ralph Metcalfe also qualifying if the meaning of "sprint champion" was extended to include relay victories. These were well known athletes, and knowledgeable sports fans would have spotted the falsehood.

More egregious was the claim that Claybourne was *also* an intercollegiate wrestling champion. By 1941, a Black wrestler had yet to qualify for the NCAA championship tournament, let alone win it. That feat would go unaccomplished until Simon Roberts won the NCAA wrestling championship in the 147-pound weight division in 1957.

As for Jones, it would be in Sandusky where Jones put another of the finishing touches on his standard wrestling formula. In a main-event match at Fisher's Hall, Jones absorbed the discomfort caused by Gorilla Pogi's hair-pulling attack and finally "began slugging and then bumping heads." Rufus succeeded in putting Pogi down for the first fall with headbutts, and then he concluded the match by putting Pogi away with what would very soon become his signature submission hold.

"Promoter Fishbaugh, in the role of referee for the main event, was instrumental in paving the way for Jones' victory," observed *The Register-Star-News*. "Pogi again began hair-pulling. He socked Fishbaugh when the latter demanded that he refrain from such tactics. Unable to gain attention, Fishbaugh slammed Pogi to the mat. Jones then took over the situation and succeeded in adjusting a crab hold to win in seven minutes."

The Boston crab — perhaps not so coincidentally adopted by a native of the Greater Boston area — would become nearly as synonymous with Rufus as his headbutts.

Jones continued to utilize his head in a novel way as his act reached additional cities, providing writers with fresh opportunities to paint imaginative pictures about the way Rufus meted out violence upon his adversaries. The sportswriter from *The Fremont News-Messenger* got in on the fun when Jones squared off with Lefty Pacer, opening his match report by saying of Jones' head that it "is so hard he uses it to send opponents to dreamland," and that Jones ultimately "won the match by a head — his own."

While technically legal, Jones' headbutts came with an implicit illegality. They represented a flip from boxing, where headbutts were strictly forbidden. Ironically, the use of fists was frowned upon in wrestling, but somehow the destructive use of one's head fell within the rules of what was designed to be a grappling-based competition.

This ambiguity with respect to the legality of headbutts is evident in *The News-Messenger*'s description of the bout, where it is expressed that the first fall won by Jones "was about as dirty as any seen here." Pacer evened the match by matching Jones' level of aggression in the second fall, and then Rufus brought the evening to a close.

"The third fall started out with some clean, hard wrestling, but Jones doesn't like to play that way," continued *The News-Messenger*. "He caught hold of Pacer's noggin and started bumping it against his own, and Pacer folded up like a picnic camp stool, and Jones followed with a crab hold."

From this point forward, just as Jones' reach was extending into Indiana during the summer of 1941, it would become increasingly rare for Jones to win his matches through any means other than some combination of headbutts and crab holds.

Now operating throughout a large stretch of the contiguous Rust Belt states, Jones continued to sew himself into the fabric of the historical development of wrestling in the region. Within the same week, he became one of the first Black wrestlers to participate in Indiana pro wrestling matches since Mitchell had wrestled there years earlier, while also participating in only the second tag team wrestling match in the history of Detroit.

Jones further demonstrated the unsettled nature of the discussion surrounding headbutts when he challenged Irish Pat

Riley to a boxing match at Fisher's Hall in Sandusky. The two staged what was reported to be a respectable approximation of a true boxing competition for six two-minute rounds, only for Jones to end the match in the exact manner that the fans familiar with his antics had probably predicted he would.

"Going into the seventh, the pair continued their slugging tactics, and action was at a high pitch when Jones suddenly used his head to butt his opponent," reported *The Register-Star-News*. "Riley was jarred for a moment, and immediately the two judges stopped the bout, disqualified Rufus, and awarded the victory to Riley."

The lack of crossover coverage between cities that were relatively close to one another enabled Jones to wrestle with completely different sets of stylistic expectations from one night to the next. Over in Anderson, Indiana, Jones and Mitchell reunited their tag team to defeat Bob Cassell and Ali Pasha in a cleanly contested bout. Back in Sandusky, Ohio, Rufus resorted to every trick in a heel's arsenal to dispose of Pasha in a single's contest.

Jones began his predictable use of illegal tactics by rubbing a piece of the adhesive tape from his wrists into the eyes of Pasha. When Pasha succeeded in removing the tape from Jones, it suddenly appeared as if Jones was "grasping at something under his tights" and then "rubbing Pasha's face with it."

"Fisher's Hall attendants said later that Jones may have used alcohol to help subdue the Calcutta grappler," reported *The Register-Star-News*. "Head butts, body slams, and a crab hold defeated Pasha. The crowd yelled disapproval at Jones' tactics."

In Fremont, Jones implemented these same infuriating tactics, and his match with Prince Nihalakis appeared to be headed in a similar direction until it was suddenly interrupted and the show was brought to an abrupt end.

"The colored boy arrived and began the mean stuff as quickly as he got in the ring with the Prince," said *The News-Messenger*. "Jones used a piece of tape, covering a supposed injury, to rub the Prince's eyes. Nihalakis countered Jones' mean plays with a few left and right swings, and grabbed the first fall with a toe hold. Jones didn't miss a foul tactic in the second fall. [Referee] Fishbaugh was manhandled as the third man in the ring, and the fans began to show their indignation by climbing onto the ropes. Fishbaugh awarded the match to the Prince as the spectators threatened to come into the ring. Jones remained on the canvas until the fans' wrath subsided."

In Sandusky, Jones' spread his use of illegal chemicals throughout his match with Paul Orth, resulting in a hotly contested ending. *The Register-Star-News* explained how the crowd "became aroused" early in the bout when Orth began to rub his eyes to indicate that he was feeling discomfort in them.

"There was a hint that oil of wintergreen was being used by the colored grappler," suggested the report. "Later, it was found that Jones used the oil for rub-down purposes, and it had been absorbed by his wrestling tights. When the last fall was scheduled to start, Orth demanded that Jones rub the oil from his hands. He refused, and then Referee DeMore attempted to award the match to the Toledoan. [Orth] refused and plunged into action with Rufus."

Jones captured the final fall and the match by countering Orth's attempt to toss him out of the ring by pushing both of his own feet into the ropes, sending the duo crashing to the mat with Jones' back on top of Orth, and in perfect position for the referee to count the pinfall.

When Jones began wrestling in Muncie, Indiana in October, he was first described as an "African Negro," only to have that place of origin discarded in favor of the more common location of Atlanta, Georgia. Oddly enough, the Muncie papers supplied Jones with a backstory that was far more aligned with his authentic upbringing in Greater Boston.

"Jones, one of the few colored wrestlers in the business, attended Boston University and was active in athletics there before leaving school to enter the pro wrestling game," stated *The Muncie Sunday Star*. "He won the New England pro championship at 175 pounds in his first year of competition and has been a top-notcher since."

This latter statement was completely true, but was only recognizable as fact to those who were aware that Jones had debuted in New Endland as Ed Flowers.

In the week following the Japanese attack on Pearl Harbor, and as the U.S. braced for war, *The Marion Star* stated that Jones had wrestled in Madison Square Garden and appeared in many wrestling movies. Curiously, the only times that it appears Jones would even have been performing within spitting distance of Madison Square Garden would also have been when he wrestled as Tiger Flowers.

The stylistic differences between Jones and the Panther came into sharper focus when they each won their respective bouts in Marion. Jones won his bout with Joe Ferona "with a headlock and body press, accompanied by signature headbutts." The two then traded additional punches after the bout. Panther dispensed with Nick Billins by taking him down with a bulldogging headlock, and then forcing him to submit to a hip headlock.

The by-the-numbers approaches to wrestling adopted by Mitchell and Jones may have been very different, with one being more brutal and the other being more technical, yet they managed to set a bizarre precedent when they both competed in Fremont's Christmas battle royal.

"Jones set out to soften up all his opponents, butting them with his head, and then [Joe] Ferona thought he could do the same thing, but he picked the wrong fellow to try it on," explained *The News-Messenger*. "When he bumped noggins with the Panther, he knocked himself out. When the others saw Ferona on the floor, they all jumped on him, and he was through for the evening."

A segment of a match that was clearly intended as a harmless bit of fun managed to communicate a clear message. The Black Panther — who had discarded his regular headbutts years ago and was not a truly prolific headbutter as far as Midwest fans were aware — possessed a cranium that was suggested to be of equivalent thickness to that of Rufus Jones. This cranial thickness was a trait that now seemed to be universally shared by Black wrestlers, suggesting that Blacks in general had thicker skulls than Whites.

The assertion that Blacks had thicker skulls than Whites had persisted for at least a century despite repeated attempts by medical experts to debunk the claim. In 1893, an unnamed surgeon provided an interview that eventually wound up in syndicated reports, stating that Africans' skulls were actually thinner on average than those of Europeans, but that other common Black phenotypic features had contributed to the development of the stereotype.

"The negro's head is covered with coarse, curly wool, which being matted closely over the skull, forms a cushion and proves a constant shield or protector of the cranium, and thus deadens the force of a blow upon the head," the expert was quoted as saying. "Hence the negro is given credit for a skull of abnormal thickness, capable of withstanding the crack of a policeman's club, or even a blow with an ax."

As retroactively preposterous as such claims appear, the skulls of Blacks were credited with supernatural levels of invulnerability in early 20th-century news reports. In 1901, *The St. Louis Republic* devoted considerable space to the story of Dan Oates, a Black man whose life was spared when his thick skull managed to flatten a .38-caliber bullet, resulting in him only suffering a bruise.

"The bullet disarranged a few kinks in the wool at the back of Oates' head, knocked off his hat, and fell to the floor flattened out," reported *The Republic*. "It is perhaps needless to say that Oates is a negro."

More than a decade later, in 1913, another syndicated story circulated of George Wern, who was allegedly shot during an altercation that occurred on July 4th. Wern was supposedly fired upon at point-blank range by an unidentified assailant; the bullet deflected off of his skull and struck Mrs. Edward T. Smith, who was passing in a street car. Mrs. Smith was taken to a city hospital for treatment.

"Wern, after mopping his brow, went about his business of celebrating the Fourth," concluded the article. "The negro who fired the shot escaped."

As expected, the stereotype also thrived when placed in an athletic context. In 1914, it was reported that boxer "Battling" Jim Johnson — who wasn't a particularly successful fighter — was assaulted by fellow fighter Kid Hawkins while seated in a Parisian cafe. Hawkins hurled a water bottle in Johnson's direction, and it shattered against the heavyweight fighter's forehead.

"Jim Johnson suffered no injury save a scarcely noticeable swelling where he was struck," informed *The Ottawa Journal*. "He was annoyed at the incident, however, and has sent a message to Hawkins intimating that if the manners of the latter do not improve, he will decline his acquaintance."

*The Journal* published the piece under the title "Negro's skull able to defy most anything," and included a statement that "the thickness of the negro skull was practically demonstrated" by the incident.

With stereotypes of such magnitude being delineated as fact in the early 20th-century press, it is altogether unsurprising that the public was so quick to believe that Black wrestlers would have an innate physical advantage when it came to head-oriented offense.

The surprise attack by Japan upon the U.S. naval base in Pearl Harbor, Hawaii rapidly shifted the priorities and orientation of the nation, since pre-existing international alliances guaranteed that the U.S. would be fighting a war on multiple continents and oceans against all of the Axis nations.

As America was revving up its war machine to prepare to fight a full-scale war primarily in Europe and Asia, Claybourne returned to Ohio with the local newspapers stating that he was resuming his pursuit of a regional championship, and specifically the Midwest Wrestling Association's version of the world junior heavyweight championship owned by Speed LaRance of Canada. The hint was also dropped that it would be an incredible milestone for a Black wrestler like Claybourne to win a world wrestling title.

"Unlike the fight game, there are few colored athletes competing in the wrestling game," explained *The Dayton Daily News*. "During the past 15 years, only four men of the race have appeared in the local ring. But all of them were outstanding stars. First to come here was Reginald Siki, the heavyweight star of 12 years ago. Then came Gorilla Parker of Louisville, Ky., and after him was Jimmie Mitchell of Louisville, Ky., known to the game as the 'Black Panther.'"

*The Dayton Journal* added gravity to the occasion, stating that if Claybourne managed to dethrone Speed LaRance, "Not only would the accomplishment give [Claybourne] championship prestige, but it would allot him the additional honor of being the first Negro to ever garner a major mat title."

This observation would probably have been true in the eyes of many U.S. residents, at least with respect to race-neutral championships. As Samara's USWA championship reign in Boston may have been nominally a "world heavyweight championship," it was the top championship of what was clearly the promotion running a distant second to the most popular company in the city, and after three short months, it was blotted out of existence the instant those organizations merged.

Also, there is a heap of context that is missing from the attribution of world-title status to different wrestlers prior to the late 1940s and early 1950s. Due to a glaring lack of regulation over the use of the term "world champion," there were almost no prohibitions on promoters referring to the top championships in their areas as world titles, even if the entire wrestling territory was confined to Maine, and more than half of the territory's wrestling events took place in Portland, a city with just over 70,000 residents.

With the passage of time and the high esteem reserved for world title reigns even if they were only world titles in a nominal sense, the fact that some wrestlers were the top gate attractions and champions of large, vibrant territories that did not promote "world champions" is frequently held against them in legacy discussions.

Because his challenge for the title was preceded by an introduction that drew upon the history of Black wrestlers' struggles in the region, along with an explanation of the symbolic significance that such a victory from Claybourne would hold, many fans may have felt that an eventual victory from the Gentleman would have been a foregone conclusion. Yet, the extent to which mysterious forces would seemingly conspire to keep a respected championship belt from finding its way onto Claybourne's waist bordered on the absurd.

In his early matches against Speed LaRance, Claybourne repeatedly took the champion to time-limit draws while failing to achieve victory. Speed then lost his championship to Billy Thoms, at which point he defeated Claybourne soundly in a qualifying match, then immediately regained his championship from Thoms.

After Speed repeatedly wriggled his way out of losing his championship to Claybourne by hook or by crook, the Gentleman appealed to MWA officials in order to get special referees assigned to oversee their matches. The MWA reportedly acceded to Jack's wishes, and designated three different referees to officiate a title bout — one for each fall that would presumably take place.

"This will mark the first time in local wrestling history that such a plan has been used in assigning referees," stated *The Dayton Sunday Journal-Herald*. "Both Claybourne and LaRance have agreed to the plan, and indications point to their battle being the highlight of the current indoor season."

The resulting match between the two resulted in a classic instance of fans having their joy retroactively crushed after believing they had just witnessed wrestling history. The match began with Claybourne achieving the first fall with his usual flurry of dropkicks, only for LaRance to square the tally with three flying headscissors and a pinfall. This set the stage for the final exchange of the match.

"Speed took an impromptu trip over the ropes on an attempted flying headscissors," remarked *The Dayton Journal.* "He regained the mat before he was counted out, but was in no condition to cope with the tiger-like Claybourne, who promptly flipped him to the canvas and tallied the fall on a body smother."

It was only at this point that the fans in attendance at Dayton's Memorial Hall were made aware of what Claybourne had presumably already known. The announcer informed the audience that Claybourne had weighed in that evening at 203 pounds — three pounds over the 200-pound weight limit — and was therefore ineligible to win the championship. Therefore, Claybourne had physically vanquished Speed LaRance, but by way of a technicality, he would be denied the opportunity to make his case as what the fans believed to be the first Black holder of an American pro wrestling championship.

Unbeknownst to Jack and the rest of his cohort, there was a wrestling promoter in his home state who had just broken away from his partner, and he was about to make an attempt to prioritize and validate Black wrestlers in a way that had never been attempted before. The only question was whether or not the promoter could execute his plans before the repercussions of war caused them to fall by the wayside.

## 8 - Meet Me in St. Louis

In April 1942, Jack Claybourne was advertised to return to Louisville to face Seelie Samara, with the latter inexplicably identified as the reigning Negro world champion despite the fact that Jack had won all of the most recent matches between the two, including their latest title match in Louisville.

It's probable that all of this was a promotional ruse, as Claybourne was replaced in the match by LeRoy "King Kong" Clayton, who was making a rare appearance outside of the Rocky Mountain region. Louisville's wrestling fans were told that Clayton had bested Claybourne to earn the right to challenge Samara.

In Clayton's most high-profile feud with a fellow Black wrestler — as such bouts were nigh impossible to present in the state of Montana — he defeated Samara to capture the Negro world title. Clayton and Samara engaged in a quick multi-state feud before Clayton dropped the belt back to Samara and reported for military duty after being drafted into the U.S. Army.

The drafting of Clayton into the military nearly interfered with St. Louis promoter Sam Muchnick's plans to legitimize a world Negro championship on a grander stage. Muchnick had already arranged an impromptu tournament amongst who he was touting as the four best Black heavyweight wrestlers in the country — King Kong Clayton, Seelie Samara, Rufus Jones, and Jack Claybourne.

Jones' path to the Negro title tournament in St. Louis began with a by-the-numbers victory over Billy Rayburn on New Year's Day. *The Marion Star* played up the supposed regional rivalry between the two Georgian wrestlers, although Rayburn was the only true Georgian of the pair.

"Getting the upper hand shortly after the first rest period, Jones took the second fall in 10 minutes with hammerlocks and head-butts, followed up with a perfect jackknife which did the trick," said *The Star*. "The third fall was a rough and tumble affair and was virtually even until Jones maneuvered a crabhold at the end of eight minutes and forced Rayburn to concede the victory."

**Leroy "King Kong" Clayton spars with Eddie Wenstob**

Incensed at having lost to Jones, Rayburn attacked Jones after the final bell until referee Nick Beavens separated the two.

In Hammond, Indiana, Jones was correctly labeled as a Boston native, which provided a unique angle for the advertising of his match with Lee Jenson of New Orleans.

"Jones is said to be a confident colored lad who features a strong right-hand uppercut when the referee isn't looking," said *The Hammond Times*. "This matching of a northern Negro with a white man from the deep south sets some kind of precedent."

Even with a world war actively underway, angles capitalizing on racial strife in the American South continued to play a central role in the booking of U.S. wrestling shows. Jones would prove to be very valuable with respect to the Hammond Civic Center's box office, with *The Times* later stating "Jones has been one of the Civic Center's best drawing cards on the wrestling program, although fans have sneered at decisions he has won."

One of the least popular of those decisions occurred in April when Jones' dirty tactics once again led to a near riot, and caused his opponent Flash Clifford to become so incensed that he assaulted the referee in response to the latter's refusal "to intervene with proper celerity."

"The colored Jones eventually won the bout, although losing the first fall in 19:15," continued *The Times*. "Clifford fell victim to Jones' famed head slam, a maneuver in which Jones bounces his foe's skull off floors, ring posts, etc. A dozen or so women fans milled around the ring after the bout had ended, but police moved in quickly to prevent violence."

In Marion, Ohio, in order to compete against the duo of Billy Rayburn and Steve Nenoff, Jones and Panther resurrected their tag team combination in early March, albeit with a twist. The pair had never teamed together in Marion before, and in that city they sat on opposite sides of the heel-babyface dynamic, with Jones being the unquestioned rulebreaker of the pair.

"Of the quartet, Rayburn and Nenoff are by far the most popular, while the Panther also is regarded by local fight followers as an excellent scrapper," opined *The Star*. "He has been fighting in Marion rings under the management of Promoter Les Fishbaugh and others for more than seven years. Jones is the not-so-popular scrapper of the four men, resorting to unorthodox procedure when the going gets tough."

Working as a heel-face pair, Jim and Rufus managed to defeat the previously undefeated team of Rayburn and Nenoff, but *The Star* disclosed how a matchup between Jones and Panther appeared to be in the offing considering the contentious interactions between the two as they pursued victory.

The Black team fell behind quickly, with Rayburn forcing Jones to submit to a crab hold, and then dropkicking and pinning Mitchell. In the second fall, Mitchell evened the score just as single handedly, immobilizing first Rayburn and then Nenoff with his favorite hold, the hip-headlock. That's when Jones ambushed his opponents to put them at a marked disadvantage during the third stanza.

"Just after returning for the third and deciding fall, Rayburn was jarred from the ring twice by the highly unorthodox Jones," recounted *The Star*. "The second drop from the four-foot ring put Rayburn out of commission. He was jolted hard on the first fall, but the second, even harder, kayoed him. Fighting alone with one half of the third fall already charged against him, Nenoff buckled down and pinned the Black Panther. With all the vengeance of a prehistoric beast, Jones came to the Panther's rescue, and made quick work of Nenoff with a body press accomplished on a spring from the ropes."

In April, *The Hammond Times* printed a quote that had supposedly been issued by Jones as the wrestler responded to the suggestion that he should wrestle rising star Farmer Jones by saying, "The Farmer will have to get hisself a reputation before I rassles him."

To their limited credit, *The Times* named wrestling promoter Buck Estes as the true source of the quote, and stated that it was Estes who claimed that Jones had said it. To their eternal credit, *The Times* reissued the quote two weeks in the following form:

"'I would not wrestle him until he established a reputation,' Rufus answered when fans inquired why he did not persist in matching Farmer. 'Now that he's pretty good, I'll get credit for beating a good man,' Rufus added."

It was still a lamentable practice that quotes from Black wrestlers of the era were repeatedly printed in North American newspapers in forms that mirrored the speech patterns wielded by the performers of the popular radio show *Amos 'n' Andy*.

As a consequence of this, Black wrestlers often had a contrived form of Blackness created by White producers imposed upon them for the sake of ensuring that their characterizations were molded to the expectations of what many Whites believed Blacks to sound and act like. These mannerisms generally mirrored what uneducated Blacks were presumed to have sounded like upon release from Southern plantations upon the abolition of slavery.

The result of this was that Joseph "Rufus Jones" Godfrey, a Black man born, raised, and educated in Malden, Massachusetts, had his manner of elocution set 80 years in the past for the sake of appealing to audiences' misinformed conceptions of what many Blacks sounded like, especially in the North.

When Jones made his way to St. Louis to participate in Sam Muchnick's tournament, his appearance coincided with the arrival of infamous wrestling promoter Jack Pfefer in the same city. *The St. Louis Star-Times* touted Pfefer as wrestling's "trust buster" from New York, who "operated a booking office that supplies pachyderms for promoters who desire his wares."

Even in the local newspapers, Pfefer's appearance was viewed as an unmistakable sign that he was taking sides in a wrestling war between Muchnick and Tom Packs, who Muchnick broke away from to break up Packs' local monopoly and start his own wrestling promotion.

It may just be a coincidence that the debut of Rufus Jones in St. Louis was perfectly synchronized with the participation of the promoter who had a heavy hand in amplifying the Tiger Flowers wrestling identity, but this is unlikely.

As far as Muchnick was concerned, Samara had already advanced to the finals of his Negro-title tournament, with Jones and Claybourne filling out the other side of the bracket. On May 1, 1942, Claybourne defeated Jones at the St. Louis Municipal Auditorium with a dropkick and a cradle hold to satisfactorily advance to the finals of the tournament.

Of the bouts on the card, the match between Claybourne and Jones was said to have stood out "for good wrestling" by Ray Gillespie of *The St. Louis Star-Times*, who noted that the show was held "under the protection of a restraining injunction against interference by the police or the state athletic commission," which was apparently a realistic threat during interpromotional wrestling wars of the times.

"The boys spent no idle moments in their tasks and even added a little comedy to their skit with their quick recoveries after hard thrusts to the mat," Gillespie wrote of Rufus and Jack.

Unfortunately, no final bout between Samara and Claybourne — at least not one that can be definitively linked to Muchnick's tournament — appears to have taken place.

By May 1942, the term "headbutt" wasn't even a universal term within the areas Jones regularly wrestled. In struggling to identify the maneuver, a sportswriter for *The Hammond Times* referred to a headbutt as "Jones' famous skull trick," which he used by holding his opponents by the shoulders and "bouncing his own kinky head" off of theirs.

With Russian Ivan Kalimikoff as his tag team partner during an era where Russians were viewed as America's wartime allies, Jones also demonstrated how his teammates could take advantage of his unusually hard head even when they weren't the ones wielding it with violent intentions during the first fall of the pair's bout with Billy Venerable and Martino Angelo.

"Jones was in top form in gaining a fall over Italian Angelo with his self-styled cranium cracker, a combination of a sound crack with a sledge hammer tamed down to an old-fashioned Dutch rub," described *The Star*. "Kalimikoff picked off Venerable to complete the first fall advantage with a body spread after ramming Venerable headlong into Jones' skull."

Once again, the message being communicated was that Jones' cranial advantage had almost nothing to do with the pinpoint accuracy with which his headbutts were administered, and everything to do with the supernatural density of Black bones.

With the Black Panther having been drafted into military service, the two wrestlers whose public relationship situationally vacillated between that of best friends and arch enemies depending on time, place, and location would be required to have their final interactions for the foreseeable future.

Seemingly in an effort to make their final feud memorable, Jim and Rufus engaged in an exchange at the tail end of a battle royal at the Marion Armory that *The Star* referred to as "a back alley fight" that didn't conclude until after both wrestlers reached the locker room.

"The Panther, officially the winner of the regulation ring tiff, but loser in the eyes of more than a few of last night's house, came out on the short end of a locker room climax," the article elaborated. "Jones, whose unorthodox tactics have brought about a strong sense of disapproval among the local fans, battered the Panther's head with a dress shoe, knocking the Panther senseless, and ultimately resulting in the intervention of Patrolman Smith."

The publication elaborated by delving into how Jones had been harboring "bitter hatred" toward the Panther for having deserted him during a prior tag team bout during which Rufus engaged in disreputable tactics that caused Mitchell to walk out on him in disgust.

In response to the brawl, promoter Les Fishbaugh arranged for a no-holds-barred match with a two-hour time limit to be held at next week's event in late June. What materialized was a brutal match that lasted just under an hour, including the 10-minute intermissions between falls.

"The low-built Rufus, whose one ambition is to gain the support of the ring gathering, however, couldn't play fair when almost every shady practice was allowed," wrote *The Star*. "He indulged in a session of eye-gouging or low hitting whenever he was placed in a tight spot. Rufus gained the first fall with a devastating series of head punches, climaxed by a body press after a rough and eventful 31-minute tussle."

The Panther evened the match very quickly by coaxing Jones into submitting to his vaunted hip-headlock, and then battered Jones' ribs with a barrage of punches during the final fall until Jones collapsed and was pinned.

As physical, dramatic, and seemingly conclusive as the climactic bout between former partners was, the wrestling fans of Marion, Ohio would have been absolutely astonished to learn that the two men would be teaming together just four nights later in Detroit. The two partners handily defeated Martini Angelo and Nick Billings in the main event of the Arena Gardens show.

Three nights after *that*, the two were back in Marion competing against one another in a boxing match, which concluded with a 10-round decision won by Mitchell.

When the Panther received a classic wrestling sendoff, losing his departure bout to Ivan Kalimikoff so that he could report for induction into the U.S. Army on July 24th, he joined King Kong Clayton as another Black star who had been called to join the U.S. Armed Forces. With their numbers being thinned by wartime activity, the value of the remaining Black wrestling stars rose by default.

For the majority of Black Americans drafted into military service during World War II, what awaited them were support roles. This included Black wrestler Johnny "Cyclone" Cobb, who served as a mess hall cook in Ft. Benning, Georgia.

With a wrestling career that had flown almost totally beneath the radar until that point, Cobb was discovered for all intents and purposes when the Associated Negro Press found him during his military service and interviewed him about his life as a wrestler in a traveling circus that toured Texas.

By percentage, only a select few Black soldiers saw action during World War II in segregated units, including the famed 92nd Infantry Division, also known as the "Buffalo Soldiers," the Tuskegee Airmen, and the 761st Tank Division — coincidentally known as the Black Panthers — to which famous baseball player Jackie Robinson was assigned. It wouldn't be until 1948 that President Harry Truman would formally desegregate the U.S. Armed Forces, eliminating the practice of maintaining segregated units.

Noting the absence of a second Black wrestler in the area, *The Fremont News-Messenger* said that Jones would be obligated "to uphold the prestige of colored wrestlers." Curiously, this notion that Jones inherited the responsibility to uphold the favorable representation of his demographic came from a mainstream, non-Black publication that presupposed Blacks shouldered a unique burden and an obligation to uplift an entire demographic without the freedom to simply act independently without such pressures.

This sort of utterance also acknowledged a sentiment that the pressure Blacks bore with respect to setting a standard for the sake of others of their race was not a pressure commonly carried by other races, ethnic groups, or nationalities within wrestling circles.

Furthermore, the notion that Blacks collectively constituted their own nationality — regardless of their actual countries of origin — was a common conception in wrestling at the time. During a show in Detroit advertised to feature "five nationalities," the supposed nationalities listed were Hungarian, Polish, Russian, Jewish, and Negro.

The term "Jewish" has enjoyed a degree of flexibility over the centuries; it applies to adherents of the religion originating in Ancient Israel, and also to the genetic descendants of the citizens of that nation. With the dissolution and renaming of Israel at the hands of Rome in 136 AD, Jews had essentially been without a homeland, and functioned more as an ethnic group.

Meanwhile, the term Negro was broadly applied to anyone with traceable descent from Sub-Saharan Africa, regardless of their actual place of birth. By classifying Negro as a nationality, wrestling promoters were taking a continental identifier and applying it to Black wrestlers whose ancestral presence in North America may have predated the 1700s.

Back in Dayton, Claybourne defeated Speed LaRance in a best-of-three-falls match now that the Canadian had just lost his world title in Claybourne's absence. The two junior heavyweights then competed in a series of five matches, which Claybourne won 3-2, but it was a hollow victory as all of these wins against LaRance were stockpiled only after the title was no longer available to be captured.

In October, LaRance regained the title, inviting yet another challenge from Claybourne. As usual, with the world title on the line, Claybourne returned to his habit of losing when it mattered most. Then, when Martini Angelo managed to defeat LaRance for the junior heavyweight title, Claybourne challenged Angelo for the championship and lost to him as well.

Before the end of July, Rufus Jones had competed in the first-ever mud battle royal held in Detroit, outlasting Joe Ferroni, Ivan Kamikoff, and Martini Angelo in the process. Then he truly became a standout in Hammond, Indiana — as a babyface of all things — working for promoter, wrestler, and referee Dory Funk.

Stated by *The Hammond Times* to possess "ape-like muscles and lighting speed," Jones formed a highly successful tag team with Buddy Knox, and conquered several villainous pairs. They were granted the unofficial title of "tag team champions of Hammond" when they defeated the top-ranking villains Wild Bill Zim and Soldier Thomas with some assistance from the referee, who was Dory Funk himself.

"The Knox-Jones team won the first fall in 20:44 when the opposition was disqualified for foul tactics," reported *The Times*. "Zim had pinned Knox with the help of some slugging by Thomas when Referee Dory Funk ruled that the Zim-Thomas twosome was out of order. The deciding fall arrived at 10:07. Knox pinned Thomas, and Jones threw Zim in a simultaneous move which met with general fan approval."

Meanwhile, Jones was also spending time in Dayton teaming up with none other than Jack Claybourne. The two partnered on what was advertised as "the first all-Negro team" to compete in Dayton, in what turned out to be a losing effort against Bill Venable and Whitey Walberg.

Temporarily breaking off his pursuit of the MWA World Junior Heavyweight Championship, Claybourne traveled to Buffalo, New York at the end of 1942. There, Claybourne was referred to as "the Black Phantom," and *The Buffalo Evening News* praised him as "the best colored grappler since Regis Siki used to draw large crowds at Broadway Auditorium."

The Buffalo area had been starved for Black wrestlers to such an extent that it identified Claybourne as "the only Negro wrestler in the pro ranks today," while attributing to Claybourne the statement that Black athletes "never took to wrestling because it lacked the spectacular" as an explanation for why there were so few Black wrestlers.

Gentleman Jack made his debut in Buffalo by living up to his stage name. After supposedly dislocating the shoulder of his opponent Pat Flanigan, Claybourne directed Referee Carr to tend to Flanigan's injured shoulder, and refused to attack his Irish adversary any further. This display of sportsmanship elicited loud applause from the crowd, resulting in *The Buffalo Evening News* declaring Claybourne to be "the star of the show" solely for that ethical act.

Overlapping with this period was Claybourne's entry into Toronto, where *The Toronto Star* made a barely veiled racist reference in the promotion of Claybourne's match with Al Dunlop, stating that Dunlop had been "complaining about a colored gent in the local woodpile," and was now going to be required to wrestle "'Gentleman Jack' Claybourne, a colored gentleman in anybody's woodpile."

The common phrase that was obviously being danced around was "nigger in the woodpile," which was a plainly racist way of referring to a fact of some importance that went undisclosed, with the analogy being based on the idea that wood piles were natural hiding places for presumably lazy Black people to nap.

Completing the analogy, the writer from *The Star* was suggesting that Dunlop had a penchant for complaining about problems, and that Claybourne presented a clear threat to any wrestler he faced.

*The Toronto Star* was also in the practice of stylizing the "Gentleman" in Claybourne's stage name as "Gemman," which presents a classic case of ethnic incongruity. The bizarre implication was that the Black ring star would still speak in the stereotypically inarticulate manner associated with plantation-dwelling Black Americans in the antebellum South despite supposedly being a native South African.

The practice had picked up steam ever since the release of the 1939 film epic *Gone With the Wind*, which went on to receive 10 Academy Awards from 13 nominations. Perhaps the most surprising of these awards was the receipt of the Best Supporting Actress award by Hattie McDaniel, whereupon she became the first Black American to win an Academy Award.

Winning an Oscar may have been a landmark achievement, but McDaniel's portrayal of "Mammy" had a downside to it, as the depicted mannerisms and utterances of the Black slaves portrayed in the film became commonly applied to 20th century Blacks. As such, Claybourne was degradingly referred to as "Massa Jack" in *The Brantford Expositor*, in an exaggerated approximation of the way "Master Jack" would have been uttered by the plantation dwellers in the award-winning film.

In actual combat against Dunlop, Claybourne proved to be impressive. Cy Kritzer of *The Buffalo News* described how Claybourne "sailed over (referee) Goodrich's shoulders in a flying dropkick and floored Al Dunlop for victory in 19:28." That's when the shenanigans began.

"Dunlop claimed Claybourne bit him when he had his fingers pulling the Negro's mouth apart," wrote Kritzer. "It was a roaring encounter and continued after the bell. Dunlop offered to shake hands; instead he smacked Claybourne with a right-hand punch. There was a towel around Dunlop's neck and the Negro grabbed it and pitched the Toronto huskie all over the ring until Goodrich stopped it."

Following the bout, local promoter Jack Herman was quoted as saying that the 32-year-old Claybourne was "the best prospect I've seen in the last five years," while comparing him to Scottish wrestler George "Dazzler" Clark. Clark's popularity had peaked in the region several years earlier, and he was known for his size, strength, speed, and well-rounded attack.

Claybourne was quickly promoted into the main events of Buffalo's wrestling events, with *The Evening News* promptly reminding fans that this marked "the first time a Negro grappler has been on top since the days of Regis Siki."

Quickly transitioning back to the name of "the Black Panther," Claybourne did something else reminiscent of Siki and lost his main event bout, this time to "Irish" Pat Fraley. Claybourne also did something that was very rare for him, and temporarily played the role of an outright heel, although *The Evening News* stated that he was "far less than dastardly in the unfamiliar role."

The ending came when the two wrestlers attempted simultaneous dropkicks and missed, only for Fraley to recover first and floor Claybourne with a second attempt at a dropkick to score the win.

Prior to the bout with Fraley, Claybourne offered reporter C. Kritzer of *The Evening News* an exclusive interview, the contents of which appear to have been entirely made up. In the article, Claybourne is quoted as saying that he began wrestling in 1939 after wrestling promoter Al Haft spotted him sparring in a Columbus, Ohio gym and told him he had the physique and athleticism to be an outstanding wrestler.

Claybourne added that Haft paid him the ludicrous sum of $2,500 just to undergo the training process.

"Imagine getting $2,500 for just training and working out," Claybourne told Kritzer. "Why, I said, 'yes sir,' before he could change his mind. Mr. Haft hired two professional wrestlers, and for the next ten months, I wrestled every day, sometimes for four or five hours. Then he called me into the office again and said, 'you're ready.' He also said that he was guaranteeing me $3,000 for my first year of wrestling. I never had hopes of making $3,000 a year."

Adjusted for inflation, Claybourne was suggesting that he was paid that 2020s equivalent of nearly $60,000 just to train for 10 months, with a first-year guarantee of nearly $70,000. Of course, the story is complete nonsense anyway, as Claybourne debuted in the states immediately surrounding his home state of Missouri a full seven years before the date he proposed to Kritzer.

The plain truth is that Claybourne was never coaxed into wrestling by Al Haft, nor did he claim anything to that effect in the most genuine interview he ever provided. In his retrospective interview with *The Afro American*, Claybourne credited Kansas-Missouri promoter Gus Karras with offering him the opportunity to wrestle.

"I started as a fighter in Kansas City, Missouri, but I quit after a few months to wrestle," revealed Claybourne during his interview with *The Afro American*'s Joseph A. Owens. "I envisioned more money in wrestling."

Back in the ring in Buffalo, Claybourne wrestled the future world heavyweight champion "Whipper" Billy Watson to a time-limit draw in 30 minutes during an April bout, but then lost their May rematch two falls to one.

When Claybourne departed from Buffalo and began wrestling in Toronto with greater regularity, promoter Frank Tunney introduced Claybourne as the "Senegambian champion." He also reacquainted the Gentleman with his fictitious South African tribal roots, apparently not realizing or caring that the Senegambian region is nearly 4,000 miles away from South Africa — the same distance separating Claybourne's home state of Missouri from Hawaii.

"Claybourne you know as the son of a Zulu chieftain and a Wabezi mother," declared Tunney. "He gets his strength from his father's tribe and his ferocity from the other."

Never mind that "Wabezi" is not the name of *any* African tribe, or that Tunney appears to have made up the name entirely on the spot.

This wouldn't be the only time such a clumsy naming practice would be employed, as Claybourne's mother was subsequently referred to as a member of the "Geetze" people — an equally fictitious African tribe — prior to a late-August bout in Ottawa between Gentleman Jack and Earl McCready.

Writer Gordon Headley of *The Ottawa Journal* further revealed how Claybourne wore the gold-and-silver ring of his father — the Zulu chieftain — on the middle finger of his right hand.

"Across the broad surface of the trinket are three coursing dogs in flight, and there is also a posed figure with folded arms who Claybourne claims is the grand chief of the Zulus," wrote Headley.

Presuming Headley had direct access to Claybourne, then it's likely that the story Headley included about how Claybourne was a veteran of 50 professional boxing matches, *and* was a sparring partner to Joe Louis prior to the Brown Bomber's 1938 rematch with Max Schmeling, was supplied by Claybourne himself.

As funny as all of these false attempts to provide a social or professional link between a Black professional wrestler and the world heavyweight boxing champion had been, there actually was *one* Black wrestler who managed to achieve such a career boost through his military service.

In the fall of 1943, the U.S. Army's Bureau of Public Relations circulated a photo to all news outlets of Joe Louis driving a U.S. Army Jeep. Seated right next to the reigning world heavyweight boxing champion was none other than the Dark Angel of wrestling, "Dynamite" Don Blackman.

Identified across the country as "Sergeant Don Blackman of the Fort Dix Military Police, former wrestling star" while riding next to arguably the most famous Black athlete in American history up until that point, Blackman had his career furthered more by that single photo than hundreds of in-ring victories could have accomplished for him.

Later, Claybourne sat for a second interview with Headley, this time insisting that the reason he transitioned from boxing to wrestling was because he didn't wish to share any of his earnings with the trainers or any of the other handlers who managed boxers' careers.

"I found out that a pro fighter had to have about a dozen managers," Claybourne told Headley. "I took a beating in that bout (against George Dixon), and by the time my managers cut up my purse, there wasn't much left for me. Now I wrestle two or three times a week, and make more money with no managers or trainers to take it all away from me."

Claybourne was then asked about how a professional wrestler would fare in the ring against a professional boxer.

"That's easy; a wrestler will get to a boxer much easier than a boxer will get to a wrestler," stated Claybourne. "Once the boxer is off his feet. He's through."

Surprisingly, Claybourne balked somewhat when asked if he could discard the reigning world heavyweight boxing champion — with whom he had supposedly sparred — with such ease, and instead chose to comment on the skill of Louis' golf game, as well as the fighter's taciturn nature.

"He's too doggone quiet," Claybourne added.

Outside of the areas he was wrestling in, Claybourne's name was being invoked favorably when other grapplers were debuting in territories and needed to be compared with a wrestler whose name the fans could relate to. In Dayton, it was said of "Tiger" Jack Moore that his dropkicks "and many of his other high flying holds stand him out as even more sensational than 'Gentleman' Jack Claybourne, popular Negro star."

While the quote may seem uncomplimentary at first, the notion that a Black wrestler was being referenced as the comparative standard by which a White wrestler could qualify to be esteemed as impressive spoke volumes. Not to mention the fact that Black wrestlers were usually only ever compared to one another, even if their sizes, dimensions, or their approaches to wrestling had little in common.

**Rufus Jones in the 1940s**

As 1943 opened, Rufus Jones began his annual campaign by continuing to wrestle in the Midwestern states,

along with Ontario. As further evidence that things were distinctly different from one town to the next, Jones found himself working in Hamilton on the opposing team of his beloved tag team partner in Indiana, Buddy Knox.

During a match involving Jones and his partner Soldier Thomas competing against Knox and his partner Jimmy Sims, the firmness of Jones' head turned out to be the deciding factor in leading to the downfall of the Knox-Sims team.

Thomas dragged Knox over to Jones, slammed his opponent's head against the head of his own tag team partner, which was protruding through the ropes, and then covered the unconscious Knox. *The Hamilton Spectator* remarked that trying to put a dent in the head of Jones was "like bumping up against the proverbial stone wall."

Finally appearing in Cincinnati, Jones was given the intriguing title of "The Black Tiger of Boston." The name accomplished the task of aligning Jones with the other Black wrestlers who adopted feline sobriquets, and while it is unlikely that a great deal of thought went into the name, it may also have been a clever allusion to his prior identity as Tiger Flowers.

In Marion, Jones engaged in a match with Greek grappler Nick Billins, and the two men seemingly attempted to reenact a real-life lynching. After throwing Jones out of the ring once during the bout only to have him return, Billins then wrapped a towel around Jones' neck, and hurled him over the top rope while grasping the towel. Incredibly, Jones shook off the strangulation attempt, and won both falls of the bout with headbutts.

It is impossible to know if the intent of the act was to conjure images of anti-Black violence. However, following the development of the American frontier and the conclusion of westward expansion, lynchings of White Americans declined precipitously, to the point where lynching had become seen as a form of violence that was almost exclusively inflicted upon Blacks.

According to statistics on lynching collected by the Tuskeegee Institute, 185 White Americans were lynched between 1901 and 1943, in comparison to 1,671 Black Americans. As overall numbers of lynchings dropped, the percentage of the number of lynching victims who were Black increased. Between 1933 and 1943, 94 percent of all lynching victims had been Black.

As is often the case, repeated exposure to a wrestler whose actions are entertaining — even if they're intended to engender anger in the fans — can eventually provoke cheers. In Jones' case, his repeated efforts to inject comedy into his performances, evidenced by occasions when he would feign ignorance after blatantly fouling an opponent behind an official's back, increased the fans' appreciation of him.

One example of this occurred in Windsor following the defeat of Jones at the hands of Soldier Thomas in a best-of-three-falls match at the Market Building. After Jones had submitted to a leg lock by Thomas, Jones "went berserk and tried to attack Thomas."

"Referee Lauzon endeavored to stop him, and Rough Rufus turned on him with the fury of a wildcat," added *The Windsor Star*. "For several minutes, they slugged, clawed, gripped and grunted. They were still going at it when several policemen climbed into the ring, pried them apart, and escorted Jones, still fuming, back to the locker room. That was the grand finale to a bout in which, for once, Jones was the favorite of the fans."

As *The Star* later went on to elaborate on the style of Jones, "Half the time Rufe is a bit of an imp, the other half a most villainous villain. All of the time, he is a master showman."

Still, earning the admiration of the fans didn't mean that Jones was suddenly immune to having his bouts interrupted. *The Star* began its description of one of Jones' March bouts against Maurice Shapiro by providing a way of differentiating between crowds that were merely engaged or fully outraged within the border city.

"It isn't unusual for three or four over-heated fans to rush the ring's edge and berate the villain, but when three or four of said fans go so far as to climb up on the apron, and enough of the remaining fans get excited enough to crowd each side of the ring, from corner to corner, four, five, and six deep, then something definitely is in the air," explained *The Star*.

This is how *The Star* described the crowd on the night of the Jones-Shapiro bout. Observing that "a wrestling fan's bark is a lot worse than his bite," the writer of the piece stated that "the deep respect" that the Windsor fans had for the toughness of Jones is the only reason why Jones remained safe after the bout despite his violent actions toward referee Joe Lauzon.

"Twice [Jones] floored Joseph via that pet trick of his, bumping his ebony noggin against the more fragile cranium of the white man, and besides, went so far as to throw the ruffled referee out of the ring," concluded *The Star*.

That same month saw Jack Claybourne displaying his willingness to get rough with his opponents, and he did so in a manner that bore an alarmingly striking resemblance to the style of combat employed by Rufus Jones. *The Courier-Express* declared that "the agile Negro... made badman tactics pay off" when he "butted skulls with (Joe) Christy several times, and evidently Jack's noggin was the harder, for Joe sank to the canvas."

Claybourne then twisted Christy's head in a manner similar to Jim Mitchell's famed hip-headlock, causing Christy to submit.

In the aftermath of this aberrant display of headbutting from Claybourne, he was described as a wrestler who "uses his head as a battering ram" by *The Buffalo Evening News*, and even followed up on why his newest trick was "to butt skulls with his opponent and knock him out."

"I have the toughest skull in wrestling," bragged Claybourne.

Fittingly, Claybourne only seemed to break out the headbutts during the rare occasions when he was playing the role of heel, as if seasoning his high-flying style with the head-cracking flavor of Rufus Jones was the easiest way to communicate to the crowd that he was engaging in villainous behavior.

During this stretch of 1943, Jack engaged in a series of matches with "Whipper" Billy Watson, who was being hailed in Buffalo as "the best young wrestler" in the business, who had already captured the British Empire heavyweight championship. Clearly, Claybourne's role was to make Watson appear even more impressive, as he lost nearly every bout he had with the regional favorite, while only occasionally managing to secure draws with the inventor of the Irish whip.

Results aside, for entertainment value, the bouts were apparently unmatched. After burying the quality of a semifinal bout involving the singularly rotund Martin "The Blimp" Levy, *The Toronto Star* gushed that a March bout between Claybourne and Watson "shattered all standards in the main bout for remaining suspended in the air without refueling."

"These two enacted the strangest tableaus before the Whipper emerged the winner via the Immelman with a falling leaf," added *The Star*. "Several times during the aerial clash, they passed each other while flying in opposite directions."

During a separate match with Watson held months later, Claybourne played the role of a subtle heel and once again demonstrated his fusion of high-flying and roughhousing tactics during another loss to Watson in Buffalo. It was yet another bout where the two "did most of their wrestling in midair."

"Watson shook off two body slams, but a series of head butts had him dazed when he reached for a toehold," described *The Evening News*. "Throwing his right leg full length on the outside of Tiger Jack's right leg, Watson whirled Claybourne overhead. The result of this tricky application produced a human cartwheel about 10 feet high, but Watson worked it so cleverly that Claybourne was the one who whirled high in the air and then crashed on his back. Three of these slams finished the Negro."

*The Evening News* also described two different instances in the match where Claybourne and Watson attempted simultaneous dropkicks only to wind up recovering on the mat when they both crashed to the canvas.

As Claybourne's summer rolled along, so did championship opportunities. *The Expositor* explained how "Jack's friends feel that, presented with the chance of breaking the white monopoly on the crown, he will be the first colored rassler to wear the mythical memento of his prowess."

No such title acquisitions came to pass for Claybourne, at least not during 1943. In addition to losing his opportunities at the British Empire title held by Bill Watson, he also lost to the other prominent holder of that championship, Yvon Robert, when Robert caught Jack in mid-air during a third-fall dropkick attempt and dropped him on his head for the win.

Of far more significance was when Claybourne was offered a title shot at National Wrestling Association world heavyweight champion Bill Longson in Hamilton, Ontario during October 1943. Of the world championships in existence at the time, those of the National Wrestling Association were among the most prized. The organization had the benefit of being established by the National Boxing Association, and its titles were widely recognized throughout the wrestling world.

"The match is pregnant with possibilities, for if Gentleman Jack beats the Salt Lake City slasher, he will be the first negro to enter the heavyweight throneroom," observed *The Hamilton Spectator*, once again teasing the cultural and historical ramifications of a potential Claybourne title win. "Coloured athletes have won the topmost crown in many different fields of athletic endeavour, but it remains for Claybourne to reach the top in wrestling. And right now his chances loom up as plenty strong."

Once again, despite the illusion of hope that saturated the promotion of the match, Claybourne was defeated by Longson in 34 minutes with a piledriver.

Similar to Claybourne, a true race-neutral championship outside of his first months of activity eluded Jones through the first 10 years of his wrestling career. Up until this point, most attempts at bestowing a championship on Rufus had been inaccurate, or embellished.

As a case in point, while promoting a bout between Jones and junior heavyweight champion Frankie Talaber at Cincinnati's Music Hall Sports Arena, *The Cincinnati Enquirer* described Jones as "a former champion, having held the middleweight title for several years, increasing weight forcing him to give it up."

Jones would lose his match to Talaber, but the claim that "the New England Cobra" was a former champion became embellished even further within the pages of *The Cincinnati Post*. The claim was delivered over the course of an article explaining how Boston native Jones was trained to wrestle by former world middleweight champion Ted Germaine.

"How well Germaine taught Jones is shown by the fact that after several years of tutelage, Rufus took the middleweight crown away from him," continued *The Post*. "With the championship under his belt, Jones toured the country until too much fine living started to show in his weight, and he had to relinquish the title. Jones misses the acclaim he received when champion and will shoot the works in order to have another crown on his head after Friday's bout."

As preposterous as the longevity granted to this title claim is, it does offer the best hint available as to how Rufus Jones had been taught to wrestle. Aside from being a frequent opponent of Godfrey's when he wrestled as Ed Flowers during the earliest stages of his career, Germaine probably trained with Godfrey behind the scenes to help him achieve his mastery of the wrestling craft.

Just as important, Germaine was well known for his ability to transition seamlessly between straight grappling and wild brawling antics. A career-retrospective article about

Germaine printed by *The Boston Globe* in 1964 explained how Germaine's bouts "nearly always ended up outside the ropes, with ring-side patrons scattering and the police moving into action."

More to the point, since there is no record of Ted Germaine having wrestled in Ohio, his name would have meant next to nothing to the wrestling fans of Cincinnati, meaning that there would have been no reason to invoke his name if there hadn't been at least a kernel of truth to the tale.

*The Cincinnati Enquirer* later added that Jones was also a former Hollywood extra, but "he couldn't eat regularly waiting for assignments." While there is no clear evidence that Jones ever made an appearance on the silver screen, it's possible that there is some connection between this reference and the past statement that Tiger Flowers was in high demand as a model in New York City.

# 9 – Dancin' and Lena Horne

As U.S. troops overseas were contending with the hardships of war, Rufus Jones was coping with physical inconveniences that were far less perilous but nonetheless troublesome. In multiple cities at the end of March, it was announced that Jones would be forced to miss a few events due to an injury to his ear, while the Akron press reported a similar story, with the slight difference being that Jones' ear had become infected and needed to be checked by a specialist. Like Tiger Flowers, the left ear of Jones was well known to be cauliflowered, and was even described as such on Jones' World War II draft registration card.

When Rufus ultimately did return to mat action against Farmer Jones, the ear factored heavily into the reasoning for Rufus' loss, as Farmer Jones reportedly targeted the ear of Rufus, leading to a stoppage by the official.

In another match against Farmer Jones in Hamilton, Ontario, Rufus provided one of the first instances of his headbutt being used to draw blood during a match. Eventually, the bleeding of Rufus' opponents would become a common sight in the wrestler's bouts, except in this case the blood spilled was that of the wrestler who was doubling as a referee, Archie Smith.

"During the heated action between the Jones boys, Rufus bumped his head against Smith's eye, and three stitches were necessary to stop the flow of blood," reported *The Hamilton Spectator*. "However, Smith has been in the wrestling wars often enough to realize that a little thing like a split eye is not going to matter much."

Rufus' most entertaining match against Farmer Jones was probably their early May bout at the Municipal Pool in Hamilton. Rufus took the first fall via pinfall after aggressive back-and-forth action by both men. Following the intermission, the action became even more exciting for the fans in attendance.

"When the action resumed, Farmer started using his elbows to advantage and then tossed Rufus into the pool," said *The Spectator*. "The coloured man had no sooner reached the dry canvas again when they both took a tumble into the pool, evidently feeling that the cool waters might help soothe their tempers. They got back in the ring again and Farmer started a rush that resulted in his evening up the count in three and a half minutes. The deciding fall came six minutes later when another top spread by the ebony-hued one did the trick."

In April, Jones was brought to Muncie, Indiana, and recognized in *The Muncie Evening Press* as "Rufus Jones of Boston College, classy colored boy who is recognized as the world's light heavyweight champion." This made Boston College the second college in the Boston area that Jones had allegedly attended, although census records indicate that Jones self-reported as having only completed high school and never attended college, unlike his wife Ursaline.

Jones was an instant hit with the Muncie fans, teaming with Joe Ferona to demolish Nick Billings and Wild Bill Zimovich. As reported by *The Muncie Morning Star*, Jones' unique brand of offense represented a style that had never been seen by the fans of the East Indiana city.

"Jones, a newcomer to the Muncie Arena, seized his opponents in both hands, and then butted them into submission with his forehead," described *The Morning Star*. "It was the first time this method of attack ever had been seen here."

Hopefully Jones enjoyed his very short time as being referred to as a world light heavyweight champion without any racial constraints being imposed on that claim. Within one month of Jones being advertised as a full-blown world champion, the claim was amended in Muncie to "world's lightweight colored champion." In addition, the advertisement included the incorrect attestation that Jones was the "originator of the headbutt."

In Cincinnati, the press was going so far as to suggest that Jones' head was even immune to headlocks, "as he does not seem to be bothered at all by pressure being applied to his cranium."

In Muncie, Jones' entire offense had seemingly been reduced to his use of the headbutt as a weapon. As *The Star Press* stated, "Jones' favorite hold is a simple one. He merely seizes his opponents by the head and then butts them into submission, using his own skull as a battering ram."

However, there were some items around the ringside area that proved to be even harder than Jones' skull. Facing Pierre DeGlane in Windsor, Jones snatched the ring bell from the timer and brought it down on top of DeGlane's head. As a result, three men had to carry the unconscious body of DeGlane back to the dressing room.

The incident came at the tail end of a brawl outside of the ring. After Jones took the first fall with a Boston crab, the two men exchanged punches so close to the fans that *The Star* reported how "only the alertness of attendant police prevented the crowd from pitching in to help Pierre." Jones' use of the ring bell resulted in his disqualification, and DeGlane was awarded the match.

In June, *The Spectator* issued a warning to the Hamilton fans that they had better catch the act of Rufus Jones while they still had the chance, as there was a strong likelihood that his time on the wrestling circuit was drawing to a close.

"Jones, who is one of the greatest drawing cards in the game, may not appear here many more times, for he expects to be inducted into the United States army at any time now," declared the publication.

This was a threat with a rather low likelihood of occurrence since both Jones' size and accumulation of ring injuries were likely to disqualify him from military service. Regardless, wrestling fans on both sides of the Ambassador Bridge would soon have far more pressing concerns.

Just a few days after Hamiltonians were encouraged to catch Jones' act before he departed, fights broke out between youths on Belle Isle Park, an island that sits in the middle of the Detroit River, and is accessible by bridge from the American side of the river.

After police broke up the fighting and the youths dispersed, two separate rumors — that Whites had thrown a Black mother and her baby off the Belle Isle Bridge to their deaths, and that Black men had raped a White woman by the same bridge — resulted in large scale violence and rioting.

It was in this manner that the Detroit Race Riot of 1943 unfolded. When the violence was quelled by military intervention nearly two days later, 34 people — nine Whites and 25 Blacks — were dead, and more than 400 were reported injured. Of the dead, 17 Blacks were killed by the police, while there were no White deaths resulting from police intervention.

Following the Windsor wrestling show held in the aftermath of the riot, the writer of the article summarizing the action for *The Windsor Star* proposed that the wrestling held at the Border Cities Arena on that night was an indication of the greater racial tolerance practiced by the Canadians on the southeast side of the Detroit River.

"Under the circumstances — meaning in view of what transpired in Detroit at the beginning of this week — one might have expected trouble," began the article. "But Canada is a pretty conservative country, and the average sports fan — even the one who follows wrestling — is a pretty fair-minded individual. So last night, when white man met Negro, even though the crowd was predominantly white, the applause was at least evenly divided. As a matter of fact, there were probably more cheers for the colored man than the white man, and Jones was given what sounded like an almost unanimous ovation when he turned out to be the bout's winner."

While the writer may have been attempting to content Canadians by offering them a pat on their collective backs for their assumed racial tolerance, this simple critique minimizes the stark differences between the life circumstances of Blacks on each side of the river.

In Detroit, the 150,000 Black residents comprising 10 percent of the city's population had been packed into two poorly serviced neighborhoods, while restrictive housing practices prevented them from acquiring homes in most of the predominantly White neighborhoods of the city.

In contrast, the Black Canadian population in Windsor accounted for well under five percent of the much smaller city's 100,000 residents. With such a small population, there were fewer measures taken to control them, allowing for Black Canadians to live more or less in whatever neighborhoods they could afford to occupy.

Ironically, this meant that the house at 859 McDougall Street — less than 500 meters from the entrance of Border Cities Arena, and not at all unlike the rest of the homes in Windsor — could provide housing for young Black Canadian Lawrence Shreve, who was two years old at the time. Shreve would eventually grow up to become a brawling, headbutting, blood-spilling wrestling legend in his own right, going by the ring name Abdullah the Butcher.

Jones' became so well known for his headbutts that *The Star* jokingly accused lightweight boxers Julio Cesar Jiminez and Lupe Gonzales of "copying Rufus Jones" when they bumped heads, and their fight was quickly ruled a draw due to a cut on Gonzales' head.

However, things went differently when Jones competed against Windsor referee Joe Lauzon in a boxing match of his own. In the third round of the bout, Rufus began to break the rules that the pair had agreed upon before they donned gloves and entered the ring to settle their differences.

"Famed for his noggin-busting ability, the colored grappler knocked referee-fighter Lauzon on the forehead, sending him sprawling on the canvas," said *The Star*. "Referee Ted Greise disqualified Jones for this infraction of the rules and ordered him out of the ring."

Upon being informed that he had lost the bout, Jones quickly landed a left hook to Greises' jaw, "sending the arbiter crashing to the floorboards." Promoter Bill Thornton then leapt into the ring in an attempt to halt Jones' rampage, only to be knocked horizontal by the enraged wrestler. Rufus was quickly corralled and calmed down, but what happened next was by no means part of the show.

**Rufus Jones prepares to headbutt an opponent**

"The ring activity excited a squabble among a few colored and white fans in the ringside section, and it might have developed into something serious had not police and other wrestlers waded in and separated the opponents," continued the report from *The Star*. "Naturally, this activity vastly overshadowed the three scheduled events on the wrestling card, although all three produced enough activity to satisfy the most rabid fan."

Apparently, the sportswriter from *The Star* had spoken too soon when he'd written about the fair-mindedness and tolerance of average Canadian wrestling fans being superior to that displayed by their American counterparts. In fact, *The Star*'s own sportswriter Don Brown had a few occasions when he dove deep into his bag of insulting racial imagery when writing about Rufus Jones.

In one September column, Brown wrote that Jones' actions against Frankie Hart made the crowd "think of doing a tar-and-feather job on the pudgy colored boy." While not exclusively racist, tarring-and-feathering had developed a strong association with Ku Klux Klan activity during the prior two decades.

The next statement from Brown carried far less ambiguity. When Hart succeeded in putting Rufus Jones to sleep by wrapping his highly effective sleeper hold around Jones' chin, Brown remarked that Jones "dropped to the canvas dreaming of a big slab of Southern fried chicken and a big slab of watermelon."

An unnamed writer from *The Star* — but quite possibly Brown once again — also made a comparison between Jones and Charley "Gorilla" Grubmier. In stating that comparison, the writer posed a question to the readers, asking, "Who is to deny that Rough Rufus Jones, when he looks and acts his worst, doesn't come even closer to the most manlike of apes?"

Apparently, the writer was leaning into the common racist comparisons rooted in early evolutionary theory that presumed Blacks — as the humans inhabiting the African lands where gorillas and other large primates originate — were more closely related to apes than other humans, and therefore more primitive, savage, and unintelligent.

Ironically, it would become very apparent who was the more apelike of the wrestlers involved in *The Star*'s comparison in less than a year. In May 1944, Charles "Gorilla Grubmier" Eastman broke into the home of his estranged wife Geraldine in Michigan City, Indiana with a gun in his hand. He then hid in the master bedroom of the house until his wife came home.

After surprising Geraldine and narrowly failing in his attempt to shoot and kill their 15-month-old child, Eastman dragged his wife into the basement and killed her by shooting her three times in the head. From there, Eastman took his own life by hanging himself while simultaneously shooting himself in the head.

## Gentleman Jack and Rough Rufus

Jack Claybourne returned home to New England in November, where he was once again praised as a crowd-pleasing wrestler with an inimitable style. In Fitchburg, Claybourne's unique approach to wrestling was credited with rescuing a show that had, up until that point, been "a dull, drab, listless affair" during his match with George Linehan.

"Claybourne, a sepian ballet master, demonstrated all types of steps and dances, doing a Charlotte Greenwood leg-lift over the bogeyman Linehan's bald head a short time after the match started; then going from a Fred Astaire flying poise drill to a Gene Kelly heel click before the half-hour time limit was up," illustrated *The Fitchburg Sentinel*.

*The Sentinel* also added that Claybourne "used his old trick of jumping over the referee's head to get at his adversary," and joked that Linehan "thought he had been dive-bombed."

The pair also wrestled to a draw in Portland, Maine, with *The Portland Press Herald* declaring that the bout between Linehan and Claybourne overshadowed and upstaged the main event, which had involved a title change resulting in the crowing of Lester "Cement" O'Neil as the new New England junior heavyweight champion.

"This was a really riotous affair with Claybourne, the best acrobat to hit the Expo this winter, putting on a top-notch exhibition of tumbling and circus stunts while Linehan baited on the fans with some neat and diabolical dirty work," wrote Frank Curran. "The combination worked to perfection and the hour's end came too soon for most of the fans."

Down in Louisville, with Seelie Samara sliding into his role as Negro heavyweight champion for a new season of wrestling, *The Courier-Journal* informed the local wrestling fans that Samara had taken the Negro title from Claybourne, and that Claybourne was now serving " in the Army."

That certainly would have been news to Jack, who was busy wrestling in locales far closer to his Roxbury home than Louisville, Kentucky.

As predicted, Rufus Jones was called up for his U.S. Army medical inspection, missing a scheduled bout in Hamilton in the process, while *The Hamilton Spectator* lamented on November 3rd that Jones "might be lost to the wrestling realm for the duration."

Any fears that Jones would be called up for military service were immediately dispelled. Three days later, *The Spectator* served up the seemingly incongruent announcement that Jones had "failed to pass the U.S. army test," and would therefore be free to resume violent exchanges with his mat foes in the ring on a nightly basis.

In Dayton, Rufus was pulled aside by *Dayton Herald* reporter Marj Heyduck, and provided what was ostensibly the most direct and honest interview of his wrestling career, with all quotes directly attributed to him, and with the reporter's name fully on the record.

Heyduck opened the piece by saying that Jones, "the grinning 205 pounds of jumping jive on a 5-foot-7-and-a-half-inch frame, is not the Baron of Beall Street, as he has been called," and then included Jones' admission that he had never traveled further south than Louisville, Kentucky in his life. He then continued on to ask Jones what he liked.

"Nothing but wrestlin', eatin', dancin', and Lena Horne," Jones answered.

Jones added that his favorite meals were chicken and steak, "but mostly steak," that his favorite musicians were Duke Ellington, Fats Waller, and Hazel Scott, and that he did attend Boston University for two years before turning to wrestling, even though that claim contrasts with Jones' own reports to census takers. As for injuries, Jones stated that he had "only got one broken leg, a broken collarbone, and a couple broken ribs in the last 10 years. Yeah, man."

Certainly, the accumulation of that many injuries would have gone a long way toward disqualifying Jones from military service. Also, based on Heyduck's writing, Jones appeared to have had a distinct habit of punctuating his sentences with "Yeah, man" at the end.

In Adrian, Michigan, Jones displayed his toughness by outlasting five other grapplers in a "wrestle royal." Six men started out in the ring, and all five had to be pinned or forced to submit in order to eliminate them from the contest. After Abe Coleman and Buddy Knox were eliminated, the remaining four fighters — Rufus Jones, Bob Casselle, Frankie Hart and Tex Riley — quickly paired off into ad hoc alliances.

"Casselle and Jones teamed up against Hart and Riley, but Jones, over-anxious in his head-butting tactics, accidentally rapped his partner on the head, and the Kansas City entry was counted out," explained *The Adrian Daily Telegram*. "Jones then went after Hart, and pinned the Canadian. Riley tried to pull him off, but failed. It wasn't long after that Jones did away with Riley. For the 90-minute event, Rufus clamped a Boston crab hold on Tex Riley, which, counting his final fall in the wrestle royal, ended the bout in 17 minutes."

Jack Claybourne's 1944 campaign once again opened in New England, with Jack continuing to wrestle in locations that were within a relatively short drive of his Roxbury home. At this stage, publications like *The Portland Evening Express* were focusing their attention on the impressiveness of his "tumbling tactics," and how sensational they were for "a man of his stature."

Along these lines, the newspapers of Springfield, Massachusetts regularly compared Claybourne to one wrestler in particular, "Count" Nicholas Zarnyoff of Russia, who was a frequent main-event wrestler during the 1920s and 1930s, competing against the likes of Gus Sonnenberg and Hans Schroeder.

From a stylistic standpoint, Zarnyoff was known to regularly take to the air during matches, attempting flying headscissors, rapid sunset-flip takedowns, acrobatic rolls from his back to his feet, and most impressively, full front-flip counters to flying mare takedown attempts. To so favorably compare Claybourne with Zarnyoff — or in the case of *The Springfield Union*, to flat-out call him "the colored Count

Zarnyoff" — was to equate Claybourne with one of the elite mat showmen of the prior era.

"Jack Claybourne, Lawrence heavyweight mat ace with a million tricks, fastest and speediest of the wrestlers today, has taken the place left vacant by Count Zarnyoff, Russian nobleman-matman," insisted *The Union*. "Count Zarnyoff retired several years ago, and despite the imitative ways of some heavyweights, none of them came close to duplicating his mat trickery until Claybourne moved into the heavyweight ranks. The Negro speedster has showed the same qualities that made the Count in a class by himself. His speed, his lithesomeness, his score of tricks and his ability to give and take make him one of the outstanding performers of the mat."

*The Fitchburg Sentinel* also pitched in with praise. The publication stated that the "colored bolt of lightning" was the fastest wrestler to ever appear in the local ring, and added that "to see him sailing over the referee's head and landing on his opponent's shoulders is worth the price of admission."

Claybourne readily displayed these athletic gifts in matches with the likes of Robert "Rebel" Russell in Hartford, Connecticut. Russell was able to nail Claybourne to the canvas for the first fall of the bout before Claybourne predictably took to the air to take control of the action.

"The second stanza was a bit different as far as Russell was concerned when Claybourne returned the punishment he took in the opening frame with added flips and flops that had his opponent anything but happy," reported *The Hartford Daily Courant*. "With the falls even, the matmen started out for the winning fall and it looked as if Claybourne was in for his first real licking as Russell had the 'fare-thee-well' Negro hanging onto the ropes. No sooner than it takes to wink an eye, Claybourne dashed out from his daze, and with a series of jumpin' dropkicks, spilled the 'Rebel' for the count of three."

Also in January, Claybourne engaged in his first bout that actually involved the presence of world heavyweight boxing champion Joe Louis, albeit with Louis playing the role of arbiter rather than opponent. In Portland, Maine,

Claybourne faced off with Manuel Cortez, with Louis serving as the referee.

As a condition of his military service, Louis had been making almost daily public appearances to rally support for the U.S. war effort. These engagements often bestowed refereeing duties at boxing and wrestling events upon the world heavyweight champion. Although Claybourne and several other Black wrestlers had been referred to as associates of Louis for nine straight years, not to mention his wrestling equivalents, this would be the first time that Claboure was confirmed to have been within arm's reach of the famed Brown Bomber.

"Cortez took advantage of Louis' obvious unfamiliarity with the mat rules to give Claybourne a beating in the first fall, and won it in 13:32 on a lift and slam," reported Frank Curran of *The Portland Press Herald*. "Claybourne wasn't doing much better in the second till he landed a drop kick and ended things at 6:36, but he went to town in the finale. Here, Cortez egged Louis on with every trick in the book, but Louis evidently didn't see any enjoyment out of punching a mere wrestler, so Claybourne captured the melee in 12:21 with a double-arm press."

Claybourne's match against Cortez with Louis serving in the role of referee turned out to be a rehearsal for the feature event in Boston, which was a bout for the "duration world's heavyweight wrestling crown" between Jack Claybourne and the massive masked champion known as the Golden Terror.

"After taking the first fall in the match which Louis refereed, Claybourne dove for the Terror, missed, catapulted off the ropes, and landed on his back," reported *The Springfield Daily News*. "He was carried away unconscious and taken to a hospital, where attaches said today he was resting comfortably."

The authenticity of Claybourne's injuries notwithstanding, the night was additionally memorable due to the riot that ensued at the arena. Attracted by an opportunity to see the reigning world heavyweight boxing champion in person, 7,200 spectators showed up, overwhelming the capacity constraints of a building that was never intended to hold more than 5,000 persons. When rioting fans broke down the doors to the venue in their attempts to gain entry, mounted police had to be summoned to restore order.

The real name of the Golden Terror, a truly large man for the era, was Bobby Stewart, and he was billed at the time as weighing 379 pounds. By bodyslamming the Terror to win the first fall of the bout prior to resorting to his established routine of plummeting to his peril outside the ring, the highflying Claybourne was conveying the physical strength that had earned him the additional name of "The Black Samson" from several sportswriters.

That was perhaps one of the greatest ironies of Claybourne's career, inasmuch as he was routinely referred to as a "giant Negro," and a man of atypically large muscles for the period, but he still felt compelled to engage in a ring style that would have been far more easily adopted by smaller grapplers.

A related irony of Claybourne's career was pointed out by Bill Cunningham of *The Poughkeepsie Journal*, who observed that Claybourne and the Golden Terror, promoted as two of the most physically imposing combatants in the Northeast, "are a couple of brethren the armed forces didn't want."

"Claybourne was tested physically and waived out for some reason, but they didn't even test the Terror," added Cunningham. "He weighs a grand total of 379 pounds, and that's more than the army can uniform."

While Claybourne may have been beset by injuries that he could still figure out ways to work through, he apparently could not conceal them during a military evaluation. It is also possible that Claybourne had a criminal record that interfered with his draftability.

This last suggestion is entirely speculation, but it stems from the fact that the sole instances of Elmer Claybourne grabbing attention in his hometown newspaper — *The Mexico Intelligencer* — prior to the beginning of his wrestling career stemmed from problematic circumstances. In April 1928, the 17-year-old Claybourne was cited for "peace disturbance," and in November of the same year he was charged with reckless driving while chauffeuring around his brother James Claybourne and his friend Tyler, who were both charged with drunkenness.

Back down in Dayton, Rufus Jones received a rare title shot against Frankie Talaber, the world junior heavyweight champion as recognized by the Mid-West Wrestling Association, to open 1944. The statement was attributed to Jones by *The Dayton Herald* that many other champions had sidestepped him specifically because of his color, and that he intended to make the most of his opportunity.

More realistically, the scarcity of Black champions had to do with a combination of three different factors. First, traveling Black champions would have been categorically banned from making appearances in several cities in that era, including the entirety of the former Confederate states.

Second, wrestling was built on filling dates in both large cities and small towns, and a Black champion would have presumably been a poor attraction in exclusively White towns in the North.

Finally, to the extent that a Black champion would have been perceived as an exceptionally strong attraction among Black fans, the average annual income of Black men in 1939 was $639 in comparison to an average earnings of $1,419 for White men. In other words, promoters in most areas would have questioned whether or not Black families had the disposable income required to support a Black champion to their liking, especially if the presence of a Black champion was a turnoff to White audience members.

Of course, all of these points presume that promoters were looking at the situation through a purely objective, dollars-and-cents lens, and weren't having their actions influenced by prejudicial beliefs of their own, or the presumption of prejudice amongst viewers.

According to *The Herald*, Talaber had requested that Jones' headbutt be banned prior to their title bout on the grounds that Jones' head was seemingly "made of iron," but the officials retorted that "they can find nothing in the rule book against such tactics."

Both the action and the outcome of the January 4th title bout went according to script. Talaber submitted Jones with a "figure-four leg strangle" to take the opening fall, while Jones evened the bout in the second fall by headbutting the champion into unconsciousness. In the third fall, with fans beginning to surround the ring and stationed policemen on the alert, Talaber finished the bout.

"Frankie rallied and made a grab for Rufus. He connected with Rufus' head, which connected with the floor in a neat piledriver," concluded *The Herald*. "Frankie won the match. Pandemonium broke loose."

*The Herald* also added the detail that the three-pound weight advantage Jones had going into the match was "all bone in his head." Apparently, all of that extra bone did not make Jones immune to the effects of piledrivers.

While a true wrestling championship eluded him, Jones was forced to settle for the consolation prize of competing against Gorilla Grubmier for the honorary "rough-and-tumble title of junior heavyweights now campaigning in the middle west."

With Grubmier only months away from committing the heinous act that would end his own life and the life of his estranged wife, Jones brutalized him to claim the honorary championship of bad men in Ohio.

In Muncie, Jones had his status upgraded to that of colored light heavyweight champion *and* "football star at Boston University," although a misunderstanding with the printer resulted in Jones humorously being named as the "lightweight Colorado champion" on at least one event poster.

For a time, it appeared that Jones would have no fellow Black wrestlers in the region to compete against, but then "Black Panther" Jim Mitchell returned from his stint with the

U.S. Army to engage with Jones once again. Promoter Al Ross informed *The Adrian Daily Press* that the Black Panther and Jones were both "head-bunters," and that their bout would be decided by who could more effectively crack the other man's skull with his own.

As Jones and the Panther brought their act to Benton Harbor in the spring, Jones was forced to contend with a fair amount of writing from *The St. Joseph Herald Press* that stretched the boundaries of racial sensitivity.

In one article, the writer proposed that "Rufe, with all due respect to his ancestors, looks not unlike an ape," and suggested that his match would therefore "have all the aspects of a visit to the zoo." In describing how Rufus preferred to deliver his headbutt, the article further elaborated that Jones would stand upright "with the backs of his hands all but touching the mat," as if he dealt with postural struggles caused by arms of primate-like length.

If anything, the thickly muscled arms of the 5'7" Jones skewed toward the shorter end of the spectrum, but this writer certainly wasn't going to allow something like the truth to interfere with a racist analogy.

During a description of Jones' match against Tiger Jack Moore, *The News-Palladium* of nearby Benton Harbor got in on the act, saying of Jones that "he bit, he kicked, and he slugged his foe… and he did it with all the grace displayed by 'Cheeta,' the chimpanzee in Tarzan films."

After the bout ended with Jones suffering a loss, *The News-Palladium* continued to describe how referee Sammy Price had to shove around "the happy savage," and then the writer expressed surprise when Jones "seemed to resent one fan who kept asking him if he wanted a banana."

That fan is lucky that Jones never got within arm's reach of him. During a match against the Panther in Hamilton, Ontario the following month, a fan got much too close to Jones after the match reached its conclusion and the show was presumed to have ended.

"When Rufus was on the way to the dressing room, after hostilities ceased, an irate spectator made a pass at him to his sorrow, for Rufus retaliated with a stiff right to the face which left the man with a souvenir to carry around for a few days," reported *The Spectator*.

At the very beginning of June, Jack Claybourne had an interaction with a wrestler that was glossed over at the time, but which should be treated with far greater significance in retrospect. As Claybourne was occupying the main event of a show in Holyoke, Massachusetts with Tiger Tasker, and being praised as a grappler whose "unique styles" and "peculiar holds" had made him "the most unique wrestler" in the professional ranks, the undercard would feature a disguised appearance by Reginald Siki.

It's quite possible that the Holyoke fans had no idea who they were seeing in the ring, or what his significance to professional wrestling had been two decades earlier, as Siki was never even introduced by his original ring name.

"The Arena card is unusual in itself for Kemil Abdul el Rahman, American Negro who wrestled for a half-dozen years in Europe, and who spent 20 months in a Nazi concentration camp before he was swapped with other American 'nationals' to this country last March, will make one of his rare appearances," reported *The Evening Union*. "He will meet Les Ryan of New York in the 60-minute semi-windup, best two of three falls."

It's difficult to discern which is more unfathomable: The fact that Reginald Siki was never identified by the name that made him a figure of national interest in the United States for a solid decade stretching from the 1920s into the 1930s, or the fact that there was another Black wrestler on the card wrestling in the main event, and the American-born wrestler who first filled major venues as a main-event wrestler had no involvement with him.

*The Portland Evening Express* would get it right one month later in July when Claybourne and Siki once again competed in matches on the same card. However, even though

Siki was identified by his famous ring name, he competed in the opener against George Linnehan while Gentleman Jack battled Cement O'Neil in the semifinal.

Outside of Michigan, Jones and the Panther resumed their pattern of wrestling as a team in Ohio while competing against each other in Ontario. During an appearance of their reunited tag team in Marion, Ohio, Jones and Mitchell both collected falls with headbutts, proving the superior and universal thickness of Black men's skulls once again.

During their next team-up in Marion, Jones apparently leaned on Mitchell to do the bulk of the dirty work, as the Panther disposed of both Angelo Martinelli and Irish McGree with headbutts while Jones watched from the apron of the ring.

In the Midwest, and Canada, Jones had spent a great deal of time in the company of Mitchell, his ally and adversary, who had one of the most overused feline pseudonyms in all of combat sports. During 1944, Jones would turn back the clock and treat a select few audiences in the Northeast to a deadlier version of a large cat by a different name who once prowled their region.

## 10 - The Tiger Hunts Again

The seeds that would inevitably sprout forth to yield the surprising return of the original Tiger Flowers were sown when Rufus Jones and Jim Mitchell teamed together one final time in Hamilton, Ontario. Due to Jones' insistence on cheating, the Panther became annoyed with him and deserted him in the ring, resulting in Jones being pinned twice. The second fall occurred while the Panther conversed and joked with the fans at ringside.

At the tail end of these interactions with the Black Panther in Ontario, Jones once again made a few appearances in Montreal under the name of Tiger Flowers, and with the Black Panther right there by his side. In late August, the pair participated in a handicap bout at the Exchange against Blimp Levy, a wrestler promoted by Jack Pfefer who was advertised to weigh 700 pounds. They also teamed up at the Saint-Jacques Market to face the team of Monte Ladue and Harry Madison.

One month earlier, Jones was reportedly at the Montreal Baseball Stadium participating in a wrestling exhibition alongside Jean Prisie and Tiger Delisle as part of the sport and musical conference offered by Palestre National, according to *The Montreal Gazette*. At the very end of the following month, he appeared in New Brunswick under the guise of Tiger Flowers, just as he'd done in Montreal and Ottawa in the past.

Then, on August 24th, *The Moncton Daily Times* announced that "a bit of color" would be added to one of their bouts, and that it would be owed to the presence of Tiger Flowers, "one of the best known colored grapplers in the game today," who possessed "a wide knowledge of wrestling holds through extensive campaigning in the United States."

To ensure that the wrestling fans of New Brunswick were suitably prepared for Flowers' debut, *The Daily Times* provided them with a fair warning of what they should expect to see in the ring on the occasion of the veteran wrestler's arrival.

"Flowers is another of those wrestlers who raises the ire of the fans the minute the going gets underway, and when the going gets tough he leans back and butts his opponent's noggin with his own dome," explained *The Daily Times*. "His head butt is distinctly different; the fact is he has just the kind of head to butt with. At times he amuses the fans with his comical gestures."

In the wake of Flowers' debut, the sports page of *The Moncton Transcript* was critical of the grappler's performance in a way that was atypical to what he was accustomed to hearing in the Midwest. The report from *The Transcript* outright declared that Flowers' performance during his bout with Mike Demetre had "failed to live up to expectations."

"Flowers came here with a big reputation, but aside from some tricky tactics, he displayed little in the way of real wrestling," complained the reviewer. "The bout reached a climax when it showed both wrestlers 'bowlegged,' presumably punched that way by the pseudo heavy gong."

Flowers lost the match by way of a disqualification in the final fall. Even if the show hadn't been a critical success in the eyes of *The Transcript*'s sportswriter, the publication's editor Bill Hutchinson said that the show featuring Flowers had drawn one of the largest crowds ever to the Moncton Arena, but then added that the presence of wrestling star Yvon Robert at the next show would be "needed to atone for the show put on by Tiger Flowers, the colored gripper," which had clearly left him feeling underwhelmed.

The writer from *The Daily Times* was of an altogether different opinion, declaring that the match between Flowers and Demetre was "easily the best performance presented here in a long, long time." *The Daily Times*' report included the observation that Flowers was also "one of the fastest wrestlers to appear in the local ring," and also regarded the first use of Flowers' famed headbutt as a major unveiling.

"For the first time in Moncton, fans were treated to the head butt, a novelty which Flowers uses extensively, in which he holds his opponent's head in his hands and then butts it with his own. This drew a big laugh from the fans," added the article.

Clearly, Joe Godfrey was making absolutely no effort to mask the fact that Rufus Jones and Tiger Flowers were one and the same.

One week later, in early September, *The Daily Times* announced the presence of "plenty of color" at the next show, when Flowers' faithful comrade Jim Mitchell arrived in New Brunswick. As for his opponent, Flowers was granted an opportunity to wrestle against world junior heavyweight champion Paul Lortie. Flowers took the first fall "with a series of punishing holds, most of which were on the illegal side, followed by the Boston crab."

Lortie won both the second and third falls of the match, even resorting to illegal tactics to win the third fall, "pinning the Negro with the ropes," which *The Transcript* interpreted as the champion repaying Flowers for his foul play.

From there, the original Tiger Flowers returned to the New England area for the first time in more than five years, and took up residence in the wrestling rings of Vermont, marking the longest absence of the name Rufus Jones from the wrestling scene in seven years. However, the images of Rufus Jones circulating in the press certainly didn't disappear, as the promotional photos used to advertise the appearances of Tiger Flowers were totally identical to the promotional photos used to market Jones in other states.

As for why Godfrey would return to the Tiger Flowers persona in 1944, it was probably a matter of promotional logic. Despite the smashing success Godfrey enjoyed under the name Rufus Jones in the Midwest, Godfrey had seldom appeared east of Ohio and Ontario under that name prior to 1944. Therefore, the Flowers name had greater recognition and resonance with fans in those areas.

Further, Godfrey's only appearances as Rufus Jones in a familiar Tiger Flowers stomping ground had been in New Jersey in 1941, and only in the town of Bayonne, where Flowers had never made any appearances in the 1930s. In short, the promoter and Godfrey may have agreed that the Flowers name retained enough of its promotional allure in New England that it would be more worthwhile to reintroduce him under his original name than under the unfamiliar pseudonym of Rufus Jones.

On Saturday, October 14th, *The Burlington Daily News* introduced Flowers to Vermont's wrestling fans as "a 224-pound colored giant" who would face Lucien Leblanc at the Memorial Auditorium.

Rather unsurprisingly given the knowledge of what sort of wrestling presentation would be popular with fans, the marketing for appearances by Flowers left fans under no illusions that they were going to see a vintage Tiger Flowers wrestling display from 1936.

While Flowers had always been described during the early to mid 1930s as a clean-cut wrestler who got by on his technical wizardry, *The Daily News* introduced the returning Flowers as "a rough and rugged wrestler who will use all the bad tactics he knows to try and pin his opponent's shoulders to the mat."

Conversely, *The Burlington Free Press*, which apparently received a different set of notes regarding Flowers, offered a throwback description of the grappler as "a scientific wrestler with tremendous muscles who hails from Tuscaloosa, Ala."

According to descriptions of the first match, what fans ultimately got out of Flowers was a mixture of the two approaches, as he defeated Luze in a bid to reestablish himself as a wrestler to be reckoned with in New England.

"It was a rough and tumble affair, which had the 300 fans on edge throughout," stated *The Daily Times*. "Punches and kicks were frequently exchanged. Flowers took the first fall with a grip hold after 37 minutes of wrestling. Luze took the second fall with a top body press in 11 minutes. After nine minutes of wrestling for the last fall, Flowers hurled Luze out of the ring and was declared the winner."

*The Montpelier Evening Argus*, while adding that Flowers was introduced as "The Detroit Detonator" prior to the bout, also noted that Luze grabbed his ring robe and attempted to strangle Flowers with it to the applause of the fans until his attempt at ending Flowers' life was thwarted by the referee.

At an event hosted by the Memorial Auditorium just one day later, Flowers seemed to settle into more of a technical groove, defeating Paul Gaudette two falls to one, and using a Boston crab to gain the pair of submission victories.

Just like that, Flowers had earned his way into the main-event picture of Vermont against Greek star Mike Demitre. *The Daily News* opined that in just two short matches, Flowers "left the fans with an intense desire to see someone wring his neck," and suggested that the popular Demitre would be "just the man to do it."

In what was described as "a knock-down, drag-out affair," Demitre was able to draw first blood in the rivalry by defeating Flowers two falls to one after Flowers had captured the first fall through unspecified means.

On November 2nd, *The Daily News* printed yet another unmistakable photo of Rufus Jones labeled as Tiger Flowers, and stated that Flowers had "in a remarkably brief time, earned for himself the undying hatred of the paying patrons, who are still looking for the man who can do unto him as he has been doing unto others."

In this instance, the Burlington fans were sent home happy as authentic "South African English" wrestler Maurice Letchford managed to defeat Flowers in dramatic fashion to win the third fall after the score had been knotted at one fall apiece.

In describing an opening fall that reads like a perfect summary of a Rufus Jones match, *The Free Press* analyzed how Flowers "used his cranium as a human sledge hammer to batter Maurice's skull, dropping the Englishman to the mat on several occasions" before he "used his very effective crab hold to force Letchford to say 'uncle.'"

Letchford eventually weathered the storm, taking the next two falls with a body slam and a leg hook, followed by his variation of an Indian deathlock.

For his next main-event joust, Flowers would be invited back to Burlington to tussle with Babe Kasaboski on November 30th. However, massive snowfall in New England brought traffic to a grinding halt. This delay likely prevented Flowers from being able to drive in from Boston even with the show delayed by two days, and ultimately resulted in him being replaced on the card by Legs Langevin.

The match between Kasaboski and Flowers was further delayed by an alleged injury that Kasaboski suffered in Quebec City. Instead, Flowers would face Jacques Trudeau on December 7th — the third anniversary of the Japanese attack on Pearl Harbor — in what was called a "War Bond Match."

The participants of the bout would be required to purchase a $25 war bond for every fall they lost in order to support the Allied war effort. In essence, it was one of the most altruistic matches ever designed, practically guaranteeing that a babyface would lose in order to be perceived as a hero by the crowd for contributing money toward a worthy cause. In the end, that's exactly what happened, as Flowers defeated Trudeau two falls to one.

Over the course of what was described by *The Daily News* as a wild melee, replete with "much hair pulling and eye gouging," Flowers managed to slip his Boston crab hold onto Trudeau twice, thereby winning the bout and forcing Trudeau to pay up.

In addition to the war bonds purportedly purchased by the wrestlers, "three $100 war bonds were sold along with 100 war stamp corsages from the ladies who generously gave up their time to sell these at the matches."

In the fallout from this event, local Burlington sportsman and service center employee Arthur Lacharite contacted *Daily News* reporter Charlene Sullivan and informed her that he was willing to wager $50 that he could defeat Flowers in a wrestling match. There is no indication that Flowers ever acknowledged the challenge posed by Lacharite.

Next up for Flowers would be a rematch with Maurice Letchford, in what promoter Jack Carter stated was a finish match made at Flowers' request, because he wanted there to be a clear winner without the pressure of a time limit.

*The Daily News* chimed in to refer to Flowers as "the heavyweight colored champ from Detroit," in concurrence with other publications in the region that listed Detroit as the hometown of Flowers, rather than Georgia, Alabama, or Cuba.

While this may have been a nod to the fact that Detroit was the birth of the Rufus Jones gimmick, it had the humorous side effect of turning Tiger Flowers into "The Detroit Tiger," in an unintentional allusion to the city's Major League Baseball franchise.

Just as he had in the first meeting between the two, Letchford won the best-of-three-falls brawl two falls to one, winning the conclusive fall with an airplane spin and slam. It was a night that was considered noteworthy for the fact that multiple heated exchanges broke out between wrestlers and fans, resulting in at least one Burlington wrestling fan being arrested and hauled off to spend the night in jail.

Further proving that he was altogether immune to the effects of losses due to the entertainment value of his bouts, Flowers was right back to being advertised as a main event participant in the next show. This time, he was set to do battle with Tiger Delisle in what was branded as the "Battle of the Tigers" in the main event of the big Christmas spectacular.

Because of the overwhelming weight advantage enjoyed by Flowers, it was decided that he would be required to defeat Delisle twice in 45 minutes without dropping a single fall in order to be deemed the winner.

As much hype as there was for this bout, it never took place. *The Daily News* reported that a head-on crash involving a car bringing several wrestlers from Montreal to Burlington had caused them to miss the event. Jack Carter later announced that the match had been postponed while Flowers enjoyed the holidays in Detroit, but said that he would arrange the match early in 1945.

By no means were fans of Rufus Jones kept in the dark about where he was and what he was doing, or at least the wrestling fans in Hamilton, Ontario weren't. A mid-November edition of *The Hamilton Spectator* informed fans that Jones was "plying his trade in the Maritimes where he travels under the name Tiger Flowers."

If Ontario's wrestling fans had missed Rufus Jones, the first line of the first article announcing his return to Canada would have suggested otherwise. In what was probably the most racially insensitive opening to an article announcing the return of a Black wrestler ever written, *The Windsor Star* opened its December 14, 1944 edition with the line, "Get out your lynching ropes, boys. Rough Rufus Jones is going to be in town."

While this certainly wasn't the welcoming homecoming reception that most main-event wrestlers would have been offered, it's likely that Jim Mitchell was pleased to have Jones around again, as the two quickly resumed their routine of appearing together as both partner and opponents.

Storyline consistency was upheld when Jones and the Panther teamed together in Hamilton, and the fans were reminded that Mithcell had walked out on Jones during the badman's summer swansong. As such, Jones was said to harbor resentment and distrust toward his partner.

"The last time the four-man act was put on here, Jones accused the Panther of taking a 'tablet' and refused to sign unless his partner put up $50 of real money to guarantee his appearance until the finish," reported *The Spectator*.

Closing out 1944 with his return to Dayton, Jones supplied *The Dayton Journal* with what has the ring of a truthful response to the question of why he chose to wrestle so roughly.

"I tried clean wrestling, and I was lucky to get cake and coffee money," Rufus remarked. "One night up in Detroit, I got mad at Bull Curry and cut loose. From that time on I have been in demand and have found that rough and tumble pays."

Meanwhile in Cincinnati, promoters added additional details to Jones' backstory. While the city's papers had previously declared him to be a former Hollywood extra and a trainee of Ted Germaine — the latter claim likely being truthful — the question they were seeking an answer to apparently had to do with the original source of Jones' prodigious muscles, which by this time were covered by substantial layers of body fat. Jones' answer led *The Cincinnati Post's* writer to opine that he had earned his muscle "the honest way."

"He got (his muscles) working at day labor. It didn't come from heaving barbells around," continued *The Post*. "Black Rufe used to be a stevedore on the fish docks at

Boston. Now he tosses wrestlers around instead of hogsheads of fish."

Throughout 1944, Jack Claybourne had competed in several championship qualifying bouts and title bouts, and was unsuccessful in every belt-winning opportunity he was presented with. The closest he came to appearing capable of swiping a top title from a reigning champion was when he defeated New England junior heavyweight champion Johnny Iovanna at the Portland Arena in a non-title bout. Siki also appeared on the same card, and lost to Cement O'Neil in the opener.

At the tail end of 1944, Claybourne would finally make his first significant appearances in California in several years when he wrestled for promoter Ad Santel in Oakland, and then headed south towards Los Angeles. Immediately, the local press was replete with comparisons between Claybourne and the most recent Black star to appear there, Seelie Samara. In their efforts to promote the newest Black wrestling star, *The Los Angeles Times* went so far as to report that Claybourne had defeated Samara "and all the other Negro grapplers" in one-on-one matches.

While this was true inasmuch as Claybourne had defeated every Black star he had wrestled against at least one time, he had never wrestled against Reginald Siki, Gorilla Parker, or King Kong Clayton, despite appearing on cards with at least two of the three.

All of the comparisons between Claybourne and Samara were clearly by design, as a match was finally signed for the pair to square off at the Pasadena Arena in front of a California crowd for the first time in January 1945. However, on a scary night in Culver City, it appeared that an injury might prevent a bout between the two wrestlers from happening.

Claybourne performed his regular stunt of leaping over the referee to attack his opponent Sandor Szabo, but the spacing between the grapplers in this instance was apparently not what it should have been. Claybourne clipped Szabo awkwardly and landed on his head, putting him out of commission, and leading many of the fans in attendance to believe that the impact with the mat had broken Claybourne's neck.

"Santa Monica police told us this morning that all that happened was that Claybourne misplaced a vertebrae in his neck," reported a relieved Bob Needham from *The Evening Star-News*.

With his loose vertebrae apparently snapped back into place, Claybourne was cleared to wrestle against Samara. This time, there would be a physical trophy up for grabs, as a belt that Samara had allegedly won in New York City would be at stake.

**Jack Claybourne – Colored world heavyweight champion**

"It is the first time that Promoter Morrie Cohan has ever matched the two leaders of the big fellows in a showdown," offered *The Monrovia Daily News-Post*. "This bout was the apple of the eye for every big club in the country. Pasadena got it because it is the testing place of the heavies. Both Samara and Claybourne have headlined in the Crown City spot. Fans figure they are a toss-up as to which is the real champion of the Negro race."

At the conclusion of a match that was knotted at one fall apiece, Claybourne dropkicked Samara clear over the top rope, out of the ring, and into the audience. When Samara failed to return to the ring prior to being counted out, Claybourne was awarded "the New York belt" and the title of colored world heavyweight champion along with it. By all appearances, it was the most sophisticated handling of a colored championship match ever conducted up until that time.

Just days later, in early February, Claybourne and Samara participated in a rematch in San Bernardino that essentially served as a replay of the championship match that had occurred in Pasadena, with Samara once again entering the match as champion despite the title change in Pasadena.

"Jack Claybourne of South Boston won the world colored heavyweight championship last night, defeating Seelie Samara of Kansas City in two straight falls at the San Bernardino Club," reported *The San Bernardino Daily Sun*. "Claybourne won the first fall after 25 minutes of clean and fast grappling with a dropkick and body press, and repeated in 11 minutes."

At the beginning of 1945, and with the U.S. Armed Forces now fully engaged in warfare in both Europe and Asia, the expectation that all men who were physically competent to serve in the military would be actively engaged in the war effort cast an air of suspicion over able-bodied men who were not serving.

It is possibly for this reason that when Jones made his return to Kokomo, Indiana after a long absence, *The Kokomo*

*Tribune* reintroduced him to fans as "the head-bonking Negro who only recently was discharged from the army."

Throughout the early part of the year, Jones continued with his usual act, and even appeared in new towns within his familiar states, including Muskegon, Michigan. As had become their custom, Jones and the Panther appeared on cards together, as both friends and foes.

Unfortunately, there were occasional interruptions to their schedule. In March, *The Hamilton Spectator* wrote about how easily Rufus healed from injuries. This wasn't in reference to an in-ring injury, but instead came in response to an unfortunate incident that happened during travel.

"The coloured wrestler, who was badly injured in an automobile accident in Windsor one week ago last Thursday night, saw action in Windsor last night, and may be available for a bout here shortly," said *The Hamilton Spectator*.

In fact, Jones and the Panther had *both* been involved in the car accident, but only Jones' injuries warranted an overnight stay at a Windsor hospital. Jones did return to Hamilton quickly, and just one month later, he was involved in a tag match that was said to have introduced a new wrinkle into tag team wrestling after he and Pat Riley fell behind Pat Billings and Monty Ladue in the fall count.

"To gain the equalizing fall, Riley and Jones worked a neat trick," wrote *The Spectator*. "Jones stuck his leg through the ring to form a knee rest, upon which Riley crashed Billings several times. The punishment hurt Billings plenty, and after he was pinned at the ten-minute mark he was unable to retire from the ring unassisted, Ladue being forced to carry him out."

Between the falls, Billings was allegedly examined by Dr. Gerald Lunz, who refused to permit him to return to the ring due to the risk that he might suffer an even more severe injury. Ladue bravely returned to the ring, and quickly succumbed to the most efficient and effective team maneuver in any match involving Rufus Jones. Riley grabbed Ladue by the head and rammed it into Jones' stationary head, which immediately ended the match.

Meanwhile, Hamilton promoter George Hills was still coming up with ways to exaggerate Jones' backstory to add legitimacy to it.

"Rufus Jones, who wrestles for me, was christened Rufus Godfrey, and he is a nephew of Sam Godfrey, the great coloured boxer of some years back," Hills told *The Spectator*.

As is the case with much of what wrestling promoters said, the majority of Hills' statement to *The Spectator* was untrue. It was true that Jones' true surname was Godfrey, but he was certainly not christened with the forename Rufus.

More importantly, of the two famous Black fighters to carry the surname Godfrey, only one was born with that name, neither was named Sam, and neither was any relation to Joseph "Rufus Jones" Godfrey.

George "Old Chocolate" Godfrey — the former world colored heavyweight boxing champion — was born in Canada in 1853 and passed away in 1901. Feab Smith Williams, who borrowed the name George Godfrey from the Black Canadian fighter and carried it to worldwide fame, was a native of Alabama, and was also of no relation to Rufus Jones.

Of course, it is merely assumed that it was one of these fighters that Hills was alluding to in order to make his claim; there was no famous Black fighter by the name of Sam Godfrey.

It was fortunate that the car accident in which Jones and the Panther were found to be traveling together occurred in Canada, where they were now partnering regularly, and not in either Indiana or Ohio, or devoted wrestling fans would have wondered why such bitter rivals could bear to ride with one another in between their brutal encounters.

By the summer, the two men were facing each other everywhere, battering one another and exchanging victories at all points between Marion, Ohio and Kokomo, Indiana. In Canada, the two men were best friends and ruthless heels, as Jones had finally succeeded in swaying Mitchell over to the dark side.

In other California matches outside of his feud with Seelie Samara, Jack Claybourne continued to be mostly competitive. In April, he got a measure of revenge on the Golden Terror for his lack of championship success against the masked wrestler throughout New England by permanently unmasking him after defeating him in Pasadena. Then, at the Wilmington Bowl in San Pedro, Claybourne won a one-night, eight-man tournament to determine the number-one contender for the state wrestling championship by defeating Myron Cox, Craig Jaras, and Hardy Kruskamp in three separate matches.

Claybourne more than held his own against three men on the same night, but then he struggled mightily with the California state champion, "the Mexican mat idol" Vincent Lopez. The champion struck first in 13:03, and Claybourne immediately fired back with a dropkick to win the second fall in 7:03.

"The deciding fall was taken by Lopez with a toe hold in 8:12," reported *The Wilmington Press*. "As Lopez started to leave the ring, Claybourne knocked him down with a rabbit punch. A rematch is promising, according to Jack Guben, promoter."

This moment of uncharacteristically ungentlemanly behavior from Gentleman Jack sparked a rematch, prior to which *The Wilmington Press* acknowledged the fact that "should Claybourne wrest the laurels, he will rate as the first Negro ever to hold a State mat championship in the West."

The accuracy of that distinction would have depended on how the writer chose to define "the West," since King Kong Clayton had already held the state championship of Montana. Regardless, none of the hype mattered, as the injured Lopez was a no-show, and Claybourne defeated the untitled Brother Jonathan in his absence.

Instead of Lopez, Claybourne's next title test would be provided by wrestling superstar Jim Londos, the reigning world heavyweight champion. *The Monrovia Daily News-Post* did its best to position Claybourne as a major threat to Londos' world title in the fans' eyes, explaining that while "Jumping Joe" Savoldi had created the dropkick as "a showmanship trick," Gentleman Jack had "developed it into a real weapon."

"For weeks, Pasadena has seen Claybourne kick his opponents high, wide, and yonder," illustrated *The News-Post*. "He sends them over the top ropes like he was kicking for the point after a touchdown. Claybourne says he is ready for Londos."

The results of the match would suggest that Claybourne was not, in fact, ready for Londos. The world heavyweight champion bested Claybourne in straight falls, ending the bout in a total time of just over half an hour. Both falls were captured "via double leg-breakers," and the fact that Claybourne failed to register a single fall meant that the seed of hope that a title change was afoot was never even given an opportunity to take root in the minds of fans who watched the match in person.

Nevertheless, Claybourne won yet another one-night tournament — this time at the Olympic Auditorium at the end of May — to continue to look like a viable title contender. He also perfected a new submission hold, known as both a rolling leg lock and a rolling toe lock.

Late in the summer, Claybourne moved to Northern California for the first time since he had performed there strictly at the Black Panther in 1937. He was now significantly bigger than he had been in the 1930s, and was being billed as a 222-pound heavyweight rather than a 175-pound speedster.

Soon after Claybourne reached Salinas, promoter Mickey Casper enticed *The Californian* into teasing that Claybourne was going to unveil his new "atom-smashing" hold when he wrestled against Joe Benicassa at the Salinas Armory.

When Claybourne returned to Northern California, a specific variation of his trademark dropkick acquired the colorful name of "The Atom Smasher." That "atom" was a play on words, as Max Gordon of *The Salinas Californian* described Claybourne's dropkick as a two-footed strike to Adam's ("atoms") apple of his opponents.

Gordon later elaborated on this specific version of Claybourne's dropkick, and applied it solely to the dropkick variation Claybourne used when he would vault over the referee's head and "plant his feet firmly against his opponent's neck or head."

It goes without saying that this nickname for Claybourne's match-ending maneuver was inspired by the devastation wrought by the public unveiling of America's atomic arsenal, which leveled the Japanese cities of Hiroshima and Nagasaki during the final stages of World War II. Claybourne's dropkicks may have possessed nuclear properties, but he was still defeated in straight falls by former world champion Dean Detton when the two squared off in Oakland.

When the summer ended, Rufus Jones disappeared from the Midwest once again, but instead of retreating to his hometown on the East Coast, he traveled to the opposite side of the country, as announcements in Oregon heralded the arrival of one of the greatest superstars in the wrestling world. However, the Oregon promoters inflated his accomplishments well beyond being "one of the finest showmen and all-around matmen in the business."

"Jones, who hails from Birmingham, Alabama, is an all-around athlete, and a former professional football player, baseball player, and boxer," stated *The Eugene Register-Guard*.

Certainly, it would have been possible for Jones to have been a professional boxer, or even a professional baseball player; organized Black professional baseball leagues had been in existence since 1920. However, there was no organized Black football league, and the color lines of the major professional football leagues had not yet been broken as of 1945. Therefore, anyone possessing any familiarity with football who reviewed *The Register-Guard*'s statement would have quickly spotted the lie.

*The Oregon Statesman* was far more accurate with its take that "the negro meanie is said to be the hottest piece of torso twister to come out of the Detroit-Chicago-Cleveland area in some time." Yet, Jones was not going to be able to debut the headbutt-heavy style in the Pacific Northwest, as he had been beaten to the punch by the Grey Mask, a hooded wrestler who had first performed in Oregon just one year earlier.

The newspapers in the region began teasing an eventual showdown between the two prolific butters of heads, one of whom clearly came about the sturdiness of his head honestly, and the other who was rumored to conceal objects beneath his mask to amplify the damage of his blows.

Jones was similarly positioned as a threat to surpass the most dastardly heels of the region, including Danny McShain, Bulldog Jackson, Sailor Moran, and "Gorgeous" George Wagner, with *The Register-Guard* noting that Jones was arriving in Oregon "with a reputation that surpasses the villainy of anyone in the grappling business."

*The Register-Guard* further heaped nicknames on Jones — like "Pinky," "The Birmingham Bomber," "The Alabama Assassin," and most topically, "The Black Atom Bomb" — and included that most of the interest stemmed from the fact that Jones was "the first Negro villain ever to show here."

"Jack Claybourne, the last dusky matman to appear here, was a great favorite of the local fans, but Jones is apparently as different as day and night," added the article. But, unlike Gentleman Jack, who relied on uncanny athleticism accompanied by a bright smile, Jones met his opponents with "battering-ram headbutts, accompanied by foaming at the mouth."

The segmentation of Oregon into several cities managed by different promoters created the opportunity for each location to develop a separate origin for its wrestlers, much as Northern California had once managed for Claybourne. As such, even though Jones had received as many as four separate nicknames reliant on the premise that he was born in Alabama, the fans in Portland received a steady diet of articles stating that he was from Detroit.

In comparison to the relatively playful match descriptions provided for Jones in many of the cities of the Midwestern United States, as well as Ontario, the writings of the newspapers in Oregon seemed to lean more heavily into the violence of his actions. Such was the case when he defeated Jack Kiser during one of his early matches in September.

"Kiser made good use of his limber tricks to avoid any powerful approach, and it enabled him to stay on even terms with the 'Alabama Assassin,'" reported *The Register Guard*. "After 21 minutes of hectic action, Kiser fell victim to deadly headbutts, and was easy prey for a body press, losing in the first fall. In five minutes' time, the Birmingham Bomber easily overpowered his groggy opponent with a brutal onslaught, leaving Kiser limp on the mat to give Jones a straight-fall award by Referee Walk Achiu. The arena crowd stormed around the ring in zealous hatred for the mat meanie."

Following the bout, *The Herald and News* alleged to have intercepted a message from Jones to promoter Mack Lillard expressing his refusal to participate in any more wrestling bouts unless he received top billing. The paper also stated that Rufus' headbutt "overshadows any similar attack ever seen in the local ring," and reminded fans that he "cold-cocked Kiser," resulting in the grappler being unable to leave the building under his own power.

Jones was treated with such acclaim that promoter Don Owen announced that he was offering the winner of a forthcoming bout between Tex Hager and Georges Dusette the choice of whether to face Pacific Coast junior heavyweight champion Jack Lipscomb, or newcomer Rufus Jones. Owen's reasoning was apparently that "beating the Negro villain is more of an honor than copping the junior heavy title."

A bizarre facet of Jack Claybourne's tenure in Northern California during the fall of 1945 is that he seemed to be competing exclusively for the money in the eyes of the fans as opposed to chasing a title himself. Or, to put it another way, his priority was to attain strings of main-event matches for the sake of securing the attached payday from each.

Ahead of a bout with former world champion Sandor Szabo, it was printed in *The Post Enquirer* that Claybourne was due to receive a series of three main-event matches in Oakland if he was victorious. Surprisingly, even with this relatively low level of a stipulation attached to the match, Claybourne still lost.

Another curious component to Claybourne's appearances in Northern California is the methods that were used to explain why he was carrying around his Negro championship belt. Although Claybourne had procured the championship and the physical belt from Samara through a visible victory in Southern California, publications like *The Fresno Bee* reported that Claybourne had "won the Negro mat crown in a tournament in the South a few months ago."

As most wrestling writers of the era were well aware, matches even between Black wrestlers were banned in most states south of the Mason-Dixon Line, and certainly in the states of the Deep South. Furthermore, those writers were equally aware of the dearth of Black wrestlers with name recognition.

Years earlier, just prior to a Greeley, Colorado bout between King Kong Clayton and Seelie Samara in early 1941, a sportswriter expressed his ardent belief that half of the Black wrestlers in the country, regardless of skill level, were present on the card, adding that the only other two Black wrestlers in existence who were unaccounted for were Gorilla Parker and Rufus Jones.

At a minimum, Jack Claybourne, Jim Mitchell, Don Blackman, and Alex Kaffner would have taken issue with their absence from this list, along with probably a dozen other Black wrestlers who enjoyed less fame, and whose exploits went uncovered. Still, the fact that it certainly came within a few names of capturing all of the Black wrestling names that could be presented as competent main eventers during that period is an indication of the general paucity of major Black performers, and the commensurate value that they represented to promoters.

In other words, to yank even four Black wrestlers from their respective territories for a title tournament would have taken substantial planning to work around their schedules, not to mention the assurance that the financial payoff from arranging the tournament would have been worth the effort required to organize it.

Of interest at the very end of 1945 was Claybourne's pursuit of the Pacific Coast championship held by Dean Detton. The story being told heading into their main event at the Oakland Auditorium was that Detton considered Claybourne to be a very dangerous challenger, and he would only accept a title match with Claybourne under the condition that Claybourne would be forced to defend the championship against him just two weeks later.

*The Oakland Tribune* added that if Claybourne successfully defeated Detton, he would be the proud owner of two championship belts, as he already carried around a belt acknowledging his position as the world Negro heavyweight champion.

With a built-in stipulation making it easy to take the Pacific Coast championship from Claybourne just two weeks later, the stage was set for promoter Ad Santel to make Claybourne the first Black holder of the title. Instead, Detton took two straight falls from Claybourne in just over 30 minutes "before an unanticipated crowd of five thousand rabid pachyderm enthusiasts," resulting in another crushing defeat for Claybourne in a championship setting.

The fact of the matter is that it was the prevailing belief that placing championships around the waists of Black wrestlers wasn't considered smart business, and it was a fact that was publicly discussed even within Black news publications. In 1941, *The Atlanta Daily World* answered a question posed by a Cleveland reader as to "why the two or three top-flight Negro wrestlers" who appeared regularly in other parts of the country were never offered opportunities to appear on major wrestling cards in New York City.

"There is scarcely any box-office appeal in the city for Negro grapplers," answered the editor. "Even when Regis Siki and George Godfrey were headliners, they still didn't possess the all-important drawing power or the gate appeal."

Theoretically, this was an answer supplied by the editor of a newspaper who had a vested interest in Black success in the field of professional wrestling. Presuming that his opinion was widely shared even among Black Americans, then the Black wrestlers of the era were still being handicapped by impressions generated during the U.S. phase of Reginald Siki's wrestling career, which had truly come to a halt back in 1933.

Also, in the case of George Godfrey, this simply wasn't true. Godfrey had been an exceptional draw during his earliest wrestling matches, outdrawing several of the most well established wrestling stars who were active during that same period in the 1930s. United Press correspondent Dixon Stewart took great pains to point this out while following Godfrey around during his first wrestling tour, beginning with his first appearance in Jersey City.

**Reginald Siki and George Godfrey**

"Whereas such stars as Londos, McMillan, Sonnenberg, and Don George never have been able to draw more than

1,100 fans at Jersey City, Godfrey's appearance resulted in a sellout of the 6,000 capacity arena, and more than 5,000 fans were turned away," Stewart wrote.

A similar story emerged from Godfrey's debut in Camden, where 5,500 fans packed the Camden Convention Hall to watch Godfrey dispose of Andy Zaharoff in straight falls. Despite the incessant tease that Godfrey had a mystery hold to unveil, no such unveiling occurred, as Godfrey won both falls with bodyslams according to *The Every Evening* of Wilmington.

Of course, the majority of these fans were lured to the arena by Godfrey's boxing fame, as the converted boxer barely knew how to wrestle at all. In *The Knoxville News-Sentinel*, sports editor Joe Williams stated how after one of his first U.S. wrestling matches, "the snarling, snapping, vicious black panther" stated that it was "impossible for him to recall any of the technical phases" of his matches, nor did he know what holds he had used.

"I just grabbed hold of the man and threw him," said Godfrey.

In fact, it was George Godfrey's early 1930s success that went a long way toward convincing promoters that a Black face could serve as the feature attraction at a pro wrestling event.

Other Black wrestlers of the era who lacked the sort of name recognition that Godfrey had accumulated for himself as a big-time fighter were not accustomed to performing in front of audiences of that size. That was all about to change when Jack Claybourne took his talents to a land Down Under.

## 11 - A Big Wad of Dough

Similar to the scenarios he dealt with in the Midwest, Rufus Jones found himself dealing with the same situation that Claybourne and his other Murderers' Row peers dealt with in the Pacific Northwest, working in a region where a majority of the small towns had no Black populations to speak of in 1945. Unlike in the Midwest, the large cities in the Pacific Northwest also had no Black populations to speak of, with Blacks accounting for a barely detectable 0.2 percent of the Oregon population.

Perhaps it was because of this that publications throughout Oregon maintained their habit of turning to analogies that would have drawn backlash in part of the nation where the Black population had higher representation.

Regardless as to the reason, publications like *The Roseburg News Review* made highly unflattering allusions to Jones' race, including when they insisted that Jones was "a perpetual motion of tactics that matched his color" as he disposed of Chinese wrestler Walter "Sneeze" Achiu.

After Jones "paralyzed" Achiu with his "noggin attack" to win the first fall, he succumbed to Achiu's "shoulder attack" in the second. In the final fall of the bout, Jones righted the ship by dropping Achiu to the mat with headbutts once again, and then flipping him over into a Boston crab for the submission victory.

For the record, prior to becoming a professional wrestler, Walter Achiu played for the Dayton Triangles, one of the founding teams of the National Football League, and thereby became the first player of East Asian descent to ever suit up in the NFL.

Jones was also the recipient of the same derogatory nickname that was applied to Claybourne during his earliest visit to the Pacific Coast, and was dubbed "Snowball Jones" by a writer from *The Oregon Statesman*.

Against crowd favorite Buck Davidson at the Roseburg Armory, Rufus was ambushed at the outset of the bout, absorbing a pair of dropkicks, a series of punches, a bodyslam, and a Boston crab to lose the opening fall in only 45 seconds. From there, Rufus turned the bout into the first of many bloody wars he would eventually participate in throughout the Pacific Northwest.

"Buck paid heavily in the second round when the Negro stunned him with head butts, twice kicked him out of the ring, and subdued him with a toe hold at the end of 14-and-a-half minutes," said *The News-Review*. "Bleeding badly from the area of his left eye, which had suffered previous injury, Buck was in bad shape, but he spurned urgings to retire from the battle and gamely reappeared for the third stanza. Jones displayed no mercy, centering all of his efforts with head and fist on the injured optic until Buck lay in the ropes almost helpless. At that juncture, referee Owen, who had repeatedly wanted Jones to cease headbutting, halted the match and raised Buck's hand in victory at the end of five minutes."

Apparently Owen — who was both referee and promoter — had not counted on the fans fully understanding the rules of wrestling when he scripted that finish to the match. Because there was no rule in professional wrestling that prohibited the use of headbutts, that also meant that there was no reason for Owen to disqualify Jones simply because he had headbutted his opponent. This resulted in the unanticipated protests of the fans, who felt like the heel wrestler Rufus Jones had been cheated out of a legitimate victory over Buck Davidson.

"To a group of ringsiders who protested, Owen explained that Jones was less interested in defeating Davidson by 'legitimate' wrestling than in dealing injury to his eye that might blind it for life, and that he was justified in halting the bout both on that account and because Jones ignored warnings to change his style of attack," concluded the article.

Perhaps realizing that this decision was still without grounds according to the articulated rules of wrestling, Owen refrained from ever using this particular finish in a Rufus Jones match ever again.

In a rematch between the two men in Roseburg, Jones was paradoxically described as both the "dusky demon of Detroit" and "the Ethiopian," and he evened the score with Davidson, beginning with a pinfall victory in the first round following three consecutive headbutts. After Davidson surprised Jones with a quick takedown and pin, the two men thoroughly brutalized one another as soon as the bell rang to start the third frame.

"Foaming at the mouth, spewing blood, and raging around the ring like one in an insane frenzy, the Negro absorbed enough punishment to paralyze a half dozen men, but in the end he emerged victor," described *The News-Review*. "Buck was knocked out of the ring once, and shortly after returning to the fray, he missed a shoulder butt and again landed on the floor. The succeeding battle on the mat was a test of endurance, with the book of rules tossed out for the duration, and the armory resounding to the roar of the crowd. In the end, it was Buck who became exhausted, the Negro finally pinning him with a simple body press."

At Portland's Labor Temple just one night later, on October 8th, the final layer of red-tinted polish was applied to the finish of a Rufus Jones bout. Against Pacific Coast junior heavyweight champion Jack Lipscomb in a non-title match, Jones emerged triumphant while conveying precisely how threatening his headbutts could be to the champion.

"After Lipscomb had won the first fall with a body press, the colored boy came back to butt Lipscomb till the Hoosier's eye was cut wide open, and won the fall by the simple expedient of applying a half-crab on his groggy foe," explained *The Oregonian*. "Jones continued the 'heady' antics in the final fall until Referee George Kitzmiller gave the fall to the colored lad as Lipscomb's eye was badly cut."

This correct interpretation of the rules served to add an extra layer of drama to Jones' matches. If Jones succeeded in opening cuts to the foreheads of his opponents through the legal use of a headbutt, his foes would be at the ever-present risk of having their matches ended by the referee without them consenting to it. It was a phenomenal loophole within the rules that allowed Jones to achieve legal victories through methods that seemed profoundly cheap.

Justifiably, Jones requested a title match with Lipscomb on the basis of his rather dominant victory over the Pacific Coast champion. Surprisingly, *The Register-Guard* reported that Lipscomb "flatly refused to put up the belt against Jones," in an action that defied the expectation that champions should be willing to defend their titles against all comers.

Instead, Lipscomb agreed to face Jones in yet another non-title match, which yielded a similar result. The two wrestlers traded the first two falls, with Jones copping the first round with a headbutt and half-crab, and Lipscomb evening the tally with a chokehold and body press. However, Lipscomb made a perilous mistake at the beginning of the final stanza.

"The mustachioed Indianan made the mistake of punching the darkie on the head in No. 3, fracturing his right hand," said *The Statesman*. "He was duck soup for the unpopular 'Snowball' from there in, and another session of butts, followed by a half-crab, won it for Jones."

Giving credit where it's due, Jones' non-title victory over Lipscomb is the first clear case of a match following the logical consistency that if Rufus' head was thick enough to damage the heads of opponents without suffering any ill effects of its own, it should also have caused appreciable damage to the hands of anyone striking it directly.

If Lipscomb's refusal to put his championship up for grabs against Jones had been questionable and eroded his favorability with Oregon's wrestling fans, the reason publicly offered for his decision only caused his popularity to plummet further.

"Lipscomb, the hated Indianan, had been guarding his belt zealously for the past few weeks, using every means including refusing to put his belt up," reported *The Register Guard*. "He has refused to wrestle Jones for obscure reasons of racial prejudice, but has been forced to defend the title by the city wrestling commission."

Subsequent articles in *The Register Guard* depicted Lipscomb as doubling down on the reasons behind his refusal, stating that he had "drawn the color line" and was "refusing to put up the belt because of Jones' race."

Perhaps even more stunning than Lipscomb invoking the I'm-a-racist defense in order to duck a title challenge was the fact that this act of prejudicial cowardice did not result in Lipscomb being universally disliked, or cast as the unmistakable villain of the match. In this climate of the 1940s, being a racist did not automatically turn a wrestler into a heel, and the press made sure to stress how equally unpopular Jones remained with the wrestling fans of Eugene.

In fact, Jones was so unpopular that he was attacked at a Klamath Falls dining establishment by a fan of Lipscomb's who spotted Jones peacefully eating his dinner.

"Rough Rufus Jones has a split skull, rendered that way by a Jack Lipscomb booster as the dusky boy was consuming a plate of ham and eggs in a Sixth Street cafe after the fights last Friday night," reported *The Herald and News*. "The embittered Lipscomb fan entered the cafe, saw Rufus at the counter, and promptly bounced a chair off the Detroiter's dome. The railbird was taken to the city lockup, and five stitches were taken in Jones' pate."

For the few Jones' fans in attendance at the Roseburg Armory, the ending of the bout between Jones and Lipscomb was bitterly disappointing, especially if they were hoping that Jones would punish the brash racism of Lipscomb by relieving him of his Pacific Coast title. Instead, Lipscomb slipped lead into his shoes, and relied on a loaded boot to punt Jones in the head and pin his shoulders to the mat.

Even more inflammatory than the depths to which Lipscomb stooped to retain his championship was the quote he was reported to have uttered by *The Register Guard* in response to the request that he defend his title against Jones a second time.

"I've already beaten that nigger once for the belt and see no reason why I should give him another chance," insisted Lipscomb.

**Rufus Jones in the Pacific Northwest**

Before Jones would receive another crack at Lipscomb, he would first have to suffer through his first encounter with the Grey Mask. The match between the two prolific headbutters played out exactly as advertised, with Jones falling victim to the same ending that had worked to his advantage in his first bout with Lipscomb.

"Although the third fall was as advertised — a lulu for action — it took the gladiators the first two flops to get tuned up," explained *The Statesman*. "They tried their vicious head butting early, but found it only scrambled the brains of both men. They didn't bust loose with the head ramming until the final heat. Jones won the first fall in eight minutes with a full crab after slugging the hooded hoodlum around the ring. Stoneface came back with an identical dosage to win the second in 11 minutes, capping it off with a barrage of head butts while the Negro was flat on his back. These started Jones' blood flowing."

In the third fall, Jones and the Grey Mask traded headbutts with vigor, and both remained upright until the commissioner ordered the referee to halt the bout to prevent Jones' injury from getting worse.

Enduring the loss to the Grey Mask without having his stock lowered, Jones faced off with the Pacific Coast junior heavyweight champion once again in mid-December, with Lipscomb once again declining to put his title on the line.

Although the bout was advertised as an opportunity for Jones to exact revenge on Lipscomb for the deceitful manner in which he had downed Jones to hold on to his championship, it was Lipscomb who came out of the gate with aggression, strangled Rufus into submission, then applied knee pressure to Jones' throat and kicked him in the ribs after winning the first round.

"Rufus went berserk in the second round, using head, fists, and feet on the Indiana villain," described *The New-Review*. "He finally snared Lipscomb's head between two of the ropes, downed referee Owen with a head-butt, then turned on the helpless opponent and hammered him without mercy. When Owen regained his feet and freed Lipscomb, the Negro nearly paralyzed Jack with kidney punches, then turned him over with a Boston crab hold; time 9:04."

In between falls, Lipscomb spent his time writhing on the canvas, selling the damage to his back caused by the flurry of kidney punches as well as the Boston crab. As soon as the bell rang to start the third fall, Jones charged at Lipscomb and continued to punish the champion relentlessly.

"The referee intervened for the gong, and Rufus quickly threw Lipscomb face down onto the mat and began another tattoo in the region of the kidneys," the report continued. "Lipscomb made no effort to fight back, tacitly acknowledged he was whipped, and Owen at once pronounced Jones the winner; time 1:25."

The year 1946 would begin with Jones and Claybourne essentially passing like proverbial ships in the night. Jones, who had begun 1946 in Oregon, quickly returned to the Midwest and teamed with the Black Panther once again. He also had a serious brush with the wrestler who perhaps most embodied the ongoing shift from straightforward, blood-and-guts wrestling to entertainment, Gorgeous George.

Presenting himself as a well-to-do wrestler who adorned himself in the trappings of success — from his sequin robes to his theatrical ring entrance and mirror-toting entourage — George Wagner displayed himself as a wrestler whose behaviors bordered on effeminate. This made him a box office attraction whose exhibitions seemed strikingly discordant with the comparatively barbarous and hypermasculine roots of pro wrestling.

In short, the pairing of Gorgeous George and Rough Rufus — a highfalutin White parvenu and a ruthless Black sadist — represented a compelling clash of styles that fans filled the Windsor Market Building to see. The combatants did not disappoint, treating the audience to a 60-minute draw in the main event of an early February show.

*Windsor Star* reporter Jack Dalmage stated that Rufus was "intent from the opening gong to tear Gorgeous George into little pieces," and that "Hollywood's gift to the fashion parade took a tremendous pasting" after he finally finished stalling and removed his $10,000 robin's-egg blue robe.

"The black-skinned grappler from Atlanta threw off all vestige of gentlemanly restraint and sent George reeling with those terrible 'Jones' head-dusters," continued Dalmage. "For a time it appeared that the battle might end right there, as fists, knuckles and elbows flew in a staggering slugfest that left both men slap-happy and careening wildly. While Rufus inflicted his paralyzing skull-benders, George took a frightful toll with repeated kidney smashes, and the frequent hair-yanking episodes seemed mild in comparison. This was battle in the raw, and the wide-open fistic attacks were still going strong when time ran out and Joe Lauzon had to lay down the law to prevent further mayhem."

Feeling that he had been cheated out of a potential victory by biased officiating administered by Lauzon, Jones publicly demanded a rematch with George with a different referee in charge. Jones' request was granted, but with the condition that the bout would be demoted from a best-of-three-falls main-event contest into a one-fall match.

Just like last time, Jones got the jump on George at the start of the match, with *Star* writer Dalmage noting that it appeared as if "an overzealous female spectator tripped the bell in this reporter's corner to send Rufus into action while George was still folding a luxurious fern-splashed robe of wine." To Rufus' dismay, the referee that Jones had personally requested to call the action — Speedy Schaeffer — pulled Jones off of George so that the Hollywood fashion plate's valet could collect his employer's belongings and abscond with them.

"Rufus waded in with a fury possessed from last Monday's frustration," proceeded Dalmage. "Delivering brutal body attacks and fearful head-to-head busters, Jones staggered his opponent and wheeled him into a Boston crab within eight minutes, but George paddled the ropes and safety. That was as close as Jones came to victory."

Ultimately, the one-fall nature of the bout worked decidedly against Jones, as Gorgeous George was able to weather the storm, counter with body blows, and eventually trap Rufus in a quarter-nelson armbar for the submission win.

While this was transpiring in Ontario, Jack Claybourne had reestablished himself in Oregon, where he was once again greeted as "the St. Louis Black Panther" to connect him with his earliest appearances in the region. This reattachment of the feline appellation to Claybourne's name was completed in spite of the fact that the Oregon publications had done everything but dismiss Claybourne as a fraud when it was time to introduce Jim Mitchell as the *real* Black Panther in Claybourne's absence.

The story told to the Portland fans by *The Oregon Journal* was that Claybourne had been "one of the game's most deadly Negro menaces prior to doing war work," although Claybourne had been deemed ineligible for service, and there were also zero gaps in Claybourne's career that would suggest that he was engaged in any sort of military activity whatsoever.

In fact, in stark contrast to King Kong Clayton and Jim Mitchell, it seems as if Jack Claybourne, Rufus Jones, and Seelie Samara experienced minimal career interruptions resulting from U.S. involvement in World War II.

*The Journal* also described Claybourne as being "faster and younger than Seelie Samara," underscoring the perceived need to compare Black wrestlers primarily with one another. Aside from complexion, the two wrestlers didn't have a great deal in common with respect to their wrestling styles.

Depending upon the night, the location, or the opponent, Claybourne could be promoted as everything from a "high-flyer" to a "scientific specialist" to a "giant Negro" of immense strength. When *The Times Herald* of Vallejo made it a point to describe Claybourne's power, it told the tale of the night Claybourne wrestled against Flash Rogers, and with 15 seconds remaining in the bout, Claybourne launched Rogers so high into the air for a backdrop that it resulted in "the latter kicking out the overhead light with his heel."

On most nights, Claybourne was displaying his two most cited attributes, like when he wrestled against the popular Hollywood stuntman Lee Grable in March. *The Seattle Star* disclosed how "the colored boy used a leg lock" for the first fall — more than likely his variation of a rolling knee bar — and then won the bout with his usual dropkick in the finale.

Although he seemingly possessed every performance trait that would be desired of a top babyface performer, the booking results indicated that Claybourne was still treated as fodder for the true superstars of wrestling. *The Oregonian* reported that Claybourne was "flattened" by football and wrestling legend Bronko Nagurski during their March matchup in Portland, dropping two straight falls in under 26 minutes, and succumbing to the force of Nagurski's bodyslam and running tackle.

The very next night, Claybourne was manhandled by Nagurski once again. This time the match lasted closer to 40 minutes, but the result was essentially the same. *The Sun* of Bremerton, Washington described how Nagurski "flipped Claybourne into the ringside section and followed with an airplane spin" to end the first fall, then crushed him in the second fall to send him home with "misery in his back."

All of this was seemingly a prelude to a mid-April match between the two at the Empire Theatre in Edmonton, Alberta. *The Edmonton Bulletin* opined that Claybourne lived up to his description as a "jumping sensation" as "the colored boy managed to wriggle loose from Nagurski half a dozen times in a way that thrilled the crowd." What's more, Claybourne actually managed to score a fall on Nagurski, when he "came off the ropes to smack Nagurski" with a dropkick.

In the grand scheme of things, it was all for naught; Nagurski won the first and third falls by stretching Claybourne's arm and forcing him to submit.

In March, Claybourne and Jones were both included on a list of all-star Black professional wrestlers that had ostensibly been supplied to *The St. Louis Argus* by promoter Sam Muchnick and wrestler Ray Steele. Steele was particularly complimentary of the Black wrestler who had paved the way for the acceptance of other Black wrestlers, and who spent large stretches of the 1930s in Europe, and well over a year in German custody.

"Siki, in my book, is the outstanding colored wrestler of today, who ranks with the topnotchers in the ranks," opined Steele. "Not only is he a wizard at holds and leverages, but is an aggressive worker."

Also named were King Kong Clayton, Seelie Samara, and Gorilla Parker, and of the six men named in total, it could be argued that only three had ever enjoyed even the briefest of reigns with the top titles of any North American territories — the one-month reign of Clayton with the championship of Montana, Jones' two-month reign in Boston as Tiger Flowers, and the short reigns of Samara in Montreal and Boston, along with a five-month reign he had added as the Pacific Northwest champion.

Then at the very end of April, it was Samara who returned to Seattle to duel with Claybourne over the title of best Black wrestler. *The Seattle Star* reported that Samara laid claim to Negro supremacy east of Chicago, while Claybourne was considered to be the best Black wrestler west of the Windy City.

No mention was made to the fact that Claybourne had defeated Samara in California just one year earlier, and for the physical championship belt he carried with him no less. Presumably, the belt was Claybourne's personal property, and it remained with him despite the fact that Claybourne lost a best-of-three-falls match to Samara in Seattle.

In the closing stages of the match, Samara grabbed Claybourne when the latter attempted a dropkick, and slammed him to the mat for a resounding third-fall triumph. With no official championship mentioned as being on the line in that bout, *The Seattle Star* still reported that Samara would be filing a claim with the National Wrestling Association to be recognized as Negro champion of the world.

Even though he had an ongoing feud brewing with Samara, not to mention the fact that he had first publicly laid hands on the belt following a victory over Samara, Claybourne started what would become a longstanding practice of insisting that he secured his personal diamond-studded Negro world heavyweight championship belt by defeating Rufus Jones in New York City, even though such a match never took place.

One of the first clear instances of this occurring was when Claybourne visited Calgary in April and informed *The*

*Albertan* that he had beaten Jones in New York "several months ago" to win the belt.

In May, Jones made his postwar return to Sandusky, Ohio, and *The Sandusky Register-Star-News* gave Jones far too much credit for his relatively brief tour of Oregon. While rightly claiming Jones "is a top attraction wherever he appears," the publication added the absurd claim that Jones "has frequently outdrawn world champion Jim Londos on the West Coast."

With all due respect to Jones, Londos had attracted several crowds exceeding 10,000 fans, and had at least one match in Greece against Bronko Nagurski that was reported to have attracted a crowd of 100,000 fans. While the smaller sizes of the venues Jones performed in certainly factored into the number of fans he performed in front of, he seldom appeared in front of crowds larger than 2,000.

As for the results of that return to Sandusky, it went exactly according to script. *The Register-Star-News* recorded how Jones "applied his famous headbutt and slipped in a Boston crab hold" to defeat Lefty Pacer in 11 minutes and 24 seconds.

Coincidental with the Ohio activities of Jones from late May through early July were matches involving a wrestler going by the name "Tiger Jack Flowers" in Oregon and Washington. This particular Flowers — referred to as "a speedy Negro wristlock artist" — arrived in the Pacific Northwest alongside promoter Jack Pfefer.

According to *The Oregon Daily Journal*, Pfefer was being brought in by Don Owen to resurrect wrestling in the Northwest — and in Portland in particular — while incumbent promoter Ted Thye was taking a hiatus.

Marking the debut of the Tiger Flowers name on the West Coast, at least as far as wrestling was concerned, this particular version of Flowers won none of his matches in just over one month of activity, and was never heard from again. While neither photos nor substantive descriptions of this Tiger Flowers exist, there is ample reason to believe that the wrestler portraying him was not the original Tiger Flowers, and certainly *not* Joe Godfrey, especially since he appeared in environs where Rufus Jones had already made a name for himself and was quite recognizable.

With Jones and Claybourne both well into the second decades of their wrestling careers, it was clear that they and their Murderers' Row contemporaries had made an indelible impression on the landscape of the industry, even if the topmost titles of most territories consistently evaded them.

The September 13, 1946 edition of *The St. Louis Argus* — a well-established Black newspaper — listed Claybourne, Samara, Jones, and Clayton as well known Black wrestlers, and then offered an invitation for aspiring wrestlers weighing at least 180 pounds and possessing well-muscled physiques to sign up for pro wrestling classes at the Pine Street YMCA if they wished to "make good money."

Readers were told that a "skilled, experienced professional wrestling coach" would be on hand to contribute to the courses as an instructor. It is unknown whether or not any of the students who enrolled in those wrestling classes went on to achieve an iota of success or name recognition.

Ironically, the writer of the article included an assertion that St. Louis really wanted to see "its own local boys" in action, hence the encouragement for qualified athletes to visit the local YMCA and train for careers in the wrestling business. If Claybourne — one of the minority of wrestlers who actually wrestled under his real name — had ever bothered to reveal the location of his actual hometown, St. Louisans might have been enthused by the fact that he was born and raised within a two-hour drive of their city.

Shortly after their skirmish in Seattle, Claybourne and Samara both traveled overseas, with Claybourne appearing in New Zealand, and Samara competing in Australia. When it was time for the two wrestlers to switch places in September 1946, the Australian newspapers alerted their readers that a brand new Black American wrestler was inbound, except that Claybourne was the rightful world champion of his race even though he had lost his most recent bout with Samara.

"This laughing negro, with a tremendous width of chest, has arrived from New Zealand, where he was sensational," glowed *The Age* of Melbourne. "For a man of such weight, he moves with the litheness of a panther, and is the greatest specialist of the 'Drop kick.' In his execution of the feat, he leaps six feet from the ground to apply the 'knockout,' which was a specialty of 'Jumping Joe' Savoldi and Paul Boesch when they were here."

*The Age* included that Claybourne would be arriving in Australia after accumulating a stellar record of 26 wins, two draws, and two losses during his time in New Zealand, and added that he had competed in more than 1,200 total contests to date. This was probably a fairly accurate match estimate for a full-time wrestler of Claybourne's stature with well over 14 years of activity under his belt.

*The Sunday Mail* of Brisbane described Claybourne as "an entirely different animal" from the recently departed Samara, noting that Claybourne's forte was blinding speed that was best displayed through the use of dropkicks and flying tackles.

Just as in the United States, the Australian press explored the links between Black American wrestlers and boxers. As *The Mail* drew a physical comparison between Claybourne and former Black American world heavyweight boxing champion Jack Johnson, *Sydney Morning Herald* reporter Ken Hardy asked Claybourne what Joe Louis was like in real life.

Claybourne is recorded as describing Louis as a "nice, quiet fellow," which may simply indicate that the world heavyweight champion didn't have much to say to Claybourne either before or after the riotous evening they shared together inside of Boston Arena's wrestling ring.

Prior to his Brisbane appearance, Claybourne demonstrated his leaping ability to the press by dropkicking the hat of stadium manager Bern Potts as flashbulbs exploded all around him. Claybourne then sat for an interview, and supplied the Australian press with an original backstory. Although

Claybourne admitted that he grew up on a Missouri farm, he professed that he had also been both a professional baseball player and — of all things — an ice skater.

It just so happens that Jackie Robinson had already signed a contract to play baseball for the Brooklyn Dodgers of the National League, and the first stage of the experiment required that Robinson play a season for the Dodgers' affiliate in Montreal.

Robinson had just completed a season in which he batted .349 and was voted the Most Valuable Player of the International League. As such, Claybourne's sudden profession that he had been a professional baseball player was likely provoked by Robinson's success, and the anticipation that his big-league debut would open new frontiers for Black athletic achievement.

In comparison to the baseball reference, Claybourne's ice skating comment seems to come totally out of left field unless you realize that 1946 was one of the peak years of popularity of Mabel Fairbanks, the first Black figure skater to achieve significant fame. Apparently no members of the Australian press offered to take Claybourne to an ice rink to test his abilities.

In a *Brisbane Telegraph* article from the middle of October, Claybourne repeated the story that he had won "the coloured championship of the world" from Rufus Jones in New York at some point in 1943. In fact, Claybourne and Jones hadn't sparred with one another since their St. Louis match for Sam Muchnick in 1942, which had no titles on the line, and which was part of a Negro title tournament that never arrived at an official conclusion.

It is likely that Claybourne never felt like a grander star than he did when he wrestled in Australia. On top of headlining in front of crowds that reportedly topped 11,000 spectators — the largest crowds Jack had ever wrestled in front of — Claybourne's every move was seemingly chronicled by the Australian newspapers.

*The Daily Telegraph* followed Jack to the horse racing track of the Boys Town Sports Ground, where the wrestler rode a trotter named Mark Robert while competing head-to-head with career horsewoman Cecilia McGarten.

Reporters from *The Sun* also tailed Claybourne to the Rushcutters Bay Oval, where they observed him whirling around "a pokerwork boomerang, four feet long, with his portrait in the center." *Sun* reporter W.F. Corbett advised Jack to bring the boomerang with him to the ring and use it to bash Abe Kashey, John Katan, and his other opponents.

Strangely, the coverage of Claybourne's Australian travels included a lengthy story about steady thumping sounds emanating from the wrestler's hotel room, the source of which was initially implied to have been far more provocative than its actual source.

"The first time it happened, the manager thought Elmer had a wrestling partner in his room practising back slams," reported *The Daily Telegraph*. "When he put his head to the door to say 'shush,' Elmer was standing in front of the mirror peacefully shaving himself. There was no other person in the room."

The housemaid apparently discovered "strange chalked hieroglyphics" on the wall, some of which were six feet from the ground. The marks were first attributed to an African religious ritual that Claybourne was suspected of engaging in.

"Elmer is partly to blame himself for this legend," continued *The Telegraph*. "On the third finger of his left hand, he wears an enormous ring. It weighs six ounces. It is made of silver and gold with sacred symbols engraved on the stone. Elmer told the staff that it had been in his family for more than 200 years. He had got it from his grandfather, 'Toby' Claybourne, who was a direct descendant of the famous Zulu tribe of warriors."

As for the marks on the hotel room's walls, *The Telegraph*'s sports reporters surmised that the presence of the smudge marks on the wall was either due to Claybourne's habit of rehearsing his dropkicks indoors, or attempting to practice his boomerang throwing form by using a walking stick.

"He goes down to Rushcutters Bay each day with a veteran boomerang coach, and practises throws out over the water," added *The Telegraph*. "After a fortnight, he is now able to make the boomerang return, and has caught it a number of times. He uses an outsize boomerang with his picture stenciled on it between the images of a kangaroo and an emu."

**Claybourne provides a dropkicking demonstration in Brisbane**

Then, as if the story hadn't been bizarre enough, *The Telegraph* got down to the topic of Claybourne's broad smile and bright teeth. The wrestler attributed both qualities to eating apples, and especially to drinking milk, the favorite source of which was his Jersey cow, Rebecca.

"During his travels, [Claybourne] carries a picture of Rebecca in his wallet to remind him of home," concluded the story.

Presumably Rebecca remained on the Claybourne family property in Mexico, Missouri, as there wouldn't have been much room for a cow in Claybourne's Roxbury neighborhood.

Fresh from his experiences down under, Claybourne stepped off of an Australian Skymaster airliner on Sea Island, British Columbia in late October 1946 absolutely gushing about the favorable treatment he received from the Australians.

"I won myself a big wad of dough," Claybourne told the reporter from *The Vancouver Sun*. "Don't ask me how much, fella!"

Adding that he had won 30 of his 35 matches, Claybourne "pointed happily to his Aussie-style blue shoes and dapper purple serge suit." Claybourne said that the Australians had "treated him royally," and that he hadn't been forced to suffer through anything approximating Jim Crow racism. This is to broadly say that there was no codified system of segregation that restricted his access to facilities or amenities, or enabled him to be legally denied access to rights afforded to others on the basis of skin color.

Making his way to New England, Claybourne wrestled in Hartford, Connecticut, and made one of the first East Coast unveilings of "the diamond-studded belt which rates him as champion among the Negro heavyweight wrestlers."

During December in Hartford, Claybourne participated in yet another match against his Murderers' Row peer Jim Mitchell, which matchmaker Frank Perry advertised as the first time that the two well-traveled Black wrestling stars had ever faced one another. This was certainly not the case; Mitchell had beaten Claybourne in his hometown of Louisville more than seven years prior.

For the sake of long-term recordkeeping, it could be said that Claybourne evened the score between them in Hartford, taking two falls out of three from Louisville's Black

Panther. After surrendering the first fall to a "head-over-shoulder headlock," Claybourne won the second fall with a dropkick, and the third with a backdrop.

As far as Rufus Jones was concerned, the most noteworthy thing to happen during the remainder of 1946 was when he set aside his earlier differences with Gorgeous George to successfully team with one of the top draws in wrestling in front of a Canadian crowd. In front of more than 2,500 fans at the Windsor Arena, the pair of unlikely allies turned back the challenge of Danny Savich and the Great Balbo, leaving their adversaries wiping blood from their faces.

Rufus and George traded the first two falls with their opponents, losing the initial round when Jones was pinned by Balbo, only for George to even the score in the second fall by hurling Savich into the front row, and then body slamming Balbo for the pinfall. This left Balbo ripe for the picking when the third and final round began.

"Balbo, whose sensational forays carried him from wild sorties across the ring to an apeman perch on top of one of the corner supports, was first to go," reported *The Star*. "George cut him down in the midst of his charging act, then sneaked out of a corner moments later to smash Savich to the canvas. Rufus, who had been in trouble with the Utah terror, quickly seized the opening and pinned Balbo with ease. [Referee Joe] Lauzon then spent the busiest five minutes of his life trying to persuade the boys to depart. That he succeeded, despite a few brief clashes, was a tribute much less to himself than to the nimble footwork of Rufus and George."

At the holiday show at the Windsor Arena, Jones went straight back to playing the role of heel during a bout with Gordon Hessel. The tension of the crowd had crescendoed over the course of the evening thanks to intervention by the police in depriving two fans of water pistols that they had used to squirt the wrestlers, and also a ringside brawl between Buddy Knox and Frankie Clemons.

The match between Jones and Hessel unfolded uneventfully enough through the first two falls, with Rufus smashing Hessel's head with his own and forcing him to submit to a Boston crab, only for Hessel to respond six minutes into the second round with a flying headscissors for a pinfall.

Midway through the third fall, one of the turnbuckle pads broke beneath the weight of Hessel, and sent him sprawling to the mat. It was more than likely at this point that the three men in the ring — Jones, Hessel, and referee Joe Lauzon — realized that the show-closing battle royal would not be able to proceed as planned, and that they needed to improvise a finish that would give the fans their money's worth right then and there to salvage the evening.

"Jones got busy with the dangling rope right away," wrote Jack Dulmage of *The Star*. "He wound it around Hessel and used his neck for a snubbing post. Lauzon, attempting to halt this fearful display, was hurled from the ring twice to come up bewildered and bleeding. Hessel was choked into unconsciousness. With hundreds of roaring patrons threatening to invade the scene, Matchmaker [Bill] Thornton bulled his way into the ring, removed his spectacles, and proceeded to lambaste Rufus with several highly professional elbow slams. With the aid of Lauzon, Wild Bill managed to bring Jones under partial control, but he underwent a severe beating in the process."

Dulmage closed his piece by saying that Jones "barely escaped being mobbed by outraged customers" on his way back to the locker room, and that "hordes of would-be ambushers skulked in the doorways" after Rufus completed his successful retreat.

To close out his wrestling coverage for the year, Dulmage also wrote an article about how the professional wrestling industry had experienced a tremendous post-war boom. In the case of the wrestling market in Windsor specifically, the promoter had been required to move from the Market Building into the Windsor Arena to keep up with demand. The peak attendance of the year was registered in the summer, when "Whipper" Billy Watson headlined a show that attracted 3,500 fans.

More significantly, Dulmage's piece exposed one of the problems wrought by the sudden increases in revenue that were being enjoyed throughout the wrestling profession.

"Such was the demand for top-flight mat entertainment, that in November, two well-known Windsor sportsmen, Blake Robertson and Cliff Head, peeled off their own hook to bring the city a second grappling market," added Dulmage. "Operating in the Market Building, they are currently enjoying near-capacity crowds, employing matmen of three weight divisions from a Michigan circuit under the matchmaking of Harry Light of Detroit."

While Dulmage expressed his excitement for the idea of continued appearances from the wrestlers Light provided his Canadian partners access to — including Maurice Tillet, Lou Klein, Bert Ruby, Flash Gordon, and Ivan Kamikoff — and the entertainment value that more shows could provide to fans, promoters who relied exclusively on revenue from ticket sales were less enthused when competitors sprouted up.

With families having limited disposable income, doubling the number of wrestling shows ran the risk of eventually halving the revenues earned by each promoter, or burning out the fans on wrestling altogether.

The fear that a wrestling promotion might eventually die is one of the primary reasons why wrestlers would accept bookings in a diverse range of territories in order to broaden their appeal in a geographic sense. Jack Claybourne had already reaped the benefits of venturing outside of his comfort zone, and Rufus Jones was about to travel further from home than ever before in his attempts to do the same.

## 12 - Greatest Negro Wrestler

Even though he had received star treatment in Australia during the fall of 1946, Jack Claybourne's booking in North America during 1947 would follow a similar pattern to what he had grown accustomed to in years past. This meant that Claybourne would continue to draw rave reviews everywhere he appeared — including states he had never performed in before like Vermont — while being shut out of the title picture.

In Boston, in the middle of January, it was reported that Claybourne attended a women's basketball game between the Boston Giants and the West Medford Vets to open the local winter basketball season, and grabbed the spotlight by tossing up the ceremonial jump ball at the beginning of the game. It was included in the report that he then went "dashing to the arena to tangle with the Black Panther."

The only problem with this description of the evening is that Claybourne and the Panther weren't booked to wrestle one another for another month. Since Claybourne lived in Boston inside of an apartment building that he owned and rented out units to tenants from, it's quite possible that he was speeding home to tangle with the Panther over a home-cooked meal.

In Burlington, Vermont during a mid-February event, Claybourne reportedly stole the show from world heavyweight champion Lou Thesz, who wrestled in a by-the-numbers bout against George Linnehan "without extending himself to any degree."

"This lag was more than made up in the semi-final when Promoter Jack Carter unveiled a new hero in black skin for the approval of the large crowd of mat addicts. They approved, and how," proclaimed *The Burlington Daily News*. "The new ebony express, Jack Claybourne, lived up to his advance booking and then some."

The ending to Claybourne's bout was described as spectacular. While Chick Garibaldi was conversing in the center of the ring with referee Mike Futa, Claybourne sprang completely over Futa's head, crashed on top of Garibaldi, and won the bout cleanly with a body press. *The Burlington Daily News* then heralded Claybourne as the "answer to the clamor of local mat fans for Don Eagle to return, or someone who moves around like him."

In Vermont, there would be no attempts to associate Claybourne with African tribes in order to hint at some form of latent savagery lurking within him. Instead, Claybourne was labeled as "a gentleman in and out of the ring." To effectuate this aura, he was declared to have been a graduate of New York University, one of the most elite academic institutions in the United States.

After making appearances in Ottawa, where the newspapers affirmed that Claybourne hadn't lost a step, Gentleman Jack returned to defeat Frederic Von Schacht at the Memorial Auditorium of Burlington with a dropkick in the first fall, and a disqualification victory in the second. With the victory, Claybourne earned a shot at Montreal's version of the world heavyweight crown, which was held at the time by Bobby Managoff.

The first match between the two was slated to take place in Burlington, Vermont. In front of the largest crowd to attend a wrestling show in Burlington that season, Managoff defeated Claybourne in a best-of-three-falls encounter to retain his title.

In St. Albans, the pair wrestled yet again, drawing a crowd of 1,000 fans — the most to attend a wrestling show in the town that year, and accounting for more than 50 percent of the town's population. The two were praised in *The St. Albans Daily Messenger* for their refreshing use of "clean breaks, orthodox holds, and general wrestling knowledge." With that said, Claybourne still lost the bout after seizing the advantage during the third fall.

## Gentleman Jack and Rough Rufus

"The Harlem hustler got a little overconfident as he thought the end was near, and after connecting with one dropkick, he had the tables turned on the second attempt when Managoff caught him in his arms and laid his shoulders down on the mat in six minutes," concluded *The Daily Messenger*.

The battleground of the two men shifted to Ottawa, and *The Ottawa Journal* declared it to be the first mixed-race championship match ever staged in Ottawa.

Claybourne dominated the action for nearly 30 minutes, and landed two successive dropkicks to the chin of Managoff. When Claybourne attempted to land his third consecutive dropkick, Managoff slid out of the way, and Claybourne's groin straddled the top rope. Once Claybourne rebounded back into the ring, crashed to the mat, and seemingly lost consciousness, the referee halted the action and declared Managoff the winner.

"In the Ottawa Senator medical room, the injured grappler was diagnosed as having a severe groin injury and a slight concussion," wrote Dan Mackintosh of *The Ottawa Citizen*. "Ice packs and first aid brought Claybourne from a coma, but he was delirious and in no condition to return to the ring."

It needs to be mentioned that in several New England publications during this time, Claybourne was repeatedly advertised as "Harlem's Bouncing Black Boy." In the United States, the term "boy" assumed a widely recognized racial undertone when applied specifically to Black adult males. The inherent racism of the term implied an automatic subservient relationship between the usually White individual uttering the term, and the Black recipient of the expression.

Uses of the term during the earliest stages of Claybourne's career — while almost certainly derogatory in their intent — have the smallest bit of wiggle room to be marginally less offensive due to Claybourne's youthful appearance and disposition. At this stage of his life, with Claybourne bordering on 37 years of age, the belittling nature of the term cannot be so artfully explained away.

Halfway through May, Claybourne made an appearance in St. John, New Brunswick, where *The Telegraph Journal* introduced him as "Negro champion of the world," and told wrestling fans that he was "being groomed for a world title bout."

**Claybourne traps the arm of his opponent and crossfaces him**

Fans were also informed that although Claybourne was "famed as Gentleman Jack," he was capable of becoming "as rugged a fighting machine as the next man if necessary." By every appearance, it would seem that Claybourne's debut match in St. John was crafted to prove the veracity of this statement.

At the St. John Forum, Claybourne was dueling with the rugged George Calza, with the fall tally between the two knotted at one apiece. That's when both men slid outside of the ring and out to the floor, and then Calza bolted into the audience with Claybourne hot on his heels.

"While the customers were spilled right and left, and police and others tried to separate the participants, the fans first scattered, and then, bolstered by rush seat holders who leaped over barriers, closed in on the ringmen, pushed them back into the squared circle, and cheered wildly as Claybourne pounded his opponent into submission for the deciding fall of three," described sports editor Doug Costello.

*The Evening Times-Globe* of St. John would capture another important detail from the bout when it described exactly how the final fall was recorded. Calza was the first to reenter the ring, and when Claybourne tried to make his way through the ropes, "Calza tried to kick him in the face but only succeeded in getting a head butt that put himself out of business."

This amounts to the first clearly recorded instance in five years of Claybourne concluding a match with the sort of thunderous headbutt that Rufus Jones would have endorsed.

Throughout the next month, Claybourne logged very few marks in his win column as he concluded his time in New Brunswick. In the meantime, on the other side of the world, *The Melbourne Age* was apparently queried as to why there were no Black wrestlers present for that year's summer wrestling tour. The dumbfounding explanation proceeded as follows:

"Although the colored black wrestler Jack Claybourne desired to visit Australia again, the white wrestlers here this season drew the color line and refused to meet him or Seelie Samara."

It's difficult to fathom a more puzzling explanation for the absence of Black grapplers than to accuse nearly an entire roster of wrestlers — both heels and babyfaces — of racism, while expecting that answer to satisfy the fans.

Opening 1947 in Sandusky, Ohio, Rufus Jones was booked in a boxing match against Sandusky's own former world light heavyweight boxing champion George "Johnny" Nichols. By this point, it had been 15 years since Nichols had won the championship and then lost it by failing to defend it within the mandatory eight-month period. It had also been eight years since Nichols had officially retired from competitive fighting altogether.

To add an air of legitimacy for Jones' skirmish with Nichols, he was provided with a backstory as an "ex-big-time pugilist" who "had a colorful boxing career behind him, having battled many of the top eastern boxers during his heyday."

"Sure sign that the Link's Hall fight will be filled with action is Jones' determination to stop the Sandusky leather-pusher in order to settle a long-standing dispute between the two performers," continued *The Sandusky Register-Star-News*. "The husky grappler switched to wrestling after being barred from boxing because of rough tactics in the Boston area. Jimmy 'Black Panther' Mitchell figured prominently in Jones' change to the mat game."

Even if Jones had been a boxer at one point, which is a claim there is no clear evidence for, it is unlikely that he would have had skills that could match those of a former world champion fighter, albeit one 15 years removed from his prime. Fittingly, Jones lost his predetermined fight with Nichols by way of a third-round TKO after a flurry of punches from Nichols sent him to his knees and the referee called a halt to the action.

Jones had undoubtedly gained a great deal of weight over the course of his wrestling career, which different publications took note of along the way. However, in describing one of Jones' bouts with Alex Kasaboski during July 1947, the word selection of *Windsor Star* reporter Jack Dulmage suggests that weight, age, injuries, or some combination of the three had slowed Jones considerably over time, and that certain moves that had once been commonplace in his repertoire were becoming increasingly rare.

"There was gasping and eye-popping as ol' Rufe erupted with a speed that compared favorably with his licks of yesteryear when he was hailed as the swifty of the circuit," described Dulmage. "At one stage, he even launched a flying drop kick. Matchmaker Bill Thornton was flabbergasted. It was a wonderful sight to behold…"

Jones wasn't the only one whose appearance had changed with time. As the summer of 1947 progressed, Jack Claybourne returned to wrestle in Rochester, New York. It was here that *Rochester Democrat and Chronicle* reporter Frank Lillich echoed sentiments previously expressed of Jones in his observation that Claybourne "appears to have added considerable poundage around the midriff since his last showing here three years ago."

This was yet another acknowledgement of the change in Claybourne's appearance that would soon begin to influence his performance style. Now tipping the scales at an advertised weight of 235 pounds, Claybourne was being promoted as a true heavyweight who was 65 pounds heavier than when he debuted. If the reporting of *The Democrat and Chronicle* is to be believed, it's quite possible that the figure was accurate.

In the meantime, an extended feature article on Claybourne printed in *The Niagara Falls Evening Review* revealed that Claybourne had made some interesting additions to his repertoire of offensive maneuvers, not to mention his backstory.

It was stated that Niagara Falls promoter Sammy Sobel "only recently discovered" that Claybourne had been awarded the honor of being named "the world's Negro wrestling champion" by the New York Wrestling Association in 1941. The two major issues with that statement were that Claybourne made no claims to being a world champion when wrestling in New York in 1941, and more importantly, the New York

Wrestling Association was a completely phony wrestling organization.

The article said that Claybourne had been married to his wife Lillian Smalls for eight years, when they had actually tied the knot only five years earlier in Minneapolis. Lillian had grown up in Roxbury, Massachusetts, and met her famous husband once he moved into her neighborhood.

Claybourne apparently also stated that he was originally from South Africa, and had first been a major star on YMCA wrestling teams before turning professional 10 years earlier.

This final point may mark one of the first attempts to conceal Claybourne's true age; he had been wrestling professionally for 15 years at this point, and had just turned 37 years old over the summer.

It's possible that Claybourne's rising age was a contributing factor to the set of statements that followed, which described Claybourne's favorite in-ring holds and tactics.

"Claybourne, like most grapplers, has pet holds," the article continued. "One is the standing leg split, and the other is 'the Koko bump,'" said *The Evening Review*. "The latter scarcely can be described as a hold as it only calls for Jack to bump his head against his opponent's head, and as Jack's noggin is an unusually hard one, this weapon can prove a very handy one in a close bout."

Overlooking for a moment the fact that this is the first extensive article written about Claybourne in more than a decade that failed to mention his penchant for leapfrogging over referees and dropkicking his opponents' faces, the description of his supposed love for headbutting and the proffered reason for its effectiveness — thus far almost totally absent from Claybourne's recent match reports — reads like a carbon copy of every analytical piece written about Rufus Jones.

The suspicion is that some combination of age, injuries, declining athleticism, or the desire to add variety to his arsenal had prompted Claybourne to at least strongly consider transitioning to the use of a style that more closely resembled the headbutting style popularized by his Malden-born contemporary.

Regardless, the piece made very little sense in the context of what had transpired in the location where it was written. Claybourne's documented matches in Niagara Falls had been won with dropkicks up until that point, with no mentions of headbutts included in the reports. Instead, the advertisements for his appearances stressed Jack's "kangaroo legs" and acrobatic proclivities.

Curiously, Claybourne never received an opportunity to unveil his proposed brawler-friendly persona in front of the audience to which it was advertised. One week later, he went on to wrestle primarily in preliminary matches in Windsor, Hamilton, and Cleveland, leaving Niagara Falls promoter Sobel to declare that he had made the decision to sideline Claybourne for failing to win a match against the Masked Marvel.

With Rufus Jones likewise seeming to lose some of his mobility, and with there seeming to be a looming sense that he had already been used in every feasible wrestling capacity during his 10-year run in the region, Rufus continued to participate in an outsized number of boxing matches.

At the Memorial Hall of Lima, Ohio, Jones competed in yet another simulated boxing match, this time against his familiar opponent Gil LaCross. *The Lima News* described how LaCross finally "knocked Jones cold" in the sixth round of a fight scheduled for 10 rounds, continuing Jones' career-long losing streak in boxing matches.

Returning to Sandusky, Jones was knocked out by Billy Fox in the seventh round of a boxing exhibition, with *The Register-Star-News* stating that Fox "jarred the headbutting Jones to the Links Hall canvas."

Finally, Jones returned to New England late in the fall of 1947, this time making his first appearance in Maine. *The Portland Evening Express* described Jones as "a newcomer from Detroit, who is reported by the powers that be as something bordering on hysteria for the fans."

## Gentleman Jack and Rough Rufus

In Portland, Jones treated the fans to the sort of signature bloody performance that Midwestern wrestling fans had grown accustomed to from viewing a decade of his work. On the undercard of a show headlined by a women's world title defense from Mildred Burke, Jones brutalized Jack Kelly and rearranged his face.

"Jones forced Kelly to succumb from the pressure of a reverse arm lock in 2:30, then shifted his attack to Kelly's head, butting him repeatedly with his own skull until Referee Fred Moran stepped in at the eight-minute mark to stop the affair," wrote *The Portland Press Herald*. "Kelly was bleeding freely from a gash over the eyebrows."

This tour through New England reunited Jones on cards with his early opponent and the man who was credited with his development, the Boston legend Ted Germaine. The descriptions of the matches seem to indicate that Jones still remained capable of delivering the same level of action as he did in the Midwest, like the summary of his bout with Johnny "Moochy" Muccaccario at the Hartford Auditorium by *The Hartford Daily Courant*.

"The squatty Negro was the fans' choice, and he came through to take the first fall in 14 minutes and 10 seconds with a headbutt and leg hold," wrote Max Liberman for *The Daily Courant*. "Moochy seemed fully qualified to even the score, but Jones stopped whatever ambitions Moochy had with a series of butts. Both struggled through the remaining 26 minutes without success as the gong ended their 45-minute time limit bout. It was a lively set-to."

Jones also treated Hartford fans to one of his signature Detroit-style brawls, battling Bull Curry all over the Hartford Auditorium.

"Curry took the first fall in 10:45 with a series of smashes and a top body press," wrote Liberman. "In this set-to as well as in the following two frays, both plunged in the hard wooden aisles in a blur of flailing, flying fists and arms to culminate a steady procession of heave-hos by one or the other combatants. In the second affair, which Jones took to even the score, he headbutted Curry into defeat, needing but a top body press to win. In the final fall, which Curry took in 8:30 with a series of elbow smashes and a crab hold, action went sky high requiring the assistance of the attending policemen to keep things in order."

Rufus also had his first hometown match under his most frequent stage name in November, finally wrestling under the name Rufus Jones in Boston Arena, and dueling Chuck Montana to a draw. This means Joe Godfrey wrestled in his home state of Massachusetts under all three of the identities he would adopt during his career.

Jones also succeeded in appearing in a main event at the Boston Arena, losing yet another bout to Bull Curry as one of Jones' most common badman rivals defeated him to earn a title shot against Frank Sexton.

Simultaneous to activities of Claybourne and Jones, both of whom were active in the Northeastern U.S., 1947 was a year that would mark a major turning point in the career of Reginald Siki, whose treatment since returning from German imprisonment had been a very mixed bag.

Throughout the first three months of 1947, Siki wrestled in Minnesota and lost almost every match he appeared in. It must have seemed like a completely different business to a man who had regularly wrestled in multi-fall matches with the Zbyszkos that lasted well over an hour a quarter of a century ago, only to be losing single-fall bouts to the likes of Hans Kaempfer in less than 10 minutes.

A mid-March edition of *The Minneapolis Star* provided some insight into what Siki was doing during his downtime in between matches. The paper revealed that Siki had been volunteering extensively for the Red Cross of Hennepin County — of which Minneapolis is the county seat — in the organization's effort to raise $300,000.

"The Red Cross saved my life when I was interned by the Germans as a prisoner for 20 months during the war," Siki told *The Star*. "My fellow prisoners and I absolutely would not have lived on the meager rations provided by the Nazis had they not been supplemented by American Red Cross prisoner of war food packages."

Siki added that he had worked as a barge captain in New York harbor following his repatriation, and before he returned to the ring on a full-time basis.

In April, Siki returned to Southern California — the site of some of his most favorable booking — and his fortunes took a 180-degree turn. He quickly accumulated victories against Jules Strongbow, Al Billings, Otto Von Bussing and Dutch Schultz throughout April and early May. Then in mid-May, he defeated Maurice LaChapelle in a best-of-three-falls match at the Pasadena Arena to capture the California State Heavyweight Championship.

Since Siki's career had in all likelihood started in 1921 under a different name, it had taken 26 years for him to finally capture his first authentic race-neutral championship on American soil.

That's when Siki finally embarked upon a winning streak commensurate with his legendary status, as he dominated all comers throughout the summer of 1947, turning back every challenger to his championship. He wasn't relieved of his title until October, and even then, the loss had the appearance of a fluke.

"Vincent Lopez tossed Reginald Siki out of the ring last night at the Olympic Auditorium, and when Siki couldn't continue because of an injured back, Lopez was awarded the state heavyweight wrestling championship," reported *The Valley Times* of North Hollywood. "The two heavies grappled for 20m. 4s before Siki was tossed out of the squared circle."

Liberating Siki of his official state championship may have been done so that fans could focus on the subtext of his next encounter, which was a match for the metaphorical colored heavyweight championship between Siki and "The Black Panther" Jim Mitchell.

"Leading claim to the colored heavyweight wrestling championship of the world is expected to be settled here tomorrow night when Jim Mitchell, 'called the Joe Louis is wrestling,' faces Reginald Siki, former California state title claimant, in a three-fall to a finish special attraction at Municipal Auditorium," reported *The Long Beach Press-Telegram*. "Mitchell is favored to win over the veteran Siki, despite the latter's experience."

**"The Black Panther" Jim Mitchell**

Unsurprisingly, Mitchell won the match and the symbolic championship that Siki had already supposedly lost against two separate opponents — George Godfrey and Seelie Samara. In fact, although Siki's claim to being the world colored heavyweight champion was often mentioned throughout his career, documented cases of him being successful in any matches where any championships bearing that title were up for grabs remain elusive.

Siki bounced back from his loss to Mitchell and continued to be competitive in Southern California wrestling rings, but Siki would be put back in his proverbial place in December when he faced Gorgeous George less than a month after the national television appearance that made Gorgeous George a bona fide celebrity and a household name.

In that match, Siki was selected as the figurative tomato can used for George to showcase his dominance; George quickly dropkicked and pinned Siki right after the opening bell sounded, resulting in Siki suffering a humiliating defeat in only 12 seconds.

Siki persevered in spite of the crushing loss and continued to be booked rather favorably in the Los Angeles region. In early January 1948, Siki also teamed with Jim Mitchell in March during a bout against Chris and Babe Zaharias, which the two lost.

During the first week of June, Reginald Siki dueled to a draw against Vic Holbrook, and then promptly disappeared from the ring without any updates or statements about what had contributed to his absence. The answer would come around Christmas, and it would arrive in devastating fashion.

In the meantime, Claybourne began 1948 wrestling in Buffalo, New York, for the first time in several years while competing under the unusual name of "Tiger" Jack Claybourne. He then returned to appearing in Toronto and Windsor. When victories were earned, they were secured with dropkicks, and when defeats were experienced, they typically occurred long after Claybourne had already displayed his vaunted athleticism. Against Hi Lee in Toronto, Jumping Jack — who *The Toronto Star* had been comparing to an aircraft in flight — ended his night with a spectacular crash landing, followed by a shower of grocery aisle produce.

"On the last test flight, [Claybourne's] landing gear became fouled in the ropes, and he landed with a 'binnnnk,' head first on the mat," exclaimed *The Star*. "His immediate and subsequent actions led all of the 5,500 to believe he had broken his neck, or severed the jugular, or shattered his spinal column. Always ready to help a fallen foe, Hi Lee probed Claybourne's injuries — with his boots. Maybe he was trying to kick the jangled vertebrae back into place. The fans didn't like his methods, oddly enough, and said so with samples of fruits and vegetables. At current prices, they must have been incensed indeed!"

Acting aside, Claybourne was perfectly fine, and only a few nights later, he made his debut in Syracuse by deposing the city's reigning mat king Hans Schnabel at the State Fair Coliseum. The bout ended in just over 25 minutes when Schnabel submitted due to the discovery of "a broken knuckle on his left hand."

"A crowd of 1,000 fans, amused by Claybourne's bouncing tactics and semi-waltz weave while on attack, were surprised at the sudden finish, for when Schnabel was forced to say 'Uncle' he seemed to be in command," reported *The Syracuse Herald-Journal*. "The decision achieved by the negro matman enabled him to gain final booking next week with Jim "The Goon" Henry in a Ladies Night special."

*The Post-Standard* provided the detail that Schnabel appeared to be on the verge of victory when he swung at Claybourne while Jack was standing next to the ring post, and "the Gentleman ducked the punch," causing Schnabel's knuckles to make sharp contact with the steel.

Claybourne's victory earned him a match with Jim Henry, and the following week, Claybourne bowed out in 26 minutes to a series of Henry's airplane spins, and immediately began packing for a trip back to the Pacific Northwest.

As Claybourne made his return to the West Coast at the beginning of February 1948, it appeared that he had made a significant career breakthrough when *The Tacoma Sunday Ledger* reintroduced him to local fans as a claimant to "the world's heavyweight championship," without any mention made of his title claim being restricted to his race.

In the 1940s, the average size of American men was 5'9" and 143 pounds, and at 6'1" and a fairly muscular 220 pounds at the beginning of 1948, Claybourne was easily on the bulkier end of the distribution when it came to the weights and sizes of professional wrestlers during the era.

This is a fact underscored by a statement from *The Vancouver Daily Province* evaluating Claybourne upon his return. The publication described Claybourne as one of "the largest heavyweights to hit the local wrestling circles in years."

The elevation of Claybourne to an all-races championship still appeared to be largely intact, when *The Vancouver Sun* not only introduced Claybourne as "the U.S. heavyweight champion," but even acknowledged that he had successfully defended the title against Russian wrestler Abe Yourist at the city's Veterans' Memorial Center, suggesting that it had been on the line.

*The Vancouver Daily Province* described Claybourne's victory as one of the most spectacular ever seen live. For Claybourne, it was just another night hurdling the referee and dropkicking his opponent in the face.

"Claybourne, who was subjected to underhanded tactics throughout the eight 10–minute-round bouts, finished off Yourist with a tremendous jumping smash," glowed *The Daily Province*. "While the referee remonstrated with Yourist for his dirty wrestling, Claybourne sprang from behind, cleared the six-foot arbiter's head, and felled the New Yorker with a devastating drop-kick smash."

Even if the intention had initially been to present Claybourne as a full-fledged champion without a racial modifier applied to it, these plans quickly fell by the wayside; by early March, Claybourne was back to being advertised as the "U.S.A. colored champion" in the Vancouver area.

However, Claybourne's breakthrough would be coming shortly, and it would seemingly arrive during what was intended to be a short stopover on the way to his return engagement in Australia.

When 1948 opened, Rufus Jones teamed with frequent Boston mainstay Les Ruffin to wrestle the villainous duo of Ted Germaine and Tiger Tasker. *The Portland Evening Express* made the observation "Negro wrestlers are rare, and this is the first time that two have ever appeared together on the same card at the Expo."

"The Ruffin-Jones duo scored with the first fall in nine minutes, but the roughnecks bounded back for a four-minute toss, and then assaulted not only their opponents, but occasionally the referee Fred Moran, in the final sprint to win in 19 minutes," printed *The Evening Express*.

The item that stands out in the promotion of this match is the use of the word "Negro" to describe Les Ruffin, whose nickname in Pennsylvania was "The Boston Indian." Carrying none of the common phenotypically Black features, Ruffin was never referred to as Black either before or after this affair, over the course of a wrestling career spanning more than two decades when factoring in Ruffin's time as a matchmaker and promoter.

Throughout New England, Jones continued to lose spirited brawls against Bull Curry. For years, wrestling promoters had done their best to shoehorn Jones — who had always been thickly muscled, but who now possessed an equally thick waist — into the 190-pound weight category for the sake of preserving his contendership for light heavyweight championships, which were the industry norm. In Hartford, Jones' weight was finally listed, and probably quite accurately, at 220 pounds.

Rather than returning directly to the Midwest, Jones made an effort to appear before a completely fresh audience. In the middle of March, *The Santa Barbara New-Press* announced the California debut of Jones, offering a description of Jones' in-ring demeanor that would have left fans familiar with the antics of Rufus wondering if *The News-Press* staff had gotten the nearly 35-year-old Jones confused with someone much younger.

"Rufus Jones, one of the few Negro wrestlers in the United States, will make his Pacific Coast debut at the Mission Athletic Club Arena Thursday night according to Don Sebastian, promoter," declared *The News-Press*. "Jones has been wrestling for about seven years, and has built up a large following in the East, where he has become somewhat of a sensation among grunt and groan fans."

In a separate article on the same page, *The News-Press* stated that Jones would be making the first Santa Barbara appearance by a Negro wrestler, and that he was "considered by his people as the uncrowned mat champ." They also listed him as weighing 210 pounds, and standing 5'10", while also laughably describing him as "a rugged but clean fighter."

In truth, Jones was now a 15-year mat veteran who was barely taller than 5'7". Not to mention, by telling wrestling fans that Jones was essentially a clean fighter, Sebastian must have been setting them up for a startling turn of events once the headbutts and blood began to fly.

It also isn't difficult to identify who it was that probably had a hand in convincing Jones to travel to Southern California. Simultaneous to the advertisement that Jones would be debuting in Santa Barbara, *The Ventura Weekly Post* announced that Rufus Jones and the Black Panther would be forming a tag team partnership to take on Gino Garibaldi and Bulldog Clements.

Unfortunately, the closest Jones would ever get to wrestling in California would be a visit to the ringside seating area. *The News-Press* explained that when Jones appeared in Santa Barbara, his presence was announced to the fans, who were then told that Jones would be unable to wrestle until he got his license cleared by the California State Athletic Commission. Instead, the Black Panther substituted for Jones, and promptly lost his match to Martino Angelo.

By this point, Jim Mitchell had become quite the headbutter in his own right. Likely motivated by Jones' success in the Midwest, Mitchell reintroduced headbutts into his arsenal in New England, and transitioned from a wrestler who occasionally slipped in a headbutt to a combatant who — like Jones — used an excessive number throughout his bouts, and then at the conclusion.

This practice of Black wrestlers "borrowing" Jones' style in certain situations would become increasingly more common, as Mitchell would continue this headbutting practice primarily in California and New York, but would also seem to scale back its use in places where Jones had previously popularized it.

Apparently unable to get himself cleared by the Athletic Commission of California under any circumstances, Jones instead found himself booked in a few shows at Phoenix's Madison Square Garden. Introduced first as a claimant to "the Boston championship" — a claim that was quickly amended to that of "Boston Negro champion" — Jones faced Jose Lopez of Mexico, and in the words of *The Arizona Republic*, "used his hard head to knock Lopez into Tamale Land."

Speaking of wrestling in unfamiliar locations, Jack Claybourne was first advertised to appear in Hawaii on March 30, 1948, through a prescient statement that he was "the world's greatest Negro wrestler" who "should make a big hit here."

In his debut match on the island, Claybourne competed against California junior heavyweight titleholder Maurice Chapelle on the undercard of an event presented by promoter Al Karasick at Honolulu's Civic Auditorium. It was the same Maurice LaChapelle, using a slightly different surname, that Reginald Siki had wrestled the California heavyweight championship away from one year earlier, and the same LaChapelle who Tiger Flowers had dueled with in New York in the mid 1930s.

Chapelle and Claybourne wrestled to a 45-minute draw in a contest that *The Honolulu Advertiser* described as "sensational" and "breathtaking."

"The two matmen displayed skill and sportsmanship the likes of which will seldom be seen at the auditorium," gushed *The Advertiser*. "It was evident from the start that they were well matched. Chapelle relied on his agility and speed while Claybourne amazed the crowd with neat tricks, which enabled him to slip out of some tight holds. The match proved exceedingly popular."

Seeing the outpouring of support that Claybourne achieved during his match against Chapelle — along with the fact that *The Honolulu Star-Bulletin* referred to the Chapelle-Claybourne bout as "the best straight wrestling match seen at the auditorium in months" — promoter Al Karaskick wasted no time in promoting Claybourne to the main event of his April 11th show at the Civic Auditorium.

This time, Claybourne would be facing established veteran of the Hawaiian mat scene Ted "Tiger" Travis, who was also the holder of the Hawaii Junior Heavyweight Wrestling Championship.

Although it possessed a territorial essence and an association with a lighter weight division, the Hawaiian junior heavyweight title was no ordinary championship. Not only was it the most cherished singles wrestling title in the Territory of Hawaii, but it was also the only championship in the professional wrestling world to carry the official sanction of *Ring Magazine*.

As a result of this distinction, the Hawaiian title belt around Travis' waist carried a grander implication of legitimacy than nearly any other championship in the wrestling world since its creation in January 1943.

To commemorate the creation of the title, *Ring Magazine* editor Nat Fleisher delegated his associate William Schulkin to present the diamond-studded belt to the winner of a single-elimination tournament. Fleisher added that his intention was for the belt to enhance the quality of the matches that were being presented to the many American servicemen who were stationed in Hawaii.

## Gentleman Jack and Rough Rufus

In October 1943, Charley Carr became the inaugural champion and holder of the *Ring Magazine* belt, knocking off Chester Hayes in the finals of the tournament, which culminated in a bout in front of "13,000 soldier fans" at the Schofield Barracks military base, located roughly 20 minutes northwest of Honolulu.

Claybourne would be turned back by Travis in his first attempt to separate him from the *Ring Magazine* belt. During the first fall, Travis forced Claybourne to submit to a reverse leglock a little more than eight minutes into the match. That's when Claybourne mounted "one of the most spectacular comebacks seen in local rings."

"Roughed up by Travis, Claybourne appeared out on his feet, but springing high into the air, he leap-frogged over the referee and dropkicked Travis," recounted *The Advertiser*. "And before Travis could recover from his surprise, Claybourne used arm whips to slam him around before applying a body press for a fall."

From there, Claybourne continued the onslaught and succeeded in rendering the champion groggy, but an errant dropkick sent Claybourne crashing onto the back of his head, rendering him easy prey to a pinfall loss at Travis' hands.

With that, Claybourne departed from Hawaii to fulfill his commitments in Australia, but Ted Thye, who helped Karasick with the booking of qualified talent, quickly assured *The Star-Bulletin* that Gentleman Jack would be returning to the Hawaiian Islands as soon as his stint in Australia reached its end.

Even with Claybourne appearing in only two Hawaiian matches, the level of fame he had achieved was already sufficient to be worth reporting about on the U.S. mainland, at least within Black news circles. While Claybourne had already moved on to Australia, an Associated Negro Press writer based in Hawaii — Hubert H. White — published a syndicated article informing the ANP's readership about the popularity that Gentleman Jack had rapidly achieved in the heart of the Pacific.

## Gentleman Jack and Rough Rufus

"Jack Claybourne, world famous wrestler, arrived here from California two weeks ago and has become the greatest drawing card of wrestling events, given every Sunday night at the Civic Auditorium," wrote White. "He is one of the cleverest and fastest mat men ever to appear here. When he made his debut two weeks ago with Maurice Chapelle, junior heavyweight champion of California, he demonstrated unquestioned ability to use holds and tactics far superior to many of the wrestlers seen here."

Now back in Australia after a two-year absence, Claybourne went straight back to headlining shows in what had clearly become one of his favorite places to wrestle. This time, the presence of a companion by his side was rather conspicuous, and rapidly became a topic of interest to the Australian press.

"World champion negro heavyweight wrestler, Elmer (call me 'Jack') Claybourne, would rather talk about his wife's prowess at bowls than what he does in the ring," printed *The Sun* of Sydney. "'Yes, I've got the champion's belt — but, listen, you ought to see my Lillian operating in the bowling alley. She's mighty good,' [Claybourne] said today when he arrived in Sydney from the U.S. by ANA Skymaster. Mrs. Claybourne beamed broadly."

Lillian Claybourne humored the members of the press who asked her how much she weighed after confirming the weight of her husband at 17 stone; *The Sun* actually printed Lillian's weight of 13 stone, or a little over 180 pounds.

As with his first tour of Australia, Claybourne once again wrestled in front of packed arenas, with his seasonal debut in Melbourne against Billy Kuusisto ending in a draw, and attracting a packed house of 10,000 fans.

In Newcastle, Claybourne was similarly well received when he defeated Babe Smolenski at Newcastle Stadium. The reporter from *The Newcastle Morning Herald and Miners' Advocate* — writing under the mysterious pseudonym of "The Onlooker" — seemed thoroughly impressed with Claybourne's athleticism. The anonymous reporter referred to Claybourne as "a spectacular drop-kicker" and "the highest flyer Australian wrestling enthusiasts have ever seen."

"Claybourne leapfrogged the referee (Joe Dawson), springing over his head after he had run about three yards and gained impetus by placing his hands on the shoulders of Dawson, who seemed to buckle under the weight," wrote the Onlooker. "Clearing Dawson, Claybourne hit Smolenski with his boots and flattened him to secure a fall. This manoeuvre was in contravention of Dawson's edict that no wrestler should lay a hand on him. He ignored Claybourne's two hands."

Although he was clearly wowed by Claybourne, the Onlooker added a curious criticism of Claybourne's methods, stating that Jack was "a fairly good wrestler, but a poor showman" who benefitted from the use of the Australian system that included rounds. Had Claybourne wrestled without rounds, the Onlooker argued, "Smolenski would have won easily," but he "always secured his best holds too near the bell each time."

Claybourne's growing popularity in the diverse islands of the Pacific was made further evident by the arrival of the New Zealand All-Blacks Rugby Team in Sydney prior to a subsequent match there between Claybourne and Smolenski. Hearing that Claybourne would be in action, several wrestling fans within the team decided to take the opportunity to attend the event live.

In *The Sun*'s coverage of the Claybourne-Smolenski match, more details were added to the backstory of Claybourne's wife Lillian. While reinforcing the idea that Claybourne's original sports background was as a baseball player, *The Sun* added that Lillian had been a professional softball player in her own right.

By this point, Jackie Robinson had fully broken the color line of Major League Baseball, starring for the Brooklyn Dodgers and even receiving Rookie of the Year honors while leading the National League in stolen bases. Whether true or not, this doubling down by the Claybournes on their participation in American bat-and-ball sports seemed to be a strategy to further capitalize on Robinson's international notoriety.

Upon making his return to Newcastle for a bout against Danny Dusek, Claybourne was apparently asked how he went about perfecting his dropkicking method. In response, Claybourne said he painstakingly practiced the dropkick for two years in order to develop the dangerous and powerful match-ending weapon that he was widely known for.

"Claybourne can kick as high as 6ft. 4in.," printed *The Herald and Miners' Advocate*. "His method of training is similar to that of a high jumper. He kicked at a string drawn across a wall with a mat underneath to break his fall. As he improved, he raised the height of the string."

Apparently, Claybourne didn't find that story to be satisfactory, so when he was posed the same question by reporters in Brisbane, he was prepared with a slightly different answer.

"Claybourne set up a high-jump apparatus in the gymnasium, but instead of trying to clear the bar, he aimed at kicking it off," reported *The Brisbane Telegraph*. "He says that he can now reach six feet with a flying dropkick."

Expectedly, some members of the Australian press got around to discussing the tremendous popularity that Black American wrestlers had achieved in Australia in recent years — Claybourne and Samara in particular — and racked their brains searching for explanations. *The Newcastle Sun* bluntly opined that the frequent rivals, who had yet to face one another in Australia, were the two most popular wrestlers to have appeared in Australia, excepting no one.

"Reasons for this favoritism are not hard to find," offered *The Sun*. "The negroes are non-stop matmen, very agile, and able to use all the recognized holds. Good showmen, they keep their temper in the face of the greatest provocation."

Eventually, Samara and Claybourne *did* get around to facing one another in Australia, with *The Sunday Mail* crediting them with motivating a new wave of Black wrestlers to begin working in the United States.

## Gentleman Jack and Rough Rufus

The extent to which Samara, Claybourne, Jones, Clayton, Mitchell, Parker, or any of the other wrestlers of their generation inspired future Black wrestlers to try their hands at professional wrestling is difficult to gauge. However, a new generation of Black wrestlers was beginning to take shape, and the Murderers' Row members would soon be forced to contend with their presence, for better or worse.

Claybourne and Samara headlined a show in Sydney as Jack was making his exit from the country, and Samara gained the victory in what can be presumed to have been a non-title match, since Claybourne was still repeatedly referred to as the Negro world heavyweight champion in the aftermath of the contest.

"Coloured wrestlers Seelie Samara and Jack Claybourne staged one of the most scientific and clever bouts seen at the stadium in a long time, Samara winning by two falls to one in the sixth round," stated *The Newcastle Morning Herald and Miners' Advocate*. "Samara gained a submission fall in the third. Claybourne equalised in the fifth with a series of dropkicks and a body press. Samara clinched the match with a crotch hold and press in the sixth round."

Leaving Samara to continue headlining in his absence, Claybourne once again departed from Australia after what was presumably another prosperous tour and returned to Hawaii. Without question, Jack wouldn't have flown back to Hawaii if he didn't think he would make money. He probably had no idea that he was about to make history.

## 13 - Island Fusion

The short-term limbo Rufus Jones found himself occupying after his anticlimactic exit from California didn't last long. As soon as Jones could get himself booked in Oregon, it appears that he quickly traveled back to the West Coast to wrestle for Don Owen. *The Coos Bay Times* informed fans that hadn't seen Jones during his initial tour of the state that he was "the head-buttinest Negro" in these parts, who combined "unusual tactics" with a "red-hot wrestling style."

Jones' first major bout in his return to Oregon was a textbook dismantling of George Dusette in Salem. Jones dropped Dusette with headbutts and applied a Boston crab to win the first fall, lost the second fall to a full nelson, and then pinned Dusette to conclude the match after repeatedly butting his head. According to *The Statesman*, Jones then "took leave of the crowded premises in the escort of city cops, as he had the customers ready to help, as usual."

*The Coos Bay Times* described Jones' actions against the masked Phantom at the North Bend Community Building as "an exhibition of animal brutality." During the bout, the two men "spent most of their minutes in the ring slugging, gouging, kicking, and head-butting, with the Phantom ending up with a badly split forehead that streamed blood over wrestlers, referees and fans."

"The bout ended outside the ring, where Jones ran the Phantom's head into a heavy ringside bench, finishing the job he started with head-butts," added *The Times*. "[Referee] Williams managed to get between the men long enough to pull the bloody and almost unconscious Phantom and award him the match on fouls. As he and spectators were carrying the Phantom to the dressing room, Jones attacked him from behind again, trying to head-butt him further."

When Jones arrived in Vancouver in May, it was *The Vancouver Daily Times* that informed fans that Rufus had no plans to stay in the Pacific Northwest for very long, as he intended to return to the East after the summer. Still, Rufus confirmed that he had designs on the junior heavyweight title, which would have sounded like a ludicrous desire for him to harbor; anyone who had seen Rufus in person could have confirmed on sight that he was well over the weight limit to qualify for a junior heavyweight championship match.

Of course, a top-tier wrestling promoter would never let something like reality interfere with a money-making opportunity. Jones was quickly booked against an even lighter opponent, the Pacific Coast light heavyweight champion Gordon Hessell, with it being said that Jones was too heavy to qualify for a shot at Hessell's title that had a far lower weight limit, but would attempt to leverage that opportunity into a shot at Frank Stojack's junior heavyweight championship.

The weight difference wouldn't matter. It was reported that Jones' aggressiveness worked against him and ultimately cost him the match against Hessell. After Jones was disqualified for "persistent headbutts" in the first fall, he evened the match in the second fall. Jones continued his domination, but Hessell surprised him with a headscissor takedown to wrap him up for the deciding fall.

A report from one of Jones' early matches against Jack Kaiser in Vancouver indicates that he was able to retain some of the humor in his matches on the West Coast of Canada despite what also seemed like a general amplification of the violence factor.

"Jones, a colored, cigar-smoking citizen from Boston, used head butts to subdue Kaiser in the semifinal," reported *The Vancouver Sun*. "Mr. Jones proved to not only be the master of Kaiser, but of buffoonery as well."

In the interest of providing fans with further insight into what made Jones tick, Vancouver promoter Jack Whelan obliged *The Vancouver Province* with an interview to discuss the newest wrestler in British Columbia.

"Just because it takes four policemen to escort him to his dressing room, there is no reason to think he has a bad disposition," remarked Whelan. "After all, I have seen worse than that on the street cars in rush hour."

Whelan then laughed and declared that the true source of Jones' bad attitude was his lousy golf game, joking that "when he misses a couple of putts, he takes it out on the wrestlers."

The match that finally seemed to earn Jones a crack at the Pacific Coast junior heavyweight title was another gory bout against the Phantom, which left "a trail of blood from one side of the ring to the other." Rufus had to rally for the victory after succumbing to the attack of the Phantom in the first stanza.

"From there on, it was all Jones as he slammed the Phantom with his murderous head blows, finally opening a blood gusher on the loser's head, and a few minor cuts on his own," described *The Register-Guard*. "The second and third falls went quickly to the toughie as he relentlessly pursued his victim, pinning him both times with body presses, and all the while keeping the Phantom in a dazed state with his head-butts."

Instead of facing Frank Stojack, Rufus would face Hungarian wrestler Al Szasz, the man who defeated Stojack for his championship almost simultaneously to Jones' dissection of the Phantom. The title bout between the two in Eugene followed the familiar pattern of Jones seeming to defeat himself, as his refusal to halt his overly aggressive attacks at the urging of referee Jack Poppenheimer led to a first-round disqualification.

"Jones came back heated and got real revenge, pinning the titleholder with a Boston crab to even the score and come close to Szasz's wrestling crown," said *The Register-Guard*. "Jones went all out in the final meeting, nearly putting Szasz down for the long count with his battering head-butts, but swiftly Al, in one last uprising, slipped into his 'Al Szasz Special' and it was all over for Jones, Szasz gaining revenge for earlier beatings and retaining his crown."

## Gentleman Jack and Rough Rufus

A few nights after Jones' loss in the title match, the Phantom took his own brand of revenge on Rufus. Battling in Eugene once again, the pair engaged in yet another brawl that left the ring and the surrounding area stained in crimson.

"Jones drew first blood in less than a minute when he tied the Phantom's leg in the ropes and beat the hooded man's head against the planks several times before the referee could come to the rescue," wrote *Register-Guard* reporter Glenn Snyder. "The same tactics cost the Negro the fall four minutes later when he refused to break after being told the second time by Referee Poppenheimer."

In the second fall, the two combatants exchanged headbutts as the Phantom's blood continued to leak right through his mask. Eventually, the hooded wrestler withered and crumpled to the mat beneath the continuous onslaught from Jones' headbutts, and Rufus applied his Boston crab for the second-fall victory.

"It looked like the match was over when Jones knocked the Phantom outside the ring where he lay dazed and unable to get up," added Snyder. "He finally regained his feet, lunged back in the ring, and floored the Negro with a crunching head-butt and body press to win the final and deciding fall. The Phantom's knees buckled and he almost collapsed when the referee raised his arm in a token of victory."

Losses aside, the consistent message being sent in these matches was that if Jones could simply manage to restrain himself at critical moments, he would avoid losing falls by disqualification, and potentially never lose a multi-fall match.

The fans also sent a consistent message to Jones: "We don't like you." It was a message that was delivered loud and clear when a fan attempted to snipe Jones with a hunting knife in the middle of a late-July show in Salem.

"His aim was poor, and no damage was done, but someone threw a long-bladed pocket knife at wrestler Rufus Jones Tuesday night during the wrestling program at the Salem armory," reported *The Oregon Statesman*, providing a wrestler with rare front-page coverage. "Jones was just leaving the ring after taking a fall over an opponent when the knife, believed by the police to have been thrown from the balcony, sailed toward Jones and missed him by a few inches. Although city police went into action immediately, they did not apprehend whoever threw the dangerous missile. Jones has wrestled in Salem many times, and is extremely unpopular with the armory fans."

**Rufus Jones headbutts his opponent**

The flinging of edged weapons in Jones' direction wasn't the only hazard he was forced to contend with. In Salem, Jones had to deal with two sets of ringside distractions caused by the hostile crowd. *The Capital Journal* reported that while Jones was in the midst of combat with Jack Lipscomb as the two were standing close to the audience, Jones was "hit in the head by an outsider while a firecracker exploded." Despite initially fearing that someone had fired a gun at him, Jones still completed the match by headbutting and pinning Lipscomb.

Apparently, none of these incidents could compel Rufus to tone down the level of hostility he displayed during his matches. In Coos Bay, Jones temporarily teamed with light heavyweight champion Gordon Hessel to empty the ring of competitors, only to dramatically turn on him, split his eye open with headbutts, and then eliminate him as well.

In the beginning of August in Portland, Jones defeated the Phantom in a way that once again conveyed the unique danger that headbutts presented. After the Phantom won the first fall with a piledriver, Jones administered his headbutts to the Phantom, knocking him out of action and causing him to be counted out. What's more, the Phantom was so concussed from the headbutts that he was unable to return, culminating in a medical disqualification before the third fall could begin.

In essence, the act of headbutting when behind in the fall count could enable Rufus to score two falls consecutively if he did sufficient damage to incapacitate his opponent and render him unable to continue.

Compared with the derogatory comments in the press that were often used to describe Jones during his first swing through the Pacific Northwest, the frequency of their use during this return visit was significantly scaled back. With that being said, there were still occasions where Jones was referenced in less than flattering racial terms.

For example, when quotes were attributed to Jones' teammates, like "Bully of the Balkans" Tiger Nenoff, a certain degree of tacit racism — very common for the time — was implied in the words that were used.

"I've wrestled against Negroes, Indians, Japs, and all other kinds of matmen, and wrestling with Jones as a teammate is okay with me," Nenoff was quoted in *The Register-Guard*. "I draw no lines in race or creeds, and the only stipulation is that I be the captain and make all decisions."

The irony here is that Jones and Nenoff were being cast as the good guys in this bout against the villainous holders of the world tag team championship Jack Lipscomb and Glen Knox. To be charitable, it is not inferable from Nenoff's statement that he would necessarily have been a more agreeable partner to a teammate who did not represent a member of a minority group in the United States, but his words certainly lean in that direction.

Far more overt were statements from some of Jones' opponents. When a late-September match between Rufus and Farmer Jones was being advertised in *The Register-Guard*, the utterance attributed to Farmer Jones was that he'd have "nothing to do with the Nigger," but later decided that he'd "like nothing better than to toss Rufus around for a bit."

This was the second consecutive tour that resulted in Jones being called a nigger in the Oregon press. While the second use of the racial epithet had been credited to a supposed pig farmer from Arkansas, the first had been assigned to a straightforward grappler from Indiana.

In his daily life, Farmer Jones was Cecil Murdoch of Waxahachie, Texas, the brother of wrestler Frank Murdoch, and the uncle of future wrestler Dick Murdoch. For what it's worth, the younger Murdoch had several accusations of racist behavior leveled against him throughout his career and following his death, including tales that he drove fellow wrestlers to KKK rallies, and proudly displayed his Klan membership card.

Because of his family ties that actually point to a racist legacy, the idea that the N-word could have actually come out of Cecil Murdoch's mouth during an interview isn't particularly far-fetched.

## Gentleman Jack and Rough Rufus

By all appearances, a few Oregon newspapers — and *The Register-Guard* in particular — seemed to harbor a peculiar fondness for the N-word. When "King Kong" Clayton debuted in Oregon in 1939, wrestler Babe Small was quoted by *The Register-Guard* as saying that he would "be damned if he'd wrestle a nigger." The same month, Bill Kenna's promise to "get that nigger" Clayton during a battle royal was allegedly overheard by a writer from the same publication.

The following month, *The Register-Guard* made further attributions of the appalling racial slur to Small. Before another bout with Clayton, Small once again said that "he didn't need any help beating the nigger," and when the two wrestlers were preparing to face each other in tag team competition and were soliciting partners, Small supposedly added, "Just give me one more chance at the nigger, and he can pick anyone else as black as he is."

On the one hand, Eugene had been one of the most active outposts of Ku Klux Klan activity in Oregon during the 1920s, with parades, cross burnings, and public initiations all a matter of public record. On the other hand, none of the uses of the word nigger that appear in *The Register-Guard* were ever assigned to a babyface, other than Farmer Jones.

Therefore, it could also be deduced that Eugene's wrestling promoters believed that reserving use of the N-word and other racist behaviors for heels was one of the most potent tactics for communicating their villainy, or for wrestlers hailing from the former Confederate states, within which Jim Crow racism was the order of the day.

As Rufus began his feud with the bearded and barefoot Farmer Jones, and as the scene of the action shifted to Pasco, Washington for the debut of pro wrestling in the Tri-City area, *The Tri-City Herald* described the lengths Rufus would go to in his attempts to communicate the hardness and durability of his cranium to fans before the shows even got under way.

"Rufus himself is a popular drawing card, mixing his expert wrestling ability with a good dose of ring razzle dazzle, including a demonstration of his head, claimed to be the hardest in the world," insisted *The Herald*. "Before matches, Rufus allows bystanders to break boxes over his head; during a match, he uses his incredible cranium as a battering ram against his opponent."

From a momentum standpoint, the feud with Farmer Jones was devastating to Rufus, who was constantly pinned to the canvas after being on the receiving end of the Arkansas farmer's mule kicks night after night. It is worth noting that the decision to cast the Arkansas farmer as the winner of the feud with the Black man may have had something to do with the demographics of places like Roseburg — essentially 100 percent White at the time — and the sort of crowd that Farmer Jones was reportedly attracting to the wrestling venues.

"The pig-raising farmer was not equal to the head-butting black boy and eventually bowed out via a drop kick and body press in the third fall," recounted Dan Mindlovich of *The Roseburg News-Review* following a late October bout between the two Joneses, and a rare scuffle that Rufus actually won. "The decision brought loud boos from the pro-pig-man portion of the patrons, and they milled about the ring as if waiting to dispatch the Detroit boy in traditional southern fashion, but they were spared in the effort because referee Ray Steele, an ex-heavyweight wrestler from way back, began throwing forearm jabs at Rufus when the Detroit senegambian got in an extra jab at Farmer after the match was over."

With there being no other records of Rufus Jones being referred to as a native of the region comprising Senegal and Gambia, Mindlovich seems to have been using "senegambian" as a catch-all synonym for Black. Regardless, the more troubling portion of the sentence is the somewhat casual suggestion that there was a potential lynching threat present in the aftermath of the match, and false violence directed at Rufus by Ray Steele was needed to help satiate the crowd's desire to administer Southern-style vigilante justice against the Black grappler.

In the heart of the Pacific, when Jack Claybourne was set to reappear in the wrestling rings of Hawaii, *The Honolulu*

*Star-Bulletin* made the announcement on October 4th that the "colored mat artist" was due to arrive from Australia, where he had been touring for the prior six weeks.

Promoter Al Karasick immediately proclaimed that Claybourne would team with established star Oki Shikina against the team of Jimmy Lott and Lee Grable at the very next Sunday night show at Honolulu's Civic Auditorium.

Karasick also noted that Hisao Tanaka, the reigning Hawaii junior heavyweight champion, was supposed to have defended his title against Claybourne's tag partner Shikina, but had requested two additional weeks to prepare himself for the title defense due to a fall that had resulted in an injury to his back.

"Claybourne showed here in two matches en route to Australia and impressed local fans with his power and skill," added *The Honolulu Advertiser*. "He is agile and clever. He and Shikina should form a tough team."

When Claybourne's plane landed, the red carpet was rolled out for both him and his wife Lillian, while the pair posed for photos while wearing Hawaiian leis. *The Advertiser* referred to Claybourne as the "undefeated Negro heavyweight wrestling champion of the world," which was a false commendation no matter how creatively a promoter might have attempted to manipulate the words in that sentence.

At that very moment, Claybourne's record in Hawaii stood at no wins, one draw, and one loss in a Hawaiian title bout. In Australia, he had not only lost on more than one occasion, but he had dropped his final bout in the country to Black American heavyweight wrestler Seelie Samara.

In addition to landing in Hawaii with his wife and an exaggerated claim to being undefeated, Claybourne also arrived in Hawaii in the possession of something else that was of equal interest to the press.

"Tiger" Jack Nelson

"A veteran of 10 years in professional wrestling, Claybourne said he won the Negro heavyweight title in 1943, and is the proud owner of a jewel studded gold belt presented to him by the New York Boxing and Wrestling Commission," reported *The Advertiser*. "Only two others wore that belt before Claybourne. They were Tiger Nelson in 1941 and Rufus Jones in 1943. Claybourne has turned back all challengers since he won the title in 1943."

Becoming something of a wrestling legend in California — and in the Los Angeles area in particular — "Tiger" Jack

Nelson had retired in 1939 after wrestling George Godfrey in what was advertised as a match for the colored wrestling championship belt that Nelson had carried around with him in California for years, despite seldom winning any matches there, and almost never competing against any Black opponents.

Nelson claimed to have captured the title in New York once he arrived in California, but he had started the practice of carrying around championship belts in 1930, and when he first began making appearances as a "colored champion," he told a very different origin story as to how he had acquired his trophy.

According to a 1933 article in *The Detroit Tribune*, Nelson arrived in Toledo, Ohio and entered a tournament "to decide a colored heavyweight champion of the universe," and when it was over, referee Raymond Laraux of Montreal "was tapping him on the shoulder" to present him with "the gold belt, emblematic of the World's colored heavyweight championship. This was in 1930."

The fictitious tournament was allegedly held by "the Terminal Athletic Club of Toledo" and was sanctioned by the National Wrestling Athletic Club of Toledo, within which Nelson was purportedly "one of the seven Negroes holding membership."

Setting aside for a moment that the belt in Claybourne's possession first emerged when he defeated Seelie Samara for it in Pasadena, the matches required to have substantiated Claybourne's false chain of custody for his title would have been impossible. Rufus Jones had never wrestled Nelson, so there is no established connection between the two men, and Jones and Claybourne certainly hadn't wrestled one another since 1942.

Even more provocative is the fact that Claybourne was making a direct claim that his Negro world heavyweight title was sanctioned by the New York State Boxing and Wrestling Commission, more commonly referred to as the New York State Athletic Commission.

While it was true that the NYSAC had recognized a world heavyweight wrestling champion beginning in 1929, the Commission had fallen out of the practice of formally recognizing a world wrestling champion by the late 1930s. This actually created some embarrassment for wrestling legend Jim Londos in September 1939 when he produced a diamond-studded wrestling title belt to the press — in Honolulu of all places — and claimed that it was sanctioned by the NYSAC.

"It seems to be that the New York commission recognizes no wrestling championships, and therefore could not have given [Londos] that 'international' title trophy," reported *The St. Louis Dispatch*.

Regardless, Claybourne was seemingly following in the footsteps of Londos and claiming phony NYSAC recognition of his world Negro title on Hawaiian soil.

"Claybourne makes his home in Boston, Mass., and played prep baseball before he became interested in wrestling. He followed the mat sport closely, and his idol was Ed (Strangler) Lewis," added *The Advertiser*. "He prefers straight wrestling and uses the drop kick and other modern tactics. One of his best holds is the leg and body sweep."

As evidence of his conquests in Australia, Claybourne showed off newspaper clippings, with the contents of some articles suggesting that he received "250 fan mails" after his matches.

On the day of Claybourne's return in the main event tag team bout at the Civic Auditorium, *The Advertiser* shortened the name of Claybourne's championship for simplicity's sake, referring to it as "the New York heavyweight championship belt."

"Powerful and strong, Claybourne specializes in leverage holds and uses dropkicks to set up falls," added *The Advertiser*. "In Shikina, he has a partner who combines judo with leverage holds."

The Claybourne-Shikina tandem enjoyed a successful debut, with Claybourne scoring the deciding fall to capture his very first win on Hawaiian soil.

"Claybourne, recent arrival from Australia, seemed to have adopted some of the down-under kangaroo style, as his jumping and versatility against the Grable-Lott duo made him look like a Mexican jumping bean," observed *The Star-Bulletin*.

Grable and Lott got off to a quick start, scoring a pinfall on Shikina at 14:55. Eventually, Shikina was able to even the score before handing things over to Claybourne.

"At this point, Claybourne furnished the action and was chasing Lott around the ring with flying drop kicks," continued *The Star-Bulletin*. "He pinned Lott for the deciding fall."

No sooner had the October 10th contest reached its conclusion than Al Karasick announced that Claybourne would be headlining at the following Sunday's show against Red Vagnone. Shikina had been the established number-one contender to Hawaii's top title, but Claybourne had leapfrogged him in one night, relegating Shikina and Grable — both former holders of the Hawaiian championship — to the semifinal slot.

"Jack Claybourne, holder of the New York State gold belt as world Negro heavyweight champion battles Red Vagnone in the top skirmish," advertised *The Star-Bulletin*. "Claybourne made a big hit with local fans in the team match Sunday. Agile and clever, he uses dropkicks and forearm blows. In Vagnone, he meets a rugged, experienced battler who is familiar with every style of wrestling."

On the day of Claybourne's October 17th match with Vagnone, *The Advertiser* printed a crystal clear photo of Claybourne with his title belt. The caption read, "Jack Claybourne, wearing the gold belt presented to him by the New York wrestling commission for winning the Negro heavyweight championship, is the latest mat sensation here. He meets Red Vagnone tonight at the Civic Auditorium."

The fact that Claybourne arrived ready-made with his own championship belt seemed to work extremely well for him with respect to his appeal and promotability. There was also the matter of his uniqueness. Of the prominent Murderers'

Row members who raised the standard for Black excellence in wrestling, he was the first to appear in Hawaii.

The only time a Black wrestler had performed in Hawaii in anything close to a featured role prior to Claybourne, it has been "Tiger" Jack Nelson — whose real name was Theodore Roosevelt Reed — wrestling under the guise of an Ethiopian known as Juan "Selassie" Amnerus. If the intent had been to uphold some semblance of mystery through the use of an Ethiopian gimmick, it failed immediately; Nelson's more recognizable ring name was exposed by *The Star-Bulletin* at the very beginning of the three months he spent in Honolulu in the spring of 1937.

"Way back in 1929, or thereabouts, Jack Nelson, as they name him in America, embarked on a promising pro fighting career," printed *The Star-Bulletin*. "He took on the tough boys in and around Detroit, Toledo, St. Louis, Omaha, and even down south. In 1929 they showed him that money flowed in pro wrestling and he turned grappler. Amnerus made such a showing that he took the world's colored heavyweight championship."

Amusingly, aside from a handful of bouts between Tiger Nelson and Gorilla Parker in Michigan and Ontario very early in the 1930s, there is little evidence that Nelson participated in many matches with a colored title of any kind up for grabs, save for his retirement bout against George Godfrey in 1939. Moreover, Nelson's bouts with Parker were contested for the colored middleweight title, as Parker — who was incredibly well-muscled for the time period — was rather diminutive in stature.

Regardless, given the fact that Tiger Nelson played the role of an untitled Ethiopian during his Hawaiian visit in the 1930s, Claybourne would represent the first top-tier Black American wrestler to be presented as both an American and a champion in the Hawaiian islands. Against Vagnone, he would acquire his first-ever singles victory in the territory.

"The main event went to the popular colored wrestler, Jack Claybourne, over Red Vagnone," stated *The Star-Bulletin*.

"By virtue of one fall, the new arrival Claybourne had his hand raised. With only about six minutes remaining in the match, Claybourne used the back-body hold coupled with slams and pinned Vagnone in 38 minutes 52 seconds."

Right after he defeated Vagnone, Claybourne was booked for a match against the man who had been his tag team partner just one week prior, Oki Shikina. The two would compete in the second of two main events on the October 24th show, sharing the top billing with a match between Hawaiian junior heavyweight titlist Hisao Tanaka, and his challenger Jimmy Lott.

"Sensational in his last two matches, Claybourne has won a big following," printed *The Advertiser* on the eve of the event. "His dropkicks, reverse body slams and other tactics should keep Shikina on his toes. But Claybourne also faces a tough test as Shikina is a cagey, experienced grappler who knows all the tricks of wrestling."

The bout between Claybourne and Shikina was ruled a draw in a manner that was strange in light of how the rules would typically have been applied under the circumstances that unfolded. *The Star-Bulletin* reported that Claybourne had uncorked a flying dropkick from the apron of the ring out to the floor, striking Shikina while the Japanese wrestler was standing amongst the spectators in the first row.

Rather than counting Shikina out of the ring when he failed to return, or disqualifying Claybourne for striking Shikina with a maneuver that might have been construed as illegal in 1948, the referee instead opted to rule the bout a draw.

No mention was made of Shikina's prior status as the top contender for the *Ring Magazine* belt, nor did it seem to matter. Despite not officially winning the bout with Shikina, the perceived supremacy of Claybourne at the conclusion of the encounter seems to have been enough to vault him into immediate title contention. The main event of the last wrestling show of October would have Hisao Tanaka defending the *Ring Magazine* belt against Jack Claybourne.

When constructing promotional materials for the title showdown, Karasick first presented advertisements bearing only the face of a smiling Jack Claybourne. Karasick also made the curious choice to double down on the claim that Claybourne was "undefeated in championship matches" over the course of his career. The claim was *barely* true from the standpoint of the Hawaii territory itself, since Claybourne had recorded a draw and a loss in his first two singles matches in Hawaii against California champion Maurice Chapelle and Hawaiian champion Ted "Tiger" Travis, albeit in non-title matches.

Outside of Hawaii, wrestling fans would have been hard pressed to find a wrestler with a worse record in title matches than Claybourne up until that point, simply looking at the raw numbers. Setting aside two dozen or so matches Claybourne had participated in with a theoretical Black wrestling championship on the line — very few of which were represented by a physical belt or trophy — Claybourne had competed for championships in many of the territories he had visited, and had *never* emerged from any of those matches wearing a title belt.

Ahead of the title bout between Tanaka and Claybourne, Al Karasick brought Claybourne with him to a meeting of the Quarterback Club, which was a weekly luncheon where all sports of note in Hawaii were discussed.

When Claybourne was introduced, he spoke up and said, "It's a pleasure to be in Hawaii. I have run into prejudices on the mainland, and it's certainly a fine thing the way different races get along here."

In his summary of the meeting, Dan McGuire of *The Advertiser* credited Claybourne with "pulling mat fans into the auditorium in increasing numbers every Sunday," and it's safe to say that with Black Americans contributing to well under one percent of Hawaii's 499,000 residents at the time, Claybourne's box office appeal could not be explained in terms of his ability to appeal to a single demographic to which he could claim membership.

Ironically, there were no news articles published in Hawaiian newspapers referencing how historically significant a Claybourne title victory over Tanaka would be with respect to racial breakthroughs on the wrestling scene in general, and on the Hawaiian title scene in particular.

This time, in his 17th year as a professional wrestler, Claybourne would successfully summit the mountain, besting Tanaka on Sunday, October 31st, and becoming the Hawaiian junior heavyweight champion and the holder of the *Ring Magazine* title belt in front of the largest Civic Auditorium crowd of the year.

"The agile and clever Claybourne, who also holds the world's Negro heavyweight title, proved too strong and quick for Tanaka, one of the outstanding wrestlers to show in Honolulu this year," observed *The Advertiser*. "Tanaka, unable to keep any of his powerful holds on Claybourne, attempted to rough up the challenger, but only succeeded in spurring his opponent to greater heights."

Claybourne's victory was also a dominant one, as he scored two consecutive falls on the vanquished Japanese titleholder without surrendering a fall in return. Fittingly, both of the falls would come by way of dropkicks set up by tried and true tactics in Claybourne's arsenal.

"Claybourne applied the first fall in 16 min. 33 seconds with a flying dropkick and a body press. He leapfrogged over the referee and caught Tanaka by surprise with his dropkick," continued *The Advertiser*. "Another dropkick gave Claybourne the clincher at 5 min. and 13 seconds later. As Tanaka attempted to kick him out, Claybourne cut loose with a flying tackle from the apron of the ring, then dropkicked Tanaka clear across the ring to set up the body press."

Gracious in defeat, Tanaka personally supervised the coronation of the man who supplanted him as champion by placing the *Ring Magazine* title belt around Gentleman Jack's waist.

Promoter Al Karasick announced the next day that Chief Little Wolf would provide the first challenge to

Claybourne's supremacy, with *The Star-Bulletin* noting that Little Wolf was a "comebacker" — a wrestler who had previously appeared in Hawaii prior to the outbreak of World War II.

Advertised as a full-blooded Navajo Indian from Trinidad, Colorado, Little Wolf was actually Ventura Tenorio, who truly was born in Colorado, but was of Mexican descent. He had toured Hawaii in 1934, 1937, and 1939 before returning to face Claybourne.

Ahead of the non-title bout, Little Wolf cited his track record as the reason why he didn't believe Claybourne would offer him a serious challenge.

"I met the champions in each division and held the heavyweight crown once," Little Wolf told *The Advertiser*. "I've met them all — Jimmy Londos, Gus Sonneberg, Man Mountain Dean, George Zaharias, Jumping Joe Savoldi, and every one of the big name wrestlers."

Little Wolf also used the interview as an opportunity to remind everyone that he is often credited with the invention of the Indian Deathlock submission hold, "one of the best holds in wrestling today."

"I got the idea for the hold from Geronimo," added Little Wolf.

Simultaneous to this announcement, Karasick also teased that Claybourne should expect to face "Mormon Mauler" Brother Frank if he successfully turned aside the challenge of Little Wolf. Frank would be exchanging holds with Oki Shikina on the undercard of the Claybourne-Little Wolf show.

The contest between Claybourne and Little Wolf went the distance, with Claybourne being awarded the victory by way of a decision rendered by referee Charlie Carr. Each combatant registered a fall during the match before the 45-minute time limit elapsed.

"The match started slow but took the turn of being one of the best matches in a long time," reported *The Star-Bulletin*. "Claybourne took the opening fall with a series of body flips and a flying dropkick. Claybourne pinned the Indian chief with a body press in 36 minutes. The Indian grappler, who entered the ring with his traditional colorful regalia, evened the match with his famous Indian deathlock hold. The chief's hold came in 6 minutes 30 seconds."

With another victory under his belt, albeit a less impressive win than the title-clincher, Claybourne turned his attention to Brother Frank. Prior to the bout, the Hawaiian newspapers predicted that the bout would be decided by the wrestler whose style dictated the action — the speed and agility of Claybourne, or the aggressive roughhousing tactics of Frank.

What ultimately transpired during that bout was a shocking turn of events, and while it may have been intended to represent a one-time ironic twist for the sake of keeping a match entertaining and unpredictable, it would definitively mark the moment that Gentleman Jack dramatically altered his approach to professional wrestling.

"The match was a torrid tussle, with Claybourne pitting his speed and skill against the Utah grappler's rough tactics," reported *The Advertiser*. "Brother Frank gained the first fall in 17:50 with a corner piledriver, followed by body slams and a press."

From this moment on, *The Advertiser*'s account of the match reads *identically* to the description of a match headlined by Rufus Jones in 1942.

"Infuriated by his opponent's wild tactics, Claybourne began butting Brother Frank with his head and opened a cut over the left eye," continued *The Advertiser*. "Claybourne kept up his butting tactics until Brother Frank began reeling dizzily and virtually helplessly. The referee then intervened and stopped the match, awarding the fall to Claybourne. Frank was unable to continue, so Claybourne was given the match on a medical disqualification."

Every element of the third fall reads as if it was lifted straight from the playbook of the most influential Black heel wrestler in history. It was Jones' custom to drop an early fall to an opponent who was well versed at the technical aspects of wrestling, only for Jones to become angry and bludgeon his adversary with repeated headbutts. The fact that a babyface aerialist like Claybourne would replicate Jones' match-ending sequence beat for beat was undoubtedly shocking.

With Claybourne showing signs of fully realizing the stylistic reimagining he had teased twice before in his career, Karasick lined up Texan Dick Raines as the champion's opponent in a one-fall, non-title match during the November 21st show. Similar to Little Wolf — who claimed invention of the Indian deathlock — Raines credited himself for the invention of the over-the-knee backbreaker submission hold.

In the end, the backbreaker of Raines proved to be a fruitless maneuver. The match between the two concluded in a time-limit draw, but Claybourne proved his resilience by repeatedly springing back to life regardless of the damage Raines inflicted upon him.

"Raines couldn't pin Claybourne with his backbreaker hold," reported *The Star-Bulletin*. "Three times he wrapped the Negro star around his knee, and each time Claybourne worked himself free."

To mount his own offense, Claybourne began the match with his customary dropkicks, and also had Raines in jeopardy with a stepover toehold. However, the coverage from *The Advertiser* made it clear that Claybourne's actions against Brother Frank had not been an isolated occurrence.

"Claybourne opened a cut over Raines' right eye when he started butting in the final minutes of the skirmish," stated *The Advertiser*.

Once again, Brother Frank would be served up for Claybourne in a non-title affair for the November 28th event, which was also the first show after Thanksgiving. Leading into the show, *The Advertiser* made its first real acknowledgement that Claybourne had a trusty new weapon in his arsenal.

"Claybourne said he was prepared for Brother Frank's roughhouse tactics and hopes to dropkick his way to victory," offered *The Advertiser*. "A clever and agile grappler, Claybourne also uses headbutts to advantage."

Essentially blending his style with that of Rufus Jones, Claybourne had created a brand of island fusion that combined his gymnastic routine of dropkicks, flips and shuffles with the brutal headbutting elements of Jones. Housed within the powerful 6'1" body of Claybourne, it was a style that was equal parts flashy and threatening.

Two days before the Claybourne-Frank non-title bout ever took place, Al Karasick declared that Claybourne would defend the Hawaiian junior heavyweight title against the winner of the undercard bout between Dick Raines and Chief Little Wolf. In essence, with Claybourne wrestling to a draw with Raines and a victory by way of referee's decision over Little Wolf, both men could claim to be worthy contenders for Claybourne's championship.

For only the second time in a long time, the report of a Jack Claybourne victory included no mention of dropkicks. Instead, Claybourne relied upon the use of his head to shed his opponent's blood and force the referee to stop the match.

"In the second part of the main event, Jack Claybourne took the measure of Brother Frank with two straight falls," recorded *The Star-Bulletin*. "Claybourne copped the opening fall in 16 minutes 20 seconds with a shoulder hold. Claybourne used his head, and Referee Rubberman Higami halted the match as Brother Frank received a cut over his right eye."

In short order, Jack Claybourne found himself perched atop the hierarchy of pro wrestling in the Pacific. It was an unprecedented position for a Black wrestler to find himself in. As justifiably optimistic about his future as Jack probably felt during that period of time, he was about to get a sobering reminder for how drastically things can deteriorate, even for those who set precedents.

## 14 - The Can't-Miss Prospect

The confirmation that Jack Claybourne would officially be defending the *Ring Magazine* belt against Chief Little Wolf during Hawaii's first December show of 1948 was accompanied by news that one of Claybourne's foremost in-ring rivals had arrived in Hawaii. Seelie Samara — referred to as "Sellie Samara" in the Hawaiian newspapers — had been brought in to face Leo Wallick on the undercard of Claybourne's title defense against Little Wolf.

Expectations were immediately established that Claybourne and Samara would be on a collision course regardless as to the outcome of the Claybourne-Little Wolf match. *The Star-Bulletin* rightly informed readers about the sort of regional wrestling history they were witnessing, stating that for the first time ever at a Hawaiian wrestling event, "two outstanding Negro stars are appearing on one show."

"Claybourne holds a gold belt presented to him in New York when he won the 'Negro heavyweight mat title,'" *The Star-Bulletin* reminded its readers. "Samara says he is after the belt."

More accurately, Samara was attempting to recover the same physical belt that he had lost to Claybourne in Pasadena, California, but which was the personal property of Claybourne and would therefore never leave his side for very long.

Karasick later held an interview alongside Samara, and as the promoter explained the significance of landing a star of Samara's caliber to the press, he also doubled down on his intention of getting Claybourne and Samara in the ring for the first bout in the history of Hawaii featuring two Black competitors.

"I know the fans will see a great wrestler in Samara, who came to Hawaii with the special intention of challenging Jack Claybourne to a match for the world's Negro wrestling championship," Karasick explained to *The Advertiser*. "Both claim the title. Claybourne has a belt presented to him by the

New York commission. The mixup will be cleared if these two sign for a match."

With his title bout against Chief Little Wolf nearly being overshadowed by the promise of a future bout between himself and Samara, Claybourne still managed to score a decisive victory over his faux Native American opponent. This occurred even though Claybourne once again fell prey to Little Wolf's Indian deathlock to surrender the opening fall of the match.

"The colored mat star evened matters after 4 minutes 38 seconds with a flying drop kick and a body press," reported *The Star-Bulletin*. "After breaking the chief's Indian death lock twice, once by grabbing the ropes and the second by butting, Claybourne won the deciding fall in 8 minutes 45 seconds."

In the featured undercard match, Samara replicated Claybourne's feat of besting Brother Frank, ending matters in a little over 17 minutes with a "flying bear hug and body press."

To no one's surprise, Samara and Claybourne were booked to share the ring during the next Civic Auditorium event on December 12th. The unanticipated twist was the revelation that the two would be paired together as members of the same team.

Before they would make Hawaii history as the first Black wrestlers to compete against one another — and in a main-event title match no less — the two Murderers' Row members would make history of a different kind as teammates on the first Black tag team in the history of the territory.

Karasick made the announcement of the team-up subsequent to disclosing that the December 12th show would be a charity event, with all of the proceeds turned over to the Honolulu Council of Social Agencies.

"I have talked to the wrestlers, and they are all anxious to appear on the big show, and they have promised to go all-out in giving the people who support the matches a thrilling evening," said Karasick.

In the pre-match hype, the respective points of origin for Claybourne and Samara were named as Boston,

Massachusetts and Kansas City, Missouri, and it's easy to imagine that the two probably shared at least one laugh about the coincidence.

While it was true that Claybourne maintained a home in Boston at the apartment building on Shawmut Avenue, he was a Missouri native. On the other hand, Samara spent the majority of his adult life in Massachusetts, began his wrestling career there, and was still claiming Boston as his place of residence in the 1940 U.S. Census despite the fact that the census taker found him in Chicago in the company of his wife and four of his children.

"We're not rough and we prefer wrestling, but we won't be pushed around," Samara warned the pair's opponents, Dick Raines and Brother Frank. "We can rough it up if we have to."

Claybourne and Samara drew with Raines and Frank, with the Hawaiian junior heavyweight champion absorbing the pinfall loss for his team after a series of backbreakers from Raines. The two Black stars then double teamed Frank to score the equalizing fall before the time limit expired.

By pinning Claybourne in tag team action, Raines earned himself another singles match against the holder of the *Ring Magazine* belt, which would be scheduled for December 19th. Samara would also be featured on the show in a semifinal bout against Chief Little Wolf.

During an event that was held for the benefit of the Salvation Army's Christmas Fund, Claybourne suffered a serious blow to his status as the best wrestler in Hawaii, and also to his position as the best Black wrestler on the island. While Samara defeated Chief Little Wolf cleanly with a double-arm stretch, Claybourne lost to Raines after 34 minutes of a one-fall, non-title match.

"Claybourne, holder of the Hawaiian mat belt, was pinned by Raines after a series of back breakers and a body press," reported *The Star-Bulletin*.

After losing to Raines, Claybourne had his follow-up match against Henry "Bomber" Kulkovich demoted to the semi-final position of the post-Christmas show featuring Raines and Samara matching power in the main event. In fact, news coverage throughout that week cast Claybourne in the now unfamiliar position as being the fighter requesting a title match with Raines if that's what it would take to lure his opponent back into the ring for a chance at redemption.

A photographer from *The Star-Bulletin* captured an image of Jack enjoying a massage in Kapahulu as part of the preparations for his bout with Kulkovich just in time for its Christmas issue.

Kulkovich happened to be making a return to Hawaii after one year away. When asked about his upcoming match with Claybourne by *Advertiser* reporter Dan McGuire, Kulkovich seemingly spent more time talking up his expertise in the kitchen, and especially when it came to baking delicious lemon cream pies.

In his December 26th bout with Kulkovich, Jack was disqualified for whipping the tough New Yorker like the very same lemon cream used in one of his pies when the action spilled to the outside of the ring, earning the champion his second consecutive loss in singles competition.

"The New Yorker was the rougher and tougher, but Claybourne made the mistake of knocking the Bomber's head against the ring post outside the ropes and dropkicking him on the ringside floor," stated *The Star-Bulletin*. "The disqualification fall came in 29:57, and the two men went the remaining distance to a 45 minute time limit without a fall."

Samara maintained his momentum with a clean defeat of Dick Raines, the very man who had pinned Claybourne the prior week. Despite the mixed success of Samara and Claybourne at the show, their overall achievements in the Hawaiian territory at that stage of 1948 were groundbreaking, and only served to underscore the tragedy of what was happening during that very same time period in Southern California.

On December 30th, *The California Eagle* offered the first report about the death of a man whose name they anglicized as

Kemal Abd-Ur-Rahman, but who wrestling fans recognized to be Reginald Siki. According to the account provided to *The Eagle*, Siki dropped dead at the feet of his wife Mildred while she was at her place of employment.

"Rahman, who was 48, and who once held the California State wrestling championship, had gone to the Bel Air home of singer Tony Martin by whom his wife is employed for a holiday visit," stated *The Eagle*. "When she opened the door, he said, 'Mildred — I—,' then he gasped and fell to the floor."

**Joe Louis with Reginald Siki**

*The Eagle* described Siki as a wrestler who'd enjoyed an excellent career that "ended last June due to an injury he received while wrestling." Siki's wife expressed "disappointment over the neglect shown her husband following his injury."

To refer to Siki as 48 years of age is to stretch the limits of his achieved age to the fullest extent. He was born on

December 28, 1899, and passed away on December 24, 1948, just four days shy of his 49th birthday.

*The Minneapolis Spokesman* supplied additional details about Siki's life, including confirming the fact that Siki had been born Reginald Berry in Kansas City. It also mentioned that he had attended Lincoln High School, which is where he first learned to wrestle and appeared as a pro wrestler, likely under the name of "The Snake" Leonard Rabinette.

"He found that American Negroes were not allowed to participate in professional wrestling in America," added *The Spokesman*. "He decided to go to Europe. Over there he changed his name and was known as Siki the Senegalese. When he returned to America, he was booked against the biggest wrestlers in the business."

Siki's funeral was held at Douglas Temple in Los Angeles, and his body was interred at Evergreen Cemetery.

Aside from wrestlers who were famous on the basis of world championship reigns, outstanding box office success, and sustained fame, there were a scant few performers within the professional wrestling business of the 1940s and earlier whose feats and accomplishments were preserved for historical reverence, regardless of race. This being the case, the passing of the man who forged the mold for how a mainstream Black wrestler could establish themselves as an appreciable draw went unappreciated at the time of Siki's passing.

Then again, the features that helped Siki to stand out during his career — possessing above average height with a chiseled physique and a unique appearance, combined with an exotic origin, technical wrestling prowess, remarkable athleticism, and the ability to competently speak half a dozen languages — would almost guarantee a main-event-level push to any wrestler in any era.

While Siki obviously happened upon some of these traits by dint of hard work and the company he kept, it seemingly required a can't-miss prospect like Reginald "Siki" Berry to make the case that Black wrestlers could effectively intrigue a mainstream audience.

As 1949 began, advertisements for appearances by Rufus Jones in Provo and Brigham City, Utah appeared in the newspapers, but both *The Daily Herald* of Provo and *The Box-Elder News Journal* divulged that Jones had telegraphed matchmaker Dave Reynold to inform him that he was injured and would be unable to attend.

When Jones returned to wrestling for promoter Jack Carter in Vermont in February 1949, he once again resurrected his persona of Tiger Flowers. *The Sunday News* of Vermont dutifully warned fans that Flowers "has lost none of his zest for the illegal means of gaining the upper hand and is one of wrestling's public enemies."

This would have been a curious statement if Flowers had completely dropped off the face of the earth as a performer since the end of 1944. However, any wrestling fans who'd traveled from the Midwest to Vermont and scanned the newspaper would have recognized the unmistakable visage of Rufus Jones being displayed in *The Daily News* of Burlington, labeled as Tiger Flowers yet again.

Accompanying Flowers on this trip would be another Black wrestler, Don Blackman. While Blackman had established himself in several regions of the country after first challenging Rufus Jones in Michigan, including a historically significant tour of the Mid-Atlantic states with Don Kindred as his opponent, he was a total newcomer to Vermont.

*The Daily News* also offered fans ample warning about the tactics Blackman might use, adding "not too much is known about Blackman, except that he is highly recommended by Flowers."

*The Burlington Free Press* added that Blackman was "the prized pupil of Flowers, educated in the ring culture that Flowers likes," and also inserted the false detail that Flowers "has been touring the world" and had just returned from Australia "where he won 28 consecutive bouts."

During this return to Vermont, Joe Godfrey eliminated any pretense that the persona of Tiger Flowers was anything other than Rufus Jones wrestling under an alternate alias. *The*

*Burlington Free Press* illustrated how Flowers, during his February 23rd bout at the Burlington Auditorium, "stunned both Referee Jacques Trudeau and his opponent by cracking them on the head with his own," thereby earning a disqualification.

After carrying out repeated bludgeonings of his opponents in like manner, the typed descriptions of Flowers' ring tactics continued to read as duplicates of the descriptions for Rufus Jones' matches, except with the name Tiger Flowers offered as a substitute.

"A real cutie in the ring, Flowers gets away with most of his rough stuff, fooling even the referee," submitted *The St. Albans Daily Messenger*. "Flowers' most dangerous weapon is his head butt, which weakens and dazes his opponents so that they are easy to pin. Holding him by the shoulders, he repeatedly cracks his forehead against his opponent, apparently suffering no ill effects himself."

Before he took on popular George Cagney in April, Flowers' style was summarized by *The Daily News* as that of a grappler who "seldom uses an orthodox wrestling hold, weakening his opponents by means of elbow smashes, eye-gouging and kicking, then finally putting the finishing touches on by means of his head butt."

The press in Vermont offered no immediate coverage as to the fallout of the April 8th battle between Flowers and Cagney, but the promotion for the rematch offered through *The Daily News* described a scenario where the match "had to be stopped by the police on hand as spectators got into the melee with one of them being KO'd." *The Daily Messenger* added that "the boys in blue" would be "on special guard" during the rematch in light of what happened during their first skirmish.

This final bout, which turned out to be Flowers' swan song in Vermont, was reportedly underwhelming in light of the battle that preceded it. Referee Trudeau "thumbed out the ugly looking Negro for illegal tactics, and for continuously assaulting the third man outside the ring."

"Flowers, as punchy as they come, persisted in using a bottle cap on Cagney's face, and when Trudeau attempted to curtail this bit of nonsense, he was dumped onto the canvas," added *The Daily News*. "Up to that time each had taken a fall."

By now it should come as no surprise that shortly after Tiger Flowers disappeared from working his relaxed schedule in Burlington, Vermont — a location within a tantalizingly comfortable drive from Joe Godfrey's hometown of Malden, Massachusetts — Rufus Jones suddenly reemerged from a multi-month hiatus.

Still holding the belt identifying him as the champion of Hawaii, Jack Claybourne received what at least appeared to be a much needed break from singles competition for his first appearance of 1949, as he concluded his second full month as the Hawaiian champion. Instead of appearing in an ordinary match, he would be one of six participants in a New Year's battle royal, alongside Seelie Samara, Leo Wallick, Dick Raines, Basher McDonald, and Bomber Kulkovich.

During his efforts to promote the New Year's event, promoter Al Karasick explained to *The Advertiser* that he sought an opinion about Claybourne's sudden and frequent use of headbutts, from Northern California wrestling promoter Frank Malcewicz.

"The only hold that is universally barred as illegal is the stranglehold," submitted Malcewicz. "Of course, eye gouging, hair pulling and such tactics are not permitted, but shoulder and head butts are rather common practices. They have been practiced here as well as all other parts of the country. The most effective way to discourage headbutting is to butt right back. So far as professional wrestling around here is concerned, it is recognized around here as part of the game."

When this question was posed, it also created a stir in parts of California where Claybourne had been a strong attraction.

"Claybourne's use of the head to butt opponents groggy has divided Honolulu into two camps, one for him, and one against," wrote Russ Newland of the Associated Press. "Professional wrestling is something in which we are decidedly inexpert, but we never heard of the use of the head as a battering ram as one of the finer points of the game. Whether legal or not, the disputed method of attack is filling Honolulu's Civic Auditorium practically every time Claybourne wrestles."

Dave Beronio, sports editor of *The Times Herald* of Solano County, California, was apparently far more familiar with Claybourne's established routine, and seemed stunned at the tactics the Gentleman had chosen to adopt in Hawaii.

"Claybourne, a wrestler well known to Vallejoans through his many appearances here in recent years, is currently the sensation of the Hawaiian Islands," wrote Beronio. "'Jumping Jack,' as he was known here through his mighty leaps around the ring, and at his opponents, is currently the hit of the Honolulu shows with his latest tactics. Seems as though Jack has quit jumping in favor of using his head as a battering ram."

Claybourne celebrated the start of 1949 by winning the six-man battle royal. As opposed to an over-the-top-rope battle royal, in which participants are eliminated by being hurled out of the ring and out to the arena floor, each wrestler needed to be pinned or submitted in order to lose.

Leo Wallick was reportedly the first wrestler dismissed from the fray, when four of his competitors piled on top of him to pin him. After Bomber Kulkovich was put out of commission with forearm blows four minutes later, Claybourne and Samara collaborated to pin Basher McDonald.

Whatever team strategy Claybourne and Samara attempted to implement against Dick Raines, it failed, and resulted in the elimination of Samara. From there, Raines and Claybourne wrestled for another 24 minutes, only for the bout to be stopped when Claybourne used his headbutts to open up a cut over Raines' right eye, prompting referee Charley Carr to call a halt to the action.

"The battle of the two finalists was a torrid affair, with Raines' rough tactics keeping Claybourne off balance for much of the time," reported *The Advertiser*. "But the acrobatic colored flash held his own with dropkicks and tricky holds, finally cornering the Texan in the blue corner to apply head butts until blood began streaming from a gash over his right eye."

With that victory, Claybourne had managed to achieve a relatively clean victory over Raines, who had bested him in a one-fall match. He also succeeded in irritating his ally Samara. Promoter Al Karasick gave the fans what they had apparently been begging for and booked a bout between Claybourne and Samara for the following week, with Claybourne's Negro world heavyweight championship belt on the line.

Karasick, in his efforts to promote the bout while ostensibly adhering to the rules governing weight classes, stipulated that only Claybourne's Negro heavyweight title would be up for grabs during the bout, as Samara was too heavy to qualify for a shot at the Hawaii junior heavyweight title.

This represents one of the few times when the weight limit was rigidly enforced; Dick Raines, who was routinely touted as a threat to the Hawaii junior heavyweight title was promoted at a weight of 235 pounds. Angered by the ruling, Samara was later quoted in *The Advertiser* as saying that he would claim the *Ring Magazine* belt regardless of Karasick's edict if he managed to defeat Claybourne.

As Claybourne and Samara prepared to make history as the first two Black wrestlers to face one another in Hawaii — and in a main event title match no less — the press positioned the contest as a duel between the speed, agility, and headbutts of Claybourne and the size and strength of Samara. They also repeated the false claim that Claybourne had defeated Rufus Jones in 1943 for that particular belt.

"Jack has brought along his championship belt for the occasion," wrote Dan McGuire of *The Advertiser*. "It was presented to him after he defeated Rufus Jones at New York in '43. Jones had been the second wearer, the original holder being Tiger Nelson in 1941, the first year the New York Wrestling and Boxing Commission had offered the belt. It is studded with 21 diamonds and is indeed a thing of beauty. No wonder Samara would like to fasten it around his middle."

**Claybourne and Samara in Hawaii**

When the day of the much anticipated showdown arrived, *The Advertiser* printed a photo of Claybourne and Samara together, along with an explanation as to why Samara had been making prior claims to being the rightful titleholder.

"Samara claims he was recognized as the champion in South Africa, and that he was trying to force a showdown with Claybourne for years," stated *The Advertiser*.

This represents an instance where indulging in some candor might have been a more effective promotional tactic. Specifically, Claybourne had won the belt from Samara in Pasadena in 1945, and the last time the two wrestled — which had been in a non-title match held only a few months prior in Sydney, Australia — Samara had defeated Claybourne cleanly.

This time, the outcome was reversed, as Claybourne triumphantly defended his championship, and made it clear that he was the most dominant wrestler in Hawaii, irrespective of race, ethnicity, or weight.

"The match went 14 minutes 37 seconds before a fall was registered. After clever exchanges and holds, Claybourne butted Samara against the ropes, and as the challenger reeled backwards, the Boston grappler cut loose with a flying dropkick," detailed *The Advertiser*. "Samara fell hard, hitting his head, and fell victim to a body press"

Nine minutes later, Samara downed Claybourne with a tactic similar to how he'd defeated him in Oregon, catching Jack in mid-air as the titleholder attempted a leapfrog, and slamming him to the mat to even the fall count at one apiece. This set the stage for a dramatic third fall with the Negro championship hanging in the balance.

"Claybourne came back strong and scored the deciding fall 7 min. 37 sec. later when he came off the ropes with a flying dropkick that landed flush on Samara's jaw," concluded *The Advertiser*. "Samara didn't know what hit him and was pinned easily."

Shortly after the Claybourne-Samara match, Hubert White of the Associated Negro Press tracked down Al Karasick to discuss Claybourne's success as a babyface in the main events of the promoter's cards, which was atypical, if not completely unprecedented.

"Claybourne is one of the greatest wrestlers of modern times," glowed Karasick. "He is as tough as they come. I only regret that at times Claybourne loses his head; when he does this you may rest assured that his opponent will get hurt."

Karasick also acknowledged that he had "yet to see one loved so much by the fans" as Claybourne, while White supplied the detail that the Samara-Claybourne tag bout had helped attract a crowd of 8,000 fans to the Civic Auditorium prior to the dissolution of their tag team and feud over the Negro belt.

As Samara crowed about wanting a rematch for the title, Claybourne would be preparing for his next test on January 16th against piledriver specialist Leo Wallick. This time, Claybourne would break his string of bad luck in non-title matches by defeating Wallick while surrendering no falls in return.

"Claybourne scored the only fall of the match with head butts and a body press after 43 minutes," said *The Star-Bulletin*. "The match was a test of skill and clever tactics until the final minutes when Claybourne opened up with slugging and headbutting tactics. In the last two minutes, Wallick almost caught Claybourne with a dropkick and a piledriver, but the clever Boston star held on until the final bell to gain a one fall decision."

Next to oppose Claybourne would be newcomer Kenny Ackles, a Canadian junior heavyweight who was billed as hailing from the champion's adopted hometown of Boston. The Saturday edition of *The Advertiser* would educate readers as to the training methods that the champion and challenger had been engaging in during their preparations to face one another.

"Kenny Ackles, newcomer from Boston, has been working out all week with barbells at the Nuuanu Y gym and was reported in excellent shape for his match with Jack Claybourne Sunday night at the Civic Auditorium," printed *The Advertiser*. "Claybourne, Hawaiian junior heavyweight champion, expects a tough match, and wound up training yesterday. He has been doing road work to strengthen his leg muscles. Both Claybourne and Ackles are among the fastest wrestlers in the country, and they should set a torrid pace"

Even when an extra five minutes was added to the end of the bout, resulting in it going for 50 minutes instead of the usual 45, the Claybourne-Ackles bout was still declared a time-limit draw.

"Their match was a thriller all the way, with both grapplers giving the crowd a fancy exhibition of what agility and skill could do to heighten the excitement," proclaimed *The Advertiser*. "Although Claybourne resorted to rough tactics occasionally, the match was a test of clever holds and skillful maneuvering. Ackles won the plaudits of the crowd with his stamina and fortitude. In the final minutes, he was caught in an Indian deathlock, but refused to give in, breaking the hold with a leg split."

Because 50 minutes hadn't been adequate time for Claybourne and Ackles to settle their differences, Al Karasick used this result as justification for extending the time limit of future main events to one hour, starting at the final show of January headlined by Claybourne and Bomber Kulkovich.

It turned out the extended time limit would be completely unnecessary. Claybourne ended the bout early, but then turned a victory into a defeat by once again conjuring up his best Rufus Jones impression.

"After using his head butts to open up a cut on Bomber Kulkovich's forehead, Claybourne was awarded the match when the referee stopped the action," reported *The Star-Bulletin*. "Claybourne, however, butted the referee, and continued to work on Kulkovich's injury. Frank Merrill, the referee, then reversed his stand and awarded the verdict to Kulkovich on a disqualification for unnecessary roughing."

Prior to the closing sequence, Kulkovich had turned the table on Jack by pinning him with a dropkick, to which the champion responded by dropping Kulkovich with an airplane spin and several flying tackles. He then headbutted Kulkovich out of the ring twice before Merrill attempted to halt the proceedings.

After the melee, Kulkovich complained to Dan McGuire of *The Advertiser*, and said, "I don't know if I was cut when Claybourne butted me, or when I fell out of the ring and hit my head on the timer's bell. Every time I wrestle with Claybourne, I wind up practically a hospital case."

Even though Jack had technically lost, he had escaped the month of January with his title reign intact, equalling the three-month reign of Reginald Siki for one of the longest individual title reigns by a Black wrestler with a wrestling territory's principal championship, and within striking distance of Samara's nearly six-month stint as Pacific Northwest champion in 1945.

Claybourne was given the following Sunday off, which is when Kenny Ackles topped Leo Wallick in a best-of-three-falls affair to obtain the number-one contendership and earn a shot at Claybourne's title on the eve of Valentine's Day.

While Claybourne and Ackles had wrestled for 50 minutes without a fall in their first encounter, they would squeeze three falls into just over 30 minutes this time around, with Claybourne pulling out moves not usually associated with him in order to win the bout.

After Ackles won the first fall by leaping over the top rope to shoulder tackle Claybourne down to the canvas, Claybourne evened the fall tally by skillfully reversing a short-arm scissors attempt by Ackles into a successful pinfall.

"The payoff fall came in 5 minutes 52 seconds when Claybourne used a combination of the giant swing coupled with a flying dropkick and a body press," reported *The Star-Bulletin*.

Claybourne was now midway through his fourth month as champion of the territory, and the irregular length of his title reign clearly wasn't lost on anyone since it came up as a topic during that week's luncheon meeting of the Quarterback Club, which was attended by Dan McGuire of *The Advertiser*.

With Claybourne, Ackles, Kulkovich, and the recently arrived Johnny Sapeda all in attendance, promoter Al Karasick addressed the room and said of Claybourne, "He's held the championship so long; I hope he gets beat."

In response, Claybourne simply said, "Everyone picks on me. Let 'em keep coming. I'm ready."

In the midst of the proceedings, someone in the audience asked Karasick about what factors were driving the sustained popularity of wrestling in Hawaii. In response, Karasick attributed the successful tenure of his promotion to the fact that he had populated his shows solely with credible male athletes.

"You can pack the house one or two times with freaks who weigh 600 pounds or women wrestlers, but in the end they kill wrestling," Karasick insisted.

Claybourne's next bout would be against Johnny Sepeda of San Jose, California. Sepeda claimed to be a former Los Angeles police officer of Portuguese descent, who learned to wrestle under the tutelage of his police department's jiu jitsu instructor.

Once again, even without his title officially being up for grabs, Claybourne defeated his opponent. Relying on his now familiar mixture of dropkicks and headbutts, Claybourne polished off Sepeda in the first fall. Presumably relying on his jiu jitsu experience, Sepeda upended Claybourne with "a spectacular reverse leg lock" to draw even with him, setting the stage for the climax.

"Claybourne came back 5 minutes 30 seconds later with body slams and a press for the deciding fall," stated *The Advertiser*. "However, he had to break out of several tight holds before he gained the clincher. Sepeda caught his opponent with the monkey flip and later with the backbreaker, but couldn't hold Claybourne down."

It's possible that Claybourne suffered some sort of injury during the Sepeda bout, as it was a rarity for him to conclude a bout with a body slam at this stage of his career. The very next week, the report of Claybourne's actions would read identically, as he defeated Kenny Ackles once again, relying on a series of bodyslams instead of either his customary dropkicks or headbutts to win the only fall of the bout.

Adding credence to the likelihood that Claybourne was nursing an injury is the fact that he was subsequently given a week off while Vic Christy and Johnny Sepeda competed on March 13th for a later opportunity to wrest the Hawaiian title from Claybourne. Christy won two falls with figure-four body scissor holds to earn a crack at ending Claybourne's title reign.

Jack would likewise become a victim to the body scissors, as he lost the first fall of their best-of-three-falls encounter in 12 minutes and 22 seconds. After suffering the loss in the first fall, Claybourne reacted quickly to save his run as the champion.

"The champion came back strong to win the second," said *The Star-Bulletin*. "Claybourne stopped Christy with a back body slam and a body press to win in 1 minute 51 seconds. The deciding fall came in 8 minutes 19 seconds as Claybourne, using his flying dropkicks, softened Christy for the body press."

The following week, Claybourne was forced to deal with the elbow smashes of newcomer Tommy O'Toole in a non-title match. Billed as an Irishman from Phoenix, Arizona with an extensive background in boxing and amateur wrestling, O'Toole earned his ring time with the champion by defeating Lofty Blomfield at the March 27th Civic Auditorium event.

The April 3rd show also featured three former holders of the *Ring Magazine* title belt who were returning to the island — Ted Travis, Lee Grable, and Jimmy Gonsalves. The clear implication was that Claybourne would have a fresh crop of qualified challengers lined up if he managed to retain his title for much longer.

Regardless of the top bout's non-title nature, Claybourne appeared to have returned to his high-flying form and had minimal difficulty with O'Toole, dispensing with him in two consecutive falls. Displaying his famed agility once again, Claybourne missed a flying tackle and went sailing through the ropes and out to the concrete floor. This resulted in a first-fall disqualification in just under seven minutes when O'Toole refused to allow Claybourne to return to the ring. It took Claybourne less than seven minutes of the second fall to bring the match to a close.

"The Boston star scored a pinfall in 6 min. 47 sec. after the rest period, using head butts and drop kicks to rock O'Toole groggy before applying a press," stated *The Advertiser*.

The next day, Claybourne's level of competition took a significant leap in perceived quality when it was revealed that his next title challenger would be Ted "Tiger" Travis. This bout would represent an opportunity at redemption for Claybourne, since Travis had handed Claybourne his first loss in Hawaii back in the spring of 1948, when Claybourne unsuccessfully challenged Travis in a championship match.

In his first title defense against the former Hawaiian titleholder, Claybourne had his hand raised in victory. The champion earned the first fall with a flying headscissors and a body press before succumbing to a reverse body slam from Travis. Claybourne then closed the show with the maneuver that had become his go-to method when things got rough.

"Claybourne, 'the champ,' came back with head butts and a body press to win the deciding fall in 4 minutes 37 second," reported *The Star-Bulletin*.

The use of the headbutt would be central to Claybourne's next title defense, which would be against "Blazing" Ben Sherman. It was proffered that if any wrestler could survive the onslaught of headbutts from Claybourne and reciprocate in kind, it was Sherman.

"Mr. Jack Claybourne, the Territorial professional wrestling champion, has been noted for dishing out headaches — and we mean it literally — to other members of the mat profession," wrote Dan McGuire in his editorial column of *The Advertiser*. "Go ahead and chortle, you sophisticated critics, but don't get in the way of one of Claybourne's headbutts if you want to keep your head."

McGuire then reminded his readers that Sherman — the reigning Pacific Coast light heavyweight champion, who had recently acquired his title from Jack O'Riley — was a prolific headbutter in his own right, and had demonstrated his headbutting tendencies in Hawaiian rings during prior visits.

The April 17th bout between the pair of titleholders was an outright bloodbath that culminated in a 45-minute time-limit draw. Even without earning a clear victory, Claybourne appeared to be dominant over Sherman, and emerged as the visual victor of the headbutting duel.

"The biggest crowd of the season saw the Pacific Coast light heavyweight champion finish on his feet despite the fact that he was bleeding from at least two cuts on his face as the result of head-butting tactics," printed *The Advertiser*. "There was no fall in the 45-minute time limit battle. Claybourne, holding a decided weight advantage over his more experienced opponent, started the head-butting tactics, and Sherman began to retaliate in the final minutes of their turbulent skirmish. The tempo of the match was so furious that both grapplers repeatedly tossed each other out of the ring and continued their brawling on the auditorium floor."

To his credit, Sherman had been scheduled to make an appearance at the subsequent luncheon of the Quarterback Club, but continued to sell the damage from his match with Claybourne. He failed to appear at the event, and in his absence it was announced that he required additional time to recover from the damage the Hawaiian junior heavyweight champion had inflicted upon his skull.

Claybourne watched from the sidelines during the April 24th show at the Civic Auditorium as Sherman regained the use of his head and battered Kenny Ackles with a series of headbutts reminiscent of Claybourne's routine.

Once again, a non-title bout between the two territorial titleholders was scheduled. Two weeks after their initial encounter, the result would be no different, as the men battled to yet another standstill. Viewed in light of the pattern that Claybourne's career had followed up until this point, the outcome could understandably be considered a moral victory for him. He had been so unsuccessful in title bouts on the U.S. mainland for 17 years that any outcome presenting him as a titleholder of equal standing to the champion of another U.S. wrestling territory was an unqualified triumph.

Claybourne was publicly gracious about the outcome. When Dan McGuire of *The Advertiser* caught up with the champion while he was waiting to have his picture taken with Joe Louis, who was visiting the island, Claybourne remarked, "That Sherman has the hardest head in the world. Usually when I butts 'em, they go down. But when I butted Sherman, *I* went down!"

Tasked with covering these events, Associated Negro Press correspondent Hubert H. White filed yet another story about Gentleman Jack. Inadvertently giving Claybourne an elevation in status to "world junior heavyweight wrestling champion" — which was not unreasonable considering how frequently that label had adorned the top titles of wrestling territories with smaller populations — White delivered word of Claybourne's exploits and his unprecedented representation of Black American wrestling success to the U.S. mainland.

"Claybourne leaves his opponents — white, Japanese, Filipino, and Negro — helpless (many times bleeding), as the howling fans call for him to 'kill 'em,'" wrote White. "He is well known for his flying dropkicks and his head butts. No wrestler so far has been able to take his head butts."

White then gleefully regaled his readers with the tale of how the White former Hawaiian champion Ted Travis had returned to the island in the hopes of reclaiming the title at Claybourne's expense.

"When Claybourne finished applying his head butts, body slams, flying dropkicks and elbow smashes to Travis' body and head, Travis was ready for the hospital instead of the championship belt," joked White.

White concluded his piece by informing readers that Claybourne had also asserted his dominance while dueling with Ben Sherman, with only the latter's "slick" tactics saving him from certain defeat at Claybourne's hands.

With his feud with Sherman temporarily behind him, Claybourne turned his attention to Antone Leone of New

York, and the fact that Claybourne promised Leone would be rewarded with a shot at the championship if he won betrayed the eventual outcome of the match.

"Sunday night's main event between Jack Claybourne and Antone Leone ended in a decision in favor of the latter," began *The Star-Bulletin*. "The match had Claybourne as the aggressor throughout, and the referee's verdict in awarding the match to Leone after the time ran out was met with howling disapproval from the fans."

To be fair, Leone had managed to pin the champion with a dropkick to the neck in just under three minutes, but Claybourne evened the score just 37 seconds later after flooring Leone with headbutts and dropkicks of his own.

Instead of getting straight to the business of presenting the title rematch, Karasick opted to place Claybourne on a tag team with Ray Daoang for a match against Leone and his Argentinian partner Rocco Toma.

Although he was presented as a Filipino — likely for the sake of appealing to the large Asian populace of Hawaii — Daoang was actually Mexican wrestler Ray Duran.

The presence of Daoang didn't help matters for Claybourne, and Leone was able to augment his claim of supremacy over Claybourne by pinning him during the tag team encounter after dropkicking the champion in the neck once again.

Karasick quickly scheduled a title match between Claybourne and Leone that would headline the May 29th show, as Claybourne looked to extend his title reign past the seven-month mark. Achieving that mark would make Claybourne's Hawaiian title reign easiliy longer than the lengthiest title reign of Seelie Samara when he was in the Pacific Northwest.

As had become his custom, Claybourne proved to be a resilient champion who always adjusted from his prior defeats at the Civic Arena. After two consecutive defeats at the hands of Antone Leone, Jack was at his best when it mattered, and turned back Leone's challenge by taking two out of three falls from him.

"A terrific leg split applied by Claybourne early in the match weakened Leone and set up a flying dropkick and a press for the first fall in 13 minutes and 45 seconds," recorded *The Advertiser*. "A series of neck choppers, followed by a dropkick to the throat enabled Leone to apply a press for the equalizing fall 7 minutes and 17 seconds later. The deciding fall came 4 minutes and 55 seconds after the rest period, Claybourne repeatedly knocking Leone to his knees with head butts."

In Hawaii, Jack Claybourne continued to smash records as reliably as his skull smacked foreheads, and as 1949 wore on, he was going to find himself getting smacked by the reality that the dawn of a new era of Black pro wrestling was on the horizon. Success attracts immitation, and Claybourne would soon meet a new crop of young, hungry Black wrestlers who were aching for their own opportunities to sample success.

## 15 - 343 Days

After a dominant stretch of activity during his long reign as the champion of Hawaii, Jack Claybourne was given a week off to await the anointing of a new challenger to his throne. In the meantime a mysterious Black wrestler appeared on the island wearing a white mask, and going by the name "The Bat."

This wrestler was none other than Ardell "Don" Kindred of Pennsylvania, who had begun wrestling during the final stages of World War II. Before making it to Hawaii, Kindred had engaged in a history-making tour of the Mid-Atlantic states in 1946.

Facing Don Blackman at every event, the two engaged in a series of matches that proved the box-office viability of Black wrestlers in those states when facing one another, as extra seating was allotted for Black fans in the balconies of several Southern venues so that they could experience the novelty of watching two Black wrestlers perform in the same rings as Whites.

Now in Hawaii, Kindred was being introduced in a fashion that had become commonplace in the territory: A masked wrestler would appear, and would remain masked until they were defeated, at which point they would unmask and reveal their true identity to the fans.

With the presence of the masked Bat providing an added level of intrigue to the wrestling territory, it would be decided that Claybourne's next opponent in singles competition would be Argentinian wrestler Rocco "The Rock" Toma, who he would compete against in a non-title match.

Labeled as a proponent of the backbreaker — albeit not the over-the-shoulder Argentine backbreaker of his presumed countryman Antonino Rocca — Toma's mastery of the move was sufficient to get his bout with Claybourne labeled as the match of "Headbutts vs. Backbreaker Slams" by *The Star-Bulletin*.

Toma did not provide an account of himself that would qualify him for a future title opportunity, as Claybourne succeeded in turning back his first challenge by taking two falls out of three, despite *The Advertiser* crediting Toma's tactics with "keeping the crowd in a sustained state of excitement."

"Claybourne won the first fall in 22 min. and three seconds with dropkicks, followed by a body press," continued *The Advertiser*. "The South American roughhouser came back surprisingly strong and outmaneuvered Claybourne to set up his famed knee back-breakers. Two powerful knee back-breakers set up a shoulder press, 6 min. and 10 sec. after the rest period."

Less than two minutes after surrendering a fall, Claybourne's hand was being raised in victory after he rocked Toma with a series of headbutts and capped off the match with one final flying dropkick.

Veteran grappler Red Vagnone was also an inconsequential challenger for Claybourne's championship. In yet another non-title match, Claybourne delivered his best imitation of Rufus Jones, turning a best-of-three-falls affair into a single-fall event decided by an official's stoppage.

"Headbutts opened a cut on Vagnone's forehead between the eyes, and Rubberman Higami stopped the match to prevent aggravating the injury," reported *The Advertiser*. "Vagnone wanted to continue, but the cut was bleeding badly and the referee acted wisely in halting the match. While the match lasted, it was touch and go, with each grappler scoring with their pet tactics. Claybourne's speed and agility offset Vagnone's roughhousing. The match lasted 20 min. and 4 sec."

Next up for a shot at Jack's title would be Kenny Ackles, and with Claybourne's possession of the *Ring Magazine* belt now nearing the eight-month mark, *The Advertiser* declared him to be "one of the most active champions to ever hold the Ring gold belt." With no title on the line in his match with Ackles, Claybourne's path to the completion of an eight-month title reign was assured, but he still defeated Ackles to maintain his momentum.

## Gentleman Jack and Rough Rufus

"Both wrestlers gained a fall each, with Claybourne stopping the blonde Boston grappler with a flying dropkick in 36 minutes and 36 seconds of the opening fall," said *The Star-Bulletin*. "Ackles retaliated with a fall in 3 minutes and 50 seconds to even up the match. At the termination of the time limit, Referee Rubberman Higami awarded the verdict to the colored mat star."

Finally, Claybourne would wrestle the longstanding Hawaii wrestler and crowd favorite Oki Shikina, and with Claybourne entering his ninth month as the top attraction in the territory, advertisements for the show stated "Jack Claybourne has established himself as one of the greatest wrestlers to show in the islands," and added that his popularity was owed to his "acrobatic style of wrestling."

Once again, Claybourne reminded the audience that he was far more than simply an acrobat who relied solely on impact-based maneuvers like dropkicks and headbutts. After Shikina took the first fall with his armbar submission hold, and Claybourne took the second with a flying dropkick, Claybourne outmaneuvered Shikina to achieve yet another impressive victory at the Civic Arena.

"Shikina gained the upper hand when he tossed Claybourne with judo hip throws," recounted *The Advertiser*. "Oki then clamped on his armbar, but before he could apply pressure, Claybourne hurled Shikina backward for a cradle hold and shoulder press."

The winning streak of Claybourne would come to an end on July 10th, when he was disqualified for dropkicking George Pencheff from the apron of the ring and out to the arena floor.

With this victory over Claybourne awarded on a technicality, Pencheff earned a bout with the Bat, who was still in possession of his mask. There were two conditions in place: First, Pencheff would be required to defeat the Bat in order to earn a title match against Claybourne. Second, if Pencheff could succeed in conquering the Bat by pinfall or submission, the Bat would be required to unmask.

Don Kindred had been able to retain his mask and his identity as the Bat by scoring either wins or draws in all of his matches from the beginning of June right up until the midpoint of July. That's when he finally lost his first match in Hawaii to Pencheff via a "reverse bodyslam."

"The Bat congratulated Pencheff, then took off his white hood and announced that he was Don Kindred — Montreal-born grappler who served in the American army for a number of years during the last war," wrote *The Advertiser*.

Kindred was *not* a Montreal-born grappler, although he had briefly been a standby player for the Montreal Alouettes of the Canadian Football League. In subsequent interviews conducted on the island, Kindred also made the hysterical claim that he opted to wrestle under a mask for all 10 of the years he claimed to have been wrestling because his family did not approve of him wrestling professionally.

The truth of the matter was that Kindred had only been wrestling for a little over four years by this time, and his short time as the Bat marked the only sustained period of time that he had performed beneath the concealment of a mask.

Kindred also added that he would prefer to be known as pro wrestling's "Brown Bomber" now that he was no longer wrestling under a mask anymore. It was a name that Kindred had adopted a few months earlier while wrestling in Texas, but if that was a reflection of Kindred's actual preference, things didn't work out that way. More often than not, he was referred to as Don "Bat" Kindred in nearly all subsequent advertisements of his appearance while he remained in Hawaii.

All of the momentum was behind Pencheff at this point, as he had technically defeated the Hawaiian junior heavyweight champion and the territory's previously unbeaten masked wrestler in back-to-back weekends. Defying expectations, promoter Al Karasick named "Sailor" Tiger Joe as Claybourne's next opponent, with Claybourne quoted as being non-committal about whom he would defend his championship against next.

"Tiger Joe is plenty tough, and I want him out of the way before I'll defend my title," Claybourne told *The Advertiser*.

Joe was famed for his "blockbuster" hold, which combined a hammerlock and a "piledriver slam" into the corner of the ring. Even though Joe would successfully apply the hold to Claybourne, it still wouldn't be sufficient to land him the victory.

"The match was torrid all the way, with Claybourne using headbutts to offset the Chicago star's rough tactics," said *The Advertiser*. "Tiger Joe slammed Claybourne against the corner ropes with his blockbuster hold to take the first fall after 11 min. 52 sec. Claybourne evened the match 16 min. 3 sec. later with a flying headscissors, pulling Tiger Joe into the ring to apply the press. The Chicago grappler was standing on the apron of the ring when Claybourne cut loose with his flying headscissors."

In the final fall, Claybourne polished off Tiger Joe with a series of headbutts and then covered him for the victory. His next bout — against California powerhouse Kay Bell — would result in him squaring off with a respected football player and actor.

Bell had a multi-year professional football career that included stints with both the Chicago Bears and the New York Giants, and he also appeared as the stunt double for Victor Mature in the 1949 film "Samson and Delilah," which earned him the fitting ring name of "Samson."

The match between Bell and Claybourne would come with the stipulation that Bell would be obligated to weigh 215 pounds or less in order for the bout to be ruled a title match. To be clear, there were several instances of Claybourne defending his championship against wrestlers who weighed well over 215 pounds during his title reign, not to mention the fact that it's probable that Claybourne walked around at a weight exceeding the 215-pound mark on a daily basis at this stage of his life.

The ending to the bout left much to be desired from the perspective of fans who desired a clear-cut winner. The match went to a time-limit decision with no falls recorded, but referee Rubberman Higami was bumped by Bell and knocked out of commission toward the end of the bout. Referee Frank Merrill replaced Higami as the official in charge, and awarded the match to Claybourne as the result of a decision, ostensibly out of spite for what Bell had done to his colleague.

Karasick ordered an immediate rematch between Bell and Claybourne, and stipulated that Bell — who weighed in at 230 pounds rather than the 215 pounds required for a title opportunity — would qualify to win the title if he could weigh in at 225 pounds, which was a serious bending of the rules. The match also featured the added presence of a special referee to maintain order, in the form of retired wrestler Count Von Buesing.

At the onset of the bout, Bell's weight was announced at 219-and-a-half pounds, but neither Bell's final weight nor his ability to qualify for a title opportunity would be an issue when all was said and done. Claybourne successfully turned back Bell's challenge, just as he had turned back every other opponent he had faced as he now entered his 10th month as the Hawaiian champion.

"The match was well enjoyed throughout, with the Negro mat star taking the opening fall in 13 minutes 7 seconds with a flying headscissors and body press," reported *The Star-Bulletin*. "Bell evened the match by pinning Claybourne with an arm swing and flying dropkick, then applying a body press. The time of the second fall was 5 minutes 15 seconds. Claybourne started using head butts and opened a cut on Bell's forehead, and as it bled the referee stopped the affair."

Jack would not be finished with Bell at this point; he would meet Bell again in a tag team bout the next week. Bell's partner was Peter Managoff, while Claybourne teamed up with none other than the erstwhile Bat, Don Kindred. The occasion marked the first time when Claybourne would team with one of the true up-and-coming stars from the succeeding generation of Black ring performers that his generation had inspired, but it would be far from the last.

## Gentleman Jack and Rough Rufus

The novelty of having an all-Black tag team present in Hawaii yet again notwithstanding, the pairing of Claybourne and Kindred would be even less successful than the Claybourne-Samara tandem. While Claybourne and Samara had at least wrestled their opponents to a draw despite Claybourne absorbing a pinfall loss during the bout, Claybourne and Kindred lost thier match outright, with both members of their team suffering individual losses.

"Kindred was the first to [lose], yielding to a Boston crab hold applied by the powerful Bell. The fall came in 1 min. 46 sec.," stated *The Advertiser*. "Head butts by Claybourne subdued Bell for the equalizing fall 11 min. 40 sec. later. The final fall came after an unusually wild session. Body slams and a press by Managoff flattened Claybourne."

Simultaneous to Claybourne's title reign entering double digits in the months column, pro wrestling expanded to the largest island of the Hawaiian island chain. In its August 2nd edition, *The Hilo Herald-Tribune* explained how travel agent Kiichi Hatayama would be promoting the first show ever in Hilo, which would take place on August 13th.

"Of special interest to local mat fans is the appearance of Harold Sakata, Hawaii's Olympic weightlifting star," reported *The Herald-Tribune*. "Sakata is turning pro and has been training diligently for his debut. Sakata goes against Don Kindred in one of three main events. Jack Claybourne, giant Negro star, is matched against Red Vagnone, and Ben Pilar, the Filipino favorite, will take on colorful Ben Sherman."

For the sake of clarification, "Hawaii" comprises a series of islands, with Oahu being the most populous island, and the home of Honolulu — the territory of Hawaii's capital and largest city. Hilo is the largest settlement on "the island of Hawaii," which is the southeasternmost island of the Hawaiian island chain, and also the largest island of the group in terms of total area.

The event was scheduled to be held at the Hilo Armory, and with tickets available weeks in advance at Hatayama's own bus terminal. The first Hatayama-promoted show on that Saturday evening attracted 1,700 fans, which was a respectable number considering the population of Hilo was only 27,000 people at the time. In the brand new environment, Claybourne once again defeated Red Vagnone and departed from the ring still in possession of the *Ring Magazine* belt.

"Jack Claybourne, junior heavyweight champion of Hawaii, took two straight falls to defeat Red Vagnone, a tough boy from Columbus, O," stated *The Hilo Herald-Tribune*. "Claybourne took the first fall on a disqualification and the second with head butts."

Back in Honolulu, Karasick declared that Claybourne and Managoff would square off in a singles match, and depicted Claybourne as a reluctant champion who refused to put his championship up for grabs during the contest due to resentment he held toward Managoff.

Once again, Claybourne won the bout even though his title wasn't at risk. The fall tally was tied at one apiece when the time ran out and the referee in charge awarded the decision to Claybourne.

"Managoff's powerful scissors holds gave him the edge in the earlier stages of the match and weakened Claybourne to the extent that he was able to clamp on his crucifix for the first fall," said *The Advertiser*. "The initial fall came after 32 min. 40 sec. Claybourne came back strong with head butts and soon had Managoff groggy enough to clamp on a reverse crucifix for a shoulder press 6 min. 37 sec. after the rest period."

On August 28th, Claybourne successfully defended his title yet again in a bout against George Pencheff that *The Star-Bulletin* said "lacked the usual color and punch of past performances." This criticism seemed to have been attributed to the fact that no falls were recorded during a bout that went the full 45 minutes and was ruled a draw. *The Advertiser*, on the other hand, related it as a compelling struggle.

"The Hawaiian junior heavyweight champion and the Australian star waged a hard-fought, bruising battle featured by powerful leverage holds and clever tactics," illustrated *The Advertiser*. "For the most part the match was a duel of holds and counterholds. However, Claybourne did use rough tactics, occasionally in an effort to slow down his opponent. Pencheff's experience and his power tactics offset Claybourne's agility and skill."

Next on the agenda for Claybourne would be one of the hottest young pro wrestling prospects of the era. Ray Gunkel was a two-time AAU national heavyweight wrestling champion, and he also finished as the runner-up to the NCAA national champion in the heavyweight division. He even served as a backup fullback for the Purdue University football team despite not being awarded a varsity letter.

The match between Gunkel and Claybourne appeared to be heading to yet another inconclusive ending, when a brawl erupted that ultimately resulted in Claybourne's disqualification.

"In one of the most exciting closing minutes ever seen here, Claybourne and Gunkel tore into each other like a couple of wildcats and had to be separated by several handlers after the referee stopped the melee," observed *The Star-Bulletin*. "The excitement began when Claybourne threw Gunkel out of the ropes and slammed him against the corner post. Frank Merrill, the referee, disqualified Claybourne, giving Gunkel the first fall."

Karasick's response was to issue an edict declaring that Claybourne would have to face Gunkel on September 11th, with the Hawaiian championship on the line if Gunkel could weigh in at 215 pounds or less.

Officially, Gunkel reportedly weighed 238 pounds ahead of his rematch with Claybourne, suggesting that he was far more interested in inflicting damage on the champion than unseating him from his championship position. To that extent, Gunkel's presumed plan worked perfectly, as he battered Jack and eventually rendered him unable to continue the contest, in a finish that contradicted the conclusion of the bout from the prior week.

"Gunkel copped the opening fall with a series of flying drop kicks and a body press in 12 minutes 44 seconds," stated

*The Star-Bulletin*, describing a scene that sounded very much like a vintage Claybourne dropkicking extravaganza. "The versatile colored star evened matters with head butts, body slams, and a press after 8 minutes 57 seconds. Gunkel then hurled Claybourne against the ring post and the referee tallied the 20 for the Gunkel victory."

To put it another way, Gunkel returned the favor to Claybourne from the prior week, but instead of being disqualified as Claybourne was, Gunkel was able to reap the benefits of ramming his opponent into the ring post and was once again rewarded with a victory, this time via countout.

There was a palpable injustice to this loss by Claybourne, but he would not be permitted an opportunity at redemption against Gunkel. Instead, Claybourne was booked to wrestle against Arthur "Tarzan" White at the September 18th show, as the length of his title reign was creeping ever nearer to the 11-month mark.

*The Advertiser* characterized the bout between Claybourne and White as an opportunity for the champion to atone for his setback. In White, Claybourne would be facing a former All-American guard from the University of Alabama, and a member of the 1938 New York Giants team that won the NFL championship.

"Claybourne is expected to use his head butts freely to offset the wild tactics of the former Alabama All-American gridder," predicted *The Advertiser*.

The gridiron accomplishments of White didn't help him in the least bit inside of the wrestling ring on this night. He was no match for the Hawaiian junior heavyweight titleholder, as Claybourne put him away rather easily in their one-fall match.

"Jack Claybourne outlasted Tarzan White of Alabama in the first main event, scoring a fall in 16 min. 55 sec. after a wild brawl," recorded *The Advertiser*. "Claybourne used head butts to set up the fall, after White had missed a flying tackle and had rammed his head against the corner padding."

## Gentleman Jack and Rough Rufus

Claybourne wouldn't have much time to celebrate; Ben Sherman had returned to Hawaii from Portland, and he was anxious for another crack at Claybourne and his championship. Karasick booked a bout that reunited the team of Claybourne and Kindred to duel with Sherman and the recently defeated White.

"Realizing that they will be giving away weight to their opponents, Sherman and White have been stressing strongarm tactics in their workouts," reported *The Advertiser*. "Sherman also plans to counter Claybourne's head butts with butts of his own."

This time, Kindred and Claybourne were successful in their efforts, becoming the first Black tag team to score a victory in Hawaii, although it was far from easy. Yet, the way the results of the bout were recorded, Claybourne appeared to be every bit the dominant champion that one would have expected him to be after nearly a year-long title reign.

"The two stocky grapplers teamed to soften up Kindred, and White put on the finishing touches with a dropkick to the throat and a body press in 9 minutes and 50 seconds of the first fall," said *The Star-Bulletin*. "Scoring with flying dropkicks, Claybourne dropped Sherman to even the match in 5 minutes and 50 seconds, applying a body press for the second fall. After both teams struggled to gain the advantage, Claybourne pinned White to cop the deciding fall in 5 minutes and 56 seconds with a body press."

The victory would earn Claybourne a brief reprieve, and he watched from the Civic Auditorium locker room on October 2nd as Bobby Managoff defeated Pat Fraley to earn a shot at Claybourne's title. Claybourne was now into his 12th month as the Hawaiian junior heavyweight champion, having won the title on October 31, 1948.

Undoubtedly, Managoff would represent the stiffest test to Claybourne's championship reign. Managoff was not only a former holder of the *Ring Magazine* belt held by Claybourne, but he had also held multiple world heavyweight championships, including the world title of the National

Wrestling Association, along with the same world junior heavyweight championship held by Seelie Samara — or Zelis Amhara — in Montreal.

Hawaii champion Claybourne stares down Bobby Managoff

From a legacy standpoint, a clear-cut victory in a title defense against Managoff would have been exactly what Claybourne required to propel himself to the next level in terms of his overall perception by the public. Unfortunately, it was not to be.

Managoff defeated Claybourne on October 9th, 1949, bringing to an end what had easily been the longest single title reign by any Black wrestler holding the top championship of a wrestling territory. The reign had nearly equaled the combined lengths of all other major title reigns by Black wrestlers that preceded it, and it would be many years before that record would be topped in a U.S. wrestling promotion.

"The match was a rip-roaring, action packed melee with the two grapplers trading clever holds until the first fall, which Managoff won with lightning quickness," recorded *The Advertiser*. "Claybourne dropkicked Managoff and whirled the challenger in an airplane spin. But as Claybourne stopped to flatten him, Managoff clamped on a double wrist lock and flipped the champion over and applied a press."

Claybourne was reportedly startled by this turn of events, and endeavored to make up for it quickly. He struck Managoff with a series of headbutts and dropkicks, and then body slammed him repeatedly before covering him for a pinfall after a further five minutes and 24 seconds had elapsed. That's when the third fall began, and Claybourne failed to pull out a title-match triumph for the first time in nearly a full year.

"Managoff came back to win the deciding fall 7 min. 3 sec. later, countering Claybourne's wild tactics with power holds and 'choppers' patterned after a judo maneuver," continued *The Advertiser*. "That quickly neutralized Claybourne's butting, and Managoff followed with knee butts to flatten the champion for a press. After the match, Claybourne congratulated Managoff and fastened the championship belt on his conqueror."

On October 11th, *The Star-Bulletin* printed word that Claybourne would be departing Hawaii to personally view the championship boxing match between Ezzard Charles and Pat Valentino at the Cow Palace in Daly City, California, and would then continue on to Boston to visit with his family. Claybourne left word that he hoped to return to Hawaii to "campaign for the belt again" after a brief reprieve in Boston.

Before word of the cessation of Claybourne's 343-day title reign reached the mainland, a photo of Claybourne with his beaming wife Lillian fastening the *Ring Magazine* belt around his waist circulated in several Black news publications, along with an in-depth article about his career written by Frank Marshall Davis of the Associated Negro Press. In the article, Claybourne supplied a number of stories from his career, a surprising number of which were probably true.

The wording of the article essentially revealed that Claybourne's departure from Hawaii was preplanned, as it was disclosed that he would next be appearing in matches in California even though he was still the Hawaiian champion at the time of the interview.

**Jack and Lillian Claybourne**

Claybourne begins the story of his career by saying he got his start in the ring at the age of 16 when he weighed 175 pounds, even though all evidence points to him getting his in-ring start at the age of 21. It's conceivable that Claybourne was attempting to conceal his true age from the interviewer, who referred to Jack as being "in his 30s" even though he was 39 years old and *very* close to turning 40.

The writer credits Claybourne with appearing in 2,000 matches, which is certainly possible, and then states that he "appeared before troops for three years as a wrestler with the USO" even though there's no gap in his wartime activity record that would have afforded him the opportunity to do such a thing.

Claybourne included the true tale of how he wrestled under the name Pablo Hernandez in Cincinnati, but added that he had supposedly been presented with the name while wrestling in Cuba. Allegedly, Claybourne assumed this gimmick to avoid the depiction as an American Black wrestler, because Cincinnati supposedly had laws in place that prohibited mixed-race matches involving Blacks.

By that logic, a Cuban as darkly colored as Claybourne would be permitted to compete against a White wrestler, while a Black American of a slightly lighter shade would have been prohibited from doing so. Regardless, Claybourne went on to say that he was presumed to speak only Spanish, and that a verbal slip-up on his part ultimately forced a change in the law.

"Then one day while training, [Claybourne] spoke several sentences in English," wrote Davis. "When the rest of the gymnasium recovered from the shock, they learned he was from Boston instead of Havana, and the whole story came out. Up to then, mixed bouts had not been allowed in the Ohio city, but officials took a realistic view. After all, Jack had already wrestled a number of opponents. So they let him continue and the ban on mixed matches was lifted."

Fluctuations in the law aside, Black Cincinnatian Chick Harris competed in several mixed-race wrestling matches in his hometown during the earliest years of the 1930s, so unless rules became more restrictive between 1932 and 1938 due to the passing of an anti-George-Godfrey law, no such ban was officially enacted. Moreover, Claybourne had not even wrestled in Massachusetts prior to the end of 1939, let alone did he live in Boston at the time.

Finally, Claybourne closed the piece with a story involving a member of his extended family that presumably took place during the earliest days of his career when he was wrestling in rural Missouri.

"[Claybourne] tangled with an opponent who was plenty tough," continued Davis. "Among the spectators was his sister-in-law, then in high school, who was there with a whole group of teenagers. When it seemed that Jack was getting the worst of it, she couldn't stand it any longer. She leaped up and dashed for the ring, followed by her crowd. Crawling through the ropes, they ganged up on Jack's opponent and got him down on the canvas before the astounded officials could stop them. They had to call the cops to restore order."

Since Claybourne emerged on the scene early in 1932 and appeared to have already been rather adept at wrestling, it is impossible to account for every circumstance he found himself in prior to when he first captured media attention. There is no way to know if Claybourne was describing an event that happened before he achieved notoriety, if he was embellishing elements of a true story for the sake of entertainment, or if he was making up the incident out of whole cloth.

The remainder of 1949 had also been full of interesting developments for Joe Godfrey. After leaving Vermont, Godfrey resurrected his Rufus Jones name and made appearances in areas of Ontario that he had never appeared in before, like Sault Ste. Marie and North Bay.

One of Jones' earliest bouts in Sault Ste. Marie, which was officiated by wrestler-referee-promoter Larry Kasaboski, was apparently used to educate fans in the area that headbutting was now a legal tactic that all wrestlers — and especially Rufus Jones — should be free to use liberally.

As a means of both proving the point and attaining a measure of revenge, Jones' first bout after the clarification of the rules was against Kasaboski himself in a show advertised as an event featuring "the black boy and the black bear," as Gorgeous Gus the black bear was also booked to make an appearance.

"Jones was dissatisfied with the decision rendered by 'Kas' when he started the headbutting in last week's show," reported *The Sault Star*. "He maintained the headbutt is just as legal as a flying tackle, and forthwith challenged Kasaboski in order to show him a few tricks in the ring. Perusal of the latest guide to wrestling revealed that the headbutt is now legal, so the fast and coming Jones will go all out to show Kasaboski how to use his head without getting bumped."

The "education" Jones offered to Kasaboski unfolded exactly as expected. *The Star* reported that Jones used his head "in an unorthodox manner" to win the match, and that by "using it in the form of a sledgehammer" he had "literally pounded out a victory."

Moments of true conquest for Jones were fleeting in the stretch of Ontario that ran parallel to Michigan's Upper Peninsula. More often than not, Jones would trade falls with his opponents, then fly into a rage during the final fall, leading to him committing acts worthy of disqualification, like attacking the referee.

The major exception to this occurred at the tail end of Jones' tenure in the area, when he was granted an opportunity to qualify for a match against international junior heavyweight champion Bob Lortie by defeating Hassen Bey. Following the familiar script, Rufus defeated Bey handily, capturing the first fall with his homegrown Boston crab.

"Foreign-looking Bey waddled back in for the next fall, and after slamming Rufus with a couple of well-timed body slams, the Terrible Turk used something new in tricky holds to even the falls," reported *The North Bay Nugget*. "Bey pushed his hairless dome into the pit of Jones' stomach and pressed until Rufus, who couldn't breathe, fell limp to the canvas. Bey threw a body spread on him to win.'"

With the score now tied, Rufus resorted to eye-gouging to gain the advantage, then headbutted Bey to the canvas and applied yet another Boston crab to record his second victory. *The Nugget* added that Bey, "who boasts he can speak seven different languages, hollered 'uncle' in all seven."

For defeating Bey, Jones was granted his shot at Lortie's junior heavyweight championship, and true to the pattern of his career, he was defeated in the season-ending show at the hands of a champion who was almost always cast as the villain except for on this rare occasion.

Lortie won the first fall with a backbreaker and a series of neck twists, but Rufus countered in the second set with his favorite combination of headbutts and a Boston crab. This set the stage for a winner-takes-all final round, with the international junior heavyweight title on the line.

"Jones went after Lortie with his damaging head butts, and for a time it appeared that Rufus was going to replace Lortie as international champ," illustrated *The Nugget*. "He had Lortie groggy and just hanging on when he applied the Boston crab twice in a row only to have Lortie shake him off, much to his astonishment. Then in a last desperate bid, Lortie came back with a whirlwind attack and tossed Jones to the mat, pinning him for the deciding fall."

Discerning wrestling fans along the Pacific Coast who traveled frequently between California and Hawaii would have been tipped off with respect to Jack Claybourne's future plans long before anyone else. The September 22nd edition of *The California Eagle* revealed that Claybourne was due to begin wrestling regularly in California that very next month, and such a tour would have certainly interfered with his duties as Hawaiian champion if his schedules were to overlap.

The Thursday, October 13th edition of *The Van Nuys News* announced that Claybourne would be the tag team partner of Vic Christy for a one-night tournament taking place that Saturday, which would have required Claybourne to have made his arrangements to participate in that tournament very abruptly had his exit from Hawaii not already been in the works for some time.

For the record, Claybourne's schedule lined up just neatly enough that it is quite possible he watched Ezzard Charles defeat Pat Valentino in person on the 14th like he said he would, and then traveled to Southern California in time for his mainland in-ring return on the 15th.

For Claybourne's return to the area, *The Wilmington Press Journal* apparently got some of its signals crossed, referring to Claybourne as "holder of the *Ring Magazine*'s belt as the Negro champion and claimant to the Australian title," not realizing that the *Ring Magazine* belt was a Hawaiian prize. *The Daily News* further referred to Claybourne — who was still in possession of his personal Negro title belt — as the "NWA Negro heavyweight champion."

At this point in time, there still might have been some ambiguity about the use of the initials "NWA." Those initials had been used for nearly two decades by the National Wrestling Association, one of the most respected sanctioning bodies of wrestling titles for decades, due in part to its relationship with the National Boxing Association.

However, with the emergence of the National Wrestling Alliance, and the rapid consolidation of world championships, the National Wrestling Association — which had never formally recognized a Negro championship — was within a month of deactivating its championships in favor of the titles sanctioned by the National Wrestling Alliance. One of the core tenets of the new NWA was that no individual world titles would be recognized by NWA member organizations aside from the NWA's world singles championships.

In accordance with this, even if a wrestling territory was not a member of the National Wrestling Alliance, the withdrawal of the National Wrestling Association's title recognition would eventually eliminate any confusion as to which NWA was being alluded to when those initials were used.

In their separate October editions, both *The Los Angeles Times* and *The Daily News* spelled out that Jack Claybourne was recognized by the National Wrestling Association as the Negro heavyweight champion in the last month that such a statement could ever have been deceptively uttered without raising eyebrows.

That particular NWA was on the cusp of withdrawing the recognition of all of its championships in favor of the regulations set in place by the National Wrestling Alliance. This included no recognition — implied or otherwise — of a world heavyweight champion other than the NWA World's Heavyweight Championship.

As the Negro world champion who prided himself on having an ornate belt to back his claim, and who often insisted that there was a sanctioning body behind his claim to the title, this would prove to be very treacherous terrain for Claybourne to navigate.

In Wilmington, Claybourne teamed with a Black wrestler known only as the Brown Bomber — likely Don Kindred — in a tag team loss in late October. A few weeks later, he was wrestling against "The Bat" in Visalia, which was also probably Kindred wrestling under the same mask he had worn in Honolulu.

On November 12th, *The Wilmington Press Journal* stated that Claybourne was in possession of "the *Police Gazette*'s world championship belt." *The Police Gazette* was famed for awarding title belts to bare knuckle boxers starting in the 1880s, and had awarded some world championship designations to wrestlers in the late 19th and early 20th centuries. However, the idea that such a distinction fell upon Claybourne in the late 1940s certainly strained credulity, and *The Police Gazette* had not been in the habit of handing out title belts to "colored champions."

*The Press Journal* quickly amended the statement, referring to Claybourne once again as "holder of the *Ring Magazine*'s championship and belt as the colored champion of the world." With the photo of Claybourne displaying the Hawaiian title belt around his waist now being used for promotional purposes — with his wife conveniently cropped out of the photo — it probably seemed like too good of an image not to capitalize upon.

In a bizarre occurrence, Claybourne faced Frank Sexton in a mid-November bout in which Sexton was labeled as the world heavyweight champion of the National Wrestling Association even though Lou Thesz had been defending that title for well over a year at that point. Regardless, Sexton pinned Claybourne in straight falls at the Pasadena Arena to eliminate the threat that a Black wrestler might capture even a phony version of one of wrestling's most cherished titles.

In the middle of December, Claybourne faced Antonino Rocca for the first time, and was defeated twice by Rocca's "famous Greek simplex hold" according to *The Independent* of Long Beach. This marked yet another occasion where Claybourne was made to appear totally ineffectual against an established White star. The fact that Rocca was said to wrestle in a manner similar to that of a young Jack Claybourne would soon be highlighted by the press.

Within two months of his return to the mainland, Claybourne was back to working in opening matches and semifinal bouts, and occasionally losing in handicap matches despite being on the side with the greater number of wrestlers. Further, there seemed to be an outright refusal to acknowledge his reign as the champion in Hawaii — let alone the impressive length of the title reign — in any of the promotional materials that advertised his appearances.

This was possibly owed to the idea that promoters did not want to have to explain how a Black wrestler who had been such a dominant champion in Hawaii could achieve comparatively so little elsewhere.

Claybourne started 1950 wrestling in the Pacific Northwestern states of Washington and Oregon. For the first time ever, his real hometown of Mexico, Missouri was mentioned by name, and he abandoned the use of headbutts and assumed his usual role as pro wrestling's most prolific dropkicker once again. He also abandoned the use of the title "The Black Panther" in the region for the first time.

"Jack Claybourne, colored heavyweight wrestler of Mexico, Mo., dropkicked his way to two straight falls to gain a verdict over Chief Little Wolf of Trinidad, Colo., in the first bout of the heavyweight wrestling exhibition on the card in the Auditorium Wednesday night," declared *The Oregon Journal*. "After losing the first fall in 21 minutes 50 seconds, Claybourne bounced back to gain the second in 2 minutes 11 seconds, and won the third in 19 minutes 7 seconds."

Stunningly, seeing the success and notoriety that Claybourne had achieved in Hawaii had seemingly inspired Seelie Samara to make some changes as well. After more than a decade and a half of being known for his use of wrestling holds that were primarily dependent upon his strength, Samara had seemingly become a headbutting specialist overnight.

"Possessing a skull as hard as ivory, Seelie delights in rapping his head against his opponent's cranium when backed into a tight corner, and this strategy always is successful," said *The Niagara Falls Review*. "The bump means nothing to Samara, but to a foe, it's generally a king's size headache. Some referees have ruled against Samara's butting tactics, but the fans always are behind him, for the big Negro never resorts to this weapon unless forced to do so."

Without the headbutt in his arsenal, Claybourne still remained agile enough at nearly 40 years of age to perform his classic trick of vaulting over the referee's back to land a "thudding dropkick" to Little Wolf's chin, according to *The Oregonian*.

In February, Claybourne returned to Hawaii once again, where he was justifiably touted as a serious threat to reclaim the *Ring Magazine* title belt that he had worn for nearly a year. In the four months since Claybourne had departed from the island of Oahu, the Hawaii junior heavyweight title had changed hands multiple times, and now adorned the waist of

Sandor Szabo, who Claybourne had wrestled multiple times in California.

Claybourne was immediately matched against the man Szabo had just defeated for the title on February 5th, Hans "Blockbuster" Schnabel. Once again back in the heart of the Pacific Ocean, Claybourne was treated as a major star relative to the comparative indifference he had received in the mainland wrestling territories.

"A sensation here for over a year until he left the Islands to visit his family in Boston last November, Claybourne won the *Ring Magazine* gold belt from Tanaka and lost it to Bobby Managoff," *The Honolulu Advertiser* reminded its readers. "He is still undisputed Negro world heavyweight mat champion. Acrobatic and agile, Claybourne is a powerful man who uses rough tactics when he has to. His headbutts have been vigorously protested by his opponents, but thus far no ban has been imposed on such tactics."

Claybourne was successful during his return engagement, scoring a decision victory over Schnabel. Both combatants claimed falls against one another prior to the expiration of the time limit.

"Schnabel took the opening fall with a back-slam and press after 12 minutes of grappling," reported *The Hawaii Star Bulletin*. "Claybourne, making his first showing in local rings after four months on the mainland, took the next fall after 1 minute 4 seconds. The colored mat star used head butts, flying drop kicks, body slams, and a body press. The bell ended the match, and the referee raised Claybourne's paw."

For Jack's next bout — a February 19th encounter with former world junior heavyweight champion Joe "Flash" Gordon — *The Star Bulletin* reported that "movie star Shirley Temple was a ringside spectator with her mother and father." If reports of the former child star's attendance were true, then the now 21-year-old Temple and her parents watched as Claybourne and Gordon dueled to a draw, with each man gaining a fall.

"Gordon gained the first fall after 35 minutes when he caught Claybourne with a series of drop kicks and a press," reported *The Advertiser*. "The fall followed a hectic exchange of drop kicks by Gordon and head butts by Claybourne. The colored star evened the match 4 min. 4 sec. later with a submission fall, grasping Gordon in a 'crystal' hold, which was a combination leg lock and back-breaker. Claybourne opened a slight cut on Gordon's forehead with head butts in the final minutes but was unable to flatten the game and clever Boston star."

After dropping a match to Ken Kenneth of New Zealand, Claybourne was given a rematch with Gordon in early May. On this night, Claybourne achieved something that had routinely eluded him on the mainland, and achieved a definitive victory over an established former world junior heavyweight champion.

"The colored mat star won the opening fall in 5 minutes 8 seconds with a flying drop kick and a press," said *The Star-Bulletin*. "Gordon came back to pin Claybourne with the same hold after 5 minutes 44 seconds. Claybourne then used head butts and a flying drop kick to end the match in 9 minutes 50 seconds."

Unfortunately, it seems as though that victory was intended to elevate Claybourne just in time to serve him up to a major star who was visiting the territory. Primo Carnera, the 6'5" former world heavyweight boxing champion, was making one of his post-fighting-career appearances as a professional wrestler, and he wasn't in the habit of being booked to lose.

"Carnera, giant Italian grappler, meets Jack Claybourne in the main event of Promoter Al Karasick's weekly mat show," announced *The Star-Bulletin*. "The ex-heavyweight boxing champion is undefeated in wrestling and is hailed as one of the most powerful men in the sport today. Claybourne, who claims the Negro heavyweight mat crown, is agile and superbly conditioned."

As was often the case when special attractions entered the world of professional wrestling, seasoned grapplers were forced to endure losses to men who were immeasurably less adept at both the theatrical and technical elements of pro wrestling. This case would be no different, as Carnera had "his opposition looking like a midget" in the words of *The Star-Bulletin*.

"Sunday's card featured Primo Carnera, 6-foot-5 Italian grappler who toyed with Jack Claybourne before using forearm blows to set up a body press for a fall in 14 min. 29 sec. It was a one-fall-to-a-finish match," added *The Advertiser*. "Giving away weight and reach advantage, Claybourne proved no match for Carnera, who awed the crowd with his physical prowess. Claybourne used his head butt only once on the Italian grappler, but after that was busy warding off Carnera's powerful holds."

By allowing Claybourne to be so thoroughly trounced by Carnera, Karasick had essentially sacrificed the holder of the longest Hawaiian championship reign in many years to a former fighter who would not be remaining behind to continually draw money.

The normal pattern with Carnera in those days was that he would enter a territory, defeat a few of the non-champions, and then wrestle the top titlists to draws. That way, the champion could claim that he had held his own against a legitimate boxing star, Carnera's undefeated streak would be preserved, and only the undercard wrestlers who lost to Carnera would endure damage to their reputations.

This pattern would hold in this instance as well; Carnera would battle to a draw with the reigning Hawaiian junior heavyweight champion Sandor Szabo two weeks later. If this same bout had been scheduled five months prior, it might have worked wonders for the reputation of Claybourne. In this instance, he was once again relegated to being the holder of a Black championship who was no match for one of the top White special attractions.

Under the circumstances, it might have been logical to think that Claybourne's importance in Hawaii had dwindled, and those beliefs would have intensified in early April when

Jack lost a one-fall match to newcomer Jesse James of Texas in much the same manner that he used to dominate his opposition at the Civic Auditorium.

"James stopped the Negro matman in 24 minutes 13 seconds with a series of flying drop kicks and a press," recounted *The Star-Bulletin*.

Shaking off the loss, Claybourne bounced back with a victory over Flash Gordon one week later, and secured a shot at reclaiming the *Ring Magazine* title belt in a match against Sandor Szabo in the latter's first defense of his newly won championship.

The result of this bout was already a foregone conclusion to anyone who perused copies of a select few Australian news publications during the spring of 1950. On March 23rd, *The Argus* printed a list of the grapplers who were set to tour Australia during the forthcoming wrestling season, which would begin on April 15th.

Jack Claybourne was included on the list, along with Francois Vallais, Leon Miquet, Ali Riza Bey, Chief Thunderbird, Joe Campbell, Jagunda Das, Dutch Hefner, Dick Raines, Carl Davis, and Johnny Mars.

Later, in the small print on page nine of the April 13th edition of *The Sydney Morning Herald*, it stated, "Jack Claybourne will meet Ted Christy in the opening match of the Sydney Stadium season next Thursday night."

In light of this, it should come as no surprise that Szabo defeated Claybourne in convincing fashion in Honolulu's Civic Arena, essentially rendering him helpless after Claybourne managed to record the first fall of the bout.

"Claybourne didn't resort to head butting tactics until Szabo had jarred him with two back-drop holds," reported *The Advertiser*. "Still fresh and recuperating fast, Claybourne turned the tables on Szabo with head butts to set up the first fall."

Claybourne continued the headbutting attack, but Szabo successfully weathered the storm. He then caught Claybourne with a backdrop, and when Claybourne's leg was left dangling over the rope, the referee counted him out and awarded the fall to Szabo.

"Still groggy and badly shaken by the fall, Claybourne was unable to defend himself after the rest period, and the referee, Frank Merrill, stopped the match after Szabo had used another backdrop on the challenger. The end came 36 seconds after the intermission," concluded *The Advertiser*.

With that, Claybourne prepared for yet another tour of Australia, but any illusions that may have been built up in his mind that Australia was some sort of post-racial paradise were about to be cruelly shattered once he explored regions of the country where the color of his skin continued to be looked upon disapprovingly regardless of his celebrity status.

# 16 - The White Jack Claybourne

Back in his familiar Midwestern stomping grounds, Rufus Jones found himself in the rare situation of having another Black wrestler other than Jim Mitchell or Jack Claybourne to wrestle during 1950. Jones met up with the former Bat, Don Kindred, in a series of matches throughout February and March, with the majority of them ending in draws.

While this was underway, Jim Mitchell made his own return to Ontario, and when he appeared in Brantford, *The Expositor* attempted to sort out the identities of Mitchell and Jones for the sake of newer fans, and probably only succeeded in confusing them even further.

"Jimmy Mitchell, the original Black Panther, who delighted many wrestling fans here some years ago, is going to break up that 'Long time, no see' thought in local minds by an appearance here Tuesday night," printed the publication. "When Jimmy showed here, he was the fastest man of them all and reports are that he has lost none of his speed. Many fans think Rufus Jones is the Black Panther. That is an error. Mitchell hails from Puerto Rico. Jones is from Georgia."

Rather than referencing the differences in height, dimensions, hair styles, skin shades, or wrestling styles between the two men, the writer instead opted to differentiate between them on the basis of where they were from, and supplied the fans with two false locations.

Making it all the more silly was the fact that Jones made his debut in Minden City, Michigan the following month, where he was referred to as "the colored mat villain from Puerto Rico" by *The Minden City Herald*. One can only assume that the prevalence of the surnames Jones and Mitchell in Puerto Rico during that time would have been exceedingly small.

Returning to North Bay, a new word was introduced into the professional wrestling lexicon. In an effort to describe the chaos of Jones' match with Dick Marshall of Quebec City, the sportswriter for *The North Bay Nugget* typed out the sentence, "The clean-cut Mr. Marshall was unable to stand up against burly Rufus' coco-butts, and finally succumbed to one of Jones backbreaking Boston crabs."

**Jones gets kicked during a North Bay bout**

So it was that a word that would frequently be used to refer to headbutts administered by Black wrestlers — and by *one* very famous future Black wrestler in particular — came into existence. According to a quote published by the paper, Jones even took ownership of the new name for his favorite move, as he namechecked it during his stated defense as to why his favorite maneuver should remain legal.

"Just because I have a harder head than the rest does not mean that my coco-butt is illegal," said Jones. "In fact, because there's so much fuss about it, I'll be out tonight to show the boys I've really never started to get rough."

While fans were introduced to a colorful new term in that article from *The Nugget*, they were also introduced to something else, or *someone* else to be specific. The writer from the paper made sure to include the detail that one of the angry spectators "went so far as pushing Mrs. Rufus Jones on the way out, but found out to his displeasure that Mrs. Rufus also packs a solid wallop, as he had a handbag cracked over his head."

The real name of Mrs. Rufus Jones was Gertrude Clements Godfrey, who Joseph Godfrey had married in Montreal on November 13, 1944. While it's downright probable that she had ventured out on the road with her husband before and watched his matches in person, this was the first reported case of her being involved in any post-match action. This report also suggests that Godrey's marriage to Ursaline had been dissolved at some point between the middle of 1940 and the end of 1944.

This wouldn't be the only time Gertrude interacted with a fan at ringside. On the first of June, Jones was wrestling Dinty Parks at North Bay's Memorial Gardens when Dinty was counted out, and several fans attempted to take swipes at Rufus. At least one fan "was kicked in the face as he tried to grab at Rufus' leg in the skirmish."

"While the spectators were still seething, Jones made his way to the dressing room while a woman fan called him down indignantly," continued *The Nugget*. "The same woman fan then became embroiled in a battle with Rufus Jones' wife. A big crowd pushed close to watch North Bay's first ladies wrestling match, an aftermath to one of the many wild-and-wooly finishes seen on a grappling night."

After a short stint in Brantford, Ontario, Jones was trotted out in North Bay once again to take multiple cracks at wrestling Gorgeous Gus, the famous wrestling bear. For at least one of those opportunities, Rufus had the assistance of his partners Benny Trudel and Alex Kasaboski in a three-on-one handicap match. In his interview promoting the man-versus-nature affair, Jones appeared to threaten the bear with literal consumption following the conclusion of the bout.

"There's no reason to worry about the meat shortage," insisted Jones. "We'll fix it so that the bear will be in no fit shape to do any more rassling with us humans."

With the numerical odds stacked against him, Gus proved to be victorious in his match with the trio of mat villains.

Back in Brantford, *The Expositor* made no bones about the fact that Jones had gained weight, declaring that he was "black as ever, and much bigger than when the wrestling fans of this city first saw him."

Jack Claybourne was performing in a far warmer climate than Rufus at the time, and without knowing precisely what Jack was being paid to wrestle in each location, it's difficult to make a value judgment as to whether Hawaii or Australia was the better financial option for him.

However, if the per-appearance pay was even remotely close, then Australia would have won that competition with ease. With events in large stadiums every few days — all of which involved main-event appearances for Claybourne — the Australian schedule made the once-a-week pattern of Hawaii's bouts seem like a working vacation by comparison.

This Australian tour of Claybourne's would last a full six months, from late April to the end of October, and Claybourne would rotate through different opponent pairings as the tour repeatedly cycled through the major Australian cities.

Judging from the recorded match results in both the mainland United States and in Australia, Claybourne's transition into a heavy headbutter appears to have been confined to Hawaii for the most part, at least at this stage. Perhaps he thought the ability to draw upon the routine of Rufus Jones would add intrigue to his bouts, but he also didn't want to infringe on the gimmick of his Murderers' Row colleague or attract accusations of appropriation.

It's also conceivable that Claybourne believed that the isolation of Hawaii from the rest of the mainland would allow him to introduce the style in a territory prior to Jones, and thus enable him to reap the full benefits of a routine that had been proven to work phenomenally well in other locations.

Prior to Claybourne's arrival in Australia, the papers reminded wrestling fans that he was the colored world heavyweight champion, and added that he had held the Hawaii junior heavyweight title until very recently. Once Claybourne touched down in Australia, he returned to working in nothing short of a main-event capacity, and immediately attracted 5,000 fans to Sydney Stadium to watch him wrestle Ted Christy to a draw.

Then the wrestling season opened in Newcastle, and the papers tempted fans with the chance to see multiple variations of the dropkick employed by Claybourne, including a particularly devastating version.

"Claybourne, who wrestled in Newcastle two seasons ago, is a master of the drop-kick and has perfected a new hold which he calls the 'throat kick,'" reported *The Newcastle Morning Herald and Miners' Advocate*. "He is regarded as one of the two best Negro wrestlers in the world. Claybourne usually wrestles quietly, but is able to take care of himself in rough exchanges."

In order to add further credibility to Claybourne's status as an authentic Black American wrestling icon ahead of the season-opening show in Brisbane, *The Brisbane Telegraph* ran a photo of Jack Claybourne sandwiched between the still-reigning world heavyweight boxing champion Joe Louis, and former three-weight-division simultaneous titleholder Henry Armstrong in its May 4th edition.

Claybourne wrestled Karl Davis to a draw in Brisbane, and finally introduced enough of the use of his head as a weapon into the match that the Australian writers took note of it.

"Throughout the bout, Claybourne had made his target a bald patch on Davis's head, and this eventually led to Davis's roughhouse tactics at the finish," stated *The Brisbane Telegraph*. "Claybourne repeatedly brought his head down on his rival's crown! And, after all, a man can only take so much."

**Henry Armstrong, Jack Claybourne, and Joe Louis**

Still, Claybourne seemed to utilize his head with far less frequency in Australia than he had in Hawaii. One reason for this may have been that the use of headbutts had been deemed illegal in Australian wrestling matches, although an occasional use was likely to result in the offender receiving only a warning from the referee instead of outright disqualification, similar to the use of punches.

As had been the case in his prior Australian visits, Claybourne's foremost selling point was his use of dropkicks, flying tactics, and other high-flying stunts of the era. This was underscored when he defeated Frenchman Felix Miquet in Melbourne.

"Claybourne, a beautifully built negro, is the most agile wrestler to come to Australia since Jim Londos, and he had the Frenchman constantly on the run," printed *The Age*. "The equalizing fall came in the sixth, when Claybourne vaulted over the referee's head and drop-kicked Miquet, who at that stage was being lectured by the referee."

This accentuation of Claybourne's aerial feats resulted in the restoration and heavy use of his "Jumping Jack" moniker for promoting his appearances. Still, Claybourne played the role of being pro wrestling's foremost gentleman to a tee, which was exhibited during his bout with Scotsman Joe Campbell.

"Negro wrestler Jack Claybourne refused to accept the verdict in his favour when Joe Campbell was injured during last night's wrestle at Leichardt Stadium," said *The Daily Examiner*. "Campbell was injured in the groin at the beginning of the seventh round. Claybourne took no advantage of Campbell's injury, and when his opponent could not continue, Claybourne would not accept the decision in his favour. The wrestle was then declared a draw."

As had been their pattern, the Australian press yearned to know more about what made Claybourne tick. During an interview with a Brisbane newspaper, ironically known as *The Truth*, Claybourne offered the story that he had earned honors as a hurdler while competing in college, resulting in his prodigious leaping ability.

Claybourne also supplied the Onlooker of *The Miner's Advocate* with a few tidbits of information about his life, starting with the previously mentioned detail that he was an avid baseball fan and participant.

"He spends as much time as possible in baseball practice," wrote the Onlooker. "Claybourne, who claims the coloured wrestling championship, is unbeaten in four seasons. He says his colour prevents him from having a chance to win the world's heavyweight title. He also believes his having defeated three men who recently held the title — in non-title bouts — is against his prospects of a title match."

Clearly nothing about these sentences were true, save for the likely possibility that Claybourne was a huge baseball fan. Claybourne had routinely been fodder for world titleholders, whether they were currently reigning titlists or former holders of those championships. He had also suffered multiple losses in his previous visits to Australia.

However, Claybourne *was* correct that his race would have kept him from achieving any serious consideration to hold a major world title in the era that preceded the National Wrestling Alliance. And, with ever more wrestling territories falling under the NWA's banner, a Jack Claybourne world-title reign approved by a vote of the NWA Board of Directors would have been an outright impossibility.

Had this interview taken place just one year later, there is a solid chance that Claybourne would have professed himself to be an ardent fan and player of basketball. October 1950 would be when the color line was broken in the National Basketball Association. However, it would still be a few years before players like Don Barksdale, Willie Naulls and Bob Russell would confirm that Blacks could succeed in the league at an All-Star level.

Over the course of his time in Australia, Claybourne seemed to have endeared himself to the nation's Aboriginal community on multiple occasions. In early June, he was on hand to bounce the ball to open a match for the Lake Tyers Aboriginal rugby team. On at least one other occasion, Jack mingled with Aboriginal Australians in their place of worship in Fitzroy, just outside of Melbourne, and was blamed for the inattentiveness of the congregation's children.

"Seated in their midst was American coloured wrestler Jack Claybourne, idol of the aboriginal kiddies of Fitzroy, and 'Uncle Jack' to a lot of them," wrote *The Argus*. "Claybourne, accompanied by American negro boxer Freddy Dawson, and his manager Mr. H.D. Rudolph, was the guest of Mr. Nicholls, who has conducted the mission in Gore St., under the auspices of the Church of Christ, for the last seven years. Welcoming the visitors, Mr. Nicholls said that the people of his church felt that they belonged to them."

**Jack Claybourne reads to children in Australia**

The sense of kinship felt between Claybourne and the Aboriginal Australians may have been at least somewhat spawned by the similarity of their complexions, and the increased experience Claybourne was having with the sort of racial discrimination that had eluded him in previous trips to the country.

Under the title "Racial discrimination practised against coloured visitors," the August 10th edition of *The Labor Call* devoted considerable space to the discriminatory treatment experienced by Claybourne upon his arrival in Broken Hill, along the western edge of New South Wales.

The writer of the article called attention to the fact that most Australians were quick to denounce mistreatment of the Aboriginal population at that point, and that most of the nation's inhabitants would have said that Australia had no color problem that could compare with what went on in other countries of the world.

"The stigma of the color bar is being applied mainly to visitors to this country who come out, or are brought out, under contract, because of their talents, and to demonstrate their prowess," stated *The Labor Call*. "These people come to Australia in good faith and are snubbed when they arrive. They are being denied accommodation and banned from hotels."

The writer then went on to say that continuing to discriminate against others on the basis of race would result in bad publicity for Australia, which had the potential to do irreparable damage to the nation's reputation.

"Australians themselves are doing something they have so often criticised," continued the article. "In Broken Hill last week, several of the city's leading hotels refused accommodation to visiting American wrestler Jack Claybourne."

The writer from *The Labor Call* then contacted the hotels to confirm that "a ban existed, and that it applied not to any particular person or type of person, but to all colored people."

"Such a ban means that no matter who the colored visitor is; no matter how well educated, behaved, popular, or otherwise acknowledged, he or she is unable to stay at the leading hotels," concluded *The Labor Call*. "Mention of Jack Claybourne was only an instance, as was the information that Chief Little Wolf's reception would be cold, and that he would be downright unwelcome. It is pleasing, at least, that such discrimination is not carried out in other parts of Australia. It would indeed be a sorry day for Australia if racial discrimination were allowed to develop."

The denial of services to Claybourne in Broken Hill stood in stark contrast to how he was advertised there, which was perhaps the strongest promotion he received anywhere in his career outside of Hawaii.

Ahead of Claybourne's bouts against French-Canadian wrestler Frank Valois, *The Barrier Daily Truth* of Broken Hill danced carefully around the wording of Claybourne being the "colored champion of the world" on several occasions, seemingly inflating his credential to being that of an outright world heavyweight champion.

"It is not every day that an international match like this — the French champion meeting the American and world champion — is staged right here in the Silver City," boasted *The Daily Truth*, before ensuring fans that Claybourne "will be bringing his world championship belt."

In a subsequent advertisement from *The Daily Truth*, Claybourne was listed as "Jack Claybourne, The Colored American, Champion of the World," with commas permitting enough strategic separation of the words to suggest that the reference to Claybourne as a full-fledged world titleholder was intentional.

Whatever mistreatment Claybourne may have experienced in Broken Hill, he still expressed his fondness for Australia regularly. A few months into the 1950 tour, he even told *The Newcastle Sun* that he would like to resettle in Australia if possible, but feared "the immigration laws might make it difficult for him to become a new Australian."

"He says he would prefer to deal in real estate, in which he and his wife are keenly interested," stated *The Sun*. "He should be, as he owns two large apartment houses in Los Angeles, and after the Australian tour, he'll devote some of his time to his business interests before fulfilling a contract to wrestle in France."

Claybourne's race was also factored into at least one of his Australian feuds in a fashion that was seldom utilized in the United States. For multiple months of the tour, race-based animosity between Claybourne and Ernie "Dutch" Hefner was played up for the sake of raising interest in their eventual clashes.

**Claybourne takes down a mat rival in Australia**

"A question now intriguing followers is whether Hefner and the negro champion, Jack Claybourne, will meet," pondered *The Argus*. "Hefner is a Texan, and with the southerner's deep-rooted prejudice against coloured people, has resolutely declined on previous visits to go into the ring with negro wrestlers. One thing certain is that if Hefner and Claybourne meet, it will be a real 'blood' match."

It is true that Hefner had been on a tour of Australia with Seelie Samara in 1948 and had not shared the ring with him, although no mention had been made of any lingering racial prejudice preventing that bout from occurring.

Whether Hefner's absence of prior Black opponents had been a byproduct of authentic racism, or merely an innocent coincidence caused by the scheduling of matches, the pairing of Claybourne and Hefner was said to have resulted from threats against the future career prospects of the latter.

"Hefner, who comes from the 'deep South' of USA — his home is in Houston, Texas — has repeatedly refused matches with negroes and objected strongly when his bout with Claybourne was suggested," stated *The Herald*. "However, Stadiums Ltd. enforced the clause in Hefner's contract which specifies that it has the right to select Hefner's opponents in Australia."

Perhaps as a means of playing up his racial hatred toward wrestlers of a different complexion, the press suggested that Hefner seemed to adopt a rougher style when facing wrestlers of different races, whether they were Black, presumably Native American Indian in the case of Chief Little Wolf, or East Indian like Joginder Singh.

"Hefner accepted the ultimatum, but insisted that he is wrestling under protest," said *The Telegraph*. "Matched with these wrestlers, Hefner completely changed from straight wrestling to a rough, rugged style."

Some of the bouts between Claybourne and Hefner were filled with such acrimonious tension that the passion emitted by the two even prompted altercations amongst the spectators, which *The Age* pointed out in one of its reports from Sydney Stadium.

"With the Stadium in uproar as Hefner crashed the negro to the canvas with punches and kicks, a brawl developed in the bleachers, and three men were ejected by attendants," reported *The Age*.

Most of the confrontations between the two grapplers ended in draws, but even when Hefner won, he was presented as a pitiable figure for allowing his racial animosity to get the best of him. Noting that Hefner had won a match against Claybourne one fall to nil, *The Courier-Mail* reported that Hefner "finished without a friend at the Brisbane Stadium last night."

"There was a revival of the age-old war between American whites and negroes in the wrestling bout between Dutch Hefner and Jack Claybourne at Brisbane Stadium last night, and the white man, Hefner, did not show to advantage," reported *The Telegraph*. "Without any provocation, Hefner indulged in an orgy of punching, jolting, and eye gouging, while Claybourne, obviously trying hard to keep his temper, concentrated on wrestling."

When Hefner won, he was booed mercilessly by the fans, and yet "Claybourne forgot and forgave at the end of the bout, went over to Hefner's corner, and shook his hand."

Surprisingly, the most far-reaching publicity Claybourne would ever receive in the United States occurred as a result of one of his matches in Australia. In the middle of a bout against Frank Valois in Melbourne, Claybourne leapt over the back of referee Bonny Muir and planted both of his feet squarely into the face of his French-Canadian opponent.

The photographer for *The Argus* snapped a picture-perfect photo of the moment, which was soon shared in sports sections across the United States, including in places like Atlanta, Georgia, where Claybourne had never wrestled before.

As Claybourne's tour of Australia was wrapping up in October, *New York Age* sports editor Les Matthews caught up with Hawaii promoter Al Karasick, who insisted that Claybourne remained the greatest attraction on the island. This belief of Karasick's essentially ensured that Claybourne would be welcomed back to Hawaii whenever he liked, even if he needed to leave every so often to permit wrestling fans to miss him.

## Gentleman Jack and Rough Rufus

Rather than touring France as he suggested he might, Claybourne went straight back to work in Southern California. What awaited him was the use of an advertising slogan that probably made sense in the minds of the promoters who introduced it, but begged further analysis.

Claybourne famously dropkicks Frank Valois

The title being applied to Claybourne — in the fall of 1950 — was that he was "The Negro Argentina Rocca." This comparison was clearly intended to portray Claybourne favorably with Antonino Rocca of Argentina, who was rapidly becoming a wrestling superstar by virtue of his acrobatic presentation, chiseled physique, and handsome face.

The inherent affront within the comparison was that Claybourne was 11 years older than Rocca, had debuted at least 10 years prior to Rocca, and had established the foundations of his style long before Rocca had gotten involved in the wrestling business. To apply a boxing analogy, it would have been like Joe Louis being described as "The Negro Rocky Marciano" right when Louis was on the brink of retirement, and the much younger Italian American champion was entering his prime.

Just as Claybourne was preparing for a match against the newly crowned holder of the version of the world heavyweight championship recognized in the Los Angeles market — Baron Michele Leone — a sports writer from *The Wilmington Press-Journal* actually had the sense to point out this anachronism.

"The Baron opposes 'Jumping Jack' Claybourne, Boston tar baby, who was performing ring acrobatics and spectacular jumping tactics before Argentina Rocca knew what the inside of a wrestling ring looked like," stated *The Press-Journal*. "The Amazing South American only capitalized on what 'Jumping Jack' has been doing for years without more than passing mention. Now they heralded Claybourne as the 'Negro Argentina Rocca.'"

From there, the approach of the publicists changed, with Claybourne receiving a larger and more appropriate share of the credit for helping to innovate — or at least propagate — the wrestling style that Rocca had so effectively monetized. In effect, they attempted to rebrand Antonino Rocca as "The White Jack Claybourne."

*The Independent* of Long Beach acknowledged Claybourne as "the original mat acrobat." *The Progress-Bulletin* of Pomona went one step further, hailing Claybourne as "the originator of the ring acrobatics that have since made Argentina Rocca famous."

In the midst of this, Claybourne did something that was atypical in his career; he won a one-on-one match against a former world champion, and in straight falls no less. While the version of the world title Babe Sharkey wore in Maryland wasn't necessarily the most prestigious of the bunch, it still permitted him to lay claim to the status of being a former world titlist even when he wrestled in California.

Out in Northern Ontario, Rufus Jones was hunting for a championship of sorts when he entered the Silver Jubilee Championship wrestling tournament — an eight-man tournament that required the victor to defeat three different opponents on the same night to emerge victorious.

The majority of Jones' time in Northern Ontario was seasoned with a storyline that involved the situational legality of his headbutts. For the most part, the maneuver was deemed illegal, requiring Jones to slip them in while the referee was distracted. In other scenarios, fans were notified well ahead of time that Jones' headbutts would be temporarily permitted in bouts with special stipulations. In several cases, this served as the modus operandi for effectuating Jones' immediate disqualification from matches he had been otherwise dominating.

It was a plot that played itself out very effectively during the Silver Jubilee tournament. In the quarterfinal round, Jones surreptitiously whacked referee Danno McDonald with a headbutt to put him out of commission, and then he "used the same weapon on [Wild Bill] Zim when the referee was slumped to the floor."

"When McDonald got to his feet, Jones had Zim writhing on the mat, a victim of the effective Boston crab," added *The Nugget*. "The referee had to count Zim out."

Fittingly, Jones was then disqualified in the semifinal round when the referee spotted him headbutting Dinty Parks, providing Parks with a clear path to the finals where he succeeded in defeating Dutch Schultz to win the Silver Jubilee championship, and the prize of 100 silver dollars.

Jones' quest to exact revenge on Parks in late September was quite memorable, as it would be held at the unusual site of North Bay's Memorial Gardens — an ice arena, with the ring positioned directly on top of the solid ice. As soon as the location for the show was announced, Jones was quoted in *The Nugget*, ensuring Parks that he'd "better bring his skates," as Rufus' goal was to "toss him right out to the blue line."

In other words, Jones was threatening to throw Parks from center ice all the way into the defensive zone, which was a distance of 30 feet in 1950. Jones neglected to mention whether he intended Parks to travel the entire span through the air, or if the length of the toss would be aided by the distance Parks would cover while sliding along the ice's surface.

In what would be one of his final appearances in Northern Ontario, Jones apparently did his best to give the fans their money's worth. This included an actual attempt to make good on his promise to hurl Parks out to the blue line of the hockey rink.

"Jones turned in one of his better displays of showmanship as he was disqualified by referee Bill Curry," observed *The Nugget*. "He danced like a dervish, he muttered and gibbered and roared, alternately. He attacked the referee and threw him around like a sack of meal. Jones sent the crowd into near hysteria with his antics, and when he was leaving the ring, with the boos of the fans in his ears, Rufus made a couple of threatening moves toward the seats. The women screamed and scattered. The men looked uncomfortable."

Preceding this scene was the bout itself, during which Rufus lost the first fall, and then resorted to all manner of cheating, including "hair pulling, eye gouging, kneeing in the groin, punching, and using the ropes to exert pressure." Jones then won the second fall with a Boston crab, and became even more aggressive as the third frame began.

"[Rufus] wanted to score the third fall right then and there, so he tore into Dinty and finally heaved him right out of the ring onto the ice," continued the report. "Referee Curry tried to warn the Dark Destroyer, but he was beyond restraint. He hurled the ref to the mat. He waited for Parks to try to crawl back to the ring, then he tossed him out again. Curry lost his temper, backed Rufus against the ropes, and flailed away at him with his fists. Then he declared Jones disqualified."

Leaving Ontario, Jones returned to the Northwest, where his headbutt remained as legal as ever in all scenarios. Upon the reemergence of "Detroit's coffee-colored nasty," *The Vancouver News-Herald* declared "Rufus Jones' headpiece is as sturdy as ever," as he earned a knockout victory over Eddie Williams at Vancouver's Exhibition Center through the violent use of his head.

The precise technique Jones implemented to butt his opponents was described in detail in the pages of *The Olympian* as Rufus prepared to make his debut in Olympia, Washington against Gordon Hessel. This technical breakdown was offered in conjunction with an authentic correction, as the paper decided to inform fans that Jones was a northerner rather than a native of the American South as originally stated.

"Jones, who makes his Olympia debut Tuesday night, is from Boston, not from Mississippi as erroneously stated on the program, and has a ruthless style that wrecks most opponents in short order," stated the article. "The 'head butt' for which he is famous, although in appearance it is as though he were making a short, quick nod, is as generally lethal as a hefty slug from a hammer, and it will take all of Hessel's agility to not be there when he 'butts.'"

As it often happened, Jones had a victory stripped from him when the referee retroactively disqualified him for using headbutts, reversed the stoppage victory for Jones, and awarded the bout to Hessel, leaving the "infuriated" Jones protesting the decision.

These proceedings once again allowed the issue to be raised as to the legality of headbutts in the areas of Washington where wrestling was being introduced. *The Daily Herald* of Everett even cited an alleged ruling by the Washington State Athletic Commission, establishing with respect to headbutts that "there is nothing illegal about them."

In the meantime, Jack Claybourne ambled along in California. Aside from a lone victory over Babe Sharkey, Jack primarily wrestled in semifinal slots as 1951 got underway, and was booked and promoted respectfully. His exploits in Australia resulted in him being advertised as the Australian heavyweight champion, and *The Anaheim Bulletin* labeled Jack as "second only to Argentina Rocca as a 'jumper,'" apparently indicating that the popularity of Rocca had given the style such credibility that it retroactively made Claybourne's high-flying approach to matches more viable.

*The Santa Ana Register* elaborated as to the specific tactics that Claybourne employed before Rocca, stating "[Claybourne] was performing high-jump knee-lifts, five-foot high-jump drop-kicks, and a half a dozen other spectacular acrobatic maneuvers long before Argentina Rocca was discovered."

It was also during this trip that Claybourne had another brush with the next generation of Black pro wrestlers, a few of whom were able to leverage opportunities that had likely eluded Claybourne. The wrestler in question was Woodrow "Woody" Strode, who had capitalized on the stardom he had achieved as a football player and used it to fasttrack his way to preferred placement and preferential treatment on professional wrestling cards.

Strode was quite literally one of the Black football players who broke the color line of the National Football League in 1946 when he signed to play for the Los Angeles Rams. All of this came after Strode had enjoyed massive success as a member of "The Gold Dust Gang" with Kenny Washington and Jackie Robinson on a UCLA Bruins football team that finished undefeated in 1939, albeit with four ties on its record.

In stark contrast to Claybourne, who lost frequently in almost every territory he wrestled in, Strode was treated as a special attraction from the first moment he ever appeared in a wrestling ring. As a result, Strode seldom lost — especially in the markets where he also played football — and he ran up undefeated streaks that were certainly exaggerated, but nonetheless believable.

After Strode made his Hawaiian debut in early April, the island's newspapers broke the news that promoter Al Karasick was desperately hoping to bring Claybourne back to Hawaii in order to pair him with the football star. A few days later, Karasick confirmed that the match had been made.

"The powerful colored stars will team up against Bobby Bruns, international star, and Gordon Hessell in a two out of three falls tag match," announced *The Honolulu Star-Bulletin*.

Meanwhile, *The Honolulu Advertiser* reminded its readers of Claybourne's past exploits, calling to mind that Claybourne "held the Hawaiian junior heavyweight belt longer than any grappler since Charley Carr," whose Hawaiian title reign had lasted well over two years.

"A comebacker to local wrestling, Claybourne is one of the most colorful men in the game," added *The Advertiser*. "His aggressive shuffling tactics, his flying dropkicks, and his mastery of holds and breaks are well known to local mat fans. In Strode, Claybourne has a capable partner who is held in high esteem in West Coast rings. Strode is fast and uses grid tactics with terrific force. His flying tackles should click well with Claybourne's drop kicks."

At the April 9th Civic Auditorium show, the team of Claybourne and Strode got off to a slow start, with Claybourne succumbing to a series of dropkicks from Bobby Bruns. That's when Claybourne resurrected the tactics that had served him well throughout his long reign as the champion of Hawaii.

"Claybourne, the former territorial junior heavyweight belt holder, used his head butts to good advantage, and after a series of body slams applied a press on Bruns to garner the second fall," recounted *The Star-Bulletin*. "The third and deciding fall came 9 minutes 10 seconds later when Strode, together with Claybourne, pinned Hessell."

As 1951 unfolded for Rufus Jones in Oregon, he earned a match against Gorgeous George by winning an elimination tournament, and defeating Jack Kiser in the finals. Notwithstanding the fact that George held no championships to speak of, his undeniable prestige as a box office attraction afforded him treatment that was typically reserved for reigning champions, and this included wrestlers occasionally being required to qualify to face him.

According to promoter Don Owen, George was a major attraction amongst female fans due to his muscles, blond hair, and robes. Owen also told *The Eugene Register Guard* that he expected all of the males in attendance to be solidly behind Rufus Jones.

If there was any truth to Owen's statement, then the men who traveled home from the Eugene Armory on that January night were indeed ecstatic, as 3,000 fans "watched the Detroit Negro head-butt Gorgeous George pratically out of this world" to win the first match between them on the Pacific Coast.

The Gorgeous One's entrance routine may have lasted longer than the actual match. *The Register-Guard* described a scene in which George entered the ring wearing "a scarlet velvet robe with gold trains," along with hair that was held in place with bobby pins. His valet carried a silver tray that held a white bath mat.

"The grand entrance over, Jones and George went to it, and in less than half a minute, George had the first fall," reported the article. "Then Rufus began to work on George's head with headbutts, which fixed Gorgeous and softened him up to give Jones the second fall. During the third fall, George's secretary entered the ring and began to help his master. Rufus began butting both of their heads, and finally Referee Harry Elliott disqualified George and awarded the final fall and the match to Jones."

## Gentleman Jack and Rough Rufus

Unquestionably, Jones' victory over Gorgeous George would end up as the most high-profile win of his career, and it wasn't particularly close. That's because the pairing of Gorgeous George with national television had enabled the native of Butte, Nebraska to achieve a level of mainstream crossover success that was virtually unprecedented, and unmatched by other wrestlers at the time.

Short of a major championship victory, there wasn't a more famous box office attraction at the time that Jones could have defeated, outside of a major sports celebrity making a special appearance in a wrestling capacity.

The victory over Gorgeous George seemed to put some serious wind in Jones' sails, as he went on a destructive tear through all of his opposition in the Northwest. The majority of his wins in the aftermath of the noteworthy victory over George arrived in a dominating fashion, and usually concluded with a few headbutts, a Boston crab, and the usual complaints about disreputable tactics.

When the mind's eye conjures up a vision of a Rufus Jones headbutt, the temptation is to imagine a headbutt administered from a standing position. This was indeed the case more often than not. Writer Jack Hewins of *The Olympian* offered his readers a detailed, step-by-step explanation for how Jones applied the move to its unfortunate recipients.

"To apply the hold, he takes his opponent's cheeks gently between his palms and brings his (Jones') head sharply into contact with his (the opponent's) noggin," explained Hewins. "He uses himself like a mallet. Whacko! The true believers feel it as far back as the third row. One large opponent, in an exclusive interview, said: 'It hoits.'"

While not as common, there were also instances when Jones was content to deliver one or more menacing butts to the head or body of a downed opponent, and a description supplied by *The Oregonian* of one of Jones' Portland bouts with Eric Pederson makes this quite clear.

Jones won the first fall with a Boston crab, and lost the second to a flurry of dropkicks from Pederson. During the third fall, Pederson knocked Jones to the outside of the ring and then leaped over the ropes to fight with Jones amongst the fans.

"Pederson, back in the ring, brought Jones over the ropes with a flying headlock, but Jones retreated outside the hemp again," continued *The Oregonian*. "When Pederson charged he was met with a head butt which knocked him down. Jones dove onto the mat, and three more head butts finished Pederson."

It's difficult to conceive of a time when the headbutt wasn't in widespread use, let alone a maneuver that was completely alien to certain wrestling audiences. Yet there's ample evidence that in early 1951 there were still regions of the wrestling world where fans needed to be educated about the nature and legality of the move.

As *The Columbian* of Vancouver attempted to educate its readers, "Jones has developed what he calls a head-butt. When possible, Jones prefers to crack heads with his opponent. To date, he is undefeated on the Pacific coast because his cranium will take more abuse than those of his opponents."

These types of assertions resulted in Jones often being erroneously credited for the creation of the headbutt altogether, which is not true even though he probably had a greater hand in popularizing the move than any other individual wrestler, possibly beyond even Gus Sonnenberg.

There were plenty of reasons to lionize Rufus Jones as an innovator in the world of professional wrestling, and students of the art of wrestling likely could have foreseen a later time when fans would be able to reflect upon the contributions of Jones to the development of the industry. The only question that remained was whether or not Jones would be alive to appreciate it.

## 17 - Head-On Collision

Departing from Hawaii, Jack Claybourne embarked upon a 1951 tour of New Zealand with plans announced that he would be appearing in Hawaii later in the year after spending the bulk of his summer in Australia. Meanwhile, a new face materialized in Hawaii to replace Claybourne as Strode's partner in the territory's Black tag team combination.

"Buddy Jackson, Negro junior heavyweight pro wrestling champion of the world teams up with Woody Strode in a tag team match against Andre Adoree and Andre Asselin Sunday night at the Civic Auditorium," announced *The Star-Bulletin*. "The 5 foot 9 inch, 210 pound Jackson also holds the Negro junior heavyweight crown in the southern states."

Ernest P. "Buddy" Jackson Jr. was the son of pharmacist Ernest Jackson and his wife Viola Walker — who were of Alabama and Arizona respectively. Jackson was born on June 21, 1921, and grew up in the area around Columbus, Ohio, resulting in him routinely being advertised as an Ohio State University wrestler, football player, and pharmacy student.

Jackson had first come to the attention of the wrestling world on the All-Negro wrestling shows headlined by Don Blackman that swung through the American South. Coincidentally, he wrestled "Black Panther" Alex Kaffner at a few of these shows, and at subsequent events in other states, in some ways mirroring the path of Claybourne during his early years.

In an intriguing bit of foreshadowing, *The Star-Bulletin* added some backstory to Jackson's introduction by including that Claybourne had been "one of the men chiefly responsible for Jackson's start in the pro mat game." While there is no clear evidence that the two men had even met prior to 1951, they would eventually find themselves joined at the hip in one of the most evident and enduring business partnerships between wrestlers of the era, and Black wrestlers in particular.

In the meantime, Claybourne did not make a professional appearance in Australia until July, and in light of the story that *The News* of Adelaide relayed from Reuters about incidents that encircled Claybourne in New Zealand, the world's most internationally famous Black wrestler may have wished he had departed for Australia sooner.

"While Australian wrestler Al Costello was resting in his hotel room over the weekend he was awakened by a man who had entered the room," Reuters reported the news out of Auckland, New Zealand. "The man said he was looking for Negro wrestler Jack Claybourne. Costello told the intruder that Claybourne was at another hotel."

Costello was aware that the maid's key had been stolen earlier in the day, so he bounded down the stairs, beat the elevator to the lobby, and turned the intruder over to the police. The man later admitted to several theft charges, but no mention was made of precisely what he'd had in mind for Claybourne if he encountered him.

Returning to action in Australia, Claybourne went straight back to his usual bag of tricks, although there was some confusion — possibly intentional — about the identity of the championship belt in his possession. In both Melbourne and Tazmania, Claybourne's championship was referred to as "the Hawaiian championship," and "the *Ring Magazine* belt," even though he had not been in possession of Hawaii's top title for nearly two years.

*The Truth* of Brisbane referred to the arrival of Claybourne as "a welcome shot in the arm to local wrestling," and recalled that he had "made wrestling history in this country last season" simply by unleashing dropkicks on his opponents from a height of six feet in the air. There would be other callbacks to Claybourne's prior appearances Down Under, as he would once again link up with his racist adversary Dutch Hefner.

*The Sunday Mail* eagerly reminded its readers that Hefner "comes from the south of America where coloured boxers and wrestlers are not allowed to meet white opponents," and that the Texan had supposedly "never wrestled a coloured man in his 20 years in the ring until he met Claybourne."

**Claybourne stomps on his opponent in the corner**

At least one statement from Hefner suggests that headbutts had also found their way into Claybourne's Australian routine even though the move had been banned from the country's wrestling rings.

"If Claybourne uses his head, I will start plenty of forearm jolting, and every one will be loaded," Hefner was quoted as telling *The Brisbane Telegraph*.

The bouts between Hefner and Claybourne often got rough, and resulted in both grapplers brawling their way through the bleachers. A few of those episodes sucked some of the fans further into the action than they'd bargained for.

"The negro, extremely popular with the crowd, forced Hefner to the ropes with a forward arm splits and threw him out of the ring. Claybourne jumped out after him," illustrated *The Examiner* of Tasmania. "Spectators in ringside seats ran in all directions as Hefner picked up a chair and attempted to hit Claybourne over the head. In doing so, Hefner struck a woman, but she was unhurt."

Inexplicably, Hefner was billed as the world heavyweight champion during several bouts in Australia — especially in Tasmania — but there was no mention of the title being transferred to any of the wrestlers who defeated him by pinfall during the tour, including Claybourne. Jack would not receive the opportunity to claim a race-neutral world championship during the tour, but he made plenty of other history in Australia that fall.

"Dutch Hefner and Dick Raines will wrestle Chief Little Wolf and Jack Claybourne in a teams 'tag' match at the Stadium next Sunday," reported Harold Balfe of *The Argus* on October 22nd. "This form of wrestling bout, entirely new to Australia, is very popular in the U.S.A."

On October 28th, 1951, the first tag team bout in the history of Australia was ruled a draw, but the match arrived at that outcome through the most memorable means possible. Longtime enemies Hefner and Claybourne shockingly teamed up and turned against their respective teammates over the course of the encounter, when Raines repeatedly struck Hefner, and Little Wolf turned on Claybourne when Jack refused to participate in the onslaught as Wolf and Raines ganged up on the helpless Hefner.

"A full house may be expected when Claybourne and Hefner pair in an effort to out-rough the 'badmen' Raines and Wolf next Saturday night," reported *The Age*.

The rematch between the four men — having swapped partners — was won by the team of Hefner and Claybourne on November 4th to conclude the season, resulting in Claybourne also being a member of the first team to win a tag team match in Australia.

Although he had achieved undeniable fame as one of the most popular sportsmen in Australia, there was still apparently some confusion amongst some of the Australians as to exactly who Claybourne was when he was spotted training in public, which he apparently engaged in with regularity.

**Claybourne training outdoors**

In the "People in the Sportlight" section of *The Truth*, a rather humorous anecdote was shared by stadium manager Harry Miller about a Claybourne sighting in Sydney.

"Last week, sweatered up and in heavy boots, [Miller] jogged road-work round King's Cross with giant negro wrestler Jack Claybourne, who looked fit to fight for a world's heavyweight championship in a white sweater, white scarf, and long white sweat pants," began *The Truth*. "A dear old lady stopped her car alongside them and said, 'Goodness me! Are you Jack Johnson the negro fighter?'"

While Claybourne and many others certainly found it humorous that he was mistaken for a legendary Black boxer who had passed away more than five years earlier — and who would have been *73 years old* at the time if he had managed to stay alive — some people apparently were far less amused by some of the depictions of Claybourne that had been appearing in *The Daily Telegraph*.

Brodie Mack, the illustrator for *The Telegraph*, had reportedly received some unpleasant feedback for the way he had depicted the wrestlers in his illustrations, and especially Claybourne, who he routinely drew with exaggeratedly thick lips.

After drawing a new comic strip that referenced past drawings of wrestlers appearing like gorillas, Mack submitted a perfect sketching of Claybourne's head and face in its "ebony symmetry" simply to demonstrate that he was capable of doing so, before immediately following that up with yet another caricature, delivered in a style that later generations would regard as unequivocally racist.

Incidentally, it is from this 1951 Australian tour that the only video footage of Jack Claybourne in action that has surfaced to date was taken. It consists of a little less than two minutes of clips from a Claybourne victory over Laverne Baxter in Sydney on August 9th.

At 41 years of age, Claybourne is clearly past his prime, having been worn down by nearly 20 consecutive years of travel, injuries, weight gain, and nightly impacts with a stiff wrestling mat.

Limitations aside, Jack can still be seen effortlessly leaping from a suboptimal, flat-footed stance to dropkick the 6'3" Baxter square in the face, jumping into the air to headbutt his taller foe, and bounding to touch his toes in a display of exuberance.

Having established that no ordinary man could stand before the unrelenting force of his headbutts, Rufus set his sights on a more threatening mammalian entity when he once again laid a challenge at the feet of Gus the Bear for the first time on American soil, in Albany, Oregon. This time, Jones was quoted in *The Greater Oregon* as saying that he was "going to headbutt the big hunk of fur."

*The Albany Democrat-Herald* offered a few more details about the arrangements made for the sanctioned man-on-bear combat, informing fans that Gus would be muzzled, and his claws would be covered, while humorously adding that Rufus would therefore have an unfair advantage because he would have the full use of his own teeth and nails. They also strongly implied that Jones believed his life was on the line, stating that he "demanded a $150 guarantee to risk life and limb, along with an additional $1,000 if he could survive in the ring with Gus for 10 minutes."

Rufus made good on his promise to headbutt Gus the bear, but he landed the blow to no effect. This may have had something to do with the thickness of the average black bear's skull being approximately three times that of the average man's, but was infinitely more likely to have been due to the bear's refusal to sell the damage of the move as generously as Jones' ordinary opponents.

"The bear, while he got several good toe holds and arm locks on Rufus, was never guilty of choking, and in 9½ minutes, had Rufus worn out and on his back for the count," concluded *The Greater Oregon*.

Competitors outside of the genus Ursus had far more difficulty contending with Jones in the ring, at least in the Pacific Northwest. *The Herald and News* described how Jones mercilessly "popped open" the head of Bulldog Clements, resulting in blood flow so excessive that "many of the ringsiders doled out more money to remove blood from their clothing than they did to buy a close-up seat."

The forehead of Clements seemed to have been a favorite target of Jones. In their rematch at the Klamath Falls

Armory, Jones split Clements open once again with a series of headbutts in the second fall, and finally put him away with a Boston crab to win the match. During a tag bout in Medford, the writer from *The Medford Mail Tribune* tabulated 12 unanswered headbutts from Jones that left the bleeding Clements lying helplessly in a pool of his own blood before he found himself trapped in a Boston crab and forced to submit.

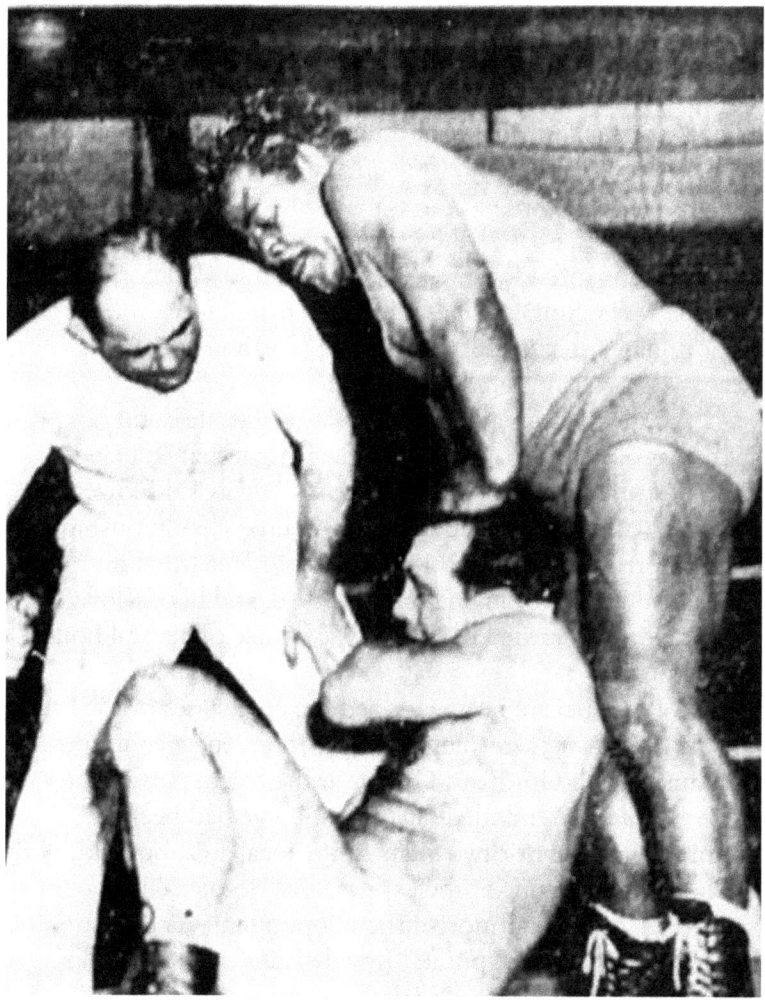

**Rufus Jones brutalizes an adversary**

Even though this trip to the Pacific Northwest hadn't inspired the same sort of overtly racist epithets or derogatory terms that had previously been used by the local papers to refer to Jones, his race still occasionally came into play for the sake of setting up feuds for matches. During a June tag team bout in Salem, Jones and his partner Ace Abbott suffered a loss because they spent more time quarreling with one another than they did with their opponents, Cowboy Carlson and Frenchie Roy.

"Abbott was substituting for Mike Nazarian, and claimed he didn't want a Negro for a partner," reported *The Capital Journal*. "So while Abbott and Jones were conducting their small-scale race riot, Carlson and Roy easily recorded a victory."

This race-based altercation between the two partners culminated in a feud where the two men traded victories, eventually resulting in Jones winning a match to earn title opportunities against reigning Pacific Northwestern junior heavyweight champion Frank Stojack.

In his 18th year as a professional wrestler, and in his 39th year of life, the one major achievement that still eluded Jones outside of his very first year wrestling as Ed Flowers in New England was a sanctioned race-neutral championship. To the misfortune of Rufus, this was the moment when his newly developed veneer of invincibility cracked, and his challenges were repeatedly turned back over the course of several bouts with Stojack.

Right before he abandoned the core states of the Pacific Northwest wrestling territory, Jones engaged in one final tussle with Gorgeous George at the Salem Armory. *The Statesman Journal* reminded fans that George had been victorious in his prior two visits to the local area, but with both of those wins coming at the expense of "cleanies," he would find Jones to be a far more difficult opponent. As the writer of the promotional piece put it, "Rowdy Rufe" possessed "a wrestling heart" that was "as dark as his skin."

The match itself played out as a rather dominant Gorgeous George victory, although Rufus was applauded by *The Capital Journal* as a performer who "stole some of the showmanship right out from under Georgie's nose — literally." Before any of that occurred, George completed his famous ring entrance while attired in a yellow-colored robe, and tossed some of his "Georgie pins" out to his elated fans in the audience.

The first fall of the contest was awarded to George after he capitalized on a flying headlock takedown, and Rufus evened the match by knocking George senseless with a series of headbutts. It was after this second fall, during the intermission period, that Jones' flourish of showmanship was put on display.

"While Jeffries, George's valet, was combing the curls in George's hair, Rufus Jones bolted across the ring, grabbed a silver cup from the valet's tray, and tossed water from said cup into George's face," described *The Journal*. "This irked George to no end. He grabbed the tray, and crowned Rufus with the same. Rufus got hold of the wayward tray, bashed George across the forehead with it, then used it to club the valet."

Jones proceeded to headbutt George out to the ring apron, but that's when George completed his "bow-and-arrow stunt" of diving over the top rope with a crossbody takedown to score the deciding fall on Jones.

One month after his latest headline-grabbing match with Gorgeous George, Jones found himself wrestling in Twin Falls, Idaho against Luigi Macera. Apparently, someone had clued in the writer for *The Twin Fall Times-News* and several other attendees that the "dark-haired, comely young woman" sitting at ringside was Macera's wife of only eight months.

According to the *Times-News* writer, it was easy to gauge the degrees of nervousness felt by Mrs. Macera by watching her chew her gum. When the "skull-denting Negro" was busy giving her husband a headache, the cadence of her chewing quickened noticeably. When Macera was in control of the action, "her chewing was slow and deliberate, almost analytical."

In a stunt that was probably agreed upon in advance by the wrestlers working in the match — if not Macera's wife herself — Rufus "butted Luigi almost into Mrs. Macera's lap near the end of the match," and "the knuckles on the hand gripping the back of the chair beside her whitened."

After Rufus collected the battered body of Macera from the lap of his wife and rolled him into the ring, he then locked Macera in the Boston crab for yet another submission victory. He then defeated light heavyweight champion Frenchy Roy in Boise with headbutts and a Boston crab.

A comical aside from the bout with Roy has to do with the alleged $150 bond that Jones, "weighing 194 pounds," had supposedly forfeited after promising to weigh in at 190 pounds before wrestling against the 170-pound Roy.

A much younger and clearly lighter version of Jones officially weighed 196 pounds when registering for the U.S. Army Draft in October 1940. Since the eyeball test indicates that Jones clearly was far heavier in 1951 than in 1940, there was absolutely no chance that Jones weighed anywhere near the realm of even 194 pounds prior to wrestling against Roy, let alone 190.

In the middle of October, Jones shifted his battleground to Utah, and in response to the rare presence of a top Black wrestler — possibly the first extended stay by one in Utah since the visit from "Black Panther" Alex Kaffner in 1931 when he wrestled as Alexis Kaffir — *The Ogden Standard-Examiner* published an elaborate piece by sports columnist Al Warden about the lack of collective successes Blacks had achieved in professional wrestling.

"The marvel to this department has been the question as to why the Negro hasn't been able to make any particular headway in the grappling game," pondered Warden. "Modern wrestling, no matter what its critics cry, is no soft touch. The average wrestler is soon scarred up with the tell-tale marks of the trade — much more so than other competitive sports."

From there, Warden shifted his approach to the recitation of common criticisms he had heard to explain away the relative absence of Black success in professional wrestling, as if the contrived essence of the business and the clandestine nature of its inner workings had nothing to do with the anointing of the sport's winners, and by derivation, its champions.

**Rough Rufus ties up his foe**

"So some say that the Negro isn't physically or mentally constituted to succeed as a wrestler," Warden continued. "A few have tried, most of them wilting under the steady pounding they must take in the scramble for the money involved. Now Rufus Jones comes as a striking exception. He succeeds by being rough, even rougher than wrestling's top roughhouse meanies. He wins most of his bouts with terrific head bumps, grasping his opponent by the head and ramming the foe head-to-head. The current issue of *Ring Magazine* describes a gory match at Portland recently in which Gorgeous George took the worst beating of his career 'at the hands and head of Rowdy Rufus Jones.'"

With that sort of an introduction, it should come as no surprise that Jones was immediately booked as a monstrous threat to all of the mainstays of the Rocky Mountain region. The papers described "the Michigan Negro" as "the biggest noise ever to hit local wrestling ranks."

In his Ogden debut, Jones "did a neat job of bloodletting" while defeating Kenny Mayne, and when Mayne made an appearance at the subsequent show to challenge Jones to a rematch, *The Standard-Examiner* reported that Jones obliged him by walking out to the ring and agreeing to the bout. Then Rufus "proceeded to meet him head-on, an obvious attempt to open the wounds."

Jones' path of destruction continued to extend into Idaho. In another of his Centennial State appearances, Jones defeated Dave Reynolds of Provo, Utah with a move that was described as "a double-stepover toehold," but was more than likely a Boston crab. Before earning the submission victory, Jones enraged the audience of 200 fans to such an extent that three of them "went as far as attempting to enter the ring," according to *The Daily Sentinel* of Grand Junction.

While Rufus busied himself in the Rocky Mountain region, Claybourne had landed in Hawaii along with Chief Little Wolf, and he was immediately suggested by the newspapers as a prime challenger to the reigning Hawaii junior heavyweight champion, Abe Kashey. Instead, promoter Al

Karasick seemed to believe it was best to hold off on delivering a one-on-one title match between Claybourne and Kashey until the former champion was seen to have earned a title shot.

"The promoter said Kashey turned down Claybourne's challenge, but added he would be willing to meet the Negro star from Boston when the latter proves his right to a match with the champion," printed *The Hawaii Advertiser*.

Instead of an immediate title opportunity, Claybourne would get his initial crack at Kashey on November 18th in a tag team match, with former Hawaiian police officer Lucky Simunovich on his side, and Peter Peterson in Kashey's corner. Predictably, Claybourne and Simunovich were victorious in the best-of-three-falls tag team match, but dropped the November 25th rematch to their opponents when the referee stopped the bout due to a Simunovich injury.

From there, Karasick was content to place Claybourne and Kashey in the ring together for a one-on-one non-title match in the next logical phase in their feud over the *Ring Magazine* belt.

"Kashey wants head butts outlawed, but Claybourne claims it's just as legal as Kashey's atomic drop, but both will be permitted in their match," reported *The Honolulu Star-Bulletin*.

Claybourne was quoted as saying that he would "demand a title shot" after he beat Kashey in the early edition of the Thursday newspaper, but the late edition of the paper reported a stunning change to the advertised main event.

"Jack Claybourne, who was to meet Abe Kashey in the main event, left town Wednesday night," amended *The Star-Bulletin*.

The next day, *The Star-Bulletin* carried the quote from Karasick that Claybourne "left town without notice," and "ran out on Kashey." The fact that Claybourne's sudden departure was a point of authentic contention was made all the more evident by the follow-up statement Karasick provided to *The Advertiser*, when he mentioned that he wired the offices of the

National Wrestling Alliance and asked them to take action against Claybourne.

"Hawaii is a member of the NWA, and unless Claybourne has a good reason for leaving Honolulu without warning, he will be suspended and prevented from working in all NWA affiliated states," Karasick told *The Advertiser*.

From its founding roster of six promoters in 1948, the list of promoters pledging loyalty to the NWA had swelled to more than 30 by the fall of 1951. Regardless as to the reason for Claybourne's sudden departure from Hawaii, a strictly enforced blackballing would severely limit his ability to continue to earn a living as a professional wrestler.

On top of that, the relative surge in the number of young Black wrestlers in the business had upped the availability of wrestlers sharing Claybourne's skin color to promoters willing to take chances by featuring Black grapplers on their shows.

It remained to be seen how the enforcement of anti-Claybourne sanctions by the NWA would jeopardize the quality of the wrestler's life and career, but a curious series of inconveniences would soon begin to stall Jack's progress whenever his career would appear to gather momentum.

In the Rockies, a far more devastating fate had befallen Rufus Jones. Through the middle of November, Jones had continued to wrestle as an absolute menace, and even managed to earn some cheers from select audiences. *The Daily Herald* of Provo, Utah described how Jones experienced the unique sensation of having crowds cheer for him when he defeated Mr. E in Provo Arena.

"The crowd went wild when 'Rufus the Terrible' won the first fall with two or three head butts and a Boston crab in 9 minutes and 18 seconds," reported *The Herald*. "Mr. E evened things up by taking the second in seven minutes and 30 seconds with a neck-breaker. When Mr. E used the ropes as an aid in applying his neckbreaker in the battle for the third fall, Referee Alexander raised Jones' hand in triumph."

One night later in Ogden, Jones did everything he could to ensure that the fans wouldn't cheer him, as he twisted Bill Melby's head in between the ropes and then began butting the defenseless man in the head while simultaneously strangling him.

"The situation obviously called for disqualification of Rufus, but Melby wasn't content to win that way," stated *The Standard-Examiner*. "He climbed to his feet and started belaboring the Negro with his fists. All about, fans were screaming for the 'kill' and wanted to be a part of it as they threw the heavy chairs — all of them probably aimed at Rufus. Police, ushers, management and others were rushed to the ring to quell the imminent riot."

It was undeniably a signature performance from Rufus Jones. Unfortunately, it would be the final description ever provided of one of his bouts. The next night, Jones wrestled in Grand Junction Colorado against the Masked Monster. During Jones' long drive back to Ogden, a catastrophe occurred.

At 8:34 a.m. on the bitterly cold morning of November 17, 1951, Joseph "Rufus Jones" Godfrey was killed in an automobile collision on Highway 84, one mile north of the forebodingly named "Death Curve" in Ogden, Utah. He was only 38 years old, and was in the midst of a solid 18-year tenure as a wrestler that showed no signs of slowing at the time of his death.

Witnesses suspected that Jones had fallen asleep behind the wheel of his car. The coroner reported that Godfrey sustained a crushed chest as a result of the collision. *The Standard-Examiner* of Ogden would add the further detail that Godfrey had "suffered a skull fracture" among his other injuries; a cruel irony if true given the celebrated invulnerability of the wrestler's head.

The other vehicle involved in the wreck plunged 60 feet from the overpass following the collision, but its occupant — 27-year-old Joseph Arrave — fortunately survived the ordeal.

Word of the tragedy spread quickly within the wrestling world. At the Roseburg Armory in Oregon, the announcement of Godfrey's death caused "a tomb-like silence" to settle over the crowd, and was then followed by a formally requested moment of silence according to *The News-Review*.

**Police examine the destroyed car of Rufus Jones**

*The Oregon Statesman* fondly called to mind the incidents when Godfrey had a knife hurled at him by a fan during one event, and believed that a fan had fired a gun at him during a separate show. The writer then praised Godfrey's versatility as a performer, adding "he could both work his audiences into a dither with his tools of mat nastiness and make 'em howl with laughter with his lighter antics."

In Tacoma, *The News Tribune* opined that Godfrey had been "an amiable chap" despite the character he portrayed, and correctly noted that Godfrey had been in the business for at least 17 years, taking into account his early years wrestling as Tiger Flowers.

## Gentleman Jack and Rough Rufus

*The Oregon Journal* added the erroneous detail that Godfrey "once held the Pacific Coast junior heavyweight title," although he competed in so many matches against holders of that title, and was awarded wins in enough non-title matches against the Pacific Coast champions that there's a decent chance the promoters truly believed Godfrey had once held the championship himself.

Godfrey's body was returned to his hometown of Malden, Massachusetts and interred at Forest Dale Cemetery. He left behind a wife and no children.

Pressing onward into 1952, Claybourne returned to his home in Boston, wrestling there for the first time in five years. While Claybourne had been billed as something of an international superstar in the region during earlier stages of his career — often as either an Australian or South African —now he truly was a world-traveled performer with international expertise.

Claybourne's stock had certainly risen in his absence. At the Boston Arena, he smashed New England junior heavyweight champion and former Rufus Jones adversary Bull Curry in just over five minutes in the main event, setting the stage for a high-profile feud between the two.

"Gentleman Jack's unemotional opinion is that he can churn Curry into beefsteak any and every night of the week, though a revenge-bound Bull can be a fierce and feared sight to spectators," printed *The Portland Sunday Telegram*. "Claybourne, a smooth-talking Negro veteran, is famous in world mat circles. He is likened to boxing's Joe Louis, baseball's Satchel Paige, and track's Jesse Owens."

Also present at the show in Portland, Maine was Frank James. Just like Buddy Jackson, James first came to prominence at the All-Negro shows held in Tennessee and Alabama headlined by Don Blackman before working his way through other territories.

Claybourne closed the show in Portland by wrestling to a 90-minute draw with Bull Curry. However, if he watched Frank James' match with Clyde Steel earlier in the program, he probably would have received his first clue that Jones' headbutting routine — which Claybourne had made liberal use of due to its effectiveness — was on its way to becoming a trademark of all Black wrestlers.

After dropping the first fall of his match with Steel, James secured the second fall, and then won the third by headbutting Steel out of the ring "so ardently that the latter was finally counted out on the floor."

At the very beginning of January, Claybourne moved on to Dayton, Ohio. It was there that he linked up with one of the most promising members of the crop of up-and-coming Black wrestlers, Luther Lindsay. In a similar vein to Woody Strode, Lindsay had been an exceptional collegiate football player. Under his real name of Luther Goodall, he had been a standout at Hampton Institute in Virginia before adopting his wife's maiden name as his wrestling surname.

If Claybourne was inclined to be nervous about the idea of some of the Black newcomers to professional wrestling eventually pushing him out, Lindsay likely added to that anxiety. While Strode was closer to being a wrestler of Claybourne's generation who had one foot squarely set in Hollywood, Lindsay was 14 years younger than Claybourne, and could satisfy promoters' demands for a young, Black babyface in ways the 42-year-old Claybourne no longer could.

It's also possible that Claybourne was totally unbothered by Lindsay's potential and didn't foresee the looming threat of his presence. Moreover, as the tag team of Claybourne and Lindsay rapidly piled up victories in Dayton, he may even have recognized the long-term value of aligning himself with a young, energetic wrestler.

When Claybourne and Lindsay made their way to Akron in March, they were advertised in *The Akron Beacon Journal* as "the first All-Negro tag wrestling team to grace the Armory in eight years," stretching back to the time that Rufus Jones and Jim Mitchell teamed up there in 1944.

Claybourne spent a very brief period in Chicago during the middle of March before moving southward in April. It would be the first time in his career that he would wrestle south of Missouri or Kentucky.

For the first time in years, Claybourne seemed to have difficulty establishing a sustained presence in any single wrestling territory, as he was now appearing in his fourth territory in a four month period. It's difficult to know if this was a result of Claybourne being hastened on his way by NWA-affiliated promoters as the news of his fallout with Karasick caught up with him, or if the steady stream of opportunities coming his way were continuously tempting him to travel onward.

Regardless as to what was prompting Claybourne's frequent migration, Arkansas is where Claybourne first latched onto Buddy Jackson on a permanent basis. Appearing under the names Sammy Jackson, Bobby Jackson, and eventually under his most frequent ring name, Buddy Jackson very quickly became a fixed presence at Claybourne's side.

Starting in the spring of 1952, Jackson and Claybourne faced one another all over the South as Claybourne defended his Negro world title against Jackson. The two were also booked to face one another in Atlanta, marking the first time either of the two had wrestled there.

For the first time, Claybourne wrestled deep in the heart of the former Confederate States, and undoubtedly encountered Jim Crow racism on a level that dwarfed what he experienced in Missouri. States like Alabama and Georgia had passed more than double the number of Jim Crow laws as Claybourne's home state. This included separate waiting rooms and ticket windows at bus stations.

Rules governing the separation of the races were so strict that White nurses could not provide care to Black male patients, and in the area of criminal punishment, Black and White inmates couldn't be fastened together while working on the same chain gang.

*The Nashville Tennessean* called special attention to the fact that Claybourne sported an actual "diamond-studded" championship belt as a sign of his legitimacy as a world Negro champion.

The pair toured several areas of Georgia and the other Southern states, with Claybourne emerging victorious in every outing. Many of their bouts were declared to have been the first matches between Black wrestlers ever held in those parts of the South.

One of the notable exceptions was in Clarksville, where Claybourne had successfully defended his world Negro heavyweight championship at the National Guard Armory against Jim Mitchell just two weeks earlier.

The papers erroneously declared that the Claybourne-Jackson bout was the second bout between Black wrestlers ever held in Clarksville, with Mitchell vs. Claybourne having been the first. This goes to show the short memories of the local reporters, the genuine dishonestly of the promoters, or both; Buddy Jackson had actually defended his world Negro junior heavyweight championship against Mitchell in Clarksville just two years prior in 1950.

In Jasper, Georgia, the fact that Claybourne had defeated Mitchell on at least one occasion was cited to underscore his title reign as a significant accomplishment, as he had clearly "defeated the best that the country has to offer," in the words of *The Pickens County Progress*. Unfortunately, the paper greatly exaggerated the degree of in-ring success that Claybourne had supposedly enjoyed over Jim Mitchell, describing it as total dominance.

"[Claybourne] beat the former champion of the colored race, the Black Panther, the first time they met, and has beaten him every time since," added *The County Progress*. "He is one of the top wrestling attractions in the East and Middle West, and on the West Coast where mixed races wrestle each other. Buddy Jackson, also a colored wrestler of the rough and rugged school will be an able opponent for the veteran champion."

It was during a promotional interview intended to drive the hype for one of his title defenses against Jackson, in April

1952, that Claybourne was asked for a list of the best Black wrestlers in the world by a reporter from *The Alabama Tribune*.

**Buddy Jackson eyes Claybourne's Negro world title belt**

After first offering a show of deference to the recently departed Black legends Reginald Siki and Rufus Jones, Claybourne went on to list Don Blackman, Seelie Samara, Frank James, Don Kindred, Woody Strode, and Jim Mitchell as the best Black wrestlers in the business. Presumably, Claybourne would also have added the names of himself and Jackson to that tally, even though such a label would have been premature in Jackson's case, as it also was in the case of Frank James.

Once Claybourne and Jackson climbed into the ring, it occasionally seemed as if Claybourne was using Jackson as a proxy for the recently deceased Rufus Jones, as Jackson appeared to be infusing elements of Jones' style into his act much like Claybourne had done. *The Jackson Sun* reported how "Jackson gave the champion a rough time, especially by using his head to batter the champion's head, but Claybourne tangled him for the count at the crucial times."

The fiction of Jackson's early career had become the truth, as he faced Claybourne nightly, as if serving as his understudy. Ideally, Jackson was compensated well, because he continued to lose to Claybourne everywhere they wrestled, from North Carolina and Georgia to Kentucky and Arkansas, and in all places in between.

It was in Arkansas that *The Blytheville Courier News* said that Claybourne "is recognized by the National Wrestling Alliance as the world's Negro heavyweight champion" who supposedly began his career by winning a 20-man tournament in 1930 consisting exclusively of Black wrestlers.

As it is more likely than not that Claybourne was performing under a formal censure from the National Wrestling Alliance, claiming to have been a world champion of any sort officially recognized by the NWA would not have improved his standing with the organization.

The fanciful stories Claybourne told about how he won his Negro world championship belt seemed to change with every stop he and Jackson made. In Paducah, Kentucky, he claimed to have won the title from Jim Mitchell four months earlier. Days later, in Knoxville, Tennessee, Claybourne told the press that he had recently won his championship at the conclusion of a title tournament held in London, England.

Claybourne and Jackson also appeared at several shows together even when they weren't facing one another. In Albuquerque, New Mexico, they split off and wrestled against separate White competitors. Days later in Texas, they faced each other to deliver "the first colored male wrestling bout ever staged in El Paso," according to *The El Paso Herald-Post*. For nearly all of these shows, Claybourne was referred to as "The Black Panther."

**Traveling Negro champion Jack Claybourne**

During their swing through Texas and the Southwestern states, Claybourne and Jackson united inside of the ring for one of the rarest of all associations between wrestlers. On an Albuquerque show in which neither wrestler was booked to perform, the two entered the ring together, and Jackson served as Claybourne's best man as "Gentleman Jack" got married to Lillian Smalls for the second time.

Claybourne and Smalls had been legally married in Minnesota 10 years prior, in 1942. Perhaps for the sake of proving the in-ring marriage ceremony was legitimate in case any journalists researched the matter, Claybourne and Smalls did file for a marriage license in New Mexico. In their eyes, the occasion probably served as a 10-year renewal of their wedding vows.

The in-ring-marriage routine had been employed to great success by Gorgeous George, who appeared in public wedding ceremonies with his wife Betty Hanson during several wrestling shows because of how much of an attraction the weddings had proven to be with wrestling fans.

This leg of the Jackson-Claybourne tour seemed to end in Los Angeles, where Jackson continued to wrestle, and seemingly ditched the Rufus-Jones-inspired headbutting routine. Instead, publications like *The Colton Courier*, when noting that Jackson had been "a big hit with the fans," also described his style as being "flashy and scientific."

As Jack Claybourne's career had seemingly continued unabated, the tragic passing of Joe "Rufus Jones" Godfrey left a clear void in the wrestling industry. Attempts to fill the void left behind by his death would be glaringly obvious over both the short and long term. One of the most coordinated of these efforts would result in a significant piece of wrestling history being recorded in the Rocky Mountains and in the Pacific Northwest — the territories that Godfrey had last touched during his life, and the places where there had apparently still been a very high demand for his act.

## *18* - The Brown Bombers

While Claybourne was in Southern California taking a well-deserved break, the ripple effects of Rufus Jones' passing were being felt in some rather conspicuous ways. After leaving Hawaii and California, Don Kindred made his way east and eventually found himself in North Bay, Ontario. In the location where the term "coco-butt" was coined, Kindred co-opted the most identifiable feature of the deceased Rufus Jones' arsenal — the interminable onslaught of headbutts — and made it a core component of his own act.

The inclusion seemed gradual at first, as the earliest reports of Kindred's use of headbutts describe him wielding them to set the stage for more technically appealing maneuvers, such as in his match against Benny Trudel in North Bay's Memorial Stadium.

"Bruising Benny Trudel had the crowd in an uproar with his continual fouling, but soon regretted it when the powerfully built Negro matman, Don Kindred, got his dander up," reported *The North Bay Nugget*. "Trudel knocked Kindred out of the ring twice by kicking to set the stage for his defeat. Kindred bolted through the ropes, used his feared coco-butts to leave Trudel dazed, and then won it with a surfboard that had bad Benny Trudel howling in pain."

Before long, Kindred was leading with his head, and being referred to as the "Negro coco-butt artist Don Kindred."

"Kindred has proven to be a top-notch wrestler in several appearances here so far, and is mighty popular with his coco-butting style when riled by fouling," said *The Nugget*.

Kindred's newfound love for the headbutt served him very well as he entered the Pacific Northwest, which was the penultimate area of the country that Jones worked during his lifetime. It was the sort of place where a link between a Black grappler making use of a headbutting style and the recently departed Rufus Jones would be acknowledged, and in many ways appreciated by anyone who thought the style of Rough Rufus had died with the grappler.

Apparently not getting the report on Kindred's most recent bouts in North Bay, the press on the West Coast announced Kindred's arrival by describing his prior style.

"[Kindred] comes highly touted as a clean, scientific matman," stated *The Times-News* of Twin Falls, Idaho. "The Negro junior heavyweight champion of the grappling world, Kindred is known as the 'Brown Bomber' of the mat."

Kindred got straight to work educating audiences in the Rocky Mountain region as to the upgrades he had made to his style. He polished off all of his earliest opponents with headbutts, frequently winning both falls of a best-of-three-falls match with a simple headbutt followed by a body press.

When Kindred partnered up with fellow new arrival Frank James — who had already been busy establishing himself as a thick-skulled stand-in for Rufus Jones — for a tag team tournament in late November 1952, there was nothing going on that would have suggested to wrestling fans that they were witnessing anything other than a routine, short-term pairing of Black wrestlers. However, all it takes is a cursory review of how the pair went about winning the tournament to identify why the partnership might have been deemed to be worth preserving.

The pair of Black wrestling stars dropped the first fall of their match with Chester and Leo Wallick, and it appeared as if they were going to be knocked out of the four-team tournament in the semis. Instead, "Kindred and James came back to take the second fall in 7 minutes and 52 seconds with a headbutt and body press."

The pair won the final fall via judges' decision after the time limit expired. Then Kindred and James asserted their dominance over Paul Degallis and Tiger Joe Marsh in the final round.

"The Negro grapplers won in straight falls, taking the first one in 15 minutes and 20 seconds with a headbutt and hangman's hold, and the second in 7 minutes and 5 seconds with a headbutt and body press," reported *The Times-News*.

Just like that, pro wrestling's first major heel all-Black tag team combination was born. By virtue of their tournament victory, Kindred and James earned a title shot at the Intermountain Junior Heavyweight Tag Team Championship held by Dald Haddock and Mike Mazarian.

The fact that the newly formed team was robbed of victory due to underhanded tactics displayed by the champions did absolutely nothing to slow their momentum, as Kindred and James continued to steamroll their competition. In some instances, they won bouts two-on-three, such as when they bested El Capitan, Buzz Jones, and Ace Abbott in two straight falls in Ogden, Utah.

Things only improved for Kindred and James once they turned against the fans in select Northwestern towns and portrayed themselves as despicable heels. Their headbutt-heavy style was more appropriate when wielded in conjunction with a set of rulebreaking tactics.

Then, when Kindred and James materialized in Albany, Oregon at the beginning of 1953 as recent signees of promoter Elton Owen, it appears that they were simply handed championship belts and presented as the Rocky Mountain Tag Team Champions.

"The colored team who hold the Rocky Mountain championship is composed of big, rugged Don Kindred, winner of last week's battle royal, and Frank James, who looks rougher than the late Rufus Jones," stated *The Albany Democrat Herald*. "These big, rugged Negro stars came into Boise at different times, but quickly formed a team and have been running roughshod over every team they have met."

The falsehoods printed in the *The Capital Journal* took the additional step of alleging that James had been "trained by the late Rufus Jones, one of the best head-butters in the business," and that "James and Rufus have been partners in tag team matches," which there is no evidence of.

*The Oregonian* simply referred to James as "another Rufus Jones," while *The Daily Journal* suggested that he was "successor to the late Rufus Jones as a head-butting operator."

It was then teased that the future bouts of Kindred and James against Northwest titleholders Sakata and Yamato would therefore be title unification matches. However, there were other challengers lined up for them first, with Luigi Macera and Tommy Martindale being quoted in *The News-Review* of Roseburg, Oregon as saying, "If those colored monsters think we're afraid of them, then they'd better think again."

James helped to cement the heelish nature of the team in the eyes of fans by his conduct in a singles match against Buck Weaver in Salem, Oregon. James was incensed when Weaver scored the fall on him using a neckbreaker.

"The angered James came back with a series of headbutts that had Weaver groggy," reported *The Statesman* of Salem. "After he had clamped on a Boston crab and Buck had given up, the colored gladiator added a couple more headbutts that brought on a near riot. Referee Harry Elliott announced that Weaver was unable to return to the ring, but said he was awarding the match to Buck, nevertheless. James, wrathy at the verdict, accused Elliott of racial prejudice, and said he would bring his friend, Don Kindred, in with him next week to see that he got a square deal."

Meanwhile, the descriptions of Kindred's singles matches now sounded almost exactly like the reports of Rufus Jones' matches. One example of this was the bloodletting of Tony Ross that occurred in Bend, Oregon once pro wrestling's Brown Bomber had begun to uncork a slew of headbutts.

"After Kindred had finished his battering ram tactics, Ross was bleeding like a fountain, and as groggy as a kid smoking his first cigar behind the barn," printed *The Bulletin*.

When the pair finally teamed up for their bout against Macera and Martindale — the men who described them as "colored monsters" — James dropped Macera with a headbutt to secure the first fall, and Kindred ended the match by bouncing Martindale's skull off the mat with a piledriver. Then

Kindred helped James gain revenge against Buck Weaver and his partner Eric Pederson, although the most interesting action seemingly occurred after the match reached its conclusion.

"The Negro tuffies actually came by their nod after the burly Kindred, a vicious exponent of headbutts and piledrivers, had applied a 'driver' to Pederson as climax to the third fall," reported *The Oregon Statesman*. "Then two unidentified women, smack in the middle of the heat-filled milling about the ringside by the fans, got into a hassle of their own. And it was a real dandy, as they swung, clawed, pulled hair, and committed general mayhem until a group of men finally separated them. So hot were the fans over the way the advertised main event turned out that both James and Kindred remained in the ring until things cooled off a bit. They really had the animals stirred up."

Lost in this colorful account of the bout's conclusion is the fact that Kindred applied the piledriver to Pederson on the arena floor, resulting in his unconscious opponent getting counted out. This is the action that fed directly into the riotous disposition of the crowd. By this point, the Rocky Mountain champs were clearly on the outs with almost all of the audiences they wrestled in front of, with *The Stateman* directly labeling Kindred and James as "the Negro villains."

Kindred and James preferred a different name, and by the end of January, they were collectively referring to themselves as "The Brown Bombers."

On top of being acknowledged as the Rocky Mountain tag team champions in Oregon, the Bombers were referred to as the "mythical" tag team champions of the Pacific Coast by *The Longview Daily News*.

Leaning even further into the headbutting theme, Frank James started getting referred to as "Oak Noggin" by the regional press, and began to draw even more comparisons to Rufus Jones, which was probably his aim.

"James has used his headbutt to advantage in bouts here and is being compared by fans to the late Rufus Jones,

## Gentleman Jack and Rough Rufus

who appeared in many local matches several years ago," reported *The Longview Daily News*.

**Don Kindred and Frank James**

Apparently the athletic commissions of different Pacific Northwestern states applied different rules to their matches. Such was the case during a bout between the Brown Bombers and French-Canadians Lou Macera and Tony Baillargeon. The fall tally was even after Kindred pinned Macera following a series of headbutts, and Baillargeon quickly scored a pinfall on James.

"Kindred and James had the upper hand when Referee Small halted the proceedings," reported *The Longview Daily News*. "Macera was injured by the 'piledriver' — where a wrestler dumps his opponent headfirst into the mat — and unable to defend himself."

In addition to their use of headbutts and general rough antics, descriptions of the Brown Bombers' matches indicate that they were highly adept at classic heel tactics of interference and misdirection. Evidence of this was on full display during their decimation of Eric Pederson and Buck Weaver in Salem after Kindred had already secured the first fall on Weaver with a piledriver, and Pederson had also been left bleeding from repeated headbutts from Kindred.

"It was at this point that James roared into the ring, only to be met by Weaver storming out of the other corner," stated *The Oregon Statesman*. "When Referee Harry Elliott took out after these two to separate them, James sneaked in a headbutt on Pederson, and Kindred again butted Pederson, and then Kindred hopped on him for the deciding fall. When Elliott got back to the work at hand, he had nothing left to do but count out the dazed Pederson."

Incensed at his mistreatment, Pederson called out Don Kindred for a match, and promoter Elton Owen obliged him.

"Eric wants to get at either one of the Negro boys alone, and since Kindred is the bigger and the tougher of the two, he's the one I've matched with Pederson," Owen told *The Oregon Statesman*. "Oughta be a whale of a battle."

Kindred won their singles encounter in straight falls, after Pederson apparently became enraged at the sight of his own blood.

"The clincher came when Kindred headbutted Pederson on an already broken nose suffered at Bend recently," reported *The Statesman*. "The blood started to flow, and Eric went berserk. He was so heated up that he got Kindred in a full nelson on the ropes and refused to break the hold. It took Referee Harry Elliott, Matchmaker Elton Owen, and two other grapplers to finally pry Pederson loose, he was so determined to squash the Negro. Elliott then disqualified Pederson, and the battering he gave Kindred forced the latter to require aid in his trip to the dressing room."

In March, the Bombers earned a shot at the Pacific Northwest tag titles by defeating Elmer and Logger Larsen in yet another match that proved how skilled the pair were at executing underhanded match finishes. The Bombers were down early, but Kindred dropped Elmer for a fall by bashing him with headbutts and a piledriver. This set the stage for the conclusion of the contest.

"The deciding fall came about when Logger Larsen tried his whirling full nelson again and caught James," recounted *The Statesman*. "This time Kindred caught James' feet. As Kindred and Logger pulled on James, Referee Peters ordered Kindred to break the hold. That Kindred did, and Logger fell flat with James on top, and the fall and match went to the Negro nasties."

Following this match, *The Coos Bay Times* printed some interesting amendments to the backstories of the most exciting tag team in the Northwestern states.

"Kindred, a graduate of Temple University and a first lieutenant in the U.S. infantry during World War II, weighs 210 pounds, and James, who runs a candy gum and gum vending business in his hometown of Baltimore, Maryland, scales a solid 197," stated *The World*.

The Brown Bombers were unsuccessful in their first high-stakes effort to take the Northwest tag title away from the team of Toi Yamato and Mr. Sakata at the Armory in Roseburg, but they were declared to be worthy of an immediate rematch with the champions. At the beginning of the subsequent title rematch, Kindred decided to interrupt the pre-match foot-stomping ritual of the champions and paid for it by being rendered unconscious with a sleeper hold to surrender the first fall to the champions.

Kindred awoke, and then roared to life, capturing the second fall just three minutes later with some headbutts followed by a piledriver.

"The final fall went to James, after the Bombers' teamwork in the headbutting department had groggied both orientals," stated *The News-Review*. "Yamata was caught in a Boston Crab in 4:57."

**Kindred and James battle Lou Macera**

With that, the Brown Bombers now simultaneously held two sets of tag team gold, and were undoubtedly the most dominant team in the region. *The Oregon Statesman* neatly summarized the situation by saying, "The Negro mat nasties hold the undisputed team title for the Oregon-Washington area," and referred to them as "not so sharp individually, but heretofore unbeatable as a team."

Apparently, that assertion was the kiss of death, as the Brown Bombers almost immediately lost their unified tag team titles to the team of Tommy Martindale and George Drake.

Placing the Brown Bombers tag team on the back burner set the table for Kindred to wage an authentic in-ring battle for Black wrestling supremacy with Luther Lindsay, where he would once again seem to serve as a surrogate for Rufus Jones.

Lindsay made no bones about what his top priority was when he was inbound to the Pacific Northwest in June 1953.

"Lindsay, former footballer and track star at Drake, reportedly has a build that equals that of Eric Pederson, and also is said to be as fast as a cat despite his 197 pounds," described *The Oregon Statesman*. "Lindsay rassles on the clean side, and his pet hates are the colored meanies, Don Kindred and Frank James. Lindsay hopes he'll eventually get a crack at one or the other here soon."

In some markets of Washington, Kindred and Lindsay made their debuts almost simultaneously, with it being explained that Kindred — described as a UCLA football star by *The Tacoma News Tribune* — was "a leading challenger to Lindsay's Negro title."

An unfortunate byproduct of the wrestling style popularized by Rufus Jones and imitated so effectively by Don Kindred and Frank James is that it added to the impression that classic wrestling, which relied on holds, evasions, and counters, was not something Black wrestlers dabbled in. That at least appeared to be the case in certain markets. In essence, Lindsay served as something of a counterpoint to reestablish that Black wrestlers could indeed win matches through clean, traditional methods.

"Unlike most Negro matmen, Lindsay is scientific and doesn't go for the rough stuff unless pushed to it," explained *The Oregon Statesman*. "He'll be up against Don Kindred or Frank James, the two Negro mat nasties of the Northwest."

In Tacoma, promoter Paavo Ketonen said that Kindred would need to prove his competence first if he wanted a shot at Lindsay's Negro title. This was stated after Kindred failed to advance his cause when he lost to Angelo Poffo by disqualification as a consequence of stretching the rules too far.

Lindsay still agreed to defend his title against Kindred, as the two were natural adversaries given the talent in the territory at the time, and the fact that there were two marquee Black wrestlers present, along with a title capable of being defended.

For whatever it's worth, from the perspective of a Washington wrestling fan, Lindsay's defense of his world Negro heavyweight title occurred only after he had been defeated by world junior heavyweight champion Danny McShain. In essence, before allowing Lindsay and Kindred to go about their business, the promoters established that the best Black heavyweight wrestler in the world still wasn't the equal of the best White wrestler in a lower weight division within the region.

In Oregon, the build toward the eventual bouts between Kindred and Lindsay was paced differently in the separate markets.

"Lindsay is hot after a match with either Frank James or Don Kindred, the two Negro mat villains who are as unpopular in Northwest rings as Lindsay is popular," wrote *The Statesman*. "[Elton] Owen wants to see if he can get by the likes of Sakata first before matching him with either of the 'Brown Bombers,' as Kindred and James like to call themselves."

While Owen teased the bout between Lindsay and Kindred, but held off on delivering it to the fans, Paavo Ketonen went right ahead and put the match in the ring. One key difference here was that Lindsay was not acknowledged as the reigning Negro titleholder in the state of Washington. Instead the two wrestlers would vie for "a silver belt emblematic of the Negro championship, an award presented by Ketonen."

"Lindsay, who carries some 230 pounds neatly distributed over a 5-foot, 9-inch frame, is regarded as one of the most powerful men in the game, and makes up in sheer strength what he lacks in the way of finesse — he hasn't picked up all the finer points in a professional mat career which is not yet three years old," explained *The Tacoma News Tribune*, offering a tale-of-the-tape. "Kindred, a 30-year-old campaigner who turned pro 11 years ago following a string of amateur successes, possesses almost as burly a physique (220 pounds, 5 feet, 10 ½ inches in height) and considerably more grappling savvy."

It was Lindsay who won the bout between the two, and solidified his claim to being the world's Negro heavyweight wrestling champion — at least to the satisfaction of the fans in Washington.

"Kindred won the first fall at 16:23 with a series of headbutts and a bodypress," recounted *The Tacoma News Tribune*. "Lindsay squared accounts at 9:52 with a devastating airplane spin and bodypress, and then won the third fall in a mere 55 seconds with a full nelson."

Away from the eyes of Washington wrestling fans, Kindred obtained a measure of revenge when he teamed with Angelo Poffo to defeat Lindsay and his partner Danno MacDonald in Vancouver.

It's possible that the National Wrestling Alliance stepped in and voided Lindsay's claim to being the Negro world heavyweight champion sometime before October, as the language surrounding the subsequent matches between Lindsay and Kindred became noticeably less official. Outright claims to titles and belts were omitted in favor of language that danced around the issue.

For example, Lindsay was now "acclaimed by the National Wrestling Alliance as the leading Negro wrestler in the United States," and he had accepted the challenge of Don Kindred to "defend his unofficial title in a match at the Fairgrounds Arena Monday night."

In Oregon, promoter Elton Owen seemingly tried to bypass the NWA's rebuke simply by lowering the weight classes of the two men who had both only recently been described to weigh upwards of 220 pounds each.

"Luther (The Tank) Lindsay and Burly Don Kindred, the Negro mat gladiators who claim the world Negro junior heavyweight title and who are as fond of one another as a kid is of castor oil, collide tonight in Matchmaker Elton Owen's Armory main event," printed *The Statesman*. "It's a brawl long anticipated by Owen, and it should be a rouser."

Back in Washington, Lindsay won what would previously have been billed as a title rematch with Kindred, and *The Longview Daily News* glossed over the significance of the win, stating that it meant that Lindsay "still rates as the leading Negro wrestler in the United States — a title handed the athlete several weeks ago by the National Wrestling Alliance." In this case, "the title" referred only to an honorary distinction rather than a literal championship symbolized by a belt like the one that he had previously been handed.

With no titles of consequence on the line any longer, the two clashed yet again in Salem, Oregon, with Kindred finally defeating Lindsay in two consecutive falls. The first fall was achieved when Kindred pinned Lindsay following a series of headbutts. The second occurred when Lindsay locked Kindred in his feared full nelson from the ring apron, then climbed the exterior portion of the corner turnbuckles and lifted Kindred completely off his feet while the latter remained locked in the full nelson.

Even though Lindsay clearly had the upper hand, referee Frank Fagetty counted Lindsay out of the ring because he would not release the hold and reenter the ring as ordered by the referee.

A rematch was held just one week later in Salem, with Lindsay emerging victorious, and with *The Capital Journal* joking that Kindred's weakness was "not in his head, which is as tough as a dried gourd for his headbutting, but in his stomach."

"[Lindsay] lifted the meanie on his shoulders and started spinning at least a couple dozen times, then slammed him resoundingly to the mat, made a diving attack, and bodypressed the helpless Kindred," recounted *The Journal*.

"After the spins, Kindred had to be helped from the ring, sick to his stomach, and could not report for the third fall."

In October, the two grapplers took a break from their in-ring feud to coexist as members of a football team composed of wrestlers. The squad of mat stars squared off against the Seattle Bombers football team in a benefit game for the local Boys Club. The star of the wrestlers' team was all-time football and wrestling legend Bronco Nagurski, and Lindsay was one of several wrestlers on the team who also had extensive football experience. Kindred filled in at guard, which may very well have been the position he intended to play in the Canadian Football League when he tried out for the Montreal Alouettes.

Meanwhile, Jack Claybourne had returned to action in November 1952 in Albuquerque, winning his bouts with arm whips and arm scissors rather than dropkicks and headbutts. He remained in Albuquerque through the beginning of 1953 as "The Black Panther of Australia," and even engaged in a match with the Goon that was refereed by boxing legend Jack Dempsey in front of 4,000 fans at the Albuquerque Ice Arena.

"The Goon, 295-pound giant, took the first fall with a Boston crab, but Claybourne came back two minutes later to win the second fall with an arm whip," reported *The Albuquerque Journal*. "Dempsey, now 57-years-old, still showed that he was the old tiger when he knocked the Goon down with a short right. The Goon had been irritating Dempsey. All Claybourne had to do was lie on the Goon to take the third fall and the match."

From New Mexico, Claybourne traveled nearly 1,000 miles away to Des Moines, Iowa to begin his next round of scheduled appearances, and gradually migrated eastward into Illinois and Indiana. Publications like *The Rock Island Argus* described Claybourne as a "rough, rugged, and speedy mauler who had skyrocketed to television fame in recent months."

Claybourne's April showing in Hammond, Indiana — which also presented fans with the homecoming match of local favorite Dory Funk — was described as the "first appearance of a Negro performer" in the city. It would have been a nice accomplishment if Jack hadn't already captured that distinction thanks to his 1941 bout in Hammond against Alex Kaffner.

Claybourne's Midwest swing also brought him through Benton Harbor in Western Michigan before taking him to Minnesota. It was while he was in Minneapolis that Claybourne sat for a thorough interview with Albert Lea of *The Evening Tribune*.

"If there is anything gentlemanly about the monstrous guy they call 'Gentleman Jack' Claybourne, it might be the way he dresses outside the rasslin' arena, or in his restaurant," the article began. "Certainly, the heavy-shouldered colored veteran would never pass an Emily Post test for etiquette while in action. As one foe put it recently, 'Big Jack makes you think of an apartment house falling when he pounces on you.'"

In the course of advertising his bout with Lionel Baillargeon on a card headlined by football star Bronko Nagurski, Claybourne spoke about his success wrestling in Australia and elsewhere, while clearly misrepresenting his age. The 43-year-old Claybourne shaved more than a decade from his age when he said that he left Georgia only 11 years earlier to begin a wrestling career that had now entered its 22nd year at a minimum.

"Jack learned some mighty good scientific tricks from Johnny Hatfield many years ago that he's always been grateful for," continued *The Tribune*. "There are times in this trade when he faces men as strong as himself. Men who are also made of steel. The factor that often tips the scale is a canny bearing."

"You can't meet 'em all with strength," Claybourne was quoted as saying. "It's the same as golf, which I play a lot of, and in baseball. I used to do some semipro catching in Kansas City. Had to use the noodle."

This was yet another claim by Claybourne that he had been a dedicated baseball player in his home state, which may have been true. For whatever it's worth, Mexico, Missouri was able to field multiple local Black-only baseball teams that competed against teams traveling around the region.

This is impressive due to the town's population of only 8,000 residents during Claybourne's upbringing, and a Black population that accounted for only 10 percent of the total. Still, Claybourne never disclosed to the press that he was a devoted baseball player until 14 years into his career when Jackie Robinson became popular.

In the middle of what was becoming a triumphant Midwest return for Claybourne, a startling edict was enforced by multiple state athletic commissions that effectively ended Claybourne's tour, and precluded any opportunities for future tours of the region.

"The State Athletic Commission Friday barred three professional wrestlers from matches in Indiana and ordered four-week rests for four professional boxers," stated the report from the Associated Press. "Suspended indefinitely from mat appearances in the state were Tommy O'Toole, Jack Claybourne, and 'the Great Scott.'"

The commission's chairman stated that Scott and O'Toole were being banned for failing to make it to appearances in Indiana, but then elaborated on the suspension of Claybourne in a way that suggested strict punitive measures enforced by the National Wrestling Alliance were probably taking effect.

"Hindman said the action against Claybourne was on the recommendation of the Illinois Athletic Commission, which barred him from wrestling in that state because of medical reasons," the report concluded.

The fact that the ban was initiated by the Illinois Athletic Commission hints that its source was Fred Kohler, the powerful and influential Chicago wrestling promoter who was one of the founding promoters of the NWA along with Hawaii promoter Al Karasick, who publicly expressed that Claybourne had wronged him.

The action against Claybourne was likely far broader in its range than stated in the report, as all appearances by Claybourne in the adjacent states of Michigan, Minnesota, and Iowa were halted as well.

As the effects of apparent sanctions imposed by the NWA appeared to be directly limiting Claybourne's potential, the continuing evolution of the wrestling business appeared to be reducing Claybourne's influence on other fronts. At the very moment that Claybourne had been left searching for viable lifelines to continue wrestling, young Black wrestlers were traveling to the places where Claybourne had helped to boost the demand for Black performers, and wowing audiences.

In Melbourne, towering 20-year-old wrestler Edward Wright — introduced to Australians as Bobo "Bearcat" Wright — was being touted as "a powerful, fast-moving negro, said to be better than spectacular U.S. negro, Jack Claybourne."

While the paucity of experienced Black wrestlers in prior decades had led to a natural scarcity of such performers, and therefore an increased demand for the few that were available, the addition of several new Black wrestlers had led to another development. Now, it seemed as if a hard limit of two Black wrestlers at a time was being imposed in most wrestling territories. Either the Black wrestlers competed against one another, or they were paired up in tag teams to compete against other duos.

Perhaps not so coincidentally, Buddy Jackson, who appeared to have taken the first half of 1953 off from in-ring activity, resumed his partnership with Claybourne in June 1953. This time, the pair appeared in Arizona and West Texas, billed in some locations as the "Negro world tag team champions."

The partnership created a scenario reminiscent of the teaming of Jim Mitchell and Rufus Jones in the Midwest, and a situation made slightly more bizarre by the presence of championship recognition. Jackson and Claybourne might appear together as the Negro tag team titlists in Tuscon on one night, and then Claybourne would defend his Negro world heavyweight championship against Jackson the very next night in Mesa. However, they *never* faced another Black tag team that they could defend their tag team championship against.

After leaving the Southwest, Claybourne and Jackson brought their touring partnership over to the Mid Atlantic states at the behest of Jim Crockett, where they faced one another on cards throughout North Carolina, South Carolina, and Virginia. In Virginia, Jackson was described as a "former footballer from Ohio State University," whereas in parts of the Carolinas, he was "a former Ohio State University great who made things tough on Big Ten college wrestlers a couple of years ago."

"A few years ago, there were very few Negro matmen working, but others of [Claybourne's] race are now flocking into the game," pointed out *The Asheville Citizen*.

Bill Lewis, the promoter for the Richmond bout between Claybourne and Jackson, glowed that the match between the two would mark the first appearance of Negro grapplers in Richmond in several years. That would suggest that a series of matches between Buddy Jackson and Don Blackman in Richmond in 1950 was the last time that two Black wrestlers had previously faced one another in the city.

In Durham, North Carolina, Jackson and Claybourne appeared on the undercard of a show at the Downtown Armory headlined by Red Roberts and Tex Riley, which would give the city "its first look at Negro male grapplers."

"The Negro grapplers are Jack Claybourne and Buddy Jackson, the best known of their race in the business," proclaimed *The Durham Sun*. "They are currently on an exhibition tour throughout the South."

As *The Sun* also declared that the Southern junior heavyweight title bout between Roberts and Riley in the main event would be "Durham's first bona fide title bout in boxing or wrestling," it's possible that the promoters balked at the idea of having Claybourne defend his Negro world title at the show to prevent the bout between he and Jackson from holding that historic distinction.

After leaving the Mid-Atlantic, Claybourne and Jackson traveled to the Midwest, where they briefly wrestled in Claybourne's home state of Missouri, and then had what was billed as the first bout between Black wrestlers in Owensburg, Kentucky. From there, they ventured into the Northeast, where they were advertised to wrestle as a team in White Plains, New York.

In Orwigsburg, recently dethroned world heavyweight boxing champion "Jersey" Joe Walcott was tabbed to serve as a special guest referee for a match between Claybourne and Jackson. Promoter John Morrison and matchmaker Bert Bertolini assigned a level of importance to the match that warranted the inclusion of Walcott to maintain order.

"A country-wide elimination tournament now is in progress between the more than 20 Negro grapplers who have entered the wrestling game in recent years," disclosed *The Pottsville Republican*. "The ultimate objective is the crowning of a universally recognized Negro champion. As a result, Morrison and Bertolini, realizing the importance of the tugfest to both Jackson and Claybourne, have 'imported' Walcott to act as the referee, and it is a foregone conclusion Jersey Joe will keep matters under control at all times."

*The Republican* added that Walcott's presence would be partially owed to the fact that he "long has been championing the cause of members of his race."

Anyone anticipating any of these Northeastern appearances of Claybourne and Jackson was in for quite a rude awakening. First it was announced that Claybourne and Jackson were being replaced in their White Plains tag team match. Two days later, *The Evening Herald* of Shenandoah, Pennsylvania made the shocking announcement that the main-event bout between Claybourne and Jackson would be canceled as a result of impropriety on Claybourne's part.

"Morrison and his matchmaker, Bert Bertolini, were advised yesterday that Claybourne has been suspended by the Illinois State Athletic Commission, and as the Pennsylvania Commission has a working agreement with Illinois solons, Claybourne's suspension also is effective in the Keystone State," reported *The Herald*.

Once again, this sudden suspension of Claybourne had all of the markings of the NWA lowering the boom on him, and compromising his livelihood. The main event between

Claybourne and Jackson was replaced on short notice by a match between Bob McCoy and Kenny Ackles. Jersey Joe Walcott still made an appearance as the guest referee, but all of the significance of the former boxing great overseeing a tournament match to crown a true Black champion was tossed aside.

Embedded within this imbroglio is the degree to which Jackson was seen as inextricably linked to Claybourne, where some logical questions were neither asked nor answered when it came to the promoter's official statement on the matter.

"We arranged the Claybourne-Jackson match in good faith, and were greatly surprised when we were informed by the state athletic commission that Claybourne was on the unavailable list," Morrison told *The Herald*. "It was too late for us to sign another Negro opponent for Jackson, so we decided to reshuffle the entire card."

This explanation might have carried weight in North Carolina, or in some other state where mixed-race bouts were infrequent. However, matches between White and Black opponents had been occurring in the Northern states — including Pennsylvania — for decades at this point. Scrapping the entire match between Claybourne and Jackson was neither a matter of legal necessity, nor a means of avoiding the setting of an uncomfortable social precedent.

In other words, while Jack may have committed a violation, Buddy appears to have been punished due to the fact that he was seen as an indispensable accompaniment to Claybourne's act.

This suspension, which ostensibly came from the Illinois State Athletic Commission, effectively locked Claybourne — and by proxy, also Jackson — out of wrestling for the remainder of 1953.

Claybourne and Jackson resumed their work in Claybourne's home state of Missouri in January 1954. When they appeared at the American Legion of Sedalia, Jackson was stated to have been the protege of Claybourne, and it was said that they "both claim the World negro title as a team."

"It is the first invasion of the Jackson-Claybourne team in the middlewest," printed *The Sedalia Democrat*. "Claybourne has appeared in matches out of Kansas City several years ago, but it's been about eight years since he was in this area."

*The Moberly Monitor* reported that the "Negro mat stars" had just concluded "an 18-month tour of Australia and New Zealand, where they became the most phenomenal ring attractions to ever represent this country in those two Western Pacific commonwealths." This lie certainly sounded a great deal better than the reality of the situation, which was that the two had finally achieved employment following a multi-month scramble that stemmed from an NWA rules violation.

This created yet another scenario in which the relationship between Jackson and Claybourne vacillated between that of friend and foe from one night to the next, as they were being simultaneously advertised as partners in some locations and as adversaries in others.

These appearances by Claybourne and Jackson were notably bereft of any claims to Negro world title status by either wrestler, including when they wrestled on the undercard of a show in Wichita, Kansas headlined by the outright NWA world champion Lou Thesz. The furthest Claybourne would now go in terms of title claims would be statements saying that he "is recognized in pro wrestling circles as the Negro heavyweight king."

Even without individual gold around their waists that they could publicly claim, the team of Claybourne and Jackson was still making history. In Atchison, Kansas, the pair was declared to have been the first Black tag team to have ever appeared in the city when they faced El Toro and Frank Hewitt.

"Claybourne is reputed to be the world's greatest exponent of the flying dropkick, and his aerial tactics border on the phenomenal side," stated *The Atchison Daily Globe*. "Jackson is also a master of mat science, and will be a capable partner for Claybourne."

Similar history was set to be made when the team was advertised to appear in St. Joseph, Missouri, where they declared that they had returned to the U.S. mainland just two months earlier after a successful series of tag team matches in Hawaii.

In Wichita, Claybourne's story was even more fanciful. During a luncheon, he told reporters that his tour with Jackson had taken them to "the Far Eastern countries, including India, Malaya, Burma, and the British Crown Colony of Hong Kong." Claybourne also added that he had become "the first American Negro athlete" to ever compete in South Africa.

This tour certainly existed only in Claybourne's imagination, especially when he stated that the tour had *concluded* in October 1953 — right around the time his suspension was first being enforced — and was followed up with a quick tour of Hawaii, during which he had supposedly reacquired the championship of the territory. While Claybourne had certainly been a strong attraction and a titleholder in Hawaii, he had not set foot in Hawaii in a competitive capacity during the entirety of 1953, as a vengeful Al Karasick would have prohibited such a visit from taking place.

Claybourne added that he and Jackson had met in Hawaii during that stint, subsequently formed their team, and dominated their competitors along the West Coast in December before traveling to the Midwest in January. Absolutely nothing about that story is true; Claybourne and Jackson were completely inactive during November and December of 1953.

Making the lies even more egregious was the fact that Claybourne and Jackson were appearing in main-event bouts against one another in Missouri during a portion of the time that all of this was said to be occurring elsewhere.

As *The Wichita Eagle* printed the claim that Claybourne and Jackson represented the first Negro team to appear in the Midwest — the truth of which was entirely dependent on how you chose to define "the Midwest" — Claybourne added the further boast that he and Jackson had been undefeated as a team since their first match as a team in November 1953. In reality, the tandem lost the very first matches in which they teamed up, when they were appearing together in Arizona and Texas.

To the surprise of many, a few of the bouts that were intended to pit Jackson and Claybourne against White competitors never occurred. The cover story given for the change — like when Claybourne and Jackson competed against one another in St. Joseph when they were scheduled to face Bobby Layne and Frank Hewitt — was blamed on their opposition failing to reach the building in time for the bout.

The truth of the matter was that a ruling had been handed down by William Theis of the Missouri State Athletic Commission declaring that Claybourne and Jackson could not wrestle against their White opponents because he did not have time to verify their credentials, but they were more than welcome to wrestle against one another if they wished.

When *The Kansas City Call*, a Black publication, discovered that Claybourne and Jackson had been banned from competing against White wrestlers, they phoned Theis directly to hear his side of the story.

"[Theis'] reason, he said, was that as teammates they knew each other, and therefore might be able to give a good performance," reported *The Call*. "It seemed that as long as they were not permitted to compete against white wrestlers, their qualifications did not matter too much."

Echoing the sentiment of *The Call*, Dave Rosen of *The St. Joseph Gazette* added, "The commissioners may repeat and repeat they barred the matches because of qualification reasons, but the actions certainly smacked of something else. We've had inter-racial wrestling in Missouri for quite some time without question before. Let's hope the commissioners can cite some specific qualification requirements that wrestlers failed to meet when they bar matches in the future."

With the adaptability of their act curtailed by an official ruling by a state athletic commission — the third such ruling to be leveled against Claybourne since he had run afoul of Al Karasick and been threatened with NWA sanctions — the Claybourne-Jackson partnership was permanently dissolved.

Jackson left the company of Claybourne and presumably went back to working in the field of pharmacology. He rematerialized in the Northwest several months later in August, working in Washington and British Columbia. Whereas Jackson had previously been described as stout and muscular during prior portions of his career, he was described as "heavy set" in *The Chilliwack Progress* by Pat Church during the final bouts of significance in his career.

Back on the West Coast, Frank James returned to the Pacific Northwest early in 1954, and the Brown Bombers picked right up where they left off, battering their opponents with headbutts. However, the pair spent their short reunion period losing to many of the wrestlers they had beaten to establish their initial momentum, and would not be able to replicate their original success.

Their partnership may not have lasted very long in the grand scheme of things, but the Brown Bombers had made good on the original promise of Rufus Jones in the Rocky Mountains and the Pacific Northwest. Essentially functioning as Jones' stand-ins while wrestling as what amounted to a tribute team, the two managed to enjoy the first championship reign of significance by a team of Black wrestlers on U.S. soil.

A bit further north and much further east of where the Brown Bombers had struck gold, Jack Claybourne would be in pursuit of some tag team gold of his own. To identify a worthy partner for his push toward tag title contentions, Jack would be forced to brush shoulders with multiple members of a burgeoning generation of young Black wrestlers who were eager for stardom.

# 19 - The Canadian Kings

After the disruption of his partnership with Buddy Jackson, Gentleman Jack rematerialized in New England in February 1954, and was once again hot on the trail of Bull Curry. Claiming to still be the Negro world heavyweight champion who was aching for an opportunity to wrestle for a world championship, Claybourne began the aggressive implementation of his Hawaiian headbutting routine on the American mainland.

*The Hartford Courant* indicated that Claybourne's "head noggin' tactics have ended many battles in his favor," and he put that on display when he disposed of Manuel Cortez in straight falls.

"The East Boston Spaniard forced Claybourne with roughhouse tactics for 20 minutes through the first fall until the Negro cut loose with a series of head butts, on the front end of a body press, at 22 ½ minutes to get the fall," described *The Portland Press Herald*.

Unlike in Hawaii, the promoters in New England seemed to have difficulty reconciling the emulation of Rufus Jones' headbutting antics with the behavior of a babyface, especially in a region of the country where Joe Godfrey — wrestling as Tiger Flowers — had once been among the most vilified grapplers.

The net result was that "Gentleman" Jack Claybourne, for the first time in his 22-year career, was forced to complete a true heel turn and fill the role of "badman." He accomplished this turn through a memorably violent assault of Jackie Nichols in late April during a bout in Capital City using "outlaw tactics generally associated with meaner maulers."

"Fortunately, several feminine fans rushed to the strangling Jackie's rescue, and Nichols was pressing the attack against his near-berserk foe when time ran out without a fall registered," stated *The Portland Sunday Telegram*. "In the dressing room afterward, Claybourne was unable to give a coherent account of his actions."

In the subsequent match between the two at the Portland Expo, *The Portland Press Herald* reminded the fans that Claybourne had "turned villain for the occasion" and "dropped his gentleman's cloak" in favor of far more aggressive tactics even before he lost the first fall of the match to Nichols.

"Returning after the rest period, Claybourne started with dropkicks, strangles, and headbutts, and it was one of the latter that stopped the bout," shared *The Press Herald*. "Nichols suffered a bloody cut over his right eye and Referee Cement O'Neil awarded the fall to Claybourne in 12 minutes and declared the bout a draw as the popular Jackie was through for the night."

That match result is interesting, as it was often the conclusion to matches involving Rufus Jones that he would surrender the first fall to his adversary, only to win the second fall via a referee's stoppage due to a cut to his opponent's forehead, and to then have his opponent immediately surrender a second fall from not being in any condition to continue the match. The variation of that ending employed here was clearly intended to protect the win-loss record of the babyface.

Coinciding with this period of malfeasance was the somewhat frequent teaming of Claybourne with "The Black Panther" Jim Mitchell. Throwing aside more than two decades of overlapping career history, during which the two men had wrestled one another several times and endured countless comparisons to one another, the two were advertised as blood brothers during at least a few of their team-ups in New England.

Out in Australia, previous Claybourne partner and former Brown Bombers member Don Kindred had begun his own tour of the nation, and continued the use of tactics that both he and Claybourne had borrowed from Rufus Jones in his own effort to establish himself as a singles attraction overseas. As *The Brisbane Telegraph* pointed out, Kindred used a headbutt known as "the Nut Cracker, which was favoured here by another coloured grappler, Jack Claybourne."

On his way out of New England, Claybourne concluded his brief run as a heel by losing definitively to Jackie Nichols in a Portland Expo bout that was advertised as a number-one-contender's match to identify the challenger to NWA world light heavyweight champion Verne Gagne.

"The Expo fans went wild Wednesday night as Claybourne seemed to be gaining the advantage of Jackie by the meanest of his bad man tactics," stated *The Journal* of Bideford, Maine. "After about 25 minutes of taking punishment, the Maine grappler suddenly exploded and chased the Negro strongman about the ring, cornering him and pounding his head on the ring post before applying his effective grapevine for the fall in 30:30. Claybourne was unable to make it into action for the next fall and the win was given to Nichols."

Around this same time, *The Afro-American* printed what was likely the most honest interview Claybourne ever submitted to during his long career. The interview was conducted by reporter Joseph A. Owens in the presence of Claybourne's "two diamond-studded belts he has been awarded, one of which symbolizes the colored championship of the world."

The resulting article makes it clear that Claybourne was vehemently opposed to the changes that the intrusion of television had forced the wrestling industry to undergo.

"The colored boys are being discriminated against," declared Claybourne. "I have wrestled all the white headliners during my 20 years in the game, but seldom do my fans see me on their home television screen. When they ask the reason, I tell them."

The reason, Claybourne stated, was because wrestlers like himself, Jim Mitchell, Bobo Brazil or Buddy Jackson would be participating in the in-ring action during the live show, but their matches "will be through when it comes time for the cameras to pick up the ring action."

"We know that many of the bouts are seen in the southern states via TV, and I believe that is the reason," Claybourne continued. "The promoters do not want to offend any of the would-be paying fans. Strange as it might seem, the same situation exists on the West Coast, though it was out in Los Angeles that a couple of my matches were beamed at the TV audience."

Once he had finished discussing the TV-match-selection process that put Black wrestlers at a decided disadvantage in comparison with their White counterparts, Claybourne explained that he faulted television for reducing the number of fans who were willing to pay to watch wrestling in person.

"All this talk about television reviving wrestling is so much bunk in my book," added Claybourne. "If anything, it has hurt our sport. I started back in the depression days when the longest lines were at relief agencies, not ticket windows, and wrestling still managed to draw good crowds. I admit that right after the war television re-interested people in wrestling, but since then, it has not helped the game."

Claybourne concluded the piece by saying he traveled to most of his engagements in his "high powered '53 Cadillac," and would enjoy a comfortable retirement thanks to the six-unit apartment house that he and his wife Lillian maintained in Los Angeles. He also said that he would compete until he could "no longer give a good, clean performance" in the ring.

Jack closed by complimenting some of his fellow Black wrestlers, saying that "Rufus Jones was great," and that "of the boys still in the game, Seelie Samara is plenty good, and Luther Lindsay is a comer, and so is Frank James."

Claybourne's claims about the unwillingness of broadcasters to upset Southern audiences was remarkably prescient. Just three years later, *The Nat King Cole Show* — the first evening talk show featuring a Black host — was canceled after just one season due to its inability to find a national sponsor. No major companies wanted to risk the backlash of Southern consumers who would be angry at any brand that contributed to broadcasting the face and voice of a respected Black entertainer into Southern households.

The next stop along Claybourne's trek through the Northeast would be in Ottawa, Canada. Claybourne was apparently recruited to the area by promoter Eddie Quinn in an attempt to develop yet another Black wrestling star, in what was erroneously described as "the first time in major wrestling that two Negro athletes have paired up, making a bid for fame."

Claybourne was partnered with Herb Trawick, generally accepted as the first Black player in the history of the Canadian Football League, who was still an active player on the offensive line of the Montreal Alouettes. It was said that he was diligently training to transition into a wrestling career "under the careful eye of Claybourne."

"Not many Negro wrestlers have starred in the wrestling ring, though they dominate the major boxing ring by fully 75 percent," noted *The Ottawa Journal*. "One of the best is, like Trawick, a football player, Wilber Strode, who starred in the West, a big figure in California rings in the off-season. Giant Bobo Brazil is another Negro star, and so too is Seelie Samara. The late Regis Siki, who succumbed to hardships inflicted on him in a Nazi prison camp, was one of the smoothest of Negro wrestlers."

Setting aside for a moment that Woody Strode's name was Woodrow and not Wilber, and no clear connection was ever established between Siki's death and his time spent in a Nazi prison camp — although it certainly didn't help matters — this report marked one of the very first times that Claybourne's name ever appeared in the same article as Bobo Brazil's.

Born in 1924, Houston Harris was raised in Benton Harbor, Michigan — a location where Black wrestling greats including Jack Nelson, Alex Kaffner, Jack Claybourne, Gorilla Parker, King Kong Clayton, Rufus Jones, Seelie Samara, and Jim Mitchell all performed — before making his in-ring debut very late in the 1940s, and then adopting the ring name of "Bobo Brazil" in December 1950.

Advertised as standing between 6'4" and 6'6" and possessing a well-muscled frame, the image of the 30-year-old Brazil communicated far more power than nearly all other wrestlers, and certainly more than the overwhelming majority of the Black wrestlers that preceded him.

The claim about the pairing of Claybourne and Trawick was later amended to the two of them being "the first Negro wrestling team to operate in Canada," and their debut was inauspicious regardless of the history-making activities being alleged. Trawick and Claybourne lost their tag team debut at the Ottawa Auditorium while their opponents — Ike Eakins and Fred Atkins — left the ring "in a shower of shattered chairs."

Claybourne and Trawick captured the first fall thanks to a pair of crossbody blocks from Trawick, but then surrendered the second fall when Trawick ran into the knee of Eakins. In the midst of the proceedings, Claybourne had been aggressively battering both of their opponents.

"Claybourne had been giving Eakins and Atkins a bad time with his 'nut-cracker,' an elementary wrinkle in which he leaps in the air and bounces his durable skull off that of the foe," described *The Journal*. "The foes were reeling from a series of these wallops when they suddenly turned, dragged Claybourne to a corner, and punished him with a prolonged series of leglocks.

Failing to capitalize on his aggressive tactics, Claybourne lost the final fall for his team when he mistimed a dropkick, crashed onto his back, and was covered for the three count. When chairs thrown from the stands rained down upon Eakins and Atkins as they made their way back to the dressing room, *The Ottawa Citizen* noted that the fans were then surprised "when the missiles were thrown right back again."

Claybourne found himself roped into yet another high-profile Black tag team when he made his way to the Upstate region of New York and partnered up with 22-year-old

Edward "Bearcat" Wright, who had dropped the "Bobo" from the ring name that he had used in Australia.

Similar in size to Bobo Brazil, and half the age of the 44-year-old Claybourne, Wright had become a main-event attraction in the Northeast, and his surge in popularity was yet another sign that Claybourne was going to have increasing difficulty maintaining his position as the top-ranking Black wrestler in territories where the competition for that spot was growing far more heated.

Wright and Claybourne teamed up for a bout against the villainous Japanese team of the Togo brothers, which was ruled a draw. Before Bearcat and Jack would get any further opportunities to partner together, Claybourne would once again find his plans derailed by a suspicious ruling from a state athletic commission.

Initially, fans were told that Claybourne had been replaced by Lucky Simunovich prior to his scheduled match against Bob Orton because the Black veteran wrestler had "failed to pass the physical examination." One week later, a more thorough ruling from the New York State Athletic Commission would be shared with the public.

"Jack Claybourne, who didn't wrestle here last week as scheduled because he reportedly failed to pass a physical examination, has been permanently suspended in New York State rings, according to the latest bulletin issued by the Athletic Commission," reported *The Buffalo News*.

With Claybourne once again chased out of a wrestling territory due to a ruling handed down by a state's athletic commission — at least the *fourth* such instance of this occurring in less than two years — he found himself in Southern Ontario teaming with Luther Lindsay once again.

Canadian fans were informed that Claybourne had recently returned from "New Zealand, Australia, and many parts of Europe," as opposed to being abruptly booted out of New York. *The Niagara Falls Review* also reminded fans that Claybourne "earned the distinction of being called Gentleman

Jack by his refusal to step out of bounds of the rules regardless of the situation."

Jack would prove this description to be false during the first night of his return to Hamilton. Claybourne made quick work of George "Zebra" Bellos, flattening him with a flying dropkick. Later in the evening, Claybourne inserted himself into the bout between the Togo Brothers and the combination of Luther Lindsay and "Whipper" Billy Watson.

"Claybourne appeared outside of the ring shouting at the officials to stop the Great Togo from strangling his pal," reported *The Hamilton Spectator*. "In the third and deciding fall, and with Watson lying flat on the canvas after taking some terrible treatment from the Togo boys, the Great One went to work on Lindsay. This Claybourne would not stand for. He tossed his coat high in the air, jumped into the ring, and started cleaning up with his 'koko' hold, which he makes by bumping heads with an opponent."

The official in charge disqualified Lindsay and Watson due to Claybourne's interference. In response, Jack "carried on with his wild tactics for several minutes before peace was restored."

Claybourne and Lindsay formed an official tag team in the aftermath of this episode, and they got straight to business by defeating the team of George Bollas and Lee Henning, and then downed the Riot Squad, consisting of Ernie and Emil Dusek.

Following those victories, Jack and Luther were quickly thrust into the running for the Canadian tag team championship held by the Togo Brothers. The title bout would take place in the main event of a show held on September 28th at the Hamilton Forum.

"Lindsay and Claybourne, both hard-hitters, feel confident that they will lift the crown, but those who make a close study of the game predict that the Togo boys will be hard to dethrone," opined *The Hamilton Spectator*.

On the eve of the match, *The Niagara Falls Evening Review* elaborated on the differences in the tactical approaches employed by each tag team combination, noting that the attack of Lindsay and Claybourne offered more variation, which might serve to sway the outcome in their favor.

**Luther Lindsay and Jack Claybourne**

"The Japs feature a judo attack while their Negro rivals, who often gain an advantage with toe holds, always switch to a dropkicking attack to win falls," noted *The Review*. "Claybourne, in addition, is adept at rapping heads with rivals and always comes out on top with his own hard noggin apparently oblivious to hard wacks."

Right before the title match, the Great Togo was replaced by Pat Fraley, but the titles remained up for grabs. Making good on their opportunity to set milestones in a way that was seldom delivered upon where Black wrestlers were concerned, Claybourne and Lindsay defeated the Togo Brothers in Hamilton and became the first Black tag team in Canada, the second in North America, and the first Black babyface tag team, to jointly hold a genuine tag team championship.

"Lindsay and Claybourne did not waltz to the crown. They had to overcome stiff opposition and some very rough handling at the hands of Fraley and Tosh before they were declared winners," stated *The Spectator*. "As a matter of fact, they had to come from behind as they lost the first fall and appeared to be headed for defeat in the second round when the upset occurred."

Facing defeat, the challengers became aggressive, with Claybourne and Lindsay simultaneously bombarding their opponents with "elbow smashes, butts, and noggin jolts." Eventually, Claybourne flattened Fraley on the mat, covered him, and won the match for his team.

Refusing to rest on their laurels, the new champions even won a rematch of sorts by turning back the challenge of Tosh Togo and a different substitute partner, Hi-Lee. Lindsay got his team off to a quick lead by twisting Togo's head, hurling him to the mat, and climbing on top of him for the three count.

"Togo evened matters with Luther six minutes later with judo chops to the throat, which rendered Lindsay 'hors de combat,'" declared *The Evening Review*. "The other team principals got into fall business for the wind-up heave when gentleman Jack Claybourne felled the mammoth Hi-Lee with a series of koko krunches and drop kicks."

After defeating a second mixed pairing involving Tosh Togo, Claybourne and Lindsay were able to battle the reunited Togo Brothers team to a draw. Then it was announced that Lindsay and Claybourne would receive a shot at the world tag team championship held by the traveling team of Art Neilson and Reggie Lisowski.

The first bout between the teams ended in a confusing one-hour draw, with the referee applying the final three-count in favor of Claybourne and Lindsay just as the bell was sounding to signify that the one-hour time limit had expired.

"Luther Lindsay and Gentleman Jack Claybourne are not holders of the world tag team wrestling title today, but they convinced slightly more than 2,000 fans at the Forum last night that they could have lifted the crown had they been given just a little more time," declared *The Hamilton Spectator*. "The popular coloured mat artists, holders of the Canadian championship, had Art Neilson and Reggie Lisowski, holders of the world belt, ready for the kill when the final bell sounded. The match ended in a draw."

So, too, ended the October 19th rematch between the two teams, with an irate Claybourne "chasing the Chicago pair right to their dressing rooms seeking vengeance" after the bout was over. The Canadian champions once again set their sights on defending their own titles against the reunited Togo Brothers tandem in front of 7,500 fans in Toronto.

As the one-fall bout deteriorated into a lawless brawl outside of the ring — and with the referee actively counting out both of the legal match participants from inside the ring — the Great Togo struck Lindsay in the throat, propelling his unconscious opponent back into the ring just as the official's count reached 10. Thus, Claybourne and Lindsay won the bout and successfully defended their Canadian tag team championship in front of their largest audience to date.

The championship success of Claybourne and Lindsay, whether intentional or unintentional — seemed to coincide with the launch of the U.S. Civil Rights Movement. It was an era that historians would retroactively agree to have begun on May 17th, 1954 when the U.S. Supreme Court rendered its decision on *Brown v. Board of Education*, and struck down the "separate but equal" clause as inherently discriminatory, thereby eliminating the racial segregation of public schools and eventually other public spaces.

Perhaps realizing that keeping Black wrestlers effectively siloed and isolated from championship opportunities had been wrong, or potentially realizing that a segment of the ticket-purchasers actively desired to see Black achievement in athletic spaces, wrestling promoters would begin to offer title opportunities to Black wrestlers with far greater frequency than in bygone eras.

Although it had been alluded to in prior publications, *The Kitchener-Waterloo Record* directly declared that Claybourne and Lindsay "hold the Canadian tag team title as well as the colored championship," leaving readers to infer that the pair simultaneously held two sets of tag team championships.

This declaration was made immediately ahead of the pair's title defense against the Soviet team of Ivan and Karol Kalmikoff, neither of whom was actually Russian. As a matter of trivia, the role of Karol Kalmikoff was played by Karol Piwoworczyk, a former bodybuilder who served as the model for the earliest sketchings of Superman that were used in the famous comic strip.

The fact that Claybourne and Lindsay were successful in defending their titles in Hamilton against the symbolic forces of communism was of secondary significance to the scene that followed the conclusion of the match. Just moments after Lindsay covered Karol Kalmikoff for the deciding fall, mayhem ensued.

"In an attempt to restore order, referee Jimmy 'Red' Sims received a deep cut in his forehead and blood flowed freely from the wound," recounted *The Spectator*. "Coming to aid was Dave Sims, brother of Jimmy. He leapt into the ring and began tackling Karol. Two exuberant fans charged the ring swinging chains. They were repelled by police. The action left the ring and moved into the dressing rooms where Big John Katan finally subdued the frenzied Russians."

Ahead of subsequent matches with the Russian pair, the champions exuded confidence in their interviews. *The Spectator* quoted Claybourne as saying, "You must be on your toes all the time when you are wrestling the Russian champions, and we will be just that."

History would show that they weren't as prepared as they purported to be. On December 9th at the Maple Leaf Gardens in Toronto, the Kalmikoffs defeated Claybourne and Lindsay to end their multi-month reign as the Canadian tag team champions.

"More than 6,000 fans roared their disapproval when referees Bert Maxwell and Bunny Dunlop announced their decision," reported *The Ottawa Journal*. "They ruled brother Ivan pinned Claybourne with a shoulder stand after 31 minutes of grunting and groaning."

In the background of this title loss was an ongoing storyline that referee Bunny Dunlop had a tendency to favor the rulebreakers during matches, and the championship loss by Claybourne and Lindsay came as a result of Dunlop wielding this favoritism against them during crucial moments of their title defense.

This partiality was also on display during a subsequent six-man tag team affair that pitted Claybourne, Lindsay, and Pat Flanagan against the heel trio of Don Lee, Pat Fraley, and Jan Gotch. In covering the event for *The Kingston Whig-Standard*, reporter Don Soutter reported that the match between the teams at the Kingston Community Centre proved three things.

"Namely: 1) That three villains instead of two can be 50 percent more dastardly. 2) That Gentleman Jack Claybourne's head is still the best weapon that the Lindsay-Claybourne duo have in their repertoire of tricks. 3) That Bunny Dunlop is sadly misplaced as an alert, impartial wrestling referee, but could no doubt play blind man's bluff quite successfully without using a blindfold," opined Soutter.

Soutter then expressed how the second point was emphatically demonstrated through a display that was intended to show how Claybourne's head was uniquely dense and rigid, even amongst Black wrestlers — which would be a distinction that would eventually be lost amongst future generations.

The trio of Lee, Fraley, and Gotch speared Lindsay's head into the ring post, resulting in Lindsay being rendered unconscious. The three then repeated the stunt with Claybourne to no effect, as it "only succeeded in making the ring shake from the impact."

"Claybourne emphasized the point quite clearly by then bouncing around the ring to give each of his opponents a bongo bonk, saving the best one for Buddy Dunlop," concluded Soutter.

Shortly after this six-man bout, Claybourne and Lindsay were joined in Canada by the youthful wrestler who had briefly been Claybourne's partner in New York prior to his suspension, Bearcat Wright. The unveiling of Wright clearly positioned him — at least initially — as the intimidating enforcer who stood behind Lindsay and Claybourne as they prepared to face the team that had dethroned them, the Kalmikoffs.

"[Lindsay and Claybourne] plan to have the gigantic Bearcat Wright in their corner, presumably to give them household hints, or to administer first aid if and when necessary, or maybe only hold their hands when matters become trying," *The Toronto Star* stated rather sarcastically. "At any rate the Kalmikoffs are quoted as being deeply concerned over the possibility and have screamed that they won't wrestle if Bearcat shows."

At least temporarily, it appeared as if the Claybourne-Lindsay-Wright trio would be positioned as a formidable stable of Black wrestlers. However, that changed rapidly, as Claybourne soon found himself wrestling in singles bouts while Wright inherited his spot as Lindsay's regular tag team partner.

The description *The Star* offered of the 22-year-old Wright — who was born the very same year Claybourne first rose to wrestling prominence — as an "elongated, six-foot-six Negro with a cement-like head" — certainly must have touched a nerve with Jack. With headbutting quickly becoming the defining characteristic of almost all Black wrestlers' routines, Claybourne's comparative lack of youth and size, combined with his declining athleticism, was starting to render him imminently replaceable.

This was ultimately the case, as Claybourne wrestled a few more dates in January 1955 before being "pulverized" by Pete Managoff in Toronto at the end of January, and then disappeared from Canada following that match.

Early in March, Claybourne rematerialized in El Paso, Texas for what was advertised to be a historic event. As a "new twist" to the card, Claybourne was signed to participate in a mixed-race contest with Danny Plechas that promoter Sam Menacker labeled as "the first wrestling match in Texas involving a Negro and White wrestler."

This claim was absolutely false, although it's quite possible that Menacker was unaware of this. White Noble, formerly a well known Black wrestler from Taylor, Texas, was trained by famous Texas wrestler Pet Brown and wrestled frequently in the 1920s in both Texas and California. The majority of Noble's bouts in the state of Texas were against White wrestlers like Gus Pappas and Gust Prokos. Sadly, Noble was tragically murdered in March 1933 while attempting to evict a squatter from a house that he owned.

Regardless, it's quite possible that Claybourne's bout with Plechas was the first match between Black and White wrestlers in *El Paso*, as Claybourne had been famously banned from wrestling against White wrestlers in El Paso in the early 1930s while still being permitted to wrestle on the other side of the river in Juarez, and had competed against Buddy Jackson when he wrestled there earlier in the 1950s.

In a bout that was at least advertised as possessing historical significance, Claybourne defeated Plechas by disqualification. The now 45-year-old Claybourne then continued his Southwest swing by losing to Plechas in areas of Arizona and New Mexico.

Suddenly, at least with respect to the booking of his matches, things took a turn in Jack's favor when a famous figure who he was often associated with added Albuquerque to his appearance schedule.

"Former World Heavyweight Boxing Champion Joe Louis last night agreed by telephone to referee a wrestling match next week between Jack Claybourne and the Golden Terror in Albuquerque's Ice Arena," reported the Associated Press.

The report of the Brown Bomber's visit to Albuquerque suggests that he and Claybourne were familiar with one another beyond mere photo opps. *The Albuquerque Journal* described how Claybourne accompanied Louis to the city's Veteran's Memorial Hospital to visit patients in the tuberculosis and general medical wards prior to the March 28th wrestling event.

The conclusion to the match between the Golden Terror and Claybourne was clearly coordinated to make use of Louis' famed punching power. To the extent that Claybourne and Louis could both be regarded as racial icons of their respective sports genres, the 5,000 fans in attendance were treated to a symbolic snapshot of the two Black standard bearers during the ending to the match.

"The finale action went this way," began the report from *The Journal*. "The Terror was holding Claybourne and reportedly poking his opponent's eyes; Louis tried to separate the grapplers a couple of times and the Terror finally hit Louis; Joe punched the Terror in the stomach, and the Terror doubled up; Claybourne then used a flying drop kick to nail the Terror for the deciding fall."

No one suspected at the time that this event was a prelude for Louis' own dabblings in the world of professional wrestling as a grappler rather than an official. However, the Joe Louis of 1955 was facing drastically different life circumstances than the man who had dominated the sports landscape in the late 1930s and throughout the 1940s.

A string of bad business decisions and unfathomable generosity had left Louis destitute, and in severe debt to the Internal Revenue Service. In order to pay back a portion of those debts, a full-fledged wrestling career would be in his near future.

Meanwhile, as this was occurring in the Southwest, Claybourne's name was being mentioned in New England in his absence. In a discussion of memorable heel turns, *The Press Herald* recalled how "Gentleman Jack" had "spoiled 15 years of local good conduct with a series of outrageous ring actions."

After the involvement of Louis, the favorable booking of Claybourne continued to such an extent that he was even successful in handicap matches, including a mid-April bout against Bronko Lubich and Count Zarnoff.

"Claybourne defeated Lubich in 22 minutes with a series of head butts, then won from Zarnoff by disqualification," said *The Albuquerque Tribune*.

Following his stint in New Mexico, Claybourne was inactive for a couple of months before rematerializing in Southern California in July. During that intervening period of time, American pop culture took another giant leap in the direction of Black acceptance with the recording and release of "Maybellene" by Chuck Berry.

Considered a perfect encapsulation of rock and roll, and the song that set the instrumental standard for what rock guitar would sound like going forward, "Maybellene" was a massive crossover hit, and set the tone for what was soon to come musically.

As Black influence was starting to reinvent popular culture, Claybourne was in need of a reinvention of his own. For a wrestler so late in his career who had wrestled his way through California several times, Claybourne had some very bizarre wrinkles added to his personal story by the promoters in San Bernardino. In *The Daily Sun*, Claybourne was called "the great colored athlete from the University of Oregon" who "excelled in track and football" and was a 10-year wrestling veteran.

Again, it's probable that references to Claybourne having barely a decade of ring time under his belt were intended to downplay his age, which was certainly advanced for a wrestler by that point. Jack was well into his third decade of in-ring activity, and no serious references to a university athletic career had ever been proposed, save for the suggestion in Australia that his high-jumping abilities were a result of his hurdling and high-jumping skill. In interviews, Claybourne usually only mentioned a failed boxing career and a fondness for baseball.

Claybourne would participate in California mat contests for less than a month before the arrival of Luther Lindsay. The two were immediately reunited in a tag team, with promoters seemingly hoping to capitalize on whatever momentum and notoriety the two had acquired during their multi-month reign as the Canadian tag team champions.

*The San Bernardino Telegram* hailed the pair as "the Canadian kings," while *The Yucaipa News-Mirror* advertised them as still being the reigning "Canadian Heavyweight Tag Champs" as they prepared to challenge familiar opponents of theirs — The Togo Brothers — for the California version of the world tag team championship.

The hype amounted to one match of significance on August 13th. It was a defeat for Jack and Luther, during which Claybourne captured a fall for his team with a maneuver from his repertoire that was becoming increasingly more rare — a dropkick — before losing the final fall by submission when Jack surrendered to an armbar.

Claybourne was suddenly on the road yet again, and by the end of that same month, he was wrestling in Salem, Oregon, and being publicized there as the Black Panther for the first time in what seemed like an eternity.

Similar to prior visits he'd made to the Pacific Northwest during his career, Claybourne came in as a force, although the wording of his arrival suggested that he now had to lean on the fame of his associates in order to garner recognition from the region's wrestling fans.

"'The 'Panther' is Jack Claybourne, a big and fast Negro star of many campaigns who holds the heavyweight championship of Australia and Hawaii, and who was for quite a while Luther Lindsay's partner in many tag events in the East," printed *The Oregon Statesman*.

Lindsay had been popular in Oregon ever since 1953, and had been the first holder of the Pacific Northwest heavyweight championship when the territory introduced the heavier weight class, defeating Roger Mackey on May 24th, 1955 to unify the championships of Washington and Oregon.

Claybourne's first significant splash occurred when he won a seven-man battle royal in Portland, finally eliminating Ivan Kameroff to seal the victory. Interestingly, Claybourne had not used either a dropkick or a headbutt to finish the match, and instead made use of a surfboard submission hold to earn the win. To show that this wasn't a one-off event, Claybourne made use of the same hold to secure a victory against Doug Donovan just a few nights later.

After battling Gory Guerrero to a draw, Claybourne was quickly thrust into the territory's title picture, with announcements on back-to-back days declaring that Jack would be receiving opportunities to capture both the heavyweight and tag team titles of the Pacific Northwest.

In his shot at the heavyweight championship, Claybourne was awarded the victory but not the championship when titleholder Ivan Kameroff was disqualified for pinning Claybourne in the third fall with his feet on the ropes for added leverage. Claybourne's disqualification win in the third fall apparently stripped the match of its potential for a championship to be won or lost.

"Kameroff won the first fall in 11 minutes with a hangman's hold after Claybourne had hit his head on a turnbuckle," explained *The Capital Journal*. "The negro took the second fall in five minutes with head butts and a reverse surfboard hold."

But Killer Kameroff wouldn't be getting off that easily; Claybourne's next title opportunity involved Kameroff as well. On Sunday, September 18th, Claybourne teamed with the same Luigi Macera who Rufus Jones had so rudely brutalized in front of his own wife in an attempt to wrest the Pacific Northwest tag titles away from Kameroff and his partner Doug Donovan. The pair was successful in their effort.

The September 19th edition of *The News-Review* of Roseburg, Oregon stated that Macera and Claybourne had "made complete their revenge on their hated rivals" by deposing the reigning Northwest tag team champs in the main event at the Armory.

"Macera and Claybourne could give referee Thor Hagen an assist however, for their triumph after the latter had disqualified Kameroff and Donovan for illegal tactics," continued *The News-Review*. "The teams split opening falls. Claybourne gave his side a one-fall lead when he throttled Donovan with head butts and a reverse surfboard at 15:20. Kameroff then applied the evener with a backbreaker and press on Macera, eight minutes and 10 seconds later."

Claybourne's triumph in the tag team ranks would be as sudden as it was short-lived. On Friday, September 23rd, *The News-Review* recapped the title win of the Claybourne-Macera team, and stated that Claybourne had all of the momentum heading into his next opportunity to now relieve Kameroff of his singles heavyweight championship.

"Kameroff, who felt the sting of defeat when Claybourne and partner Luigi Macera last week won the Northwest tag team title, has promised to spare nothing to defend his last trophy," added *The New Review*. "The Black Panther, Claybourne, has wowed fans in his first three local matches, and he will draw most of the support Saturday night. His pet hold is the reverse surfboard preceded by a few headbutts."

Two days later, with neither Claybourne nor Macera participating in any tag team contests during the intervening period, it was announced that Dick Torio and Luigi Macera would be defending their newly won Pacific Northwest tag team championship against Henry Lenz and Bill Savage.

It just so happened that the tag team title bout was repeated on Monday, September 19th, with Torio standing in for Claybourne. Macera and Torio then defeated Kameroff and Donovan and took the championship from them. Apparently, promoter Don Owen preferred the pair of Macera and Torio as champions, and continued to promote them as such.

As a result, despite the fact that Claybourne won the Pacific Northwest tag team championship in the ring — and the title win was affirmed in the newspapers several days later — he was *never* acknowledged as a holder of the Pacific Northwest tag team championship aside from the article printed five days after his triumph.

In the meantime, Ivan Kameroff convincingly defeated Claybourne in his title defense on September 25th in Roseburg, the same site where Claybourne and Macera had ostensibly captured the tag team titles, and Claybourne's win of the tag team championship on September 18th was never mentioned again.

Claybourne stuck around for one more month, and then unceremoniously departed from Oregon forever following a loss to Jack Kiser on October 16th. Without a doubt, Jack Claybourne's wrestling career was steadily creeping toward its expiration date. The only question remaining to be answered was how it would all come crashing down. The answer to that question? Catastrophically.

## 20 - More Into the World

While the wrestling career of Jack Claybourne had continued to flounder out on the Pacific Coast, tragic events were pushing the Civil Rights Movement forward. In August 1955, 14-year old Emmett Till of Chicago, Illinois was visiting relatives in Drew, Mississippi when he had an interaction with 21-year-old Carolyn Bryant — the White proprietor of a local grocery store — that may have consisted of anything from whistling at her or flirting with her to touching her nonconsensually.

In response to this, Till was abducted from his uncle's home by relatives of Bryant, and summarily tortured, murdered, and mutilated. In the aftermath of the shocking incident, Till's mother Mamie insisted on holding an open-casket funeral for her son so that the tens of thousands of mourners in attendance could lay their eyes upon his disfigured corpse and witness the horrific aftermath of racially motivated, terroristic violence.

The exposure wrought by the incident led to a direct escalation of protest efforts, including the 1955 Montgomery bus boycott in Alabama, during which the famous arrest of Rosa Parks took place as a result of her refusal to surrender her seat at the front of the bus to a White passenger.

As the push for social change was ongoing, the order of things continued to change within the professional wrestling business, although not in a way that was beneficial to Jack Claybourne. *The Kansas City Times* welcomed Bearcat Wright to the location where Claybourne first built his name by proclaiming "Wright succeeded Jack Claybourne as the No. 1 Negro heavyweight a year ago."

Even without any official efforts of NWA collusion taking place, it appeared that Claybourne was having his reputation pulled down brick by brick, and at a point where he was rapidly losing the physical tools to piece it back together.

Claybourne concluded 1955 in Los Angeles once again, wrestling in occasional show-opening matches to little fanfare. Then in the spring of 1956, Claybourne embarked on yet another tour of New Zealand and Australia, but things were noticeably different there with respect to the perception and popularity of professional wrestling. The tours attracted fewer fans than in previous years.

Whether or not Claybourne perceived his tour of his usual international Pacific Ocean haunts to have been successful or not, it was all a prelude to his return to Hawaii for the first time since a falling-out with promoter Al Karasick had seemed to spawn years of backlash from the National Wrestling Alliance that damaged Claybourne's career prospects.

With fences putatively mended between himself and the promoter, Claybourne went back to work for Karasick, and his return was heralded as a big deal by the local press. In the six years since Claybourne's nearly year-long Hawaiian title reign had ended — the second longest reign of the post-war era — no wrestler had come close to matching it.

"Jack Claybourne, probably the greatest Negro wrestler to show in Hawaii in the last 20 years, will meet Tony Gardenia in a special event," announced *The Honolulu Advertiser*. "A former champion of Hawaii, Claybourne is a colorful and spectacular performer."

Whether Claybourne had recovered from lingering injuries and wear or was feeling motivated by a return to the territory where he enjoyed his greatest successes is impossible to know. Nevertheless, he apparently found a gear that had been missing from his most recent bouts, as he turned back the clock and defeated Gardenia with multiple dropkicks and a body press.

*The Advertiser* praised Claybourne as being "a big hit with the fans" during his return, and he repeated the feat the following week, downing Ray Duran with a flurry of dropkicks to end his second Civic Arena bout of 1956 with a victory.

Perhaps noting that Claybourne still potentially connected with Hawaiian fans like few other wrestlers,

Karasick inserted Claybourne into the title picture, setting him on a collision course with reigning Hawaii junior heavyweight champion Tosh Togo. First, Claybourne and his partner Vic Christy would be required to get through Aldo Bogni and Pedro Godoy in a tag team match on September 2nd.

"Bogni took the first fall with body slams and a press in 23 minutes, seven seconds," reported *The Honolulu Star-Bulletin*. "Claybourne, using head butts and a press, equaled the count 10 minutes, 52 seconds later by subduing Godoy. Claybourne and Christy, colliding Bogni's and Godoy's heads together, took the final fall in four minutes, 12 seconds."

After this tag team victory, Claybourne was officially granted a non-title match with Tosh Togo, with whom Jack had previously wrestled in New York, Ontario, and California. *The Advertiser* made it clear that this would be Claybourne's opportunity to prove he was still a wrestler of the caliber demanded of a viable champion.

"Although the Hawaiian heavyweight title and *Ring Magazine* belt held by Togo will not be at stake tonight, Claybourne wants to prove he deserves a championship match," avowed *The Advertiser*. "By showing or making a strong showing, he feels he can establish himself as No. 1 contender. Claybourne, a former champion, combines spectacular tactics, head butts and dropkicks to weaken his opponents. He will find the going rough against Togo, a master of the judo chop and one of the roughest men in wrestling today."

The conclusion of the Claybourne-Togo bout was clearly intended to communicate to fans that Claybourne certainly did retain all of the tools required to become the Hawaiian champion once more. In fact, the only thing preventing Claybourne from defeating Togo outright was a misplaced headbutt in the closing moments of the match.

"Claybourne and Togo tussled to a wild ending after each had scored a fall," printed *The Advertiser*. "Togo took the first fall with judo chops and a press in 9m57s, but Claybourne came back strong to score the equalizer 8m37s later with head butts, dropkicks and a press. Claybourne continued to use head butts on Togo, drawing blood from a cut on the latter's forehead. But Claybourne made the mistake of head-butting the referee, and Frank Merrill put a stop to the match and called it no contest."

Two weeks later, Claybourne would battle Tom Rice with the number-one-contendership on the line. Similar to how Don Kindred had been introduced to Hawaiian wrestling fans as a masked wrestler known as the Bat, Rice wore a red mask and was known as the Red Scorpion before wrestling under his true name. When the bout between the two ended in an inconclusive draw, Rice and Claybourne both shared the distinction of being the top-ranked contender for Togo's championship.

Back on the mainland, Woody Strode — who was on the verge of receiving his first significant vote of confidence for his acting prowess due to the pending release of the blockbuster film "The Ten Commandments," in which Strode played the role of the King of Ethiopia — was being hailed as "the best Negro wrestler since the heyday of Jack Claybourne" after his debut in Kansas.

Ironically, for as much acclaim as Strode would eventually receive for his role in "The Ten Commandments," he wouldn't even be the first Black wrestler from his era to appear in an Oscar-nominated film. Don Blackman, who retired from wrestling a few years prior, beat Strode to that distinction by playing the role of Luke as he shared the screen with Marlon Brando in the Best-Picture-winning film "On the Waterfront" in 1954.

Back in Hawaii, Claybourne earned a shot at reclaiming the Hawaiian title by defeating champion Tosh Togo in their singles match on September 30th, even though he was unconscious when the non-title contest drew to a close.

"[Claybourne] scored the only fall of the 45-minute time limit battle by using head butts and a stepover toe-hold to pin Togo after 39 min. 37 sec.," recorded *The Advertiser*. "Togo applied the 'sleeper' hold in the final three minutes, but the bell ended the match before he could subdue Claybourne, who passed out after the bell had rung."

Unfortunately, Claybourne's victory over Togo would be all for naught, as Tom Rice would defeat Togo one week later — in a title match — to capture the Hawaiian championship. It had all the appearances of a scenario in which Claybourne had softened up Togo for Rice to relieve him of his championship.

When Claybourne defeated Togo yet again on October 21st by battering the former champion with headbutts until the referee halted the action, Tom Rice decided to preemptively challenge Claybourne to a title match for the sake of silencing his critics. As *The Advertiser* reported, Rice also wanted to "prove he can take head butts" while defeating the most persistent challenger for the title that he just acquired.

Rice won the match — which was ultimately a non-title affair — but his actions suggested that he had considerable difficulty absorbing Claybourne's headbutts. After Rice won the first fall in just over 17 minutes, Claybourne leveled the match 12 minutes later by repeatedly headbutting Rice and applying a cover. That's when Rice resorted to underhanded tactics to ensure that he would leave the Civic Arena with the *Ring Magazine* belt.

"Rice, some ringsiders maintained, used a hard object to protect his forehead, and, as a result, caused Claybourne to suffer a head injury and a knockout," concluded *The Star-Bulletin*.

In retaliation for being cheated out of a victory, Claybourne interfered in a non-title match between Rice and Pat O'Connor, headbutting Rice and rendering him groggy so that O'Connor could dropkick the defenseless champion and pin him with ease. Soon thereafter, Al Karasick ordered yet another bout between Rice and Claybourne. This time, the title would be up for grabs.

"The challenger is Jack Claybourne, 225 pound Negro star whose use of the head butt has made him a controversial figure in wrestling," explained *The Advertiser*. "Claybourne, however, is one of the most popular wrestlers to appear in Hawaii. Rice no longer campaigns as a masked wrestler, but may wear a mask tonight 'to protect myself from head butts.' Rice told promoter Al Karasick that if the head butt is permitted, then he must be allowed to take protective measures."

Whatever protective measures Rice implemented during his title defense against Claybourne were woefully insufficient. As the headline of *The Advertiser* proclaimed on Monday, November 19th, "Claybourne Beats Rice for Title."

"Jack Claybourne regained the Hawaiian heavyweight wrestling title and *Ring Magazine* gold belt last night by winning on a disqualification from Tom Rice at the Civic Auditorium," continued *The Advertiser*.

Claybourne captured the first fall with headbutts, but Rice evened the bout by forcing Claybourne to submit to the Boston crab. Then, when Rice applied another Boston crab to his opponent while they were entangled in the ropes, he refused to release the hold, and was disqualified.

Seemingly, Claybourne had battled his way back to the top of the mountain, but any celebrations of that achievement would be cut short by a Tuesday morning announcement. Claybourne's victory was nullified by a ruling by Karasick, who cited the rules of the National Wrestling Alliance stipulating that "a title cannot change hands except on a fall or a submission," and that "Tom Rice is still the heavyweight wrestling champion of Hawaii."

That would be Claybourne's final shot at reclaiming the Hawaiian heavyweight championship. After participating in Civic Arena matches for one more month with mixed results, Claybourne submitted to the Boston crab of the Great Zorro in a six-man match on the Christmas show. This act lost the match for Claybourne and his teammates, Dan Beitelman and young Joe Blanchard, and ended Jack's return trip to Hawaii on a sour note.

Almost as if to add insult to injury, 1956 was the year of a major release of professional wrestling trading cards by

Parkhurst Products. In a 121-card set consisting of such immortal wrestling luminaries as Lou Thesz, Bronco Nagruski, and Verne Gagne, only four Black wrestlers were included: Jack Claybourne, Bobo Brazil, Bearcat Wright, and Luther Lindsay. On the back of Jack Claybourne's card, it stated that he "is regarded as the greatest colored wrestler of all time."

Surely, Claybourne could not have been feeling like an all-time great as his career continued on an unmistakably downward trajectory.

While the career of the man who was regarded by many as the greatest Black wrestler of his era limped along, a man who was similarly praised as the greatest boxer of all time without any racial qualifications had made his own move to start wrestling.

Assuredly, when every wrestling promoter in the 1930s and 1940s was referring to the Black wrestlers on their rosters as "the Brown Bomber of wrestling," they never would have fathomed that the *real* Brown Bomber might actually show up to wrestle.

It wasn't until 1956 that the idea of Joe Louis becoming a true pro wrestling competitor became a reality, and Eastern heavyweight wrestling champion Buddy Rogers drew the assignment of training Louis to wrestle behind the scenes while the fighter refereed bouts between Rogers and "Cowboy" Rocky Lee.

The official announcement that Louis was going to wrestle detonated atop the sports world like a brown bombshell. Promoter Ray Fabiani circulated a statement to the press that Louis had inked a contract with a downside guarantee of $100,000 per year to wrestle. Louis would be booked extensively in the east following his debut match, which was a one-fall bout against Cowboy Lee.

"I haven't made up my mind yet whether I'll sign the wrestling contract," Louis told the press. "I'm going to talk it over with Fabiani in Philadelphia."

The story being fed to the fans to explain the insertion of Louis into pro wrestling affairs was that Lee had thrown an errant punch at Buddy Rogers during a bout refereed by Louis; the punch missed Rogers and struck Louis, inviting Louis to disqualify Lee.

"I'm going to fight him with my bare fists and try to knock him out," added Louis. "He'll try and throw me for one fall."

Also added to the mix was "Jersey" Joe Walcott, who was tabbed to referee the bout. Having missed his opportunity to officiate the Negro title match between Jack Claybourne and Buddy Jackson in Pennsylvania due to Jack's suspension, Walcott would receive the opportunity to officiate a match of far greater fanfare.

In an interview with Bob MacDonald of *The Delaware New Journal*, Louis confessed that he doubted he would ever be able to pay off the full debt he owed to the IRS, even though the $2,000 per week he expected to average as a professional wrestler was a very handsome sum by the standards of the era.

"They (the internal revenue service) have been very nice to me, but it just can't be done," said Louis. "I don't make that kind of money anymore."

Louis also performed his role of hyping his bout with Lee, claiming that he would "belt him out into the bleachers" the first time Lee dared to make contact with him. Meanwhile, sports editors around the United States collectively shuddered at the idea of Louis being forced to tarnish his proud legacy by participating in wrestling matches, and minced no words about it.

"Joe Louis in a wrestling ring will be a pathetic sight," printed *The Standard-Times* of San Angelo, Texas. "Louis was a magnificent athlete and a tremendous world champion. No one whoever saw him in his time will ever forget his skill, his power, and his courage. Louis is now 41 and a beefy 260 pounds. His attraction will be his name, and the degrading thrill people get from seeing a fat and 40 ex-invincible floundering around a ring. He can't wrestle — even professional, buffoon style — and he knows it."

Concerns over tarnished legacies aside, the pro wrestling debut of Joe Louis was a box office success, although official fan attendance estimates at the Uline Arena that night vary widely, from 4,000 to 8,000. The ending to the bout came after Cowboy Lee enraged the fans by illegally rubbing his taped fist in Louis' eyes, and then violently tossing referee Joe Walcott across the ring.

"At that point, Louis threw his famous right, and Cowboy flipped over the ropes and into the ringside seats," wrote Richard O'Lone of *The Washington Daily News*. "Walcott counted him out and raised Louis' hand. The crowd was wildly enthusiastic."

O'Lone's reporting also captured Louis in the locker room after the bout, receiving affirmations from Buddy Rogers.

"I've seen a lot of wrestlers in their first match, but Joe, you weren't just great; you were tremendous!" gushed Rogers.

"It was all right, except for the choking, and he scratched my eye," answered Louis. "It's an honest living, and you're not stealing."

The next bout Louis competed in that captured national interest was his encounter with young Black wrestler Shag Thomas. The former defensive lineman from Ohio State University was shuttled all the way from Ohio to Florida to serve as an opponent for Louis after the originally advertised opponent — none other than "The Black Panther" Jim Mitchell — had supposedly pulled out of the bout. John P. Carmichael, sports editor for *The Chicago Daily News*, was one of the many in attendance that night, and was depressed by how much Louis' appearance had changed.

"Joe weighed 245 pounds and looked it, especially in the arms and above his black trunks," began Carmichael. "He wore a scraggly mustache, and the bald spot seems to have grown around his pate."

From there, Carmichael described a match in which Thomas politely "maneuvered Joe into the holds of the trade" before falling prey to a right-hand knockout punch and a pinfall administered by the former world boxing champion.

Afterwards, Louis was straightforward about the fact that he was wrestling for the sole purpose of keeping the IRS at bay.

"When they present me with a bill I can pay, I want to do it," insisted Louis. "Sure, I have to earn some money."

The aftermath of the bout with Thomas — as reported by the Associated Negro Press — was indicative of just how much Louis had been forced to compromise in order to appear that night. Milton Gross of *The New York Post* reportedly confronted Louis in the dressing room of the Gable Armory with the fact that Black patrons had been banned from attending the fight.

Louis was already incensed from having been refused a dining room seat at the airport restaurant, and this revelation led to a confrontation between the Brown Bomber and his trainer Buddy Rogers. When Louis asked Rogers if he knew about the venue's prohibition against Black patrons once they entered the building, Rogers supposedly replied, "It's a small place. They don't have separate facilities."

Presumably, Rogers was referring to separate bathrooms labeled as "White" and "Colored." Then, upon hearing confirmation that Black fans weren't being permitted to buy tickets, Louis insisted that he wouldn't appear, which is when Herb Friedman — assistant to promoter Cowboy Luttrell — was summoned. Louis then asked Friedman why Black fans were banned from watching him wrestle.

"They didn't mean it that way," said Friedman. "They were afraid there wouldn't be room here for all the people if they let colored people in here."

Ultimately, the match between Louis and Thomas went on in front of an audience of only 800 fans in a building that seated 1,160. Afterward, show promoter Pat O'Hara confirmed that the option to allow Black fans to purchase tickets had never been considered.

**Joe Louis struggles with his shoulders to the mat**

"Louis should have known. It's been in the papers," said O'Hara. "Why doesn't he read the papers? I've been promoting wrestling for five years and we never sold a ticket to a Negro."

In the midst of that impromptu imbroglio, Louis also let slip that it was his understanding that Jim Mitchell had never been contacted to serve as his opponent, and that the Panther's name was used to garner greater initial interest in the bout. Either Friedman or O'Hara supposedly confirmed that Mitchell had indeed pulled out upon learning that Black fans would be barred from entry.

Later that month, Louis expressed his ambivalence toward continuing his wrestling career to James L. Kilgallen of the International News Service. Louis stated that he liked wrestling, but he detested the constant traveling associated with it, which was the most challenging aspect to life as a wrestler.

"I'm thinking of going down to Tampa, Florida to engage in a few more wrestling bouts," Louis told Kilgallen. "They're planning to match me with Nature Boy Buddy Rogers... I'd have to learn wrestling if I took it up seriously. There's a lot to it. You've got to learn the various holds and how to take the bumps and the falls."

Louis' in-ring limitations were on display and plainly noticeable during another bout from his tour of Florida. When the Bomber faced Mexican wrestler Charro Aztec in Miami Beach, Louis' repeated reliance on the body scissors hold led *Miami News* sports writer Art Grace to remark that the body scissors was "apparently the only hold he has learned thus far."

Louis ended both falls of the best-of-three-falls with punches to Aztec's chin, and was back in the dressing room in a little over 11 minutes. That's where Buddy Rogers handed Louis his money and assured him he had done a good job. Grace concluded the article by acknowledging that the spectacle was "all rather sad."

Quickly making his way back to the Midwest, Louis rapidly accumulated victories and worked his record to 15-0 in the process of beating a trail back to his hometown of Detroit, Michigan. That's where Louis added his 16th victory to his resume by defeating Jim Bernard in just under eight minutes. The Associated Press noted that fewer than 5,000 seats were occupied in Detroit's Olympia Stadium — a venue that could accommodate 15,000. It was presented as a depressing indication of how Louis' star had fallen, or at least shined far less brightly in a pro wrestling context.

Also presented as sad was the fact that IRS agents were present to collect Louis' $1,200 share of the gate for the Detroit event as soon as it was handed to him. The moment was apparently sufficient to drive Louis to put a halt to his wrestling career "until the government men lay off of me," despite the fact that he was still being advertised for other appearances.

"I don't blame the government men, because that's their job, and the government men don't want to do that to me," Louis explained to the Associated Negro Press.

Apparently, Louis' threat to retire was a hollow one, as he was back in action just one month later. By July, Louis was displaying signs that his grasp of the wrestling business— along with its holds and maneuvers — was slowly improving. His match against Cowboy Rocky Lee was described very differently from their first encounter.

"At 16:45, Louis applied the sleeper hold made famous by Vern Gagne and left Lee for dead," reported the Newspaper Enterprise Association. "It took Lee a full minute to come to, and when he did, he looked like a fellow capable of squaring the best-of-three match."

After displaying his mastery of the sleeper hold to end the first fall, Louis relied upon the skills that brought him to the dance, landing a left-right combination to Lee's jaw and covering him for the three count. Louis then spent a significant portion of his evening signing autographs by the dressing room door, while responding to questions about his financial predicament by stating, "I owe the government money and it has every right to collect."

One week later, the Illinois Athletic Commission placed a massive hurdle in Louis' path to financial solvency by declaring that he was medically unqualified to continue wrestling. The IAC's official physician Irving Slott reported that his examination of Louis turned up "an abnormal electrocardiograph." The IAC imposed a six-month ban on Louis' wrestling career, while keeping the door open for Louis to apply for a re-evaluation at that time if he wished to pursue wrestling in the future.

By 1957, Joe Louis' short wrestling career was over, and it appeared that the lengthy career of Claybourne soon would be, as Jack looked every bit like a wrestler who was short on open opportunities to wrestle. Rather than returning to the wrestling rings in and around Los Angeles, where he had permanently relocated, Jack was idle until he returned to Hawaii in April.

At that point, the writing was clearly on the wall with respect to Claybourne's future career prospects, and he was obviously there to serve as a metaphorical stepping stone for the Black wrestler who had been anointed as the premier star of the next generation, Bobo Brazil.

**Bobo Brazil**

When Brazil made his Civic Arena debut in Hawaii at the beginning of March, the local newspapers made it clear to Hawaiian wrestling fans that they had never seen anything like him inside of a wrestling ring before.

"[Brazil] is said to be greater than Jack Claybourne and Woody Strode, two of the top negro mat stars of the past decades," hailed *The Advertiser*.

After seeing one of the most popular wrestlers in the history of Hawaii being so unfavorably compared to Brazil, Hawaiian fans may have been perplexed when they opened their morning newspapers on March 26th and saw that the now 47-year-old Claybourne would soon be visiting the territory specifically to team up with a man who would clearly upstage him at his own game.

"Jack Claybourne is returning to the islands to team up with Bobo Brazil, Promoter Al Karasick announced yesterday," stated *The Advertiser*. "Claybourne, like Brazil, is a head-butting specialist, and is extremely popular with Honolulu mat fans."

The existence of a strong bond between Brazil and Claybourne was implied, with it even being stated that Claybourne had returned to Hawaii "at the request of Brazil" to help him face the reigning Hawaiian tag team champions, Tom Rice and Lord Layton.

Given the purpose of Claybourne's presence, which was clearly to help elevate Brazil even further, it's retroactively surprising that it was Bobo who suffered the first defeat of the match, surrendering a fall to Layton just over 19 minutes into the match with a reverse grapevine hold. From there, it was Claybourne who would rally the team.

"Claybourne retaliated with headbutts, dropkicks, and a press to take the second fall from Rice in six minutes 50 seconds," continued *The Star-Bulletin*. "Rice and Layton, forced out of the ring, failed to return to it in the allotted 20 seconds and referee Frank Merrill awarded the winning fall to Claybourne and Brazil."

Following the victory, it was announced that Claybourne and Brazil had "gained the No. 1 rating in tag team wrestling by beating Rice and Lord Layton," and would defend their ranking by facing Japanese stars Toyonobori and Kokichi Endo in the main event of the April 7th show at the Civic Arena.

Just as quickly as the Brazil-Claybourne pairing appeared to be ascending the ladder, they crashed straight back to earth by losing to the Japanese tandem. Claybourne submitted to a bearhug applied by Toyonobori at the 41-minute mark of the match, leaving his team with only four minutes to even the score. This led to Brazil attempting a comeback that was described very similarly to a Claybourne rally from nine years earlier.

"Brazil opened up with head butts in the remaining 3 ½ minutes of the match but was unable to gain the equalizer," concluded *The Advertiser*.

It's quite possible that the soaring demand for Brazil throughout the National Wrestling Alliance resulted in a sudden change to Karasick's booking plans. Brazil would leave immediately for California, where he would go on to simultaneously hold the separate world tag team championships of both Northern and Southern California before the end of 1957.

As for Claybourne, he would defeat Jan Gotch with headbutts on the April 14th show, fall prey to Kokichi Endo's sleeper at the April 21st event, and then battle Endo to a draw in their rematch on April 28th. During the first show in May, he would have a bout with Hawaii heavyweight champion Tom Rice in a display that *The Advertiser* said "stole the show for action and excitement."

On May 12th, Claybourne scored a victory that was reminiscent of his classic successes inside of the Civic Arena, when he "used head butts to open a cut over Rocky Brown's eyes and was awarded the match after 19 min. 5 sec." Then Claybourne was the weak link of his team with Toyonobori on May 19th, surrendering the second fall of a match against Hans Schnabel and Lord Layton that ended in a 1-1 draw.

It's conceivable that May 27th was one of the most difficult days of Claybourne's entire wrestling career, and perhaps the surest indication that the business had passed him by. While Claybourne wrestled Rice in a bout that ended in a countout draw, Bobo Brazil tussled with Lou Thesz, who had arrived in Hawaii to defend his NWA World Heavyweight Championship belt.

By this point, the NWA title was without equal as the most prestigious championship in the wrestling world. Not only would Claybourne never get an opportunity to wrestle for it — which would be an honor enjoyed by Seelie Samara, Luther Lindsay, Bobo Brazil, and others within Claybourne's sphere of influence — but Brazil had been flown back to Hawaii from Los Angeles exclusively for the match with Thesz.

Brazil would then be shipped straight to San Francisco to win the world tag team championship recognized in Northern California. It was an unprecedented level of respect and stardom granted to a Black wrestler, and it surely exceeded any form of consideration that Claybourne had ever received during his long career.

Following Bobo's second departure from Hawaii, Claybourne would team with Sammy Berg in a losing effort against Tom Rice and Lord Layton. Jack would deliver the first fall for his team 13 minutes into the match with headbutts before he and Berg would drop the next two falls to their opponents.

On June 9th, Claybourne enjoyed one final victory that was reminiscent of his Hawaiian heyday by opening up a cut over Hans Schnabel's eye with repeated headbutts, forcing the referee to stop the bout altogether. The following Sunday, Claybourne earned the final victory of his life inside of a Hawaiian ring by defeating Sammy Berg once again, this time with a simple bodyslam.

On Sunday, June 23rd, Hawaiian wrestling fans would truly witness the end of an era, with the coup de grâce delivered in a manner that was either poetic, ironic, or disrespectful depending upon one's personal point of view through the lens of hindsight. Lucky Simunovich would send Claybourne packing from Hawaii in 15:07 following a series of dropkicks and a cover.

In the end, it was a classic Claybourne aerial closing sequence — one that all evidence indicates he was no longer in any physical condition to administer consistently under his own power — that would permanently ground the high-profile wrestling career of a Jack who was no longer jumping.

After returning home to California, Claybourne would be advertised for a handful of appearances in Los Angeles County within an easy driving distance from his house, at least one of which was televised, but those opportunities would dry up before the end of October. This would bring Claybourne's 25th year of in-ring activity to a thoroughly inauspicious end.

While Claybourne's year was certainly ending on a down note, the United States had seen a major step taken toward the eradication of racist laws with the early September passage of the Civil Rights Act of 1957. The first civil rights act passed since the 19th century — primarily intended to protect the voting rights of Black Americans — would represent the falling of a major domino that would see further acts passed to criminalize discrimination across the United States.

No sooner had Claybourne left Hawaii than the newspapers were already promoting the first appearance of Ricky Waldo, the latest promising Black wrestler to come down the pike. Predictably, *The Advertiser* used language to hype Waldo's debut that added insult to injury with respect to Claybourne's moribund career, declaring that Waldo had "already established himself as the outstanding Negro wrestler to come up since Jack Claybourne."

In March and April of 1958, Claybourne had what amounted the his last stand, grinding the final few matches out of a body that had been pulverized by more than two decades of incessant in-ring wear, constant travel, and an act that required him to repeatedly leap high into the air and absorb punishing landings on the stiff wrestling mats of the early 20th century.

Claybourne won a match by disqualification against Paul Degalles in the Civic Auditorium of Albuquerque when Degalles jumped off the top rope and onto Claybourne's head. He would win a second match by disqualification when "Killer" Joe Christie insisted on "repeatedly rubbing his taped hand into Claybourne's eyes" according to *The Albuquerque Tribune*.

Those uninspiring disqualification wins were among the final victories of Claybourne's proud career. In most matches, the immobile Claybourne's role was to absorb losses. In a tag team bout with Juan Garcia as his partner, Claybourne was defeated by each of their opponents — Kurt Von Poppenheim and Hans Shultz — with a Boston crab and a bodyslam.

In Claybourne's next outing, which was the final recorded match of his career, he lost in the show's opening bout to Suni War Cloud by surrendering two straight falls.

The year 1959 would mark the first calendar year since 1931 in which there was no evidence of a Jack Claybourne wrestling match. Coincidentally, it would be a landmark year for Black advancement in entertainment across multiple genres.

In January 1959, a 29-year-old Detroit record producer named Berry Gordy would borrow $800 to found Tamla Records, which would eventually be renamed the Motown Record Corporation in 1960. The record company would achieve monumental success while presenting Black music in a format that helped it to cross over and appeal to mainstream audiences.

Two months later, *A Raisin in the Sun* premiered on Broadway. Starring Bahamian-American actor Sidney Poitier, it was the first play written by a Black woman and directed by a Black man to open on Broadway — not to mention that all but one role in the play was played by a Black actor.

Last but not least, August was the month that Miles Davis' masterpiece *Kind of Blue* was released. Regarded by many as the greatest jazz album ever recorded, with an influence that extended well beyond its original genre, it inspired innovations in other styles of music.

Sadly, history would soon show that Claybourne — whose wrestling style had similarly inspired all sorts of innovations and emulations throughout the world of wrestling — was feeling kind of blue in his own right. These emulations, it would seem, were now working against him, and of this there is no clearer example than the debut of a new wrestler going by the name Reginald Siki — a shorter and smaller, but far younger and similarly agile Black wrestler from Texas.

Not only had this newcomer taken the name of the original Black wrestling legend who bore the Reginald Siki name, but his style was practically a carbon copy to that of Jack Claybourne in his prime, including repeated dropkicks, leaping headbutts administered to the heads of his upright opponents, and a bevy of other lighting-fast, acrobatic maneuvers.

In essence, just as easily as the original Reginald Siki's name could be swiped by another Black wrestler, so could Claybourne's entire in-ring act be duplicated by the same wrestler.

After his departure from wrestling, Claybourne's name was occasionally mentioned, albeit far less frequently than when he had been active. The context for invoking his name usually involved the debut of a Black wrestler who was smaller than one of the giants like Bobo Brazil or Bearcat Wright, as a way of establishing the credibility of that wrestler.

A classic example of this occurred in 1959, with Claybourne sitting idle at his house in Los Angeles, when *The Daily Sun* of Lewiston, Maine described Claybourne's former partner Luther Lindsay — now a ring veteran and an established star in several wrestling territories — as the "newest Negro heavyweight star since Jack Claybourne."

In the meantime, as his mentees were earning accolades in his absence, Claybourne was waiting for an invitation to return to professional wrestling that would never come.

It's amazing to think about how rapidly the tide had turned against Gentleman Jack. In the span of two years, he had gone from being praised on trading cards as the greatest Black wrestler in history to disappearing from professional wrestling altogether.

Then, four years after this high praise was heaped upon Claybourne as he sat amongst prestigious company, *The California Eagle* offered a grim retelling of the final afternoon of the wrestler's life. The 49-year-old legend had reportedly received a communique that sealed his professional fate. Claybourne would not be invited on a wrestling tour of Europe — a tour that he had apparently deemed to have been the last viable lifeline capable of jumpstarting his moribund career.

When Claybourne was found lying lifeless on the bathroom floor of his Los Angeles home just before 6:00 p.m. on January 7th, 1960, it wasn't a surprise to many of his closest friends. Apparently, he had told anyone who would listen that he would take his own life if he wasn't given an opportunity to extend a wrestling career that had lasted nearly 30 years.

Clearly, Claybourne's threat of suicide had not been idle. Sometime after arguing with his adopted daughter and then calling his wife Lillian at work to inform her of the altercation, Claybourne had loaded a 12-gauge shotgun, pressed the working end of the weapon against his head, and pulled the trigger.

The Los Angeles County coroner would encapsulate the ghastliness of the scene by summarizing Claybourne's cause of death as such: "Shotgun wound of head with multiple skull fractures and almost complete evisceration of the brain."

The description provided by the Associated Negro Press was equally graphic. After setting the stage by correctly stating that Claybourne "had to fight an unwritten racial ban in professional wrestling for 20 years," the ANP described Claybourne's suicide by saying that the wrestler turned the shotgun on himself, and "blew the top of his head off above the lower lip."

"Portions of his body were scattered over the walls and ceiling of the bathroom of his home where he ended his life," added the ANP's grisly report.

Famous Irish playwright George Bernard Shaw famously wrote that a gentleman is one who puts more into the world than he takes out. When it comes to Elmer "Jack" Claybourne, he undoubtedly put far more into the world of professional wrestling than he would take out. Unfortunately, due to the crushing frustrations he endured in the aftermath of his long career, Gentleman Jack made the tragic choice to take himself out.

# EPILOGUE

In the aftermath of Claybourne's suicide, next to nothing would be said about him or his influence on the wrestling business. In fact, the business seemed more than content to move on from "Gentleman" Jack Claybourne and "Rough" Rufus Jones, with what may have originally been well-intentioned efforts to honor them ultimately coming across as blatant efforts to rip them off.

As early as 1961, Bobo Brazil would begin crediting Jim Mitchell for encouraging him to use the coco-butt, and this story remained consistent for decades. In July 1982, Bobo Brazil sat for an interview with Rick Winston of *The Hamilton Spectator*, and he repeated the tale that he had made "the coco-butt" part of his repertoire under the advice of "a guy named Jimmy Mitchell who called himself the Black Panther." Brazil also said of the coco-butt, "It's been very good to me; I've never been hurt using it, but a lot of other guys have."

The adoption of the headbutt as the core element to his own performance certainly aided the career of Mitchell in 1946 and beyond, just as it had benefited Claybourne when he chose to utilize it in 1948, and then Seelie Samara, Bearcat Wright, Bobo Brazil, and several others.

Given the timeline of events, it's quite possible that Claybourne also incorporated the headbutt into his arsenal at the behest of Mitchell, and it helped him achieve the greatest successes of his career. If this is truly the case, it's ironic to think that by continuing to share that same piece of advice with young, up-and-coming Black wrestlers, Mitchell may have inadvertently hastened along the end of Jack Claybourne's career.

While there's no reason to think that the tale Bobo Brazil was telling is necessarily false, by 1961 Jim Mitchell was the only member of the Murderers' Row's prolific lineup of headbutters who remained both alive and active in the wrestling business, and was therefore the only member of the group who could reap any benefit from the endorsement.

In 1964, George "Seelie Samara" Hardison would also pass away, leaving Mitchell as the only wrestler of the core four who would even live to see his 60th year. Mitchell would ultimately survive well beyond that, passing away in 1996 at the age of 88. This means that the Black Panther of Louisville lived the same number of years as Jack Claybourne and Rufus Jones *combined*.

In the decades following the death of Rufus Jones, more than one Black wrestler would emerge bearing the name Rufus Jones and throwing headbutts with reckless abandon. The most famous of these would ultimately be Carey "Buster" Lloyd, who actually learned to wrestle in Boston, a city that meant a great deal to the career and development of Joe Godfrey.

Lloyd's wrestling career took off after he began referring to himself as "Rufus R. Jones" and adopted a headbutt-replete wrestling style — capped off with his signature maneuver, a charging "Freight Train" headbutt — nearly two decades after the original Rufus Jones' passing.

Claybourne's name would also experience a peculiar resurgence well after his suicide. Martinican wrestler Edouard Etifier — who wrestled as Eddie Morrow in North America — would adopt the name Jack Claybourne Jr. for his tours of New Zealand, Australia, and most notably for appearances in the International Wrestling Association of Japan. This utilization of the deceased Claybourne's name would transpire a full 10 years after Jack's death.

Following the death of her husband, Lillian Smalls Claybourne would continue to live in California until the mid-1980s. She would then move back to Roxbury, Massachusetts — the neighborhood where she first met her husband in 1941 — before passing away there in 1989.

Even as the names and memories of Claybourne and Jones faded into obscurity, their influence — for better or for worse — was indelibly infused into the styles of Black professional wrestlers, and the expectations that wrestling promoters and fans had for them, and those presuppositions would continue directly into the pro wrestling media boom of the 1980s.

Interestingly, traces of the standard established by Claybourne in particular — that a Black wrestler should be strong and hyper athletic, with educated feet, a powerful right hand, and a hard head — are evident in the performance criteria for wrestlers of Polynesian descent. Many wrestlers with heritage in the Pacific Ocean Islands continue to display stylistic tendencies that seem to be directly traceable to a bygone era. And it's not just male wrestlers with Samoan ancestry: Even Savelina Fanene, who performs as Nia Jax in WWE and is Dwayne "The Rock" Johnson's second cousin once removed, has made the headbutt a core component of her repertoire.

As of this writing, neither Jack Claybourne nor Rufus Jones has been inducted into any of the several professional wrestling halls of fame. There are myriad reasons for this, including the prioritization of inductions for wrestlers whose matches were preserved by video footage and are therefore reviewable, and also wrestlers who racked up vast numbers of championship reigns. Then again, it's also possible that many of the officials who oversee the lists of nominees for such honors have absolutely no idea what Elmer "Gentleman Jack" Claybourne and Joseph "Rufus Jones" Godfrey meant to the development of professional wrestling.

Since Claybourne, Jones, and nearly all of their Murderers' Row peers had careers that were confined to the era before most matches were recorded, there is scant footage of the wrestlers in action. As a result, only a microscopic cross section of modern wrestling fans are even aware that the two wrestlers existed, let alone are fully cognizant of the influence both had on the evolution of professional wrestling in general, and on the performance styles promulgated by the Black wrestlers who capitalized on the innovations of Claybourne and Jones in particular.

As for Joseph Godfrey's time as Tiger Flowers, it is a fitting irony that a replica of his head now sits in a collection at the Fogg Museum of Harvard University. It is a reproduction of the cranium that delivered countless choreographed thrashings to opponents, thrilling wrestling fans nationwide — and more importantly, it housed the mind that pioneered a style that would define Black American wrestling for generations to come.

# AFTERWORD

The book you have just read is a meticulously researched and deeply engaging account about two iconic figures, too often overlooked. The pioneering careers of Elmer "Gentleman Jack" Claybourne and Joseph "Rufus Jones" Godfrey have, at long last, been placed into historic context.

Through their stories and the broader history revealed here, we can now — for the first time — fully appreciate their legacy. In addition to its relevance in the history of American wrestling, this book will have an impact on the sociology of sport. Scholars need exactly this kind of nuanced and detailed examination to trace the development of contemporary debates around inequities across all of American sport.

As Douglass shows, the legacies of Claybourne and Godfrey, not unlike the legacies of many Black athletes of the 1900s, have been obscured not only due to a lack of official records, but also due to willful ignorance and racism. The failure of wrestling as an institution to properly recognize stories of athletes like these two looks awfully similar to Major League Baseball's general failure (until 2024) to at least acknowledge the statistical accomplishments of Negro Leagues players.

These are the sorts of historical recokonings that are essential for many other sports to continue to have, over racist events that occurred not only in the conveniently forgotten past, but persist in the present day. Within and beyond the sport of wrestling, this book will provoke a new appreciation of today's innovative athletes and entertainers, and their ancestors from generations ago.

Now, for a moment, I want to focus on another important figure in the history of wrestling. Ian Clinton Douglass, author of this and seven additional books on wrestling, grew up with a chip on his shoulder. I should know — I helped him put that chip there, where it belongs. You see, Ian and I went to school together from first grade all the way up through graduation from Southfield High School in the Detroit suburbs.

You would be forgiven for thinking that the chips on our shoulders are entirely due to our Detroit heritage. Sure, Detroit has been underrated for our entire lifetimes. But Ian's determination to find the stories that matter about underappreciated athletes comes from personal experience. It comes from his many accomplishments as an outstanding athlete in an underappreciated sport.

I will never forget seeing Ian lead our team to a league championship in our final year as teammates on the Southfield High School Varsity Swimming and Diving Team. That championship victory barely got a mention in the school newspaper or in our cherished senior yearbooks.

Nevertheless, Ian saw how our hard work — and his own — was worth it, even if no one else seemed to notice. But an unjustified lack of attention paid to great athletes is something that Ian is naturally inclined to notice.

Ian also developed a serious capacity as a writer while we were in high school. One semester, we both took a class with the legendary English teacher, Mr. Briggs. In that class, we practiced writing with an active voice, and Mr. Briggs gave us unforgettable insights on good writing in just about every class.

Once, he explained that you should carefully consider using a word as powerful as "eldritch." In fact, you should limit yourself to using such a potent word at most ten times in a lifetime. (I think I'm up to five uses of "eldritch" now, pretty much right on schedule. Ian probably has been more careful and has only used up one or two.)

I recall reading Ian's essays in high school and seeing him rapidly improve as a writer. Whenever he reviewed one of my essays, he found plenty of places to shorten my phrases without losing any of my intended meaning. He had a knack for finding just the right word even back then, as a teenager.

Ian's high school-era dedication to swimming, writing, and more presaged his ambitions later in life, in some ways. Like many Detroiters, he has worked harder than anyone else. As more and more people have seen his dedication and many capacities, more and more people want to work with him. Ian usually has about five major projects going on at any given time, and every one of those projects gets his full attention. I don't know how he does it.

Now that I've given you some of the important context around how Ian created the book that you have just read, you can better appreciate how this project — the second single-authored, book-length work of history that Ian has completed so far — represents the culmination of several aspects of what makes Ian such a great writer. This book is thorough. It's comprehensive. It's impassioned. It's unflinching.

Ian has been a writer of quality wrestling books for almost ten years now. He's been a devoted husband for nearly ten years, as well. Two years ago, he became a father. And he's been my greatest friend, my brother, across four decades—and counting. I can't wait to see what five things he does simultaneously next.

Dr. Erik Love
Associate Professor of Sociology
Dickinson College

Gentleman Jack and Rough Rufus

# EDITOR'S NOTE

For good or ill, professional wrestling loves its simple stories and easy answers. Take Black History Month, when some of the sport's most distinguished scribes trot out the same recycled articles about Bobo Brazil, treating the burly Benton Harbor resident as wrestling's Rosa Parks — the presumed starting point of Black achievement in the squared circle. It's a comforting story that gets one thing catastrophically wrong: Black excellence in wrestling didn't begin with Brazil. It didn't even begin close to his era.

This book thoroughly excavates two extraordinary careers that demolish that comfortable fiction. Gentleman Jack Claybourne and Rough Rufus Jones weren't just athletes who happened to be Black — they were pioneering performers who transformed professional wrestling decades before Brazil stepped through the ropes. Their story reads like a thriller: wrestlers forced to compete under multiple aliases, marketing themselves as "Cuban," "Ethiopian," "Zulu," or "Aboriginal" just to suit the racist tastes of the moment even as they electrified crowds with moves that wouldn't become mainstream for another forty years.

Picture Claybourne soaring through the air with dropkicks that defied gravity, in venues where his mere presence defied local custom. Or Jones, who began as a tactician before reinventing himself as "Rough Rufus," a bad man who turned hostile crowds into paying customers through sheer force of personality. These weren't mere curtain-jerkers or carnival attractions — they were headliners who packed houses and pushed boundaries, both physical and social.

The genius of their innovation becomes clear when you understand their world. In some territories, Claybourne could showcase his technical brilliance to thunderous applause. In others, his skin color meant he couldn't even enter certain buildings. Jones responded to similar restrictions by weaponizing stereotypes, using his "Rough Rufus" persona to transform racial anxiety into box office gold.

This isn't just a wrestling story. It's an American story about artists working within brutal constraints, using creativity and courage to build careers in a system designed to exclude them. While mainstream sports slowly desegregated, wrestling remained a complex patchwork where success required not just athletic ability, but the savvy to navigate a landscape of shifting identities and regional prejudices.

All of which underscores this volume's importance. In resurrecting these overlooked careers, Ian Douglass offers us more than a meticulously researched wrestling chronicle. He offers a study of American culture — of how one corner of the "sports entertainment" world opened itself to Black athletes, but only on narrow terms that reflected a broader Jim Crow landscape.

This book forces us to confront how easily important stories get lost — or worse, get replaced with simplified narratives that make us feel better or think less about the past. Gentleman Jack and Rough Rufus deserve better than that. They deserve to be remembered as innovators who transformed their sport while navigating a system designed to deny their very humanity. Their story isn't just worth telling — it's essential to understanding one small part of how wrestling, and by extension America itself, became what it is today.

Editing this manuscript brought me the kind of joy that editors dream about but rarely find. Every page revealed something new — not just about wrestling, but about the strange, long-forgotten world inhabited by these two vagabond Black athletes. I found myself stopping mid-edit to share passages with colleagues, to marvel at the innumerable lost, strayed, or borrowed identities which these men utilized in the course of doing their life's work. I hope you find as much wonder in reading it as I did in helping bring it to life.

Oliver Lee Bateman
*The Ringer*

## ACKNOWLEDGEMENTS

This book is the product of countless hours of studying and exploring Black pro wrestling history with an intent to truly learn about its pioneers and progression. It is also the result of acknowledging my own position as one of the few identifiable Black wrestling writer and historians, and accepting the responsibility that accompanies it.

For someone who admired the work ethic and journalistic contributions of Dave Meltzer to pro wrestling for countless years, it was an honor to receive a foreword to this project from one of my foremost professional inspirations.

Likewise, Dr. Erik Love has been inspiring me to be a better version of myself for my entire life. The opportunity to collaborate with him professionally is simply the icing on the cake to four decades of a cherished friendship that was born in Mrs. Walton's first-grade classroom of MacArthur Elementary School in Southfield, Michigan.

Professionally, I owe more to Oliver Lee Bateman than possibly any other human being. It's a tremendous thrill to finally collaborate with him on something of such significance.

Thank you to everyone who encouraged and motivated me throughout this book's writing, including my parents James and Pauline Douglass, my wife Teisha, and our son Isaiah. It's impossible to complete a project requiring this level of research and attention to detail without a great deal of understanding from your family, and from your spouse in particular.

To Elmer and Joseph: Now the world knows what I already knew.

"And whatsoever ye do, do it heartily, as to the Lord, and not unto men; Knowing that of the Lord ye shall receive the reward of the inheritance: for ye serve the Lord Christ."

Regards,

Ian C. Douglass

Gentleman Jack and Rough Rufus

# CREDITS

**Author**
Ian C. Douglass

**Editor**
Oliver Lee Bateman

**Cover Art**  **Foreword**  **Afterword**
Marc W. Leitzel  Dave Meltzer  Dr. Erik Love

**Cover Reviewers**
Mike Johnson  Dr. Louis Moore

**Additional Aid and Thanks**
James Douglass  Ken Bevan
John Cosper  Jon Snowden
Khal Davenport  Janet Stechly
David Shoemaker  Phil Lions
Ohio State University  Notre Dame University
The Harvard Art Museums  Jamie Hemmings

**Photo Credits**
*The Broad Ax, The Kitchener-Waterloo Record, The Sunday Oregonian, The Courier-Mail, The Age, The Honolulu Advertiser, The Honolulu Star-Bulletin, The North Bay Nugget, The Brisbane Telegraph, The Newcastle Morning Herald, The Age, The Argus, The Daily Telegraph, The Sunday Mail, The Alabama Tribune, The Kansas City Star, The Hamilton Spectator, The Ogden Standard-Examiner, The Herald and News, The Edmonton Journal, The California Eagle, The Longview Daily News*

# ABOUT THE AUTHOR

Ian Douglass has been a contributing writer for *Men's Health Magazine*, *The Ringer*, *Splice Today*, *Cracked*, and *MEL Magazine*, and has had his material curated into the New American History project at the University of Richmond. He has also been a content contributor to *Popular Science Magazine*, *Fixed Ops Magazine*, *The Pro Wrestling Post*, *Pro Wrestling Stories*, The International Pro Wrestling Hall of Fame, and The Bahamas Historical Society.

In addition to writing, Ian was also an on-air reporter for the NBC News affiliate in Flint, Michigan. He is a graduate of the University of Michigan in Ann Arbor, earned a master's degree from Northwestern University's Medill School of Journalism, attended the Specs Howard School of Media Arts, and completed the Executive MBA program at the Quantic School of Business and Technology.

Between 2016 and 2024, Ian co-authored the autobiographies of professional wrestlers Dan Severn, Dylan "Hornswoggle" Postl (along with Ross Owen Williams), Buggsy McGraw, Brian Blair, and Steve Keirn, with multiple books earning "Best Wrestling Book – Finalist" honors from *The Wrestling Observer*.

He is also the author of "Bahamian Rhapsody: The Unofficial History of Pro Wrestling's Unofficial Territory," published in 2022.

He was inducted into the Pro Wrestling Author's Hall of Fame in 2024.

www.ingramcontent.com/pod-product-compliance
Lightning Source LLC
Chambersburg PA
CBHW071958150426
43194CB00008B/918